✶ ✶ ✶ ✶ ✶ ✶ ✶ ✶ ✶ ✶

The One Year Yellow Ribbon Devotional is a cup of cool water given in Jesus' name to anyone who faces doubt in uncertain times, particularly our men and women in the military.

DAVE RAMSEY
New York Times best-selling author and nationally
syndicated radio talk show host

✶ ✶ ✶ ✶ ✶ ✶ ✶ ✶ ✶ ✶

In over 35 years of active-duty service, I met few military spouses who matched Brenda Pace and Carol McGlothlin in their passions for God, family, nation, and fellow citizen. Join them as they pour their hearts onto these pages in daily worship—you will be blessed!

PETER U. SUTTON
Major General, USAF (Retired)

✶ ✶ ✶ ✶ ✶ ✶ ✶ ✶ ✶ ✶

The One Year®
YELLOW
RIBBON
Devotional

* * *

TAKE A STAND IN PRAYER
FOR OUR NATION
AND THOSE WHO SERVE

* * *

BRENDA PACE AND
CAROL McGLOTHLIN

Tyndale House Publishers, Inc.
Carol Stream, Illinois

Visit Tyndale's exciting Web site at www.tyndale.com

Visit Brenda Pace at www.brendapace.com and Carol McGlothlin at www.carolmcglothlin.com

Published in association with the literary agency of Fedd & Company, Inc. Literary Agency, 9759 Concord Pass, Brentwood, TN 37027.

Library of Congress Cataloging-in-Publication Data

Pace, Brenda.
  The one year yellow ribbon devotional : take a stand in prayer for our nation and those who serve / Brenda Pace and Carol McGlothlin.
      p. cm.
    ISBN-13: 978-1-4143-1929-2 (sc)
    ISBN-10: 1-4143-1929-0 (sc)
  1. War—Religious aspects--Christianity. 2. Spouses—Prayers and devotions. 3. Devotional calendars. I. McGlothlin, Carol. II. Title.
    BV4897.W2P33 2008
    242'.68—dc22   2008021677

Printed in the United States of America

14 13 12 11 10 09 08
 7   6   5   4   3   2

Dedicated to military veterans of the United States of America.

We honor you for the stand you have taken for freedom.

Preface

The meditations in this book have been composed prayerfully and thoughtfully. Our purpose in writing is to bring hope in the midst of tough times. With our experiences as military spouses, our hearts have been especially softened by the challenges facing those who are serving in our armed forces during the present War on Terror. For these, we pray the words in this book will bring encouragement. For others, our hope is that you will be reminded to take an unwavering stand through prayer for those who are serving our country as never before. As Americans, we pray your patriotic spirit will also be ignited as you are encouraged to fight the good fight for the godly principles that are at the very core of our nation's history.

We also pray that the meditations included within these pages will bless *anyone* who is facing challenging times. Each day brings crises of varying magnitudes. As Christ followers, we are called to stand firm when we are tempted to crumble under the weight of difficult circumstances. "The temptations in your life are no different from what others experience. And God is faithful. He will not allow the temptation to be more than you can stand. When you are tempted, he will show you a way out so that you can endure" (1 Corinthians 10:13).

Thank you to the American heroes in the form of military family members who have shared their hearts with us as we have had the honor to meet and talk with them during the writing of this book. To those who are serving in the armed forces, we salute you. To the resilient and courageous family members, we salute you as well. We are proud to take a stand with you and for you!

Brenda and Carol

Acknowledgments

Thanks, Rit, for always standing by me. You have listened to me process, lovingly challenged me to develop ideas, and encouraged me in every step of this project. You inspire me as I am privileged to watch you daily walk out a life of godly wisdom and integrity. I'm blessed to be your wife.

Thanks to Gregory and Megan, and Joseph and Danya for your encouragement and support. I love being your mom (and mom-in-law). Thanks for bestowing upon me the treasured role of grandma. Jolie and Noah, you have brought such joy to my life. I love you all.

Thanks, Mom and Dad, for the regular notes of encouragement and help throughout this process. I am grateful for your legacy of prayer and faith. Mom, Pop, and the Paces—I'm grateful to be one of you.

I am a woman who is blessed with faithful friends. To Karen, Ruth, Victoria, Shellie—you are so dear to me. Thanks for your encouragement during this project. Dawn, Kim, Kristen—you spur me on. Cindy and Ann, you are true heroes to me. To Patti, Sandy, Maria, Teresa, Jacquline, Cindi, Tish, Rose, Diane, Dwight, Cheryl, and John—bless you! Thank you for being willing to share your stories. Susan, your encouragement and insight were especially meaningful. To the wonderful women I have met in military communities around the world—thanks for your inspiration!

Diane and Bobby—how special to have brothers and sisters in Christ like you!

Thanks to the Tyndale House Publishers family. Carol and I are truly grateful to have worked with you on this project.

And Carol, I must thank you for being a faithful friend and writing partner. You inspire me and spur me to *write on*. I am so grateful for your generous heart. You may call it *atrial fibulation*, but I know it to be the beats of a heart that can't do enough for your Lord. It's been a fun and blessed journey.

෨Brenda

Thank you to my husband, Richard, for understanding when I asked you not to come home for lunch because I wanted to stay focused on my writing. Thanks also for understanding when I got up at 4:00 a.m. and began working on the computer. You have been my prayer warrior and my encourager through the process, and I am so thankful that you still love me so very much after thirty-four years of marriage. I am thankful that you allow me to continue to follow my dreams and take on these challenges.

Thank you to my mother, who has been the most incredible encourager anyone could ask for. You celebrated each time of completion with me, and you prayed for me when the inspiration was slow to come.

And to our sons, Neil and Alex, the answer to your question is, "Yes, I am finished with the book." You have always had an interest in the process. Jen, your encouragement and phone calls blessed my heart.

Thank you to my sister friends, Sue, Diane, Rhenee, Ann, and Reba, who would call and tell me they missed me during this time of commitment in my life. I knew you were always praying.

Thank you to my dear friend, Major Steve, who would call from Iraq and ask if he could pray for me. How humbled I was! You continued to remind me of the purpose in a project such as this and encouraged me to keep on keeping on.

Diane and Nancy, I pray that you are honored as military wives to see your words written in this devotional. I know your testimonies of faith will bless so many. Cheri, my pearl friend, you are loved, and your wisdom to others will be greatly appreciated. Bev, your positive influence in my life as a young military wife continues as we journey together in our lives. Steve and Jane, thank you for teaching and mentoring us in our faith.

Thank you, Esther, for knowing the need for a book like this and for your efforts in making things happen with enthusiasm and conviction.

Brenda, God has given us yet another opportunity to encourage and exhort. I am so thankful for our journey together.

≈Carol

Introduction

The yellow ribbon is a symbol of hope for those who are waiting. Displaying it on a car, in a window, or wrapped around a tree is a statement of support for those who are taking a stand for freedom. Our greatest source of hope during challenging times of national war or personal trials is God. We communicate with God through his Word and through prayer. Our hope is strongest when we stand together on the promises of his Word, united in prayer, believing that by his mercy he will sustain and strengthen us.

As a nation, we find ourselves at war. Yellow ribbons dot the landscape of neighborhoods from coast to coast. For those who have said good-bye to a loved one as they leave to fight a perplexing enemy, the ribbon is a symbol that this war is at the forefront of their thoughts. For others, a graphic depiction of war in the news will be a reminder of the sacrifice represented by the yellow ribbon. The call to take a stand in prayer on behalf of our nation, and for those who serve, is one we can all answer.

Scripture is replete with examples of heroes who took a stand in prayer on behalf of others. Abraham took a stand in prayer as he pleaded with God not to destroy his family. Moses stood in prayer on behalf of the entire nation of Israel. King Hezekiah took his stand in prayer for a nation under siege. God's intervention in response to these prayers gives us faith to believe he will hear our prayers too.

Paul urges us in 1 Timothy 2:1-2 "to pray for all people. Ask God to help them; intercede on their behalf, and give thanks for them. Pray this way for kings and all who are in authority so that we can live peaceful and quiet lives marked by godliness and dignity." He further encourages us in Philippians 1:27 to be "standing together with one spirit and one purpose, fighting together for the faith, which is the Good News." What better way for us to stand together than in prayer?

As you consider the devotional thoughts held in these pages, join us in daily prayer for America and those who serve. As you pray, remember that God promises to stand beside us like a great warrior (see Jeremiah 20:11), watching over us (see Psalm 121) and protecting us (see Psalm 110:5).

May he, as a result, make our hearts strong, blameless, and holy as we stand before God our Father when our Lord Jesus comes again with all his holy people. Amen (1 Thessalonians 3:13, paraphrased).

Stand for Something

Put on every piece of God's armor so you will be able to resist the enemy in the time of evil. Then after the battle you will still be standing firm. ✚ EPHESIANS 6:13

How will you face this new year? Ephesians 6:13 encourages us to face each day *standing firm*. What does that mean, and how does it happen? We're to stand firm in the power of the Holy Spirit by putting on the whole armor of God. "Stand your ground, putting on the belt of truth and the body armor of God's righteousness. For shoes, put on the peace that comes from the Good News so that you will be fully prepared. In addition to all of these, hold up the shield of faith to stop the fiery arrows of the devil. Put on salvation as your helmet, and take the sword of the Spirit, which is the word of God" (Ephesians 6:14-17).

In other words, God is saying, "Okay, I have given you everything you need to stand against the enemy you will face in this world—now stand." The stand we must take is one without fear, without hesitation, and with confidence as we encounter any crisis that may come our way. It is a stand in spiritual armor that is complete for battle, both defensive and offensive.

Because we live in a fallen world, we will encounter Satan's attacks on our mental, physical, and spiritual well-being. We must remember that he is a defeated foe and that through Christ we have all we need to stand against him. We are to stand and refuse to move from the ground that has been taken through our acceptance of Christ as our Savior.

Scripture tells us the Word of God is our offensive weapon and that we are to pray at all times in the power of the Holy Spirit. Make a commitment this year to study the Bible and learn its directives and promises. Then stand on those promises—in prayer!

Throughout this year keep in mind the stand that military men and women are taking around the world. They are standing for our nation and the principles on which our country was founded. They are standing for a better world for our children and hope for the future. Commit to keep them and their families in your prayers throughout this new year.

Take inspiration from this prayer of Peter Marshall, chaplain of the U.S. Senate in 1947: "Give us clear vision that we may know where to stand and what to stand for, because unless we stand for something, we shall fall for anything."[1]   *Carol*

✷   ✷   ✷

Father, I commit to stand on your promises in the new year. I pray for the brave men and women who have made a commitment to stand firm for freedom and liberty through their service in the military. In Jesus' name I pray. ✚ *Amen.*

---

[1] Peter Marshall, *Mr. Jones, Meet the Master* (Revell, 1952), quoted in Frank S. Mead, comp., *12,000 Religious Quotations* (Grand Rapids, MI: Baker Book House, 1989), 465.

January 2
Morning Watch

Listen to my voice in the morning, LORD. Each morning I bring my requests to you and wait expectantly. ✝ PSALM 5:3

I admit I'm not always the most congenial person in the morning. The older I get, the more time I need to ease into the day. My grandson, on the other hand, is the epitome of a morning person. He awakens with bright eyes wide open and a smile on his face. He greets the day with a cheerful and emphatic "Good morning!" Whatever misery he may have felt the night before has been crucified as he slept, and each new day is a happy resurrection.

Even with my morning challenges, I have found that the best way to begin a day is with Scripture reading and prayer. The great preacher Charles Spurgeon said about prayer, "Let us take care, while we are fresh, to give the cream of the morning to God." Giving God my first thoughts of the day helps me grasp my priorities and focus on what is truly important. Often my prayers are a natural flow from what I read in the Bible. Writing them in a journal has been a helpful tool; the physical act of writing keeps me focused and protects my thoughts from drifting. Having these written prayers also provides a tangible record of God's faithfulness as I record answers or return later to trace the work of his hand in a particular situation.

Developing the spiritual discipline of prayer is a necessity for a Christ follower. The psalmist who penned the words of today's passage obviously had a regular habit of beginning his day with prayer to the Lord. In the original language he paints a word picture of an archer shooting a bow and arrow. It can be assumed that the prayers the psalmist prayed were like arrows that he watched expectantly as they sped to the center of the target.

As a young Christian I struggled to have a disciplined prayer life. Today, I cannot boast by saying I never miss beginning a day with prayer, but the Lord has helped me develop consistency. While discipline plays a role in my prayer life, the goal is not about completing a task. The goal of prayer at any time of the day is to nurture a personal relationship with my heavenly Father. "It is good to proclaim your unfailing love in the morning, your faithfulness in the evening" (Psalm 92:2). ✍*Brenda*

✶　✶　✶

Father, I thank you for a new day to worship you. I ask for consistency in my prayer life, not as duty, but to be in an ever-closer relationship with you. I give you this day. I pray for military personnel who are on patrol during the night. Surround them with your protection as they stand watch on behalf of others. In Jesus' name I pray. ✝ *Amen.*

Living Word

The word of God is alive and powerful. ✝ HEBREWS 4:12

Do you believe the Word of God? Do you believe his Word is our offensive weapon against the enemy of our souls? Do you believe it is alive and just as applicable today as it was when it was written? I do! I have never in my life been so in love with God's Word. I have never in my life experienced such sensitivity to the relevance of God's Word for every situation today. I have never in my life experienced so many teachers and mentors who are so excited about sharing the Word with others.

In January of 2005, my mother, then eighty-three, was encouraged by her church to read through the Bible in a year. She has known the Lord since she was a teenager but had never actually read through, day by day, the entire Bible. She began that first day of January 2005. From the beginning of this experience she had a new excitement and joy that was undeniable. She would call us at night and say, "You will not believe what I just read!" Or she would tell me to go and get my husband, a loving student of the Scriptures, so she could ask a question about something she had read. It was amazing how each word, each book, and each day brought new insight as she fell in love with God's Word.

In September of 2005 my dad passed away. He was the love of my mother's life for sixty-two years. God had prepared her for what was to come as she faithfully hid his Word in her heart that year. She had such peace and such understanding of a better eternal home for my dad. She continued, letting God comfort her as she finished the last word of Revelation on December 31, 2005.

In 2006 my husband and I were challenged by my mother's renewed love of the Bible to also read it through in a year.

What a blessing to fall in love with the living Word all over again! It is his gift to us. ⤳*Carol*

✻　✻　✻

Lord, you speak to me through your Word, and I know that you are the Creator of the universe. All things are under your command. Help me to go to your Word each day for peace, understanding, and wisdom. Lead those in harm's way throughout the world to your living Word, providing for them in every conflict and every trial they face. ✝ *Amen.*

January 4
Forgetting the Past

No, dear brothers and sisters, I have not achieved it, but I focus on this one thing: Forgetting the past and looking forward to what lies ahead. ✛ PHILIPPIANS 3:13

The results of the commitment my husband and I made to reading the Bible in a year were amazing! We fell more and more in love with the Bible as we read it each day. We would sit across the table from each other and say, "Wow" many times over. We had read pieces of Scripture all our Christian lives, but to read it book by book, chapter by chapter, verse by verse was truly a spiritual experience.

Here we are beginning a new year. The Word is hidden in my heart. Just as my mother had no idea that God was comforting her through his Word in order to get through the loss of the love of her life—her husband, friend, and father of her girls—so my own year-long Bible-reading experience is enabling me to live with renewed passion for God's Word in my heart.

While reading that year, I found myself crying through the side notes I had written with names of my sons or of places we had traveled. I had recorded those notes beside specific verses in God's Word to remember how he had brought us through so many challenging times in our lives.

But I can't dwell in the past. Forgetting the past is a directive from God to let go and let him take over. He doesn't want us to dwell on our past sins or mistakes. Remembering how God led us through those times, however, gives us great comfort. He loves us unconditionally, and his presence is a reality.

I pray that you will fall in love with him every day as you are encouraged in these messages of hope and prayers of faith. I can only encourage you to go to God's Word. Let him speak to you. It is his mode of communication with us, and as we practice it we get to learn how to live in victory along the way.

Bless you today! ✑*Carol*

✶ ✶ ✶

Father God, let this be the year for me to fall in love with you and your Word. Help those who are separated from their loved ones during the conflict in the world. May they pick up your Word daily to receive the message of hope it contains. ✛ *Amen.*

Managing Time

During my time here, I protected them by the power of the name you gave me. I guarded them so that not one was lost. ✛ JOHN 17:12

My friend just said good-bye to her husband for a year as he began a deployment to Iraq. I sent her a note to ask how her first week was going. She responded that she was getting some things checked off a list of tasks that she had been compiling for the last year. She knows she has at least twelve months that her husband will be absent, and she is setting a goal to use her time wisely by accomplishing things she wants to get done while he is away.

Today we have people who are time-management experts. There are countless books, seminars, and tools to aid us in managing our time, but the reality is time can't really be saved or managed. John Maxwell suggests, "Since you can't change time, you must instead change your approach to it. Time cannot be managed . . . time just is."[1] I understand this to mean we cannot manage time, but we can manage what we do with the time we've been given.

Jesus knew his time on earth was set by the Father. His primary mission was to go to the cross, but before that happened, he wanted to use his time for positive impact on people's lives as is evident in today's passage. None of us knows the exact number of days we have here on earth. Our focus is not to be on how many days we have because that is something we can't manage or control. We can manage and control what we choose to do during the time we are given.

Perhaps it would be helpful to make a list now of those things you would like to do this year. Choose actions that are helpful to others. Spend your time wisely, and begin doing those things you plan.

My friend is turning a challenging crisis in her life into a productive time. She could have chosen to be miserable for the next year. She could easily have given in to constant worry about her husband's well-being and wasted valuable time God has given her. Instead she is choosing to turn it around and be productive even as she misses her husband. In the midst of crisis we still have a choice: to be stuck in self pity or to move forward with the task at hand.   *⮌Brenda*

✱   ✱   ✱

Father, thank you for sending your Son to fulfill his purpose here on earth. Help me to use my time wisely, making the most of each opportunity you give me today. I pray for spouses of deployed military personnel. Help them to trust you during this time of separation. In Jesus' name. ✛ Amen.

---

[1] John C. Maxwell, *Today Matters* (New York: Time Warner Books, 2004), 67.

January 6
To-Do Lists

Look here, you who say, "Today or tomorrow we are going to a certain town and will stay there a year. We will do business there and make a profit." How do you know what your life will be like tomorrow? Your life is like the morning fog—it's here a little while, then it's gone.

✝ JAMES 4:13-14

I believe in making a plan and being prepared. I am a list maker, and I enjoy seeing checks beside tasks I have accomplished. Yet as a Christian, I sometimes have mixed feelings when it comes to making a detailed plan for the future. How much do I plan for the future, and how much do I leave the future to God's divine providence? If I do not make some plan for my day, I seem to fritter it away. If I am controlled by my to-do list, however, I may miss spontaneous opportunities that would have eternal significance. My daily challenge is to not be ruled by my own plans.

In today's passage, James is addressing the mistake of those who do not even consider the will of God in their daily plans. Their mistake is twofold: first, in thinking they know what is best and can determine their own future; second, in failing to acknowledge that God is sovereign and the One who knows what is best for them.

I have found that my solution to the planning quandary is to daily commit my to-do list to the Lord. I ask him to help me discern his will for each day and make me available to accomplish his plan.

What's on your list today? Whatever it is, commit it to the Lord—and see what happens! ≈*Brenda*

Father, thank you for the plan you have made for my salvation. Forgive me for any plans I have made without considering you. I acknowledge your sovereignty, and I trust you to direct me as I commit myself to your will. I present to you my plans for this day and invite you to rearrange them if you see the need. May I glorify you in all I do. I pray for those who are directing military plans and operations. May they, too, look to you for help and guidance. In Jesus' name. ✝ *Amen.*

National Take Time off Day

Then Jesus said, "Let's go off by ourselves to a quiet place and rest awhile." He said this because there were so many people coming and going that Jesus and his apostles didn't even have time to eat. ✛ MARK 6:31

One day during a particularly physically draining season, I wrote in my journal, "After bemoaning my laziness yesterday, I decided to give myself permission to have a day of rest. It was impossible! I must not think it is okay to rest, because when I do, I feel guilty. As a result, I feel tired." The night I wrote that I got a chuckle when I read the online news banner announcing it was National Take Time off Day! On an officially sanctioned day, I still couldn't take the time to relax.

Even Jesus in his short time of ministry intentionally pulled away to quiet places for rest in order to recharge himself physically and spiritually. In today's Scripture, he directs his disciples following an intense time of ministry: "Let's go off by ourselves to a quiet place and rest awhile." The original word for rest in Mark 6:31 implies refreshment.[1] If Jesus needed rest to be refreshed in body and spirit after his labors, wouldn't you think we do as well? And if it was okay for him to do, wouldn't you think it would be okay for us, too?

For those who struggle with the idea of taking time off to rest, the term *power nap* has been coined as a management principle that claims increased productivity. Long before power naps were in vogue, however, my mother-in-law practiced a thirty-minute nap in the middle of the afternoon to feel refreshed for the rest of the day. Her energy has always put mine to shame. Whatever name you use to describe rest, the truth is that we need it to rejuvenate ourselves physically, emotionally, and spiritually.

It has been said that "if you don't come apart and rest, you will come apart!"[2] Include some rest as a part of this day. It's okay—Jesus said so! ❧*Brenda*

✯　✯　✯

Thank you, Father, for the example of Christ in Scripture. He accomplished your will in his short life on earth, yet he found time to rest and be refreshed. Help me to take time today for moments of rest, making my service to others the best it can be. I pray for military personnel in the medical corps today who are working long hours to bring health and wellness to others. ✛ *Amen.*

---

[1] *Biblesoft's New Exhaustive Strong's Numbers and Concordance with Expanded Greek-Hebrew Dictionary* (Seattle: Biblesoft and International Bible Translators, Inc., 1994).
[2] Vance Havner, *The Bible Exposition Commentary* (Wheaton, IL: SP Publications, Inc., 1992).

January 8
Wait Expectantly

When you came down long ago, you did awesome deeds beyond our highest expectations. And oh, how the mountains quaked! ✛ ISAIAH 64:3

We live in a world of expectations, and the bar is usually set pretty high. I love a challenge, and I love to continually seek to achieve great things in my life. My husband and I have great hopes and expectations for our sons, which cause us to pray constantly that God would honor them with personal, relational, and financial favor. However, we often put too high of an expectation on ourselves and those we love, and that's when things get out of order.

Psalm 5:3 says, "Listen to my voice in the morning, LORD. Each morning I bring my requests to you and wait expectantly." The expectations I have for myself should be measured by God's expectations for me. Why do we run ahead of all that God has for us? He knew we would. Often we expect an answer to come quickly, a relationship to take hold, a job offer to come in. But these expectations suggest that we have a God who simply grants wishes. We are to wait on God, not merely on his answers.

First, our prayer to the Father during times of conflict and in situations beyond our control should be that we are giving all to him. Second, our prayers and attitudes must place our expectations on him and measure them by the standard of his mercy and grace. Expectations in our humanness can only lead to disappointment and discouragement.

Finally, our expectations should be as Scripture tells us in 1 Peter 1:3: "All praise to God, the Father of our Lord Jesus Christ. It is by his great mercy that we have been born again, because God raised Jesus Christ from the dead. Now we live with great expectation." ❧*Carol*

Lord, teach me to wait expectantly on you. Give me a heart that is willing to trust, not one that is thinking *I deserve* or *I expect*. Give me a heart to continue to lift to you each day my expectations of an end to the likes of war, poverty, and disease. In your name I pray. ✛ *Amen.*

Missed Opportunity

There they will say, "Pharaoh, the king of Egypt, is a loudmouth who missed his opportunity!"

✛ JEREMIAH 46:17

There is not one of us who has never missed an opportunity. Several weeks ago, I read a story in the travel section of our local newspaper about a hotel in the heart of New York City that had just been remodeled. A special promotion offered rooms for $19.31 in honor of the year the hotel opened. It was Sunday afternoon, and I got busy—and failed to follow through in checking it out. Two days later, my husband called to tell me our friends had just made reservations for the weekend in New York City at a great hotel for only $19.31 per night! He asked me to quickly go online and make reservations for us so we could join them. But when I made the attempt, I received the message that there were no more rooms available at that price. If only I had acted on the offer when I first saw it in the paper days earlier! I had missed my opportunity.

In today's Scripture, Jeremiah speaks of Pharaoh, whom Matthew Henry describes as either a coward or a bad manager following his promise to send an army to support his people.[1] The enemy came, and Pharaoh failed to send his army to provide help. He missed a great opportunity to prove himself a powerful leader and back up his words with action.

The New Testament Epistles challenge us not to miss the opportunity to do good and bless others:

> "Therefore, whenever we have the opportunity, we should do good to everyone—especially to those in the family of faith" (Galatians 6:10).
> "Make the most of every opportunity in these evil days" (Ephesians 5:16).
> "Live wisely among those who are not believers, and make the most of every opportunity" (Colossians 4:5).

In the words of H. Jackson Brown Jr., "Nothing is more expensive than a missed opportunity."[2] Look for opportunities the Lord may send your way today! ≈Brenda

✳ ✳ ✳

Heavenly Father, thank you for making me your child. I pray that I would have eyes to see each occasion you provide for me to do good for others. Don't let me miss the opportunity to be a blessing. I pray for soldiers, airmen, sailors, marines, and coastguardsmen as they serve you around the world. Provide them with opportunities to hear your Word and be encouraged. In Jesus' name I pray. ✛Amen.

---

[1] *Matthew Henry's Commentary on the Whole Bible: New Modern Edition,* Electronic Database, CD-ROM. Hendrickson Publishers, 1991.
[2] *Life's Little Instruction Book* (Nashville, TN: Thomas Nelson, 2000).

January 10
The Power of Prayer

The earnest prayer of a righteous person has great power and produces wonderful results.
✝ JAMES 5:16

Webster's dictionary defines power as "ability to act or produce an effect."[1] As an adjective, it is defined as "of, relating to, or utilizing strength." The mere definition gives the image of strength in anything one does. The dictionary defines prayer as "an address (as a petition) to God" and as "an earnest request or wish."

I have to admit there are times when I cry out to God, "What can I do? How can I make a difference in the world?" As Christians, we cannot physically do things for our military personnel who are in harm's way. We cannot even know when danger is imminent. However, through prayer we can affect them spiritually and do battle in the heavenly realms on their behalf. Each of us has this power through the Holy Spirit. As a direct result of prayer, there are many who have come to know the Lord while fighting the War on Terror.

God honors our prayers. As we make prayer a priority, we can make a difference for those who serve our country through military or government service. Prayer in the power of the Holy Spirit can change the direction of local churches and shape worldwide missions. Being on our knees can strengthen our families for the battles we face each day.

Prayer gives hope to the hearts of mothers as their children face the bombardment of the enemy each day—because they can know that the sovereign God is listening. Discouragement and disillusionment can then be replaced with prayer. In a culture where we are constantly connected by cell phones and the Internet, we must not forget that the only connection that matters is the connection we have with God the Father through the power of the Holy Spirit in prayer. ≈Carol

★ ★ ★

O Lord, too often I find time to do lunch with my friends or be involved in many good activities but can't seem to schedule time to spend with you. Forgive me for my negligence, and give me a renewed heart of commitment to earnestly seek you. Please protect the men and women in harm's way, and help me remember to lift them up to you daily. ✝ Amen.

---

[1] *Merriam-Webster's Collegiate Dictionary*, 11th ed. (Springfield, MA: Merriam-Webster, Inc. 2003).

Lost Identity

I have tried hard to find you—don't let me wander from your commands. ✝ PSALM 119:10

As a military spouse, I am required to use a military ID card to gain entrance to any military installation. And as a military spouse, I need to gain entrance to a military installation for many reasons during the course of a week! I grocery shop, purchase gas, visit the doctor, and attend Bible study during the week and worship service on Sunday. My military ID card is a very important document.

I am embarrassed to confess that in recent months I have misplaced my card not once, but twice. The frantic search, calls to all the places I went, and discussions of what to do in the case of identity theft have all left me exhausted. I have gone through the litany of *How could I let this happen?* and *Why didn't I put it in the same place each time?* I beat myself up over my carelessness and prayed for God's mercy in the situation. It could be comical if it wasn't so serious.

My husband asked the tongue-in-cheek question, "Do you think this is God's way of telling us it is time to get out of the military?" I admit sometimes I have to have tangible lessons, but I do not think this one is about separation from the military. The mishaps, however, have not been without some spiritual application.

You see, lately I have felt somewhat misplaced spiritually. A demanding travel schedule has resulted in a loss of routine and discipline. I am amazed at how easy it is to become careless in daily spiritual disciplines while being distracted with the cares of life and the weight of responsibility. Just as I must take the extra few moments to put my ID card in its predetermined place, I must take the extra few moments to renew myself through Scripture and prayer. It is through these consistent actions that I gain my identity in Christ each and every day. As surely as I'll need my ID card the next time I drive up to a military gate, I need to have my spiritual identity firmly established in God! ❧*Brenda*

✶ ✶ ✶

"Let me live so I can praise you, and may your regulations help me. I have wandered away like a lost sheep; come and find me, for I have not forgotten your commands" (Psalm 119:175-176). Bless all those around the world who are literally misplaced because of the results of terrorism and war. May they find hope and help through you. ✝*Amen.*

January 12
Rest for the Weary

I am weary, O God; I am weary and worn out, O God. ✦ PROVERBS 30:1

There are times in my life when I become very weary. I find myself being overcome by the world or focusing on the negatives around me. I believe in sharing our burdens with one another, but my personality often takes it a little too far. I often want very much to work things out for others and fix their situations. I am convinced that is why God gave me children. He wanted me to know what it truly felt like to let go and to allow *him* to do the work he planned for them.

I am quite sure that most military members and their families experience this kind of deep weariness. I often hear young military wives with deployed husbands say, "I am just so tired." While the physical part of the deployment, with its added burdens for the one left behind, is difficult enough, the emotional part is even more difficult and often takes a greater toll. But it also affects that last and most important part of our makeup as humans: the spiritual aspect. Military families become spiritually weary.

If we are honest with ourselves, don't we all experience this at times? You don't have to be related to military personnel to become weary with all the worries and the "whys" in life that weigh us down.

We are told in Isaiah 40:31 that we are to run and not grow weary. When I am weary, I think God is saying to me, "Pick up the pace, and I will energize you with my Spirit." When weariness overcomes you, let God be your running partner. He will be with you to run the race and to fight the fight and to not grow weary in the process. ⋘Carol

★　★　★

Dear Lord Jesus, how tired and weary I get with life's circumstances. There are days when I find myself dreading to answer the phone, afraid that one more person will have a problem that I cannot handle. Then you say to me, "That's the point." I can't handle them. But when I wait on *you*, Lord, I will find new strength and be able to lead those who are also weary to you and your Word. I ask today that you give renewed strength to those families who are waiting for their loved ones. ✦ *Amen.*

Slowly Drained

I am dying from grief; my years are shortened by sadness. Sin has drained my strength; I am wasting away from within. ✛ PSALM 31:10

Living in the city, we do not drive our car every day. In fact, I can go a week without ever cranking the engine. The other day, however, I needed to run some errands. When the electronic key wouldn't work, I didn't think anything of it. But when I turned the ignition of my car, the engine wouldn't start. The battery was completely dead. Careful examination revealed that the trunk had not been closed all the way, causing the tiny light in the trunk to slowly drain the battery. You wouldn't think something so small would have such an effect. I learned the hard way that given enough time, the smallest light is enough to deplete the stored energy in a car's battery.

We often fail to realize that even small demands in life can drain our energy, our spiritual strength, and our zest for living. We can experience a slow drain that brings with it a defeated Christian life. Just as a car battery needs to be recharged by regular use, our inner spirits need to be recharged on a regular basis in order for us to live the life the Lord intends for us.

God doesn't want us to live defeated lives drained of faith, hope, love, and joy. The only way we can be energized with these spiritual qualities is by staying in communion with him through his Word and prayer. These are the battery chargers that allow his Spirit to work in us and provide fresh faith and grace for each day. Take time today to energize yourself by asking God's Spirit to renew your inner being. Be nourished by his Word today in order to live the abundant life he desires for you.
❧*Brenda*

✶   ✶   ✶

Thank you, Lord, for your power that renews me each day. Forgive me for the times I allow busyness and the cares of the world to keep me from spending time in your Word. Renew me today and fill me with your Holy Spirit. I pray for military personnel who are serving you in elite and special units. Protect them as they are required to regularly put themselves in danger. Renew their spirits as they perform dangerous missions behind enemy lines. In Jesus' name I pray. ✛ *Amen.*

January 14
Worry List

Don't worry about anything; instead, pray about everything. Tell God what you need, and thank him for all he has done. + PHILIPPIANS 4:6

I confess that I am a worrier by nature. If I don't have anything to worry about, I can easily create something. I suspect that my husband had me in mind as he prepared a sermon on the topic of worry. In the sermon, he made a suggestion that has been the most practical advice I have ever received on the subject. He suggested making a list of all the things you worry about. After the list is made, change your worry list into your prayer list. I have practiced this simple antidote to worry and can testify that it makes a difference. I have lists throughout my journals that started as worry lists but then became prayer lists.

When we are honest, we have to admit there is no value in worry. Worry in itself doesn't reverse bad situations. Worry in itself doesn't bring any solutions. Worry in itself really only accomplishes a feeling of being overwhelmed by dread. The negative scenarios in our minds that we replay end up like a record that is stuck and can never go on to complete the process.

It's normal for us to worry about issues of life, but we need to take our worries one step further by putting each circumstance into the hands of the Lord through prayer. As we put each item on our lists into God's hands, we can rest assured we have asked the most powerful person in the universe to help us with our individual struggles.

Today's Scripture directs us to take everything to God in prayer. In the original language this verse encourages us to pray through worship, specific requests concerning needs, and thanksgiving. Each of us can take these steps to victory over worry as we bring not just the big things, but everything, to God in prayer.

What are you worried about today? Why not make a list of all those things and use it as your prayer list? ~*Brenda*

* * *

Lord, you are good, gracious, and compassionate. I bring this list of things that are causing me worry today. Forgive me when I allow them to overwhelm me. I ask you to work in each situation. I ask you to give me your perspective and teach me to trust you in the process of each outcome. I thank you for the invitation to bring all my worries to you. Today I pray for parents of deployed military personnel. Give them the comfort of your peace. I ask this in your name. + *Amen.*

Standing Guard

Then you will experience God's peace, which exceeds anything we can understand. His peace will guard your hearts and minds as you live in Christ Jesus. **+** PHILIPPIANS 4:7

It is difficult to rest when you have a troubled mind or a troubled heart, isn't it? It is difficult to rest when you are overcome by worry, dread, or fear. Lately I've had some things on my mind that have caused me to lose sleep. It's as if my brain will not turn off. I think about all the things I need to get done, situations I am concerned with, and issues I can do nothing about at 2 a.m.! I read Philippians 4:7, which tells me that God's peace will guard my heart and mind as I live in Christ. What does that mean?

My soldier husband shared with me something that has helped me understand this concept: even in the midst of battle, a soldier can rest. It's hard to imagine that a soldier is able to sleep soundly in a war zone, yet my husband assures me it happens. It is possible because the soldier has confidence that a fellow soldier is standing guard watching out for him or her.

My husband remembered his first night on Iraqi soil when Operation Iraqi Freedom started. It was a former Iraqi airfield that had been taken over by coalition forces. Though my husband's unit was fairly certain there were hostile forces within the general area, when he lay down to sleep in a partially destroyed airplane hangar that first night, he could rest in comfort. Even if the enemy were around, he had confidence because his fellow soldiers were taking turns standing guard.

I remind myself as I go to bed each night that God is standing guard over my heart and mind. He desires for me to experience his peace that allows me to rest, both physically and spiritually.

If you are having trouble resting in your spirit, allow God to stand guard for you. It's an all-day, all-night guard you can trust!   *⌖Brenda*

✶   ✶   ✶

Father, thank you for the promise of your peace. Lord, I'm putting my burdens and worries in your hands today so I can rest. Help me to allow you to stand guard over my heart and mind. Remove the barriers that keep me from experiencing the peace of Christ. I pray for deep rest for weary service members who are working long hours in the cause of peace. In Jesus' name I pray. **+** *Amen.*

January 16
Writing in Pencil

So don't worry about tomorrow, for tomorrow will bring its own worries. Today's trouble is enough for today. ✝ MATTHEW 6:34

My dear friend Diane Sutton wrote a devotional and sent it to me several years ago. A woman of God and the wife of a retired air force general, she has granted me permission to share part of that devotional here.

> One of the most challenging things about being a military wife for me has been dealing with the unknowns about assignments. Much of the time not knowing where we'll be going next? to do what? when will it happen? will we be together? Or, will it be a remote tour? Pete will often tease me about something I've done almost every move we've made— We've just moved . . . lying in bed exhausted from unpacking, surrounded by boxes, and I'll ask him, "What do you think your next job will be and where do you think we'll be going next?" Pete's usual response is to wearily say something like, "Honey, let's unpack here and let me get to know *this* job before we start wondering about the next one!" You'd think after thirty-three years and sixteen moves I'd have figured this out!
>
> Because of the continual change in the military, we can be tempted to always be wondering about the future, which can keep us from living in the present. When we focus on the future, we can miss the special things God has for us *now*! We need to not always be looking to the next assignment and missing out on the opportunities and challenges of the current one. We don't want to be missing out on the joy and fun of our children's current ages and stages by thinking that life will be a little easier when they're a little older and in the next stages.
>
> My natural tendency is to not be very flexible. If I could, I'd write on my calendar in ink, but we don't live in an "ink" world. We need to be willing to write in pencil so we'll be ready for whatever God has planned for us!
>
> Psalm 95:7 says, "If only you would listen to his voice today!"

Diane told me that as she wrote those words, she was reminded of just how much God loves her and has been with her. Perhaps writing about God's faithfulness in your own life may do the same for you. ～*Carol*

✯　✯　✯

Lord, thank you that I can know I'm right where you want me to be! Help me not to look longingly to the future but to enjoy what you have for me today. Help me see and seize the opportunities before me. I pray that those whose lives are filled with transition will embrace each moment you have for them. In your precious name. ✝ *Amen.*

Chaos

I don't really understand myself, for I want to do what is right, but I don't do it. Instead, I do what I hate. ✛ ROMANS 7:15

Time—I waste too much.
Idle moments—I spend too many.
The spirit willing, but the flesh weak.
Hey, I'm fighting for even a willing spirit!
There are things I know to do—but don't.
Guilt hangs over my head like a weight,
Making rising above even harder.
Push! Heave! Thrust the weight of idleness off—
This heaviness of mind and spirit that wraps itself around me
Like a drug-induced cloak warming me
And pretending to comfort
Until I come to day's end and see—chaos.

I remember thinking that it was my job outside the home that kept me from having the clean, orderly, perfect house and family for which I yearned. But the words above were penned years after I no longer worked outside the home. Obviously, it wasn't a job that caused my chaos. I have come to realize there are struggles I naturally face that I cannot overcome in my own strength. As I look to the Lord, he alone is able to turn my chaos into order and my trouble into peace.

No one is immune to personal struggles, and we all would probably admit those struggles are things we hate to deal with. Even the apostle Paul, God's chosen minister, revealed that he struggled with those things he hated in his own life. He gives us some good guidance on how to deal with our own struggles in the context of today's Scripture.

Paul didn't deny his struggles, but he put them into the hands of God and worked through them. This process taught him to trust God. His conclusion? "So now there is no condemnation for those who belong to Christ Jesus. And because you belong to him, the power of the life-giving Spirit has freed you from the power of sin that leads to death" (Romans 8:1-2).

Give him your chaos today, and trust him to lead you to peace.   ❧*Brenda*

✳   ✳   ✳

Thank you, Lord, for your life-giving Spirit that frees me from sin. Help me to live in the power of your Spirit today, knowing I belong to you and have been freed from sin. You can bring my chaotic life into order. I pray for military commanders who are making challenging decisions today in the midst of their own chaos. Direct them with your divine hand to make wise decisions for the cause of freedom. ✛*Amen.*

January 18
A Message from God

Don't be afraid, for I am with you. Don't be discouraged, for I am your God. I will strengthen you and help you. I will hold you up with my victorious right hand. ✛ ISAIAH 41:10

This Scripture is very clear to me. It reminds me of the times when I am speaking to my sons and want them to hear and believe what I say.

Don't be afraid. . . . That is a very clear directive.

For I am with you. . . . He would never tell me that unless he meant it.

Do not be dismayed. . . . That could only mean that I am not to get down on myself to the point of hopelessness.

I am your God. . . . Yes, he is!

I will strengthen you. . . . *I will help you.* . . . Okay, double whammy. If you didn't get it the first time, he says, "Hear me; I will help you."

I will uphold you with my victorious right hand. . . . There's that wonderful, glorious right-hand reference.

He will hold us in the palm of his right hand and keep us. Not only does he hold us, but he says he will *uphold* us.

There are so many Scriptures that we ought to repeat out loud when life sends unexpected events our way. When crisis comes, when uncertainty comes, we must be ready with the Word. We receive peace and comfort from God's messages to us.

Hold on to the Word and break the Scriptures down to relate to you personally. Take heart in knowing the words that are written are just for you.   ⮜*Carol*

Lord, I am in awe that you continue to remind me that you are my God and that you will strengthen me and uphold me. Why don't I listen? I commit to you this day to personalize the Scripture that I might come to know you more intimately and more deeply. Today I ask that the many Bibles that are sent to faraway lands would give those who serve our country a desire to study and see the Word as a letter from you to them. ✛ *Amen.*

The Unseen Enemy

Stay alert! Watch out for your great enemy, the devil. He prowls around like a roaring lion, looking for someone to devour. + I PETER 5:8

The day was January 1, 2006. My husband and I sat at the breakfast table, talking about what we wanted to accomplish in the new year. We talked about practical things and then got into the spiritual things we wanted to commit to doing.

We started talking about the miracles God had performed in our family through the years—the prayers that we had prayed as parents and as spouses and the blessings that overflowed from pouring out our hearts to the Lord. Of course, these were not practices that came instantaneously but took time and perseverance.

That morning, we made a decision not to miss the blessings and the miracles of life in 2006. Since we easily get caught up in daily situations, we wanted to remind each other to step back and recognize what God has done and is doing in our lives—in other words, to become a living testimony for the Lord.

As time went on, there were many distractions from our goal, and I am sure there were many miracles missed along the way. The enemy wants to keep me discouraged and disheartened. He wants my face to be dull instead of glowing with the Holy Spirit in my life.

I found myself beginning to pray the prayer "Lord, empty self out of me. Fill me to maximum capacity so that there is no part of self left. My desire is that you are the one seen, not me." This prayer is one that I have had to go back and pray many times as self would come back into the picture.

Imagine what would happen if we truly spent time emptying self and letting God take over. We would be ready to face the enemy at any moment!

Facing the enemy hurts right now. We—particularly those who have loved ones in the military—hear of tragedy, war, and pain every day. There has always been a spiritual enemy of our Christian life; and we have come to understand an earthly parallel to that unseen enemy with the War on Terror.

But the One who defeats our enemy, Jesus, has come to give us abundant life (see John 10:10). Be ready to empty yourself, fill up with abundant life, and face the enemy.   ✑*Carol*

★　★　★

Father, I know all too well that there is an unseen enemy in the world. That enemy seeks to distract me from the ministry you have planned for me. I ask on this day for victory in my own battles and for victory for all who serve in the War on Terror. Keep the ultimate enemy from them and protect them against the physical enemy in our world, who wants to kill and destroy innocent lives. + *Amen.*

January 20
Stinking Thinking

And now, dear brothers and sisters, one final thing. Fix your thoughts on what is true, and honorable, and right, and pure, and lovely, and admirable. Think about things that are excellent and worthy of praise. ✛ PHILIPPIANS 4:8

My natural propensity is to be a glass-half-empty kind of person. I immediately imagine the worst-case scenario. I am grateful for a husband who patiently listens to me and then bluntly states, "That's just stinking thinking!"

I have discovered that I am in good company, since Scripture gives examples of those who struggled with stinking thinking. I gain hope as I study the prophet Elijah. This godly man prayed down fire from heaven and killed the prophets of Baal. Yet all it took was wicked Queen Jezebel saying she was going to kill him for him to say, "I am the only one left!" (1 Kings 19:10). In reality there were seven thousand faithful followers who remained, but Elijah could see only what was right in front of him, which resulted in a negative view of his circumstances.

When you are depressed or sad, it isn't always apparent that your thinking is distorted, is it? You may be reading this today, struggling with thinking the worst about your situation. Today's Scripture implies that you can control what you think. You can choose to think on those things that are true. Or you can choose to think on those things that are negative. I'm not just talking about positive thinking—I'm talking about thinking *truth*. Positive thinking has been proven to make a difference; however, when we go from merely thinking positive to thinking truth, we tap into God's power.

What are the results? This verse in Philippians 4:8 is sandwiched between two verses on peace:

> Then you will experience God's peace, which exceeds anything we can understand. His peace will guard your hearts and minds as you live in Christ Jesus. And now, dear brothers and sisters, one final thing. Fix your thoughts on what is true, and honorable, and right, and pure, and lovely, and admirable. Think about things that are excellent and worthy of praise. Keep putting into practice all you learned and received from me—everything you heard from me and saw me doing. Then the God of peace will be with you (Philippians 4:7-9).

Instead of having stinking thinking that brings an unpleasant odor to life, think on what is good and be filled with the sweet aroma of God's peace. ❧*Brenda*

✻ ✻ ✻

Thank you, God, for the promise of your peace. Guard my heart and mind as I live in you; may I fix my thoughts on those things that are excellent and worthy of praise. I pray for families of deployed service members who are struggling with worry. Grant them your peace of mind and heart as they trust in you. ✛ *Amen.*

Winter Blues

Why am I discouraged? Why is my heart so sad? I will put my hope in God! I will praise him again—my Savior and my God! ·I· PSALM 43.5

Winter is in full swing, and often accompanying winter is a feeling described as the blues. A Google search for beating the winter blues came up with a myriad of articles and opinions on how to combat them. The most often prescribed remedy included diet, exercise, and light therapy—the use of custom lights that mimic summer sunshine. My quick research further informed me that winter blues can be diagnosed as seasonal affective disorder, or SAD, a real condition that affects fifteen million Americans.[1] For these men and women, winter can be an especially difficult time, leading to depression, weight loss or gain, withdrawal from society, increased irritability, and even suicidal thoughts. For those with serious symptoms, medical treatment is necessary.

I am not an expert on SAD or clinical depression, but I can relate to experiencing the winter blues. I found this winter excerpt from a personal journal:

> Is there relief from this heaviness I feel? Do I bring it on myself by procrastination? Is it real physical heaviness that produces the mental tension and literally weighs my body down? I awake with my eyes feeling the need to close again. I rise with my body longing to return prostrate. I say, "Today I *will* get up and move with energy and enthusiasm." Yet no energy comes and enthusiasm is a faraway friend. Give me energy for this day, Lord. Help me make a few more checks on my list as tangible proof this day is not wasted. Provide hope that I will overcome the lethargy of spirit that lingers like the snow outside.

We can beat the winter blues more effectively when we address both physical and spiritual needs. In addition to the physical remedies of exercise, diet, and light therapy, there are some spiritual remedies that correlate. We can exercise spiritual disciplines. We can maintain a steady diet of God's Word. We can bask in the warmth of the Light of the World. Perhaps this is how the psalmist was able to respond to his sad condition and confidently state, "I will put my hope in God! I will praise him again!" *≈Brenda*

* * *

Thank you, Father, for the hope that comes through trusting you. Help me to do those things I need to do both physically and spiritually to maintain a healthy balance of mind, body, and spirit. Most of all I pray for the warmth of your love to fill my heart. I pray that you would encourage service members and their families who may be feeling sadness because of separation. + *Amen.*

---

[1] E. J. Mundell, "Shed Light on SAD to Ease the Winter Blues," *USA Today*, January 28, 2005.

January 22
Lessons Learned

I weep with sorrow; encourage me by your word. + PSALM 119:28

While my husband was stationed at Fort Leavenworth, Kansas, I had the privilege of training to be and then becoming a facilitator for the Pre-Command Spouse Orientation Program. This program was designed for the spouses of those military members who would soon be taking the command of a military unit.

One of the life lessons I took away was on the stages of grief. These commanders and their wives, the first sergeants and their wives, and the chaplains and their wives are constantly dealing with grief in one form or another. I had learned the stages of grief in my psychology classes in college:

Denial
Anger
Bargaining
Depression
Acceptance

The point was made that it is not only death that sends us into these stages but also other major life events, such as divorce, deployment, separation, and even moving, which the military in particular does so frequently.

We discussed how normal and necessary it is to go through these stages until reaching acceptance and that the only time there is a danger in all this is if you are stalled at one of the stages. Otherwise, going back and forth and continually moving from one to the next is very normal.

During these times of deployment and separation, remember that many in our country are experiencing these various stages. If you know people who are grieving, keep in mind that telling them to get over it or reminding them that this is the life they chose will not help. The way to help is to love and support them as they are experiencing their very normal grief stages.

A final lesson is that these men, women, children, and parents need a listening ear, not a wagging tongue, in their times of grief. Be there for them and be their listener, prayer partner, and supporter. They will come out being able to walk side-by-side with someone else who is experiencing grief.   ~Carol

*   *   *

Father, never let me think I know it all. I pray for a heart that is tender to *your* teaching. As I learn the lessons of life each day, help me to go to your Word as my guide. Lord, I think of those who are serving and will experience the deaths of their fellows; give them peace in the midst of their grief. + *Amen.*

A Ghost Town

Never again will you be called "The Forsaken City" or "The Desolate Land." Your new name will be "The City of God's Delight" and "The Bride of God," for the LORD delights in you and will claim you as his bride. ✝ ISAIAH 62:4

Several years ago, I was visiting friends stationed in beautiful Monterey, California. I had heard how lovely the military installation formerly known as Fort Ord was, set in its picturesque location. The setting was unquestionably stunning, but to my disappointment, the military post was like a ghost town. As I drove through the streets, I noticed that many of the houses were empty and desolate. It felt eerie and rather sad. I learned that though it was still an operating base at the time, as the installation's military mission downsized, there were fewer personnel to occupy the quarters. Unfortunately, the empty buildings could not be torn down because of prohibitive expenses associated with environmental issues. Instead they were left standing— vacant, unkempt edifices in such a beautiful setting.

Most mistakes made in life are unintentional, yet they can lead to a desolate life. In other words, sometimes we make such huge mistakes in our lives that we live with the scars of them for the rest of our days. The houses at Fort Ord weren't intentionally destined to be a wasteland, just as no one's life is intended to be wasted.

The good news is that, unlike Fort Ord, God has the spiritual resources to not only forgive past mistakes now but also restore us for a future with him. Here on earth, we get ourselves in messes we can't fix. Only God can take the desolate land of our life and make it a city of his delight. His resources have no limit. He can renovate the desolation and enable us to live useful and productive lives here on earth— a renovation that is complete and forever. *≈Brenda*

★ ★ ★

Thank you, Lord, for your renovation in my life. I pray that you would continue the process of making me into the person you have designed me to be. Strengthen the bodies and minds of those who are serving you in war-torn lands, and bring renovation to their spirits in the midst of such physical desolation. I ask in Jesus' name. ✝ *Amen.*

January 24
Blessed Hope

For the grace of God has been revealed, bringing salvation to all people. And we are instructed to turn from godless living and sinful pleasures. We should live in this evil world with wisdom, righteousness, and devotion to God, while we look forward with hope to that wonderful day when the glory of our great God and Savior, Jesus Christ, will be revealed. ✚ TITUS 2:11-13

A Blessed Hope, based on Titus 2:11-13
The weight of sin and self I feel
Is heavy in my heart.
I awaken with its pressing force
Before a new day's start.
To rid myself of sin and self—
I long for sweet release.
Your Word comes washing over me
And offers hope and peace.
I read of grace that brings with it
Salvation, and the power
To say NO to ungodliness
In this wicked hour.
It promises me the strength to live
A life that's free of stress,
As I wait patiently in this world
For a hope that's oh so blessed!
A blessed hope! A promise true—
He's coming back for me!
This heart, now clean, is eager
To wait—renewed and free!

There are times when I am overwhelmed with the evil in the world. I've learned that I must begin my day with God's Word and prayer to have a healthy focus throughout the day. It would be easy to live in a state of hopelessness if I focused only on news headlines.

But today's Scripture directs me to look forward to a day that will be wonderful! It will be a day when the evil of this world will be vanquished and God's glory will be revealed. It instructs me to live each day hopeful for what is to come.   ✎*Brenda*

✱ ✱ ✱

Father, thank you for the hope that you give each day. Forgive me when I focus too much on the events of the world and lose sight of the promise of eternity. You are my blessed hope today. I pray for those who are feeling hopeless because of events that have brought crisis to their lives. Intersect their lives with your message of hope. In Jesus' name I pray. ✚*Amen.*

A Cross in the Desert

But in your great mercy you did not abandon them to die in the wilderness. The pillar of cloud still led them forward by day, and the pillar of fire showed them the way through the night. ✛ NEHEMIAH 9:19

When my husband returned from deployment to Afghanistan, I was eager to look through the photos he had taken. There were interesting pictures of people with whom he served as well as desert landscapes and camel-dotted Bedouin camps. As I looked through the photos, I was most intrigued by at least fifty pictures of a cross. The pictures viewed the cross at different times of day and at every possible angle. I asked my husband, "Why so many pictures of the chapel cross?"

He said that the cross was not from the chapel and began to share his story. One day he was feeling especially lonely. The desert was barren, desolate, and oppressive. Ironically, even as he felt lonely, my husband also recognized his need of a secluded place to spend time seeking the Lord. He decided to climb to the top of his office building to check out the roof. What he spotted there surprised him. The Afghan workers had removed some scaffolding but stopped before the job was complete. What was left of the scaffolding was the perfect shape of a cross. That cross in the desert served him as a reminder of God's presence throughout the remainder of his deployment.

In Scripture, there are many references to God making his presence known to people in the desert. Moses spent years there as a shepherd while God prepared him to lead the Hebrews out of exile. Jacob had an encounter with God in a desert that changed his life. Elijah found himself beside a desert tree ready to die until he heard the still, small voice of God giving him hope for the rest of his journey.

The Lord allows barren times into our lives to form our character and draw us to himself. The promise to which we can cling is the same one my husband experienced in Afghanistan. His presence is always with us—even in the desert places. *≈Brenda*

✬　✬　✬

Lord, I often find myself feeling lonely. Help me to know you are with me. Help me to trust you in the barren places, knowing you are working on my behalf even when I don't see you. I pray I would make it a priority to find a place of solitude each day in order to commune with you and have my eyes open to your presence in my life. Give the men and women serving in the deserts of Iraq and Afghanistan a fresh sense of your presence today. In your name I pray. ✛*Amen.*

January 26
Hey There, Lonely Girl

Turn to me and have mercy, for I am alone and in deep distress. ✛ PSALM 25:16

There is something of a mystery in loneliness. It makes itself known at times when we are least prepared or expecting it. The greatest mystery of all is that loneliness is no respecter of situations. One may be the loneliest number, but loneliness can sometimes be at its strongest in a crowd. During a friend's husband's deployment to Iraq, she wrote in her journal, "I'm feeling very lonely today. I'm busy—people call, but I feel lonely."

During lonely times, we can be surprised at the pain we feel. In the worst cases, loneliness can lead to anger, suffering, depression, isolation, and fear. However, it is important to know that loneliness, to a certain degree, is normal. In fact, it is a part of our being human. There is not a man or woman alive who has not experienced loneliness to some extent. The wave of emotion that comes with loneliness can be debilitating. It can be described as an empty feeling and is often accompanied by deep feelings of sadness. The reasons are as numerous as the emotions that occur.

The good news is that there are benefits to being a lonely girl—or boy! We all need unscripted time to sit quietly, take a walk, read a book, or write in a journal. Times of stillness can bring comfort and refreshment to the soul. The challenge for the Christian is making the effort to change times of loneliness into times of solitude that connect us with God. Jesus himself pulled away to pray. It was a time for him to be refreshed. We are constantly bombarded with noise; it takes effort to shut out the external and concentrate on our relationship with God. The good news is that God can use our lonely times to draw us to himself.

If loneliness is the evidence that something is missing, the obvious thing to do is fill the void. We must be sure that the choices we make in the filling process are God honoring.

In times of loneliness, let others know you need their prayers, support, and companionship. Combat the temptation to become focused inward. Ask the Lord to help you use loneliness as a tool to reach out to others. ↩*Carol*

* * *

Lord, help me to not get stuck in loneliness. Give me courage to approach others as well as to seek you for companionship. Encourage lonely service members today as they serve far away from home, and strengthen the hearts of their loved ones. ✛ *Amen.*

I Can't Help It

We cannot stop telling about everything we have seen and heard. ✛ ACTS 4:20

If you are a grandparent, you understand feeling compelled to share all the cute things your grandchildren say. I am guilty of not only telling the stories, but telling the stories while attempting to imitate the appropriate voice. I can't help it—they say the cutest things! People have no choice but to be a captive audience. My husband is no exception; there are very few sermons of his without a grandchild story included.

Acts 4 records what happened to Peter and John as a result of their preaching the gospel. They were arrested and put in jail, then released and told not to preach any more. Peter responded to the ban on preaching by saying, "We cannot stop telling about everything we have seen and heard." It's as if he's saying, "We can't help it!" What had impressed these disciples so powerfully that even jail and an injunction against preaching had no effect on them?

Well, for starters, they had seen: the lame walk, the blind see, the deaf hear, the dumb speak, lepers cleansed, the dead raised, demons cast out, multitudes fed, and Christ walking on the water.

They had heard the Sermon on the Mount, countless parables, and other words of teaching by Jesus. They were doing what their Old Testament counterpart Jeremiah did when he said, "But if I say I'll never mention the LORD or speak in his name, his word burns in my heart like a fire. It's like a fire in my bones! I am worn out trying to hold it in! I can't do it!" (Jeremiah 20:9).

What is God doing in your life? Are they things that give you such excitement and insight that you are compelled to tell others? *≈Brenda*

✶　✶　✶

Lord, thank you for the personal work you do in my life. I pray that I would daily make myself available to learn from your Word. Open my ears to hear your voice. Open my heart to learn the lessons you teach. Open my mouth to share freely of your great love. Bless the reporters who are serving you in dangerous parts of the world. Protect them and use them to share truth, since they are the eyes and ears of our nation. In your name I pray. ✛ *Amen.*

January 28
A Person of Simple Faith

I am writing to you who share the same precious faith we have. This faith was given to you because of the justice and fairness of Jesus Christ, our God and Savior. ✛ 2 PETER 1:1

I am a person of simple faith. Whenever I am caught in the middle of a theological discussion and there are many directives being given on the hows and whys of our faith, I usually retort, "No one comes to the Father but through Me (Jesus)."

I am saddened each time I encounter someone who is intelligent and knowledgeable about life yet has such a difficult time understanding the simplicity of the gospel. God is love. God is all things to all men. He is our creator, our counselor, our healer, our redeemer, our provider, and more. He is our rock in times of trouble.

God gave us Jesus. God gave us his Word. God loves us unconditionally.

Many of our young men and women in the military are giving their hearts to Jesus Christ before the battles begin in faraway lands. In World War I and World War II, these were called foxhole conversions. Praise the Lord for those conversions. Often when men and women are sent to serve their country, they come to a realization that God is the only constant in their lives. The simple act of accepting Jesus as their Lord and Savior enables them to fight with confidence and the Holy Spirit's power.

Many have come to know the Lord through other crisis situations in our world. There is always an outpouring of love and support from the Christian community during these times, and prayers are offered by those who gather. Outreach and ministry come shortly after that.

I believe that God wanted our faith to be simple. He knew how very complicated our world would become, and he wanted the most important decision we would ever make to be kept simple. Become a person of simple faith.   ⁓*Carol*

★   ★   ★

Lord Jesus, I pray today that all who are experiencing difficult situations will come to know personally the Giver of life. Your Word says that no one comes to the Father but through the Son. Give hope in Jesus to those who are in conflict and crisis today. I ask these things in your name. ✛ *Amen.*

A Minute Too Late

"When the master of the house has locked the door, it will be too late. You will stand outside knocking and pleading, 'Lord, open the door for us!' But he will reply, 'I don't know you or where you come from.'" + LUKE 13:25

Yesterday I had lunch with my friend Karen at a great Italian place nearby. The prices are great, the food is good, and they even play Christian music in the background—a great plus for me! Karen parked directly in front of the restaurant and fed the meter enough coins to provide us with an hour of food and fellowship. We enjoyed our meal and were engrossed in meaningful conversation when Karen realized she needed to add another coin to the meter. Much to our dismay, she returned with a parking ticket in hand. She couldn't have been more than one or two minutes late. One coin and a few minutes would have made such a difference!

Today's Scripture is a response Jesus gave following the question of who will enter heaven. His words challenge us against having a complacent mind-set about eternity and alert us to the fact that there will come a time when it will be too late.

It is a tragedy when people busy themselves with enjoying things of this life with the intention in the back of their minds that someday they will make things right with God. I remember a conversation I once had with a college student: I asked him what was keeping him from becoming a Christ follower. He explained that he was having too much fun—following Christ was something he would do later.

Scripture states that there is pleasure in sin for a season, but the consequences of a cavalier attitude toward salvation can result in years of grief. This young man could not understand how having a right relationship with God now would make his enjoyment of life so much greater. How I wanted him to understand that the joy of following Christ is for today in addition to eternity!

As you read these words, if you haven't ever made the decision to follow Christ, don't wait a minute longer! Acknowledge that God loves you and wants a relationship with you (see John 3:16). Be aware that we all are separated from God because of sin (see Romans 3:23). Answer God's invitation to live in right relationship with him (see Romans 5:8). Accept Christ as your Lord and Savior (see John 1:12). And find a Christian who can help you from here.   *Brenda*

✦   ✦   ✦

Father, thank you for new life in Christ! I make you Lord of my life, and I commit to following you today and every day. I pray for young men and women in the armed services who are seeking spiritual meaning. May they find that meaning in the Cross of Christ. In Jesus' name I pray. + *Amen.*

January 30
Do You Remember the Time?

For God made Christ, who never sinned, to be the offering for our sin, so that we could be made right with God through Christ. + 2 CORINTHIANS 5:21

How many times do we say that life gets in the way? How many times do we get cluttered with all the to-do lists?

Amy Grant has a wonderful song called "Do You Remember the Time?" She sings about how we must take the time to remember that moment when we first let Jesus into our hearts. She sings, "Hold me close, never let me go." He is our first love in our Christian walk.[1]

So many times in the midst of difficult situations, I run to him immediately. I am so thankful that I have access to the throne of God in times of trial. However, I am to hold on to him each day, not running *to* him just when I'm in trouble but being *with* him from the moment of my salvation. Every breath I take, every decision I make, every relationship I have will be with him right beside me.

I need to be constantly reminded of my first love. Why am I going over this with you? Because there is so much going on in the world today. I want to hold on to Jesus during these times. I don't want to let go and then have to run to find him when things don't go as planned. I want him to be right there to scoop me up and put me in his lap in a moment.

If you don't have Jesus in your life, he is always waiting for you to say, "Yes, Lord, come in." In these perilous times of conflict and sorrow, we can know that he is there in a heartbeat to guide us, comfort us, and love us.   ～*Carol*

Thank you, God, for your Son, Jesus. Thank you that he is in my heart and my life today and that you have sent your Holy Spirit to dwell in me. Take me back to remember the time that I first accepted Jesus as my Lord and Savior. Keep me close to his heart so that I may never be without him. Help those who are serving our country to know that you are close at all times. + *Amen.*

---

[1] Amy Grant, "Do You Remember the Time?" *Legacy . . . Hymns and Faith*, compact disc, (p) 2002 Word /A&M.

Is It Broken?

In his kindness God called you to share in his eternal glory by means of Christ Jesus. So after you have suffered a little while, he will restore, support, and strengthen you, and he will place you on a firm foundation. All power to him forever! Amen. ✛ 1 PETER 5:10-11

I was driving with my grandson when I mentioned to him I needed to go home to fix supper. The three-year-old's response was, "Why? Is it broken?"

We want to fix things that often can't be fixed, don't we? A short time ago, I spoke to a young woman who was feeling helpless because of the discouragement her deployed husband was experiencing. The messages of help she longed to share with him seemed hollow. I was pleased when this shy wife and mother was willing to be vulnerable and shared her burden with others. Several sisters in Christ gathered around her and prayed for her and her husband. She needed to be reminded that her suffering was temporal and there was hope in the midst of the struggle.

The word *restore* in 1 Peter 5:10 means "to equip, to adjust, to fit together." It is the same word translated "mending nets" found in Matthew 4:21. Whether you use the word *restore* or *mend*, there really is some "fixing" going on. It is a fixing that creates something immovable. In the original language the words used describe something being established on a firm foundation and made firm in every part.[1]

As Christ followers, we can find hope in the fact that our troubles only come for a season. Along with the Scripture for today, 2 Corinthians 4:17 confirms this fact: "For our present troubles are small and won't last very long. Yet they produce for us a glory that vastly outweighs them and will last forever!" Small troubles and momentary suffering pale in comparison to eternity. The promise of the glory they produce provides hope.

Think about that while you fix supper tonight! ✺*Brenda*

✶　✶　✶

Dear Lord, I find myself complaining for the suffering that I feel I must endure here on earth. Forgive me and remind me of the purpose for suffering. Help me to know you are the only one who can fix my broken soul. Provide hope and help for those who are serving you in foreign lands. May they bring healing and hope to many who are broken by the ravages of war. In your name I pray. ✛ *Amen.*

---

[1] Warren W. Wiersbe, *Be Hopeful* (Wheaton, IL: SP Publications, 1983), 141.

February 1
An Unexpected Oasis

You prepare a feast for me in the presence of my enemies. You honor me by anointing my head with oil. My cup overflows with blessings. ✚ PSALM 23:5

I was cautious as I arrived in the Istanbul airport. This stop would include my second airport layover—six hours—on my international journey, and I was dreading the time in the foreign environment.

I exited the plane and felt the need to walk a while before I ventured to the domestic terminal to wait for my next flight. I decided to walk the length of the international terminal to stretch my legs. Imagine my surprise when I saw an army of Starbucks employees walking around. This welcome sight was not at all what I expected. It was as if there were a Starbucks convention at the Istanbul airport. I followed the green apron-clad crew to a brand-new, just-opened-the-day-before Starbucks. There I found hospitable, comfy couches inviting me to sit and enjoy my layover. The caffe latte I sipped as I wrote my gratitude in my journal had never tasted so good.

Here I was experiencing a challenging trip, yet I found an oasis that gave me comfort and reminded me of home. I was still farther away from home than I had ever been. I was still facing the unknown as I continued my journey. My circumstances had not changed, but in the midst of the journey, I found a comforting oasis that bolstered my stamina for what was ahead.

As we go through challenging times, we can find an oasis of comfort and strength in the presence of the Lord. Psalm 23 promises that we can be refreshed as we allow him to lead us along peaceful streams to renew our strength.

A spiritual oasis can be found in the most unexpected places as you take time to sit and look to the Lord.   ❧Brenda

✫   ✫   ✫

Thank you, Lord, for times of refreshment in unexpected places. Open my eyes to see the opportunities you give me to be refreshed in body and spirit throughout this day. I pray for those serving you in enemy territory. Provide an oasis of refreshment for their weary bodies and tired souls. In your name I pray. ✚ Amen.

Come On In

Cheerfully share your home with those who need a meal or a place to stay. ✦ 1 PETER 4:9

Some of you may read today's Scripture and say, "I will gladly do that if you give me a couple of days to clean and plan meals and buy fresh flowers for every room."

The response of a military wife is usually quite different. You see, someone is always moving out or moving in, living in housing for a short tour for school or special training—this life is an opportunity for learning to truly open your door and say, "Come on in."

I enjoyed being the person to host different activities and functions as a military wife. I always felt that the simpler things were, the more time there would be for fellowship and getting to know one another.

One of the greatest ladies I've ever known was Bev Brandenburg, who influenced me in regard to hospitality. I asked her if I could specifically use her name in this illustration because she is one of a kind. You see, when she married John Brandenburg, he was a colonel promotable. She had never experienced military life before, having been a restaurant owner. She had also been a caterer and hosted many gatherings in her hometown.

I first met Bev when she and her husband, Lieutenant General John Brandenburg, were living in Quarters One at Fort Lewis, Washington. I was amazed the first time she opened up their home to a chapel event and had all the ladies come over for lunch. In fact, there was rarely a day when someone was not sharing in her hospitality. I am very thankful for her example. I'll tell you, from that time on I was determined to keep my home open for sharing, caring, and fellowship.

Why else has God given us a home? It is not to be made into a shrine for myself or our family. It is not to be made an all-about-me house. It is for ministering to those who would enter.

Share the dwelling God has blessed you with. Be a blessing through your hospitality and love.   ⊱*Carol*

✦ ✦ ✦

Dear Lord, during this time of uncertainty and bad news, give me the strength and the foresight to share my home with others so they may see you. Give me an opportunity to open my home to someone who is separated from loved ones because of deployment. In your name I pray. ✦ *Amen.*

February 3
I Need My Mom!

You heard me when I cried, "Listen to my pleading! Hear my cry for help!" Yes, you came when I called; you told me, "Do not fear." ✛ LAMENTATIONS 3:56-57

The goal of every parent of sons is to raise them to be strong, independent men. I am no exception. I didn't realize how challenging the process would be, though—and not for my sons but for me! As a mom, I longed for them to call home from college and share all they were experiencing. Both of my boys quickly adapted to college life, making my husband very proud and me very sad. Actually, I was proud, too, but I missed them. Their expressed needs after leaving home were more in the form of financial support rather than nurturing.

One day I was sitting at my desk at work when I received a call from my oldest son, a college junior at the time. He sounded so terrible that I could hardly understand him. A bad cold had turned into something worse, and he was a very sick kid. I told him to get someone to take him to the campus clinic. Following his visit to the clinic, he called again to give me the report. Before the call ended, he became very quiet and finally said, "All I keep thinking is I need my mom." Well, that's all it took for this mom to purchase a plane ticket and be by his side before the day ended. I knew this scenario wouldn't play out many more times, if ever, his needing me in this way and my ability to be present.

As I read today's Scriptures and others like it (Psalm 145:18-20; Psalm 31:22; Psalm 40:1), I am reminded of God as a loving parent responding to the needs of his children. There are times when the help may not be as obvious as buying a plane ticket and being there by nightfall, but I am assured if I come to him in fear (holy awe) and truth (sincere dependence), he is working on my behalf.

I pray my son makes this spiritual application as he reflects on the day his mom dropped everything to feed him chicken noodle soup.   ⁊*Brenda*

* * *

Loving heavenly Father, thank you for hearing my cry for help. You, who created the universe, are attuned to the cries of your children. I stand amazed and humbled! I pray for a heart to hear the cries of others and be your hand of help in this world. I pray for veterans of war who are seeking help for emotional hurt as a result of their service. In Jesus' name I pray. ✛ *Amen.*

Family Time

I will bless those who bless you and curse those who treat you with contempt. All the families on earth will be blessed through you. ✦ GENESIS 12:3

Someday when you are on the computer and have time, google the definition of *family*. The different ways a family is defined in our society will absolutely blow your mind.

God meant for a family to be a husband and a wife and their children. He was the creator of families when he created Eve for Adam. He created us to be the family of God.

In the book *Building a Successful Family*, by Dr. Jerry Pipes, he refers to some statistics that serve as important reminders:

Only 34 percent of America's families eat even one meal together each day.
The average father spends only eight to ten minutes a day with his children—including watching television and eating meals.
Only 12 percent of America's families pray together.
The average couple spends only four minutes of uninterrupted time together each day.[1]

Many of the mothers and fathers who are serving our country right now would give anything to be sitting at the table for a meal with their families. Those who have lost loved ones in tragic situations would love to be spending hours with them this week. Some of those couples torn apart by divorce wonder if it would have worked out if they had been able to spend quality time together.

Families on earth are God's way of giving us the love and the renewal each day to help us go on in this world. Be challenged to recommit yourself while there is still time to spend quality and abundant time with those you love. Sit down with each other and talk about how each person sees your family, and make a conscious effort with them to make it happen. ✎*Carol*

✮   ✮   ✮

Lord, I thank you first of all for allowing me the privilege to be a part of your family. Thank you for families. I ask that, as so many families are separated during this time, you would continue to encourage them through your love, enabling them to remain close and committed to one another. ✦ *Amen.*

---

[1] Jerry Pipes, *Building a Successful Family*, (Lawrenceville, GA: Completeness Productions, 2002).

February 5
Around the Table

Your children will be like vigorous young olive trees as they sit around your table. That is the LORD's blessing for those who fear him. ✝ PSALM 128:3-4

During a year-long tour of military duty in Kansas, my husband and I purchased an antique dining room table. We had found some great antiques while living there, and we agreed that a table would be a worthy acquisition. We scoured stores throughout the area and settled on a round oak table that had some distress but didn't need immediate refinishing.

I would have never dreamed how dear that table would become to me. As my boys became teenagers, it developed into the symbol of family. Busy schedules for all of us meant that having a meal together was a challenge, but we made an effort to share at least one meal around that table every day. We began our morning there as I would read from a devotion book and pray over the boys before they left the house for school. Many nights after dinner, there were lingering discussions about football, school, girls, and faith. And there was laughter—lots of laughter. Laughter is important in the midst of teenage angst—for parents and for kids.

Each time my mother-in-law looks at that table, she asks when we are going to refinish it. Although that was the original intention, I'm just not sure I want to do it anymore. I like it with the flaws and distress. There's laughter in the wood. The distress reminds me of the times of prayer and struggle that took place as we endeavored to share our faith and values with those growing young men.

Parenting has proved to be the greatest joy of my life and the greatest challenge. The flaws in the table are a reflection of the table's wear; however, the wood is solid, and the base is strong. As parents, my husband and I haven't done everything perfectly, and our kids may reflect some of our errors and flaws. But the love we have for them is strong, and the foundation we laid in Jesus Christ is firm.

The Christian life is not about obtaining perfection. It is about living life to the fullest with the joys and challenges, the ups and downs, the victories and mistakes, yet knowing through it all, as a person and as a family, we can stand firm in Christ. ❧Brenda

✴ ✴ ✴

Dear Lord, you are the perfect parent. I am grateful to be your child. Thank you for loving me even with all my flaws. I pray for the strength to stand firm in you during times of distress. Help me to be a blessing to my family today. I pray for teenagers who have deployed parents. Please provide adults who will mentor them and encourage them during this critical time. ✝ Amen.

Stand by Me

"But take courage! None of you will lose your lives, even though the ship will go down. For last night an angel of the God to whom I belong and whom I serve stood beside me, and he said, 'Don't be afraid, Paul, for you will surely stand trial before Caesar! What's more, God in his goodness has granted safety to everyone sailing with you.'" ✛ ACTS 27:22-24

Natalie Gilbert knows what it is like to have someone stand beside her. In 2003, then-thirteen-year-old Natalie won a local contest in Portland that provided her the opportunity to sing the national anthem at a Portland Trail Blazers basketball game. She stepped up to the microphone and began the song with a strong, clear voice, nailing every word. But when she came to *twilight's last gleaming*, her mind went blank. She began to giggle and then looked frantically to locate her father. Fear and embarrassment were setting in quickly. At that moment she spotted the coach of the Trail Blazers, Mo Cheeks, coming her direction. Coach Cheeks stood beside her, placed his hand on her shoulder, and told her to "Come on, sing!" Together they completed the song, inviting the fans to join in. It was quite a moment.[1]

I don't know how Natalie's parents felt, but I can imagine they were quite grateful to Coach Cheeks for being the encouragement their daughter needed during a difficult time. As parents, we can't always be available to our children in their times of need. We have to trust God that he will send the right person at the right time in the right way.

Today's Scripture finds God sending help to one of his children in a time of crisis. Paul declares that an angel of the Lord was sent to stand beside him to deliver the message, "Do not be afraid." Whether it is an angel or flesh and blood, we can trust the Lord to send the help our children need. I pray regularly for encouraging people to intersect the lives of my children. I also pray that I have the opportunity to be that person for others. ☙*Brenda*

✲　✲　✲

Father, thank you for your loving care in my life. I pray today that you will stand beside my children. I pray you will send people into their lives to speak words of encouragement and blessing. I ask your grace to rest on those who are reaching out to children in war-torn lands. Use them to bring kindness and generosity of spirit to children who are experiencing deep tragedy and pain. In Jesus' name I pray. ✛*Amen.*

---

[1] Blazers, "Cheeks Anthem Assist," http://www.nba.com/blazers/features/Cheeks_Anthem_Assist-73713-41.html.

February 7
I Will Love You No Matter What

No one will be able to stand against you as long as you live. For I will be with you as I was with Moses. I will not fail you or abandon you. ✚ JOSHUA 1:5

My parents taught me what unconditional love is all about. As they watched me grow, there were times of button-popping pride when I was making hard-earned accomplishments. When the not-so-good times came, there was discipline and tears, but guess what? There was still love.

I have heard many times that young children learn how to understand the unconditional love of God through their parents. If they consistently cannot do anything right, they begin to see that in their heavenly Father also. It can be a time of wanting to be perfect but never making it, therefore feeling as if life is lived out in failure.

My favorite verse in Scripture gives me a great promise in my life. "I don't mean to say that I have already achieved these things or that I have already reached perfection. But I press on to possess that perfection for which Christ Jesus first possessed me" (Philippians 3:12).

The reference to the day of Christ Jesus is referring to the day we meet the Lord. We will not be perfect until we see Jesus. He knew that our process of perfection would never work out humanly. We are striving each day to better ourselves, but we will never get there until we meet him face to face.

What a lesson for husbands, wives, parents, and children. Why do we insist on perfection when there is no way to achieve it on this earth? Our focus should be on teaching and living out unconditional love as much as possible. We are his example on this earth. Instead of seeking to achieve worldly perfection, our goals and our lives should seek to achieve love for our fellow man.

He hates the sin of man and the sinful actions of man, but he never stops loving us. That is our challenge as humans. It is a love that will be there no matter what.
≈Carol

☆　☆　☆

Lord, as I witness the great love that those who serve our country show in their voluntary service, let me continue to strive for that in my own life. Take me from trying to achieve perfection to living day-by-day being perfected until I see you face to face. ✚ Amen.

A Good Day

Then I will sing praises to your name forever as I fulfill my vows each day. ✛ PSALM 61:8

What gives value to a day?

I cringe when the alarm clock screams at 6:00 a.m. I long to turn and ignore the incessant beep . . . beep . . . beep. My body wishes to stay in my warm bed, allowing sleep to overtake me once again. Yet, I rise. I take myself to the kitchen. I crack eggs into a skillet and insert bread into the toaster. I place this offering before my child. I read a psalm and say a prayer of blessing over him as he departs for the day.

He rises to leave, stopping to comment on his way out the door: "Thanks for breakfast, Mom."

7:00 a.m. and it's already been a good day!

I wrote these words in a journal while my youngest son was in high school. It was a time of life that found me struggling to see value in the routine of my days. I felt unproductive and frustrated. All I could see were faded dreams, unrealized goals, and unfulfilled expectations. I continually asked the Lord to reveal his will for my life. There was nothing unusual about this particular day that would have made me look at it any differently. But the Holy Spirit allowed my eyes to see and my ears to hear the value of my daily routine as I served my son.

It is easy to get stuck in the routine and lose sight of the value of the ordinary things of life. Many of the tasks we do on a day-to-day basis, like preparing meals for our families, talking to a friend, attending a Bible study, or shuttling children to various events, seem as though they are only taking up valuable time. If only the ordinary weren't draining our energy, prohibiting us from accomplishing the big and important things! When we weigh things in the balance of God's eternal perspective, we come back to what is of greatest eternal value—people. A small investment like cooking breakfast for a teenage son, who in God's eyes (and mine, too) is a priceless person, that contribution has made it a good day! What gives value to your day? ✎*Brenda*

✭　✭　✭

Lord, thank you for the people you have placed in my life. My family, my friends, and my coworkers are all priceless treasures in your eyes. Help me to have your perspective as I love and serve them today. Give me a sense of the eternal value of what I consider ordinary and routine so I may glorify you with my activity today. I pray for deployed parents serving their families while their military spouses are away. Encourage their hearts as they persevere in their daily routines. ✛*Amen.*

February 9
Flying Solo

In peace I will lie down and sleep, for you alone, O LORD, will keep me safe. ✝ PSALM 4:8

When my boys were preschool age, my husband was often called away for military field exercises. This resulted in my being a single parent for several weeks at a time. Sometimes a call would come in the middle of the night, and he'd have to leave before the boys awakened.

I got as accustomed to these nocturnal departures as I could, and my boys in time adjusted to dad's temporary absence. At least, they adjusted to it during the day. Nighttime was a different scenario.

I would read them a story, tuck them in, and even stop to view them sleeping soundly before I retired. Without fail, I would wake up in the early hours of the morning finding myself no longer alone in my bed. One little boy would be as close as possible on one side of me, and one would have my neck in a chokehold on the other side. There was something sweet about them wanting to be close; however, these conditions did not make for restful sleep.

Military parents often find themselves flying solo as they parent alone. When this happens, it is important to get the necessary rest in order to function. The reality is, one has to function, rested or not! It's easy for a vicious cycle to begin with little sleep and eventually end with a crash and burn.

During these times, it is important to make time for yourself—which is easier said than done. Recently, a gathering of spouses experiencing a second deployment shared their top priorities in being able to successfully navigate being a solo parent:

> Make plans to trade off babysitting with a friend.
> Think ahead about menus to ensure healthy eating.
> Have a bedtime ritual for your children and stick to it as much as possible.
> Get involved in a Bible study offering childcare.
> Most important of all, set aside time to pray and meditate on Scripture.

The overwhelming opinion was that structure and routine are important during deployment just as much for you as for your children. The initial time of planning may seem challenging, but the effort will be rewarded. ≈Brenda

☆ ☆ ☆

Lord, thank you for the rest for my body and soul that is promised in your Word. Help me to make good use of my time and provide routine needed for my family. Protect me from unhealthy choices that lead to exhaustion. May I rest in your promises today. I pray, too, for tired soldiers. Refresh weary bodies that labor under challenging conditions. I ask in Jesus' name. ✝ Amen.

Submit As unto the Lord

And further, submit to one another out of reverence for Christ. For wives, this means submit to your husbands as to the Lord. ✦ EPHESIANS 5:21-22

I was asked recently to speak to a mother/daughter banquet at a local church. Whenever I am asked to speak to women's groups and not given a specific topic, I always want to encourage them as women, as wives, and as mothers, by bringing up God's Word for our lives.

I refer to struggles in my own life as a woman, wife, and mother and share the heartaches as well as the victories. I often say that the times I tried the hardest to be in control were the times that were the most devastating for me personally.

After the brief time together and a thirty-minute program, the meeting was completed, and I stayed around as always to visit with those in attendance. One young woman came up to me and said, "You know, I have been fighting my husband on a move he wants to make. I will not submit to his authority, and I know now that is out of order. I am going home today to tell him how very much I love and respect him. I am going to tell him that I am with him 100 percent in his decision." Wow. That was truly a God moment for me. God had worked in her heart that day.

Then I saw three other women walking toward me. They came to me and said, "Do you realize that you mentioned the word *submit* at least twenty times in your thirty-minute talk? We do not believe in that philosophy, and we can truly tell it comes from your religious belief." After picking myself up off the floor mentally, I said this to them:

> "When I hear the word *submit*, it means freedom. Freedom to be who God intended me to be. It is the freedom not to take more than I can handle in a marriage relationship. Freedom to give it all to God and to trust that God will work through my husband. It is a word of obedience as unto the Lord."

At the end of our discussion, we agreed to disagree, but I know that what God tells me in Scripture is the only way I want to live. I can tell you that after thirty-four years of marriage, I am very thankful to have a husband who understands mutual submission and the respect that it brings between a husband and wife who love each other. ∝*Carol*

* * *

Father, on this day, I submit my life to you. Bless marriage relationships, so they may stay in order the way that you intended. Especially bless military marriages with all of the present hardships they must endure. ✦ *Amen.*

February 11
Stumbling Block or Stepping-Stone?

So let's stop condemning each other. Decide instead to live in such a way that you will not cause another believer to stumble and fall. ✦ ROMANS 14:13

One of the greatest joys of a Christian wife is having a husband who knows and loves Jesus. On the other hand, a Christian wife can experience a deep sense of hopelessness, thinking she and her husband may never be on the same page spiritually. Without meaning to cause damage, a wife will often preach at her unsaved husband instead of praying for him. She will become what Proverbs 27:15 describes as "a quarrelsome wife [who] is as annoying as constant dripping on a rainy day." A woman's desire for her husband to come to the Lord may actually turn him away from the Lord if the message is drowned out by the method. The challenge for this wife is to know how to be a stepping stone to her husband's spiritual development and not a stumbling block.

A wife can often get in the way of God. She can complain, accuse, and distract as God is trying to convict. A dear chaplain said to me lovingly, "Close your mouth. Get out of the way, and let God do his work in your husband's heart."

My husband became a Christian during his time as an active-duty soldier. The mentoring of godly chaplains and leaders who walked the Christian walk influenced him greatly. He began to understand the importance of attending chapel with me and our two young sons after reading James Dobson's book *What Every Woman Wishes Her Husband Knew about Women*.[1] This book highlights the importance of providing the example of going to church with your children so that they can decide on their own when the time comes to respond to Jesus as their Lord and Savior. As time went on and the Word began to minister to my husband's heart, he gave his life to Jesus.

During those years of transition to the Christian faith, we began to view our military orders as not just from the government but as God's appointment for a new spiritual mission. I am so thankful that my husband was saved by grace and became not only a soldier in the nation's army but a soldier in God's army.   ⁓*Carol*

* * *

Thank you for sending your Son, Jesus, to die for me. Thank you for the shedding of his blood to cover my sins. Thank you that he rose from the dead. Thank you, Father God, that Jesus can now be my Lord and Savior. I pray for Christians serving in the military as ambassadors of your Good News. Use them to spread the gospel of Christ! ✦ *Amen.*

---

[1] James Dobson, *What Wives Wish Their Husbands Knew About Women* (Carol Stream, IL: Tyndale House, 1977).

A Kind Man

But the Holy Spirit produces this kind of fruit in our lives: love, joy, peace, patience, kindness, goodness, faithfulness, gentleness, and self-control. ✛ GALATIANS 5:22-23

Several years ago, my mother became quite ill and was hospitalized for many days. I traveled to my hometown to lend a hand to my dad. On one particular day, we were both at the hospital with her. I was reading in a chair across the room, but my eyes were drawn to the scene at the hospital bed. I wrote as I watched:

> My father stands at the bed and carefully stirs sugar into her hot tea. He opens all the containers, commenting on the plate before her. He seasons each bland item to make it more palatable. A napkin is placed around her neck. She looks up at him as a little child, takes a bite, and grimaces at the taste. He stands watch over her in case she would accidently choke. It is bittersweet—just like the squash he tries to season with a little salt and then sugar.
>
> I read today a definition of kindness: "demonstrating hands-on compassion." Yesterday my mother said to me after Dad brought her a much-beloved chocolate peppermint candy, "Your daddy is a kind man." Yes, Mother, indeed he is.

Kindness is an important virtue to exhibit in a marriage. In fact, the word for kindness in Proverbs 3:3 is a word used to describe a marriage covenant. It combines the concept of a legal issue but goes beyond legality to the idea of devotion. It can also be described as steadfast love. It is the type of kindness God shows to us.

Sometimes it is hard to be kind to someone we know so well. We can be kind to everyone else and in the comfort of home allow the worst of ourselves to be exhibited. My father challenged me in the kindness department that day in the hospital. I pray I will follow his example of showing kindness to those I love. By the way, my mother recovered. In fact, the Lord used my dad to discover that some of the medications she had been prescribed were actually causing her illnesses. Today, my mother's health has stabilized, and my dad continues to demonstrate kindness.   ❧*Brenda*

✦   ✦   ✦

Thank you, Lord, for your loving-kindness. Help me to have this fruit of the Spirit operating in my life as I love and serve others. I pray for marriages that are being challenged by military deployments. In Jesus' name I pray. ✛ *Amen.*

February 13
As for Me and My House . . . We Will Travel the World

So again I say, each man must love his wife as he loves himself, and the wife must respect her husband. + EPHESIANS 5:33

My husband and I were married in 1974. By then he had served one year in the military after being commissioned from college ROTC as an artilleryman. When aviation became a branch of service in the Army, he chose to fly helicopters rather than drive tanks. We were on our way to flight school at Fort Rucker, Alabama, for our first military assignment. One short year later, military orders for Germany arrived. As newlyweds, we could not have been happier to be traveling the world together. Life was good, and the more footloose and fancy free the better. Nearly fifteen years into our marriage, with five military assignments under our belt and two teenage sons, the word came for another overseas assignment—this time to Korea—and the story was very different.

When the call came from my husband, telling me that he had been assigned to Korea, I quickly said to him, "I'm not going." Presuming this would be my response, he had already asked his superiors if he could go unaccompanied. Later in the day, we told the boys about our plan to be separated for the upcoming year. My oldest son quickly said to me, "Mom, I don't know where you are going to be the next two years, but I am going with Dad." At that moment, I knew I was to follow my husband.

Today women are encouraged to be independent even when it comes to marriage. If possible, God intends families to be together. We are to encourage, love, honor, and respect each other. As I was obedient in living out my God-given role as a wife, my initial reluctance to move to Korea grew into anticipation and even excitement for the family adventure ahead. Our assignment to Korea was the experience of a lifetime. I will be the first to tell you I am still reaping benefits in relationships with my husband and children as well as enjoying deep, ongoing friendships with people I met there. ~Carol

* * *

Lord, sometimes it is hard to drown out the voice of the culture screaming against what is best for families. Help me and my family to be an example of love and respect to one another. Father, I am mindful of service members defending our country who don't have the choice to take their families with them where duty calls. Bless them for their commitment to serve our nation and protect our liberties. In your name I pray. + Amen.

File Cabinet

Then the LORD God said, "It is not good for the man to be alone. I will make a helper who is just right for him." ✝ GENESIS 2:18

While stationed at Fort Leavenworth, Kansas, my husband and I were able to sit under powerful, anointed teaching. It was a time of empowerment through the Holy Spirit for the days ahead that only God could have known about.

George Kuykendall, the Officer's Christian Fellowship leader and chapel counselor, taught our Sunday school class the first year we were there. George talked about relationships beginning with the man/woman relationship. He said, "You know, everyone in this room today is married. I want to share with you the difference between a man and a woman to help you understand why your man is the way he is and why your woman is the way she is."

He said that the woman is like an artist's palette. Every color in her life swirls into the other. Her family is swirled into her job; her errands are swirled into her house; her faith is swirled into all of it. She can never separate these things. If she is at the store, she is thinking of when to pick up the kids. If she is at the Bible study, she is wondering how her husband is doing at work. The woman can juggle and can multitask until the day is done, a gift completely from our wonderful Creator.

The man is like a file cabinet. He has each drawer labeled. It might read *Work*, *Play*, *Home*, *Wife*, *Kids*, and *Church*. He can only be in one drawer at a time. If all the drawers happened to be open, the file cabinet would fall over on him and chaos would prevail. Therefore, he opens one drawer and works on one thing at a time. Have you ever called your husband unexpectedly to ask him what he would like for supper? He answers abruptly and even curtly, saying, "Whatever. Anything else?" It is not because he doesn't love you; he just did not happen to have the file drawer labeled *Wife* open when you called.

Man or woman, we are to demonstrate the love of Christ to one another. Understanding and appreciating our differences, though not excusing bad behavior, can help us to do that.   *≈Carol*

✯ ✯ ✯

Dear God, you are amazing! Thank you for the differences in men and women. Help me to honor you in my marriage. I pray a special blessing on parachurch ministries whose purpose is to enhance military marriages. ✝ *Amen.*

I Can Handle This

"And I give myself as a holy sacrifice for them so they can be made holy by your truth."
✝ JOHN 17:19

My husband and I have been married thirty-four years. We are so thankful to God every day that not only are we still married but we are so in love. As we look toward the future together, we enjoy spending hours talking and dreaming.

There have been times in our married life that have not been easy. Does that sound familiar? There have been times when I was at fault and times when he was. It was always hard to admit being wrong.

Upon our arrival in Korea, there was a sort of honeymoon period with the move. We were in a new place with new, exciting surroundings. We were living in a beautiful American-style hotel until our quarters became available. I didn't have to cook or clean for a month. The boys loved playing tennis and meeting new young people every day. It was such a wonderful transition time. But a reality check came very quickly.

The day we were to move into our new quarters, my husband was scheduled to be in the field. After that, he began to work longer and longer hours. I had known when we left for Korea that God meant for us to be in that faraway land, but soon I allowed that certainty to turn to doubt and frustration over my decision.

My thought was to handle it on my own, to leave Korea and go back to my family. The stirring in my spirit that I must leave became stronger every day. I had two teenagers at home, and I needed to have my husband around to support me.

I had established some very close friendships with people who loved the Lord. They began to teach me about my covenant marriage. They reminded me that the marriage was not all about me. I was there to love and support my husband, and God would fill the void for me whenever there was one.

In times of crisis, it is important to surround yourself with not only those who make you feel good as a person but those who love the Lord with all their hearts and will lead you to his Word for answers.   ⟨Carol⟩

✶   ✶   ✶

Father, thank you for friends who will lead me to you when I am discouraged, afraid, or feeling empty from times of loneliness in my life. Help those in faraway lands, as well as the families left behind, to reach out and be comforted by those who will stand with them during their times of crisis. ✝ *Amen.*

A Loyal Friend

After David had finished talking with Saul, he met Jonathan, the king's son. There was an immediate bond between them, for Jonathan loved David. From that day on Saul kept David with him and wouldn't let him return home. And Jonathan made a solemn pact with David, because he loved him as he loved himself. Jonathan sealed the pact by taking off his robe and giving it to David, together with his tunic, sword, bow, and belt. ✝ 1 SAMUEL 18:1-4

As a military family, we have moved quite often. My children have been uprooted and replanted in several different places, saying farewell to good friends each time. It was a special blessing for my son Joseph to have had his good friend Benjamin stationed at the same location four times. Joseph and Benjamin started first grade together in New Jersey, attended second through fourth grade together in Georgia, and graduated from high school together in Virginia. They stayed in touch during the times their dads were assigned to different locations, too. At the time of this writing, Benjamin is serving in the Army, stationed in Iraq, but he and Joseph communicate regularly.

Friends are important at any time, but they are especially important in a crisis. On 9/11, Benjamin called Joseph when he could not reach his dad, who was at that time assigned to the Pentagon. I am so grateful for this special friendship my son has been able to cultivate. Like Joseph, I am thankful for friends God has given me. Joseph and Benjamin's relationship reminds me that to have friends that last over the years we must be loyal, concerned about each other, and make time to stay connected.

The Scripture for today highlights the deep friendship of David and Jonathan. David often found himself in a personal crisis because of his conflict with his best friend's father, King Saul. Simply stated, King Saul turned against David because he wanted the kingship to go to his son Jonathan. However, Jonathan sided with David because their friendship meant more to him than the personal gain of inheriting the crown. That is a loyal friend!

One of the benefits of personal crisis is confirmation of who your true friends are. During a crisis, it is not unusual for some friends you may have considered to be your closest allies to fall away. Don't be discouraged by those who you feel abandon you; instead thank God for those who stand with you. ✎*Brenda*

★   ★   ★

Father, thank you for the friends you have placed in my life. Help me to be a loyal and supportive friend. I pray you would comfort, encourage, and bless my friends today. Lord, be a friend today to those who find themselves waiting for their loved ones to return from military deployments. In Jesus' name I pray. ✝ *Amen.*

February 17
Victory

Every child of God defeats this evil world, and we achieve this victory through our faith.
✝ 1 JOHN 5:4

A young military wife gave me permission to share this testimony:

> I just wanted all of the people who have loved on, prayed for, helped out, been there, and believed for me and my family to know how much I have been blessed by your loving acts of service and your faithful friendship. I have gone through some big challenges in the past couple of years, but far beyond the separation, deployment, and various challenges of being an Army wife, I have battled with my own feelings of unworthiness and self-condemnation. I could not see how God saw Steve, my children, or me because my emotions held sway over my thought life. The enemy was gaining ground in my life, and I felt unloved and incredibly lost.
>
> I finally got to the point where I couldn't see how to cope, and I called out for help. God provided people from all over the place to encourage, cheer on, and bolster me in my time of weakness. Sisters and brothers interceded for me and put on work gloves to model God's love. I was motivated and inspired to take care of myself, love myself, and love my family, . . . and I began to dig into the Word of God with a vengeance.
>
> I can now say that I have joy, peace, and victory in my life . . . in my heart. I have never felt so free. My purpose in life is to draw near to God and help others draw near as well. No matter what that looks like, I know that is something I can do with God's infinite strength.
>
> . . . On Feb. 28, 2007 I was inspired to write this down as part of my prayer during my devotional time:
>
> . . . I am not dismayed and my hope will not be spent idly . . .
>
> I am turning towards the Cross which avails me much.
>
> The expansion of my soul, through the storm which threatens to destroy me, will bring that hope to the point of unfolding destiny.
>
> I thank you for believing in me when I had no strength to do so for myself. My God is a wonderful Healer, and I am nestled safely in His arms. I pray this encourages you as you have encouraged me.
>
> With faith, hope, and inexpressible love,
> Nancy Sheridan

~ Carol

✷ ✷ ✷

Father, teach me to never give up on myself since you will never give up on me. Thank you for each victory in my life. I know they come from you! ✝ Amen.

Have You Heard?

Who may worship in your sanctuary, Lᴏʀᴅ? Who may enter your presence on your holy hill?
Those who lead blameless lives and do what is right, speaking the truth from sincere hearts.
Those who refuse to gossip or harm their neighbors or speak evil of their friends.
✝ PSALM 15:1-3

My dad used to preach a sermon titled "Gossiping Christians." He was asked to preach the sermon regularly for the chapel service at the university where he was a professor. I remember loving to hear the sermon because his usually quiet demeanor changed, and he became animated as he preached. He would dramatically begin, "Have you heard? Did you know? Would you have believed it? Don't tell anyone I told you, but . . ." He would then repeat a series of one-liners that would have the congregation in stitches about an alleged parishioner who was the typical gossiper. The monologue included such zingers as

> She could pick up more dirt with the telephone than she could with a vacuum cleaner.
> She never repeated gossip—she always started it.
> She had a keen sense of rumor.
> She thought she was very polished—because everything she said cast a reflection on someone else.
> Her tongue was so long she could whisper in her own ear.
> She was always the knife of the party.

You get the point. By the end of the preacher-turned-comedian routine, you knew that conviction was just around the corner. The verbal abuse that is suffered by words misspoken can destroy relationships, divide ministries, and bring pain that is worse than a bodily attack.

It is unfair.

It is cowardly.

It is difficult to stop. But we must stop it!

Times of personal crisis make people easy targets for gossip. This is not the time to talk about them; instead, it is the time to talk with them and pray for them. Make this a day to bless others with your words.   *Brenda*

☆   ☆   ☆

Father, I pray with the psalmist. "I am determined not to sin in what I say" (Psalm 17:3). "May the words of my mouth and the meditation of my heart be pleasing to you, O Lᴏʀᴅ, my rock and my redeemer" (Psalm 19:14). Strengthen the hearts of those who are serving in foreign lands with words of encouragement from home. ✝ *Amen.*

February 19
Deep-Spirited Friends

Then make me truly happy by agreeing wholeheartedly with each other, loving one another, and working together with one mind and purpose. + PHILIPPIANS 2:2

A result of becoming a follower of Christ is the realization that we are part of a new and wonderful family. This can be a brand-new experience for some as they develop friendships with others who become not just friends but also family.

I quickly discovered this just after my conversion. When I found myself wanting to complain and groan about my husband, kids, military quarters, the commissary not having the right cereal, or the hospital being too busy, my newfound sisters in Christ didn't say, "You deserve better!" or "He is no good for you!" or "Can you believe we have to wait two hours to get our medicine?" Instead, they began to lead me to *Scripture*. It was a new idea for me. My Christian friends helped me discover that God speaks to every situation in Scripture. These dear women led me into a deeper understanding of not only who God is but where he's directing my life!

Jerry and Mary White share seven characteristics of what could be described in today's Scripture as deep-spirited friends. These friends provide

> Spiritual stimulation,
> Prayer,
> Accountability,
> Encouragement and affirmation,
> Help and service,
> Fun, and
> Teamwork in a spiritual battle.[1]

The constant transitions experienced by military families provide challenges to building friendships. However, I daresay the members of these families would agree they have made deep and lasting friendships in spite of the transitions. *The Message* uses the words "be deep-spirited friends" in its paraphrase of today's Scripture. This description brings to mind the artesian wells that spring from deep underground. This is the purest and most refreshing water that can be found. This is the kind of friend I need and want to be!

The need for deep-spirited friends who will hold us accountable like my friends did is so important. Whether it is an ordinary day or a season of crisis, we need to open our hearts to the joys of Christian friendship.   *Carol*

* * *

Father, thank you for the friends you have given me. Thank you for the investment they have made in my life. Thank you for the greater family of God, the spiritual sisters and brothers throughout the earth. I ask for the love that only a family can give to surround military families who are in crisis during this time. In Jesus' name I pray. + *Amen.*

---

[1] Jerry and Mary White, "The Strength of Friendship," *Discipleship Journal,* 11 (September/October 1982).

The Sight of You

The brothers and sisters in Rome had heard we were coming, and they came to meet us at the Forum on the Appian Way. Others joined us at The Three Taverns. When Paul saw them, he was encouraged and thanked God. + ACTS 28:15

There are times when I don't feel like going anywhere. I just want to sit in my comfortable four walls and enjoy the solitude. I recognize that there are times when this is necessary for my mental and spiritual well-being, but I am addressing the times when I make excuses. I know when my reasoning is valid and when it is not.

Recently, my daughter-in-law, who is involved in a young moms' Bible study at her church, and I were talking on the phone. She shared that she just hadn't been feeling it and had ended up staying home more than she went. My mother-in-law radar went into high alert. I did not want to come across as preachy or directorial, but I wanted her to know of the dangers of this mind-set. I empathized with her and then shared my experience.

I have found that when I have no motivation to be involved in Christian community, I need to ask myself some questions. Is this a time of genuine need in my life to be still and get some rest? If I can't answer that question in the affirmative, it helps me to think that my presence might be an encouragement to someone else. I don't mean that there's something so special about me, but that my presence in community and support would make a difference.

Soon after this conversation with my daughter-in-law, I was reading in the book of Acts and came across the passage in Acts 28:15 highlighted today. Paul shares that when he "saw them, he was encouraged." Paul was blessed and encouraged by the very sight of the brothers who came to greet him. Their very presence encouraged him!

Have you made excuses to stay away from Christian community? Think about how *your* presence and the very sight of *you* can be an encouragement and blessing to someone today! *Brenda*

* * *

Lord, thank you for your presence that encourages and strengthens me. Forgive me when I make excuses, am led by my feelings, and miss opportunities to encourage others. Help me to show up in the places that would please you today. Encourage the hearts of those deployed military personnel who are using their gifts and talents in chapel services, and lead others there to seek that supportive fellowship. In your name I pray. + *Amen.*

February 21
Serving at Home

Stand firm against him, and be strong in your faith. Remember that your Christian brothers and sisters all over the world are going through the same kind of suffering you are. ✛ 1 PETER 5:9

There is definitely an area of the military I have expertise in. During my husband's active duty years, I enjoyed the role of military spouse. Its definition varies for each individual. It comes with much responsibility and with choices that are made because of situations like deployment and separation.

Recently, I asked a woman from our church to go to lunch with me. Her husband had served in the National Guard for many years. They were used to the monthly obligation and the times of training in the summer, but all of a sudden, she found herself sending her husband to war. She was overcome with different emotions because she had no reference point in this to hold on to. I thanked her that day for her service to this country, since she was keeping the home going while her husband was away.

Our church has a day when single moms and wives whose husbands are deployed can come in for a free oil change and car checkup. In this young woman's case, some of the men from our church went to her house and painted the trim so her husband would not have that chore waiting when he came home for R & R. This type of outreach is happening in many places around our great country.

My mother and I had a discussion about the service mentality during World War II. She said that everyone was involved then, that America was really serving together as a country along with the men and women who were serving overseas. My mother went to work in a factory in her hometown because there were not enough employees to keep the plant running during the war. For all, it was truly a time of service to our country.

Complacency is not something we can accept. It is our responsibility as a nation to support those who mourn and who need assistance in their lives.

> Service to our fellow man
> Is a phrase we often hear.
> Exactly what to do about it
> Isn't always clear.
> Find a way to help and serve
> Others who need your care.
> We're all in this together—
> See what you can share.

≈ Carol

*　*　*

Father, give me a heart of service. Help me to reach out and continue to look for those who need support and assistance in times of tragedy and emergency. Renew the zeal for service in the hearts of weary men and women in the military. ✛ Amen.

You Can Do It!

My purpose in writing is to encourage you and assure you that what you are experiencing is truly part of God's grace for you. Stand firm in this grace. ✝ 1 PETER 5:12

My son Gregory is an aspiring filmmaker. From time to time, I have asked him to prepare a film to illustrate a topic on which I am speaking. This has helped him build a portfolio of work, and it has helped me have access to some great illustrations. For the topic of encouragement, I asked him to prepare footage of my grandson taking his first steps. I was surprised but pleased when I viewed the finished product and found that not only were Noah's first steps included, but so were the very beginning of his movements—from rolling over to crawling to standing, falling, walking, and running. As Gregory thought about the message of encouragement, he decided just having Noah's first steps was not enough. He said to me, "Mom, every aspect of the process of Christian growth needs encouragement." So true!

We face daily challenges that can often keep us from moving forward with confidence. However, encouragement can propel us to stand and take a step. It can be a word, a touch, a look, or a note that speaks the message "I care. You're not alone. You can do it."

In the New Testament, the word most often translated as *encouragement* is a word that means "to come alongside." Bible teacher Beth Moore paints the word picture for encouragement as planting courage into the heart of another. In other words, we give them a courage transplant.

Encouragement is important during a crisis, but it is also necessary every day. Each of us has been through difficulties and times of discouragement and doubt that equip us to be an encourager. People need to hear from someone who has been in their shoes and lived to tell about it. They need to hear they, too, will live through diapers, teenage angst, an empty nest, retirement, menopause, caring for aged parents, deployment, relocation, _____, you fill in the blank.

In the Scripture for today, Peter says his purpose for writing is to encourage the church to stand firm in God's grace. Who needs your encouragement today? How can you encourage them to stand firm and assure them God's grace is for them? ☙*Brenda*

✴   ✴   ✴

Father, thank you for the encouragement of your Word today. Help me to stand firm in your grace and to speak words of hope to someone today. I pray for those in the military who might feel discouraged. May they look to you for help and guidance, and may they know that they are not alone when they call out to you. ✝ *Amen.*

February 23
Side by Side

When our enemies heard that we knew of their plans and that God had frustrated them, we all returned to our work on the wall. ✝ NEHEMIAH 4:15

A few years ago, I attended a conference sponsored by Precept Ministries in Chattanooga, Tennessee. The theme of the conference was rebuilding the wall. The focus was on how our nation's wall has been broken down by families who are falling apart, marriages that are crumbling, and morals that are sinking daily. The wall has been demolished in our nation, and we as Christians have an obligation to help rebuild and return to God.

Since the conference, I've found myself visualizing walls that are crumbling everywhere around me. The walls of patriotism and love for America are broken down in our War on Terror right now. When 9/11 happened, the wall was strong. The support for our military and their leadership was strong. The support for our president was strong. We realized as a nation that there was an enemy we could not see, and the best way to deal with that enemy was to unite behind those who would lead the charge.

The walls of our families are breaking down, and the Christian church statistics regarding family breakdown have, by some accounts, now surpassed those in the secular community. The Christian community is dealing with habits and challenges that compromise the body of Christ.

When Nehemiah was rebuilding the wall, the Israelites knew the enemy was going to come to try to keep them from securing their city by rebuilding their walls. Nehemiah 4:14-15 says, "Then as I looked over the situation, I called together the nobles and the rest of the people and said to them, 'Don't be afraid of the enemy! Remember the Lord, who is great and glorious, and fight for your brothers, your sons, your daughters, and your homes!' When our enemies heard that we knew of their plans and that God had frustrated them, we all returned to our work on the wall."

When we are together, God is there to fight for us. When the wall is strong, the enemy is kept from harming those who are standing side by side.

Oh, that we might be at the point that Nehemiah was at with his people! May we stand side by side against the enemy of our day. Oh, that we might go with confidence and strength and repair the broken walls in our own lives. ᴥ*Carol*

✦ ✦ ✦

Lord, be with our military as they are battling the enemy in order to rebuild the walls of broken nations. Encourage them as we stand side by side in prayer and renewed hope for their future. ✝ *Amen.*

Bulbs I Meant to Plant

So encourage each other and build each other up, just as you are already doing.
✝ 1 THESSALONIANS 5:11

During a visit to my parents' house, I commented on the lovely iris plants that were in full bloom in their yard. My dad mentioned that he had brought the bulbs from my grandmother's yard in North Carolina and offered me some of them to plant in my own yard. I was thrilled with the prospect. At that time, I was living in North Carolina, and I thought it would be especially meaningful to plant those bulbs full circle in the land from which they originated.

As our family was preparing to move away from North Carolina many months later, my husband asked me, "What are the shriveled-up, covered-with-dirt items in a paper bag sitting in the garage?" They were the iris bulbs I had been planning to transplant. The meaningful moment of planting them in their native ground had passed. My good intentions were now worthless, as were the bulbs.

It takes more than good intentions to encourage as the Scripture in 1 Thessalonians admonishes. It is obvious that the Christians Paul wrote to did not just have good intentions, but they were being intentional about the ministry of encouragement. Paul encouraged them to make sure it kept happening.

There are those who have the spiritual gift of encouragement. It is in their spiritual DNA and comes naturally. The rest of us aren't off the hook. We are all to do the work of an encourager. That work is not about doing for others what they can do for themselves. It is not taking pain or grief from their lives. Instead, it is noticing them, feeling with them, and reminding them of the hope we have in Christ as we live life on this earth.

The exhortation from Paul in today's Scripture followed Paul's encouraging the church to remember their eternal destiny. Be encouraged as you think on that today! Encourage someone else with this blessed hope!   ❧*Brenda*

✶　✶　✶

Lord, I thank you for the hope of heaven. Help me to be purposeful in encouraging others today. Make me aware of those who need a word of hope as I go through this day. Encourage the hearts of Christians serving you in the armed forces. Help the church in America to remember to support them with prayer, words of blessing, and care of their families while they are away. In your name I pray. ✝ *Amen.*

February 25
This Line Is Not Secure

So I want you to know that no one speaking by the Spirit of God will curse Jesus, and no one can say Jesus is Lord, except by the Holy Spirit. + 1 CORINTHIANS 12:3

While stationed in foreign countries, I became used to hearing a particular phrase spoken each time I called in to the office to speak with my husband. Whoever answered the phone would say, "B Company, Sergeant So-and-So; this line is not secure." However they answered, the last words had to be "This line is not secure."

What that meant to the person calling in was that you could talk about the weather, about meeting for lunch, about what time you would be home that night; but you could not talk about the mission, the assignment, or anything of military significance.

I wonder if we as Christians should think of adopting that phrase in our conversations. If we realized in our hearts and minds that God hears us and is listening not only to every word spoken but also every thought, we might change our daily rhetoric.

The next time you are having a conversation with someone, imagine God on the line with you saying, "This line is not secure." Think before you speak. Scripture tells us in James 1:26, "If you claim to be religious but don't control your tongue, you are fooling yourself, and your religion is worthless." Any questions on that?

We often remember this when we are speaking out loud, but even our thoughts can catch us in a snare. Psalm 7:9 says, "End the evil of those who are wicked, and defend the righteous. For you look deep within the mind and heart, O righteous God." Our directive from God and his Word is that we are to keep the line secure for his glory. Remember this illustration the next time you pick up the phone for a quick call or meet your friend for lunch. Let your words and thoughts be filled with his goodness so the world may come to know him.   ~Carol

* * *

Father, I am your creation. You gave me the ability to speak and to think and to influence others with those words and thoughts. Help me to be sure that what I am saying or thinking is pleasing to you. Let my words be as healing balm to those who are serving our country at this time. Let each e-mail and letter be pleasing in your sight, Lord. + Amen.

A Foreign Language

Don't use foul or abusive language. Let everything you say be good and helpful, so that your words will be an encouragement to those who hear them. + EPHESIANS 4:29

While living in Germany on military assignment, our family resided in a quaint German village. My son was to begin first grade, but I did not feel comfortable putting a six-year-old on a bus to go forty-five minutes each way to the American school. The family car was not an option since my husband needed it for getting to and from work each day. I discussed the issue with a German neighbor, who suggested I inquire into the possibility of Gregory attending the local village school. I had not even considered this an option!

My husband and I consulted the local school administrator, and Gregory was enrolled in German school. It took about four months for the language immersion to take hold, but soon he was speaking German with a very authentic accent. We were pleased and proud of our little scholar.

Learning the language helped Gregory make friends in the neighborhood. He played regularly with the other little boys in the village, and it was obvious that the play outside of school was contributing to his grasp of his second language. Imagine my surprise one day when my dear neighbor kindly shared with me that Gregory was using some words that would probably not be on our approval list. I got a quick lesson in German Unwholesome Talk 101 and had a heart-to-heart with my naive child, who had only been repeating what he heard the other boys say.

It is our normal tendency to join in conversations with coworkers, neighbors, or friends. Like Gregory, we may not realize the harmful things we are saying and how they affect others—yet we are responsible for our words. Matthew 12:36 reminds us we will give an account for every idle word we speak. There's no room in the mouth of a Christ follower for racial slurs, coarse jokes, or cruel comments about anyone, especially those who are different or less fortunate. It is important to be aware of the way words can discourage and tear down, whether intentionally or unintentionally. We need to guard our words so that what we say encourages and builds up others. ❧*Brenda*

* * *

Lord, thank you for the gift of language. May my words today be pleasing to you and encouraging to others. I pray for those serving you in foreign lands. May they speak the language of kindness and understanding to those around them, familiar and foreign alike. + *Amen.*

February 27
Triple-Braided Cord

A person standing alone can be attacked and defeated, but two can stand back-to-back and conquer. Three are even better, for a triple-braided cord is not easily broken. ✛ ECCLESIASTES 4:12

Today's Scripture is a powerful metaphor for community. I remember living in South Korea years ago. The military chapel's women's ministry chose this verse as the theme verse for the year. My dear friend Eileen Sherrill created a small quilted banner for us to hang up at each session. It had a beautiful black background with a pink, purple, and white cord wrapped tightly together. Each week as we began our meeting, we would refer to the Scripture and the beautiful decoration of the quilted cord.

The symbolism of that verse has come to mind so many times since that year. I have said to my sons, "Don't go this alone. You need to let your dad and me know so we can fight the fight in the heavenlies with you and beside you." God created us for fellowship and told us that while two can conquer, three are even better. He wants us to understand that this world we face is not to be faced alone.

Several months ago, a dear young military wife, with whom I had been talking for a while, called and said that she was finding it very hard to get out of bed. She said she just didn't want to see anyone. Oh, dear friends, that is exactly where the enemy wants us. He is seeking out any who are away from the pack so he can attack and devour those on their own.

If you are facing a difficult situation, *reach out* to others! Let someone come to stand with you. Find others who will lock arms and send prayers alongside you. Remember, "a triple-braided cord is not easily broken."   ⌁*Carol*

✱   ✱   ✱

Father, help me to reach out to find those who will stand beside me in my struggles. Keep me in fellowship in the body of believers. Help those who are fighting for our freedoms to bond together as Christian brothers and sisters and find strength in the midst of the conflict. ✛ *Amen.*

The Church Channel

And let us not neglect our meeting together, as some people do, but encourage one another, especially now that the day of his return is drawing near. + HEBREWS 10:25

The home I stay in when I visit my children in Tennessee uses an antenna for television reception. There are about ten channels that come in clearly. When I am there, I have no doubt I am in the Bible belt, since four of the ten are Christian channels. Surprisingly enough, during a recent visit to Germany, the cable television in the German hotel carried two Christian channels, including the Church Channel. Add to television such media as Christian radio, streaming audio from the computer, and podcasts, and it's possible to never have to darken the door of a church to attend a service. It's true—there are some excellent Christian broadcasts available. There are some things the church can do well from a distance.

In fact, if church were just preaching and music, you *could* stay home. But that is not what church is about. The Scripture today makes this perfectly clear. God gave a directive of more than preaching and music. Excellence in preaching and music is important, but living in Christian community is a priority. We are to love and be loved, to know and be known, to serve and be served, to celebrate and be celebrated with. It is hard to do all these things with only a television, radio, or computer.

On several occasions, the New Testament uses the phrase "one another": love one another (1 John 3:11), forgive one another (Ephesians 4:32), serve one another (Galatians 5:13). This can be done effectively by committing to be part of a church family, not just for sermons or music, but also for relationships.

Years ago, experiencing community was easier; there were no telephones, no television, and certainly no e-mail. In order to share with others, there had to be a gathering. I appreciate modern technology and all the advantages it brings; it doesn't take the place, however, of meeting together with fellow believers to encourage and bless one another. *Brenda*

✭　✭　✭

Father, I thank you for the modern technology that has provided the means for your Word to be spread around the world. I thank you for the gift of Christian community and for the church you have provided to encourage me in my relationship with you. Help me do my part in building community as I use my gifts in the structure of the church. Bless chaplains who are serving you in the armed services. Make their ministry effective as they reach out to service members and their families in your name. + *Amen.*

March 1
Close Church Encounters

I pant with expectation, longing for your commands. ✛ PSALM 119:131

As I have pondered my religious upbringing, one of the things I cherish is a sense of expectancy in the realm of worship. You see, I grew up in church. My father was a minister, serving as a pastor, church administrator, and finally college professor. I was raised in the town where our denomination is headquartered. I married one of the ministerial students who came to that town to prepare for the ministry. You could say I've had many years of close church encounters.

For me, church was a place where needs were met. Was I sick? My head would be anointed with oil and the prayer of faith prayed. If I was not healed, I was certainly encouraged. Was I sad, discouraged, or fearful? I knew God's presence would be there, often in what seemed like a tangible way. People were never in a hurry. The terms *tarry* and *pray through* are etched in my heart. Most of the time, I was happy to go and sorry to leave. The corporate experience of worship was meaningful, joyful, challenging, and life changing!

I discovered that the word *expect* in Scripture is the same word translated as "watch." It indicates watching with an outstretched head. It reminds me of times when I expect a special guest to visit my home and stand at the window, straining with eagerness for the arrival. In the original language, it carries the meaning of complete attention until the object expected is fully realized.

It is humbling to admit that my adult expectations of worship too often take the form of personal preference—as in, Will the music and preaching please me? I am challenged to enter a sanctuary each week with only the expectation that God's presence will meet me there. To know that whatever the quality of singing or speaking, if his Word is proclaimed and my ears are open, I can expect him to speak to my heart. It causes me to pay attention to the words of the songs and listen to the reading of Scripture with greater consideration.

Think about this as you prepare for worship this week. Expect God to meet you!
≈Brenda

✶　✶　✶

I praise you today, Lord, for your mighty acts. I thank you for the freedom to worship and the confidence that you will be present as your people gather. Give me a heart that looks to your Word with eager expectation, knowing it holds the precepts of life. I ask your blessings on those who assemble in military chapels around the world to worship you. In Jesus' name I pray. ✛ *Amen.*

We Are Who We Are

Then all the nations of the world will see that you are a people claimed by the LORD, and they will stand in awe of you. + DEUTERONOMY 28:10

Yes, I remember where I was when JFK was shot. I was in my seventh-grade math class when the announcement came over the loudspeaker. I was speechless. No one had ever even imagined something like that could happen. There was no point of reference in this scenario.

I also remember when a friend of ours dropped out of high school and joined the Marines. He went straight to Vietnam after training. Six months later, the word came that he had died in action. The church was packed to capacity, and the loudspeakers had to be moved to the outside for those who could not get in to hear. Someone my age had died in the middle of battle.

When 9/11 happened, I was at work. One of my coworkers pulled the TV into the conference room, and we all left our desks and gathered around to watch with our mouths open in astonishment. How? Why? Who? We remained glued to the TV during the remainder of the day and even did the same at work for the next two days until someone said, "We have to get back to some sense of normalcy."

You see, I had been brought up in a simpler time not that long ago. When I was a young girl, walking to the store to buy bubble gum for a penny or walking to a friend's house after dark wasn't an issue. I even remember picking blackberries with my sister in the woods near our house; we never thought for a moment that we might have been in danger.

While leading the Pre-Command Spouse Orientation program at Fort Leavenworth, Kansas, we did a session we called "Who You Are Is Where You Were When." In other words, your point of reference in life comes from where you were at the time those values were being established and those experiences were happening.

Today's generation is close to being numb to the violence and senselessness around us. They have seen it all, so to speak, and often the shock factor is not there.

Don't become numb to the world's happenings. Let God give you a fresh word every day from his Word so you will be able to face each trial and each situation with clear insight.   ⮜*Carol*

★   ★   ★

Father God, keep my spirit sharp and sensitive to your guidance in my life. Take away the numbness of news reports and let me continue to visualize the faces that are serving our country right now. I lift those faces to you in prayer today. + *Amen.*

March 3
I've Fallen, and I Will Get Up!

"Jeremiah, say to the people, 'This is what the LORD says: "When people fall down, don't they get up again? When they discover they're on the wrong road, don't they turn back? Then why do these people stay on their self-destructive path? Why do the people of Jerusalem refuse to turn back? They cling tightly to their lies and will not turn around."'" **+** JEREMIAH 8:4-5

Humiliating experiences seem to become etched in our memories. I have the proclivity to be clumsy and regularly find myself tripping or falling—and hoping no one is around to see me. Unfortunately, there is usually an audience to witness my awkwardness. One such time was during a church service in front of an entire congregation. The choir was dismissed from the choir loft; as I walked down the stairs, my feet stumbled, and I found myself on my hands and knees. I was humiliated and wanted to find somewhere to hide. I pulled myself up as gracefully as I could and immediately offered a curtsy. I don't think the curtsy made up for my blundering, but it made me feel better.

After a fall, it is normal to get back up. This is demonstrated on football fields around the nation every autumn. It can be seen in little children learning to walk. It's the natural thing to do. Yet for the children of Israel, there seemed to be a perpetual falling and not getting back up to follow their God. It was not a matter of "I've fallen, and I can't get up" but more like "I've fallen, and I won't get up."

Spiritual clumsiness is a reality, but spiritual rebellion is a choice. Proverbs gives guidance for keeping oneself from being spiritually clumsy through the preservation of sound judgment and discernment:

My child, don't lose sight of common sense and discernment. Hang on to them, for they will refresh your soul. They are like jewels on a necklace. They keep you safe on your way, and your feet will not stumble. You can go to bed without fear; you will lie down and sleep soundly. You need not be afraid of sudden disaster or the destruction that comes upon the wicked, for the LORD is your security. He will keep your foot from being caught in a trap (Proverbs 3:21-26). *⮞Brenda*

＊　＊　＊

Father, keep my feet firm beneath me as I follow you. Protect me from a rebellious spirit that would hinder me from walking the path you've set before me. Protect the steps of military personnel serving on the battlefield today. **+***Amen.*

Drastic Days—Drastic Measures

Oh, don't worry; we wouldn't dare say that we are as wonderful as these other men who tell you how important they are! But they are only comparing themselves with each other, using themselves as the standard of measurement. How ignorant! ✛ 2 CORINTHIANS 10:12

How do we measure ourselves today? Do we become so frustrated and overwhelmed that we say, "There is nothing I can do about the direction the world is going. I will just go live in a cave"? Instead of measuring ourselves by the world's standard, which is foolishness, let's discuss a few examples of men in the Bible who dedicated their measurement of worth to God.

Daniel is such a great example of taking drastic measures to make a difference. He would not give in to the worldly things that were offered to him. He stayed the course. He remained healthy and continued praying to the Lord. The drastic days he lived in were overcome by his drastic measure of commitment and dedication to a God he knew was bigger than any situation he would encounter. He was saved not only from the evil hand of man but from the jaws of the lion.

Nehemiah was an example of total mission focus. He knew the task before him was great. He knew the wall was to be rebuilt and that there were many who would try to keep the Israelites from doing so. He continually prayed to the Lord.

What are some of the things that these and other great men of faith had in common? They usually had to give up something. They prayed facedown, which symbolizes complete humility before the Lord. They made a conscious effort to be set apart.

We have had drastic days as a civilization:

9/11
War on Terror
High school mass killings
Virginia Tech and Northern Illinois University shootings
Pornography addiction on the rise
Divorce at an all-time high

What will our drastic measures be to challenge us to stay the course and be set apart in commitment to the Lord? ~*Carol*

✭   ✭   ✭

Father God, *you* are the answer for the world today. Keep me facedown in your presence as I face the drastic days ahead. I pray for those who serve in the military. Help them to commit to a deeper relationship with you during these days of conflict. ✛ *Amen.*

Attention!

Those who listen to instruction will prosper; those who trust the LORD will be joyful.
✝ PROVERBS 16:20

Following my graduation from college, I was awarded my first teaching job. I had a first-grade class with an interesting and colorful group of students. One little curly-headed blonde named Tina always seemed to be a step behind everyone else. She was incredibly cute but acted as if she walked in a fog. This was proven true one day when I said in my most authoritative teacher voice, "Let me have your attention!" Tina looked around bewildered and asked with widened eyes, "Where is it?" Unfortunately, Tina never found her attention that year!

Attention is a military term that requires a response. A soldier has no choice but to "snap to" when the word *attention* is shouted. This loud statement usually means that someone of higher rank is entering the area and the proper respect is to be shown.

I've also been to many ceremonies where the words *attention to orders* are spoken. The military personnel in the group stand straight and tall while something of great importance is read. The reading may be an award, a promotion, or a special commendation.

Too often, I'm like poor little Tina, unable to find my attention when I spend time apart with the Lord. My mind wanders, and my body fights sitting still. My desire is to hear the Lord's voice and snap to in reverence and respect, ready to receive my marching orders for the day. I want to be like the military personnel who listen intently when orders or citations are read. They know there is something good coming, and they readily receive the message.

I'm reminded of Samuel, who was called by the Lord as a child. The Lord in essence called out to Samuel, *"Attention!"* It took three times until young Samuel finally heard the Lord and listened to the message intended for his ears (see 1 Samuel 3:1-14). The Lord has promised to speak to us if we endeavor to hear his voice. Let's pay attention! ✒*Brenda*

✱ ✱ ✱

Dear Lord, many things distract me and cause my attention to be diverted from hearing your voice. Arrest my attention! Make me aware of your involvement in the world, and move me to join in where you are working. Like Samuel, may I hear your voice and respond, "Speak, LORD, for your servant is listening." Bless military chaplains today who are proclaiming your Word to those serving in harm's way. May they and those they minister to be attentive to your voice and obedient to your call. ✝ *Amen.*

Desires of My Heart

Take delight in the LORD, and he will give you your heart's desires. + PSALM 37:4

As a young child, I was very much a dreamer. When I would go to the movies, I would get into the story line and feel as if I were there. *The Sound of Music* was definitely my favorite. I especially liked the movies or TV shows that dealt with getting three wishes. I would ponder and dream about what my three wishes would be if I were given that opportunity. I would often wish to be a professional singer, a ballerina, and an Olympic diver.

As life went on, I would often pray, asking God to give me a desire that was in my heart. I held on to the words of Psalm 37:4 and knew that magically my wish would be his desire for me.

I have learned so much about God since then. The first part of today's verse directs us to "take delight in the LORD." He wants us to first learn to know him intimately and to take delight in our relationship with him. He knows that when directed by the Holy Spirit, our desires will change.

If the Lord had magically given me what I thought were the desires of my heart, I know now that his desires for me would not have been met. My desires will be given when his desires are identified. He knows what's best for me. He knows what will lead me to the path of honor and glory and service to him.

God knew that soon my desire as a wife would be to follow my husband around the world as an example of my commitment to him in our covenant marriage. Had he given me the request of being a professional singer or whatever else, I would not have been able to live out what God knew to be the true desire of, not only my heart, but his. My heart's desire went from being a professional singer to being a stay-at-home mother giving our sons the foundation of a loving home that they needed.

Not my desires but *his* that *he* has known since the time of my creation for this life. Praise the Lord!   ⁓*Carol*

✷　✷　✷

Father God, you are the creator of all things. Thank you for desiring only the best for me and that which will bring me to a closer relationship with you. I pray that you give the men and women who are serving our country your blessings and comfort. + *Amen.*

March 7
A Stamp in My Passport

Examine yourselves to see if your faith is genuine. Test yourselves. Surely you know that Jesus Christ is among you; if not, you have failed the test of genuine faith. ✚ 2 CORINTHIANS 13:5

Our family was living in Germany when my sister-in-law came to visit. We decided we wanted to see how many passport stamps we could get in a day. Our plan was to cross the border of each country, get our passports stamped, and eat some type of local food. We started in Germany, where we ate schnitzel, then to Austria for strudel, Switzerland for chocolate, and finally Italy to eat pizza.

I have proof in my passport that I was in Italy, but I never felt like I was really there. In Italy we stopped at a restaurant to eat pizza—what could be more Italian? We couldn't even find a place that would serve us pizza before sunset! I was not impressed with the country. I may have a stamp in my passport, but the experience was not validated by the taste of genuine Italian pizza.

Many people approach God this way. They want their spiritual passports stamped, want to taste some of the good things he offers, but don't really want to spend time with him. They call themselves Christian, but their lives are not characterized by a relationship with Christ. Then if he doesn't answer prayer—or fails to serve them pizza when they want it—they are not impressed. I would venture to say their faith is not genuine as described in today's Scripture.

It wasn't until years later on an extended trip to Italy that I really began to value, enjoy, and appreciate all the good things the country had to offer. In fact, Italy is on my list of favorite places to visit. I finally had the pizza, and it, along with other wonderful things I experienced on my visit, makes me want to return again and again. It's not until I make a commitment to spend time with God in his Word and in prayer that I can enjoy the good things God has to offer me. I am challenged to examine myself daily for an authentic faith in Christ.   ❧*Brenda*

* * *

Father, you are gracious and kind. I want my life to be stamped by a genuine faith in you. Make your impression deep, so that when others look at me, they see you. Encourage the hearts of those serving you in foreign lands. May they, too, receive impressions of your presence and your love. ✚ *Amen.*

Why Do We Wait?

This is all the more urgent, for you know how late it is; time is running out. Wake up, for our salvation is nearer now than when we first believed. + ROMANS 13:11

Why do we wait to share our faith? The military family lives in a sense of urgency. There is always the next assignment or the next move on the horizon. Often you find yourself getting very close to those around you, realizing you might never see them again in this life. You always enjoy each other to the fullest extent because time is short in your relationship.

Many times that has extended to those I knew who needed to come to know the Lord. The older I got, the more quickly and readily I came to the conclusion that I shouldn't wait to discuss my faith in Jesus Christ with others. My husband says I will always find a way to bring Jesus into a conversation. That is the ultimate compliment. I want to stand before the Lord and have him say, "You gave it your best for me."

I love the Scripture in Hebrews 13:7, which says, "Remember your leaders who taught you the word of God. Think of all the good that has come from their lives, and follow the example of their faith."

Jesus walking on this earth was our example. Now, we serve as examples of him.

At this time in history, we are all living in a sense of urgency. We are urgently encouraged to buy the next big technological gadget. Each day there is a sense of urgency to be vigilant in our watching for terrorist events to occur in public places. Even with our children, there is such a sense of urgency to get them in the right schools and the right programs so they can succeed in life.

Some of us take that sense of urgency into our spiritual lives. We must be at church when the doors are opened. I found this poem in the book *Simple Faith* by Charles R. Swindoll.[1]

> *Some wish to live within the sound*
> *Of Church or Chapel bell;*
> *I want to run a Rescue Shop*
> *Within a yard of hell.*

Our sense of urgency should be for the eternal salvation of those who are lost. We should not wait to share our faith or to give others the opportunity to know Jesus. Make a commitment to yourself to never have to say, "Why did I wait so long to share Jesus?" *~Carol*

* * *

Father God, give me a sense of urgency to share the gospel. Help me to be ready with your truth as I reach out to military families. + *Amen.*

---

[1] C. T. Studd in Charles R. Swindoll, *Simple Faith*, (Dallas, TX: Word Publishing, 1991), 53.

March 9
Good Guy or Bad Guy?

Here now is my final conclusion: Fear God and obey his commands, for this is everyone's duty. God will judge us for everything we do, including every secret thing, whether good or bad.
✝ ECCLESIASTES 12:13-14

My grandson Noah is fascinated by robots. For his third birthday, his dad and uncle decided they would surprise him with a visit from a real robot. They went through the home improvement store and gathered an assortment of materials with which they created a most amazing robot costume. On the night of Noah's birthday party, there was a knock at the door. My husband escorted Noah to open the door, where he was greeted by "003" wishing him a happy birthday. I am sorry I cannot describe the look on Noah's face as he gazed on this life-size manifestation of his little-boy dreams. When he gathered his wits about him, his first words to the robot were, "Are you a good guy or a bad guy?"

Even as a three-year-old, he understood the concept of good and bad, but he couldn't always distinguish which was which. Life is not always as one-dimensional as to categorize things as simply good or simply bad. Just as adults are able to define these things for a child, God in his wisdom will clearly define those things in our lives. That is why it is important to study and know God's Word; it is there he explains to us those things that are good and those things that are bad.

Romans 12:2 instructs us, "Don't copy the behavior and customs of this world, but let God transform you into a new person by changing the way you think. Then you will learn to know God's will for you, which is good and pleasing and perfect." This is one example of how God's Word guides us. Scripture is replete with instruction that will help us know what is good or bad for our lives. Don't depend on your ability to differentiate; depend on God's Word, and you won't go wrong. ⮜Brenda

✶   ✶   ✶

Thank you, Lord, for your Word, which instructs and guides. Give me wisdom to know the difference between good and bad choices I am faced with each day. May I bring honor to you by the choices I make today. I pray for soldiers who are having to make challenging decisions on the battlefield. Help their choices to be on the side of right. In Jesus' name I pray. ✝ Amen.

Show Them Mercy

For God said to Moses, "I will show mercy to anyone I choose, and I will show compassion to anyone I choose." ✛ ROMANS 9:15

One of my favorite gospel singers is CeCe Winans. Whenever I am asked to share a special song for events, I am always drawn to the powerful words in the songs that CeCe records. Recently she recorded a song called "He's Not on His Knees Yet."[1] The song talks about how we as humans think we are so strong and have it together and don't see a need for Jesus in our lives. People who do not know the Lord may see that need as a sign of weakness. The words of the song express that many times people are too strong to be weak, not knowing that God will give them the supernatural power of the Holy Spirit when he enters their lives.

The most important phrase of the song is "*show him mercy.*" That is where we often fail as Christians. We want to beat people over their heads with a Bible or tell them what they should be doing in a tone of condemnation rather than show them mercy.

Many who are experiencing separation and deployment from their loved ones at this time need to be shown mercy. I cannot tell you enough about the military wives who have shared their stories of coming to know the Lord during times of deployment, when the Christian community reached out to them at their times of weakness and need. I do believe in the concept of loving them into the Kingdom as well as supporting them with instruction and teaching.

Remember, they may not be on their knees yet or through the weakness they are experiencing, but God's power is there to make them strong. ❧*Carol*

✯   ✯   ✯

Oh Lord, I want to ask you a favor: when you hear me being critical or wanting to say, "What is wrong with them? Don't they know better?" Please turn that thought or those words into mercy for the individual. As I have seen from so many reports of those who are serving in this conflict and as I have heard the stories from spouses at home, this is a time of revival for them. Remind me each day, Lord, to show mercy and to pray for the Holy Spirit to minister to those who are not on their knees yet. Thank you, Lord. ✛ *Amen.*

---

[1] CeCe Winans, "He's Not on His Knees Yet," from *Alabaster Box,* compact disc, Wellspring Gospel, (p) and © 1999.

March 11
It's Not There Anymore!

I am the LORD, and I do not change. ✛ MALACHI 3:6

I will never forget the day our family was driving around in Rome, Georgia. My husband had attended elementary school there, and he was reminiscing about happy childhood moments. He was eager to drive by the school he had attended and show us where he'd spent his schooldays. His trip down memory lane took a detour when we arrived at the location of his alma mater and discovered that the school was gone. It had been torn down in the name of educational progress. The boys and I were trying not to snicker as my husband realized the drastic change that had taken place in his childhood hometown. The disappointment on his face was enough to keep us from audible chuckles.

Change is a reality of life. In the book *Future Shock*, author Alvin Toffler wrote about people needing zones of stability when they experience swift changes.[1] In other words, they need things that will not change. I can't think of too many things this side of heaven that meet that criterion.

Today's Scripture offers the greatest zone of stability there is in the declaration "I am the LORD, and I do not change." The fancy theological term for this unchangeable nature of God is his *immutability*. We can rest in the fact that he's always been the same, he is the same right now, and he will always be the same. God is perfection, and there is no need for change.

Scripture also tells us of three other things that will not change:

God's love: Psalm 136 repeats the refrain "His faithful love endures forever."

God's Word: "The grass withers and the flowers fade, but the word of our God stands forever" (Isaiah 40:8).

God's purpose for your life: "I cry out to God . . . who will fulfill his purpose for me" (Psalm 57:2).

Things in this life are made to change. Gospel writer Luke (21:33) reminded us that heaven and earth will pass away. We can count on creation changing, but the Creator will remain the same.   ✎*Brenda*

✳ ✳ ✳

Thank you, Lord, for your unchanging nature! It fills me with confidence when things around me are changing at breakneck speed. I look to you today for my stability and my confidence. I pray for military families who are experiencing rapid changes in their lives because of deployments and military training. Be their ever-present help in time of need. ✛*Amen.*

---

[1] Alvin Toffler, *Future Shock* (New York: Bantam Books, 1984).

Not Only Obedience but Trust

Today I have given you the choice between life and death, between blessings and curses. Now I call on heaven and earth to witness the choice you make. Oh, that you would choose life, so that you and your descendants might live! You can make this choice by loving the LORD your God, obeying him, and committing yourself firmly to him. This is the key to your life. And if you love and obey the LORD, you will live long in the land the LORD swore to give your ancestors Abraham, Isaac, and Jacob. ✛ DEUTERONOMY 30:19-20

My husband is a man of his word. You can trust him. You can bank on his commitment and his promise to you. He has been that way since I met him many years ago.

During his time as an active-duty military man, I watched him lead men and women in different units to which he was assigned. I listened at the change of commands as others would honor him and thank him for his commitment to their unit and to their mission. I also watched as he served under many whom he obeyed through orders, and I could always see the difference in those he felt he could trust.

Our Creator has given us free will. It is our choice whether we obey. However, if we say we trust in the Lord Jesus Christ as our Savior, there is no choice but to obey. When we choose to obey, we are choosing life and blessings rather than death and curses.

Our military members learn to obey orders very quickly. They also come to trust each other when they're in a unit together for any amount of time. Each story of those who have received a Purple Heart or a Medal of Honor comes with a story of someone who has gone back for a comrade. It is someone who has sacrificed his or her own safety in order to save another military brother or sister.

Scripture says in John 15:13, "There is no greater love than to lay down one's life for one's friends." Our military members are showing us by example every day how to obey and trust. They are leading us into what we should take as an example to follow in our Christian walk. ⟡*Carol*

✭ ✭ ✭

Father, as those who are serving our country follow their leaders, so let me follow you with obedience and trust in every situation that comes my way. ✛ *Amen.*

March 13
Peas or Peace?

Not that I was ever in need, for I have learned how to be content with whatever I have. I know how to live on almost nothing or with everything. I have learned the secret of living in every situation, whether it is with a full stomach or empty, with plenty or little. ✛ PHILIPPIANS 4:11-12

The childhood story of "The Princess and the Pea" describes a visiting princess kept from a peaceful night's sleep by a tiny pea. For each of us, that tiny pea takes the form of many things that might rob us of peace. To solve the problem of the pea, the princess's hostess tried to cover it up by stacking more mattresses on top of it. The piling of mattresses, however, didn't eliminate the problem.

It is easy for me to identify with the tendency to cover up instead of addressing irritants that rob me of peace. One of the peas in my life has been discontentment. I have struggled with being content in a situation, season of life, or new military assignment. I have whined, griped, and wished things to be different. I find such hope in the words of Paul telling me I can *learn* to be content.

Military life provides plenty of opportunities to attend the school of peace and contentment. A popular change of address card for military families uses a different translation of today's Scripture: "I have learned in whatever *state* I am, to be content" (NKJV). The numerous moves we make give ample occasion to learn invaluable lessons.

If one of the peas robbing you of peace today is discontentment, turn your focus away from yourself and look to God. Ask him to help you learn the secret described by Paul of being content.   ✎*Brenda*

* * *

Father, forgive me for allowing the irritating things of life to take my focus off you and rob me of your peace. Fill me with faith in your ability to see me through any challenge that comes my way. Teach me the secret of being content in you. I pray for servicemen and women who may feel discontented in their circumstances. Renew their vision for their work and give them a sense of your peace today. In Jesus' name I pray. ✛*Amen.*

Bitter or Better

Then I realized that my heart was bitter, and I was all torn up inside. + PSALM 73:21

Whenever I begin to dig deeper in God's Word to understand situations or emotions or relationships through his eyes, I am always encouraged. He knew at the time of creation we would be emotional beings. He knew we would deal with daily conflicts. How do I know he knew? You only have to go to the concordance of any Bible and find the word we're dealing with today: *bitterness*.

How does bitterness take root? Well, usually it begins with hurt. When that hurt is not dealt with and when we do not ask forgiveness and make amends with someone, it can take root, and bitterness begins to grow.

In the dictionary, bitterness is described as severe pain, grief, or regret; distaste.

In the Scripture for today, the psalmist Asaph had become bitter by watching those around him put their confidence and hope in things of this world. In other words, he was pained at others' not coming to the realization that only the things that affected eternity were important.

As we have learned so often through the experiences in our lives, we can become bitter when things don't go our way. When we feel that our family members don't get the things in life they so much deserve, we can start thinking about what could have been and become more and more discouraged and hurt.

Many of the young families being separated by the War on Terror could become very hurt and bitter that their families have to be apart for such a long period of time. The families who have lost loved ones to tragedies in our nation could become very hurt and bitter that they were the ones who had to go through such deep loss in their lives.

The other side of that is becoming better in spite of and because of our experiences. I have always felt that there is not one thing I have experienced through my choices that I cannot use to encourage and exhort someone else who is possibly going through something very similar. Imagine the impact of those who have been through so much choosing to be better instead of bitter by reaching out to a hurting world.

Bitter or better? Which will you choose today?   ∼*Carol*

*   *   *

Father, remind those who are hurting that they can help others along life's way by their experiences. Lord, I ask that you help me move beyond hurt and bitterness to become better in my service to you. I ask a special blessing on those whose loved ones are not with them at this time, whether because of separation or tragedy. Give them an extra measure of hope today. + *Amen.*

Empty Nest

My life passes more swiftly than a runner. ✦ JOB 9:25

The week before taking my youngest son to college, I noticed a bird's nest had been built under the deck of our house. I watched the nest each day until finally the baby birds hatched. I could hardly believe that within one week the babies were all gone from the nest! One week! I thought, *Do mother birds grieve at the launching of their babies? What does a mother bird do now that her babies are out of the nest?* Foolish questions, I'm sure. Yet I was trying to find some help for the sadness I felt in saying good-bye to my son. I had spent nineteen years with that child, and I was experiencing grief.

Returning home from the university after leaving Joseph, it felt almost as if a death had occurred as we adjusted to his absence. My husband and I moved in our circles, but it was evident something—someone—was missing. One day as we opened the garage door to leave the house, we spotted two little boys from the neighborhood playing together. They were about the same age difference as our boys and were decked out in army paraphernalia as our guys had so often played. Waves of memories rushed over my mind as I wondered, *How could so much time have already passed?*

Transitions like this are natural, but the adjustments during transition points must be intentional. For example, when the nest is empty, some couples choose to terminate a marriage while others choose to enrich their relationship and spend more time together. My husband and I quickly realized we were going to need to develop some new rituals for the two of us to aid in the transition of our boys' leaving home. One of the things we instituted was going out to breakfast on Saturday morning. It has become a treasured time for the two of us as we relax together, take time to share our thoughts, and plan for the future. We began walking together in the evenings, giving us opportunity to share the events of the day while also getting much-needed exercise.

We survived the launching of our children from the nest and can report healthy and happy results that followed. Because life passes swiftly, there will be more transitions to come. Positive planning for life's transitions will pay dividends in the future. ❧*Brenda*

* * *

Thank you, Lord, for each moment. Help me as I approach the transitions of every season of life. Make my heart open and my spirit flexible to learn the lessons that will strengthen my relationship with others and with you. Bless military families who are experiencing transition today because of deployment, relocation, or job change. In Jesus' name I pray. ✦*Amen.*

Somewhere Out There

You know when I sit down or stand up. You know my thoughts even when I'm far away.

✝ PSALM 139:2

The night was very dark. After I put the boys to bed, the house felt very lonely. I tried to flip through the channels on television to find something to keep me company. I fixed a snack for comfort. The TV was no company, and the snack was no comfort. I missed my husband.

I remember thinking that he was under the same sky that I was. We were on different continents, but the sky was the same. I needed to go outside to feel closer to him. I walked out onto the patio and realized that the stars were so bright I could see far past our acre of yard. The air was crisp and the breeze soft on my face.

I found myself sitting on the picnic table, praying that God would protect us while my husband was in a faraway land. I prayed that at this very moment as I sat under the same sky that was covering him, our thoughts would somehow be connected, and he would realize how very much the children and I loved and missed him. Stretched out on that table, looking up at the stars, I prayed that the God of the universe would protect my husband.

Our God knows everything about us. He watches us throughout each day. As people are separated because of deployment, crisis, or even mission work, he is watching and knows every move and every thought.

We can trust such a God who cares so deeply for his children. Even though his hand controls times and seasons, stars and planets, and even the destiny of nations, he cares about what concerns you. When you feel lonely, sad, or afraid, look up and know he is looking down with tender care for you.   ❧*Carol*

✳   ✳   ✳

Creator of the universe, "How precious are your thoughts about me, O God. They cannot be numbered! I can't even count them; they outnumber the grains of sand! And when I wake up, you are still with me!" (Psalm 139:17-18). Remind me of the sacrifice military personnel make being away from family and loved ones. Comfort their hearts, and give them an awareness of your closeness and care. ✝*Amen.*

March 17
Red Purse on a Bench

And we know that God causes everything to work together for the good of those who love God and are called according to his purpose for them. + ROMANS 8:28

One Saturday morning, my husband and I were in a suburb of Washington, D.C., enjoying breakfast. It was a beautiful morning, so we took our coffee and bagels to an outside bench. After we finished and were driving home, my husband's BlackBerry interrupted our pleasant morning, alerting him of a voice mail on our home phone. I looked at the number and recognized it as that of a friend. My initial thought was to call her back later, but as moments passed I decided I should go ahead and give her a quick call to make sure things were okay. As I reached for my cell phone in my purse, I realized I had no purse! I had left it on the bench several miles and minutes away. The bench was in a crowded urban area, and the purse was bright red! It couldn't have been an easier target for someone to take. We returned to the scene as quickly as we could; the bench sat empty with the exception of a bright red purse. Amazing!

I checked the voice mail from my friend. The message was not important, and there was no need to return the call. But if the interruption of her call had not come, I doubt I would have ever seen my purse, and more importantly its contents, again.

God is at work in our lives to help us when we are often unaware of his intervention. Sometimes the help comes in the form of what seems to be an interruption, an inconvenient moment, or something else that causes us to change our immediate plans. As we acknowledge the sovereignty of God and his hand at work, we can never think things happen by accident. If you love God and are committed to serving him, the Bible says he is able to work things together for our good.

As you go through your day, look for God's hand at work. What may appear to be an interruption in your schedule may actually be God's way of changing your course in order to bless you or someone else in need.   ❧Brenda

✳ ✳ ✳

Thank you, Lord, for your hand at work in the world and in my life. Help me to view today's interruptions as possibilities for a new glimpse of your loving character. I commit this day to you. I pray for National Guard families who have had the routine of their lives interrupted by deployment. In Jesus' name. + Amen.

Onward Christian Soldier

"For I know the plans I have for you," says the LORD. "They are plans for good and not for disaster, to give you a future and a hope." ✟ JEREMIAH 29:11

The word has just been given. A three month extension has been added to the deployment tour in Iraq. All of a sudden, the special month and time etched in the hearts and minds of waiting spouses and families is instantly changed. I found myself going to the calendar to find the date of departure of the five I personally know who are serving at this time.

I received an e-mail shortly after the extension was made public from my dear friend, Major Steve. I want to share a bit of what he said to help express what is on the hearts of these amazing military members:

> You probably saw on the news before I did, that we were being extended another three months. And to think that I thought one year was a long time. It's a marathon and not a sprint. I'm reminded of the extreme sacrifices previous generations made. They would go off to war for years at a time without knowing when and if they would return.
>
> My wife and I truly believe that God is our assignment manager. He uses the Army to send us places. We believe God has a mission for us at each location, and I guess I have three more months of work here in Iraq that *he* wants me to accomplish.
>
> It will be neat to look back and see what was done during these three extra months.

Next time you have to go a different way on the road because of a detour or maybe even get out of a meeting or gathering a little late, think of Major Steve and how he took the news of his extension. It is my prayer that we can learn to look at this life God has given us through the eyes of a soldier who knows who is in charge and who is directing his path!   ❧*Carol*

* * *

Dear Lord Jesus, bless those who are serving our country as soldiers, airmen, marines, sailors, and coastguardsmen. I thank you for those who know you as their Lord and Savior. I thank you that they are going forward with the power and strength of the Holy Spirit leading the way. ✟ *Amen.*

March 19
No Excuses!

Show this same diligence to the very end, in order to make your hope sure. We do not want you to become lazy, but to imitate those who through faith and patience inherit what has been promised. ✝ HEBREWS 6:11-12, NIV

My dad grew up in a cotton mill village in North Carolina. He tells a story of men who worked in the mill coming to the mill store between shifts. While there, they would spit tobacco juice and swap knives and stories. One day a great big man and a little man were there. The little man said to the big man, "If I were big as you, I'd go up to King's Mountain and I'd find the biggest bear I could find and I'd tear him limb from limb." The big man thought a moment and then said, "Little man, there's some little bears up there."

I have my doubts as to whether this was a true exchange, but it does make me think of the excuses I make where work for God is concerned: I'm too young, I'm too old, I'm too tired, I'm too busy, I'm not qualified, I'm not good enough—the list could go on.

The featured Scripture today instructs us to be diligent and not become lazy in our commitment to God. The focus of this diligence is on acting on our word, which is to be a sign of our sincerity as Christ followers.

The good news is that there are people of faith we can look to and imitate. Moses gave God an excuse when he was called to be a spokesman. Jonah gave God an excuse when he was called to be a missionary. Gideon gave God an excuse when he was called to lead an army. In spite of their initial resistance, God still had a plan for them. He used each of them to accomplish important things in the lives of people.

What's God calling you to do? What's your excuse for not doing it? There are people in need and crisis all around us, and you can help.   ❧*Brenda*

✶   ✶   ✶

Father, I thank you for the opportunity to serve you. I pray that I would have the courage to disregard the excuses I make that keep me from serving you with my whole heart. Give me a spirit of diligence. Purge me from slothfulness that would make my heart dull. Bless our servicemen and women who are diligently laboring for the cause of peace. In Jesus' name I pray. ✝ *Amen.*

Clothes Make the Man

But the LORD said to Samuel, . . . "The LORD doesn't see things the way you see them. People judge by outward appearance, but the LORD looks at the heart." ✝ 1 SAMUEL 16:7

Servicemen and women are identified immediately by their clothing. The military uniforms they wear proclaim their career paths. There are many things you can tell instantly about people in the military when you see them in uniform. First, you recognize their branch of service represented by the unique fashion and style for navy, air force, army, marines, and coast guard. When those in the military are decked out in their specific branch uniform with their medals and awards displayed, it is an impressive sight. People take notice. The uniform tells a story of assignments, battles, and achievements. It doesn't, however, communicate what is in one's heart.

The way people dress in our culture can identify them with a way of life, a way of thinking, and even a way to rebel without words. I was a teenager during the hippie days, and I wore outrageous clothes at times. When I see pictures, I am amazed at the look I tried to achieve. My children lived their teenage years in the baggy-pants era. When my husband and I finally decided to choose our battles, we realized that their outward appearance was not their heart appearance.

God saw in young David the future man after his own heart. When others only saw a scrawny shepherd boy, God saw the heart of a mighty warrior. God sees *your* potential today! You don't have to wear a uniform for him to appreciate the person he has created you to be. Give him your life, and let him take what may seem ordinary and transform it into something extraordinary. He did it for David. He can do it for you! ❧*Carol*

★ ★ ★

Lord, thank you for seeing beyond the external. Make my heart pleasing in your sight. Protect me from judging others by their outward appearance, and help me to see them as the people you created them to be. I thank you for those who wear the uniform of military service. Give me an opportunity to show my appreciation for their contribution to our nation. In your name I pray. ✝*Amen.*

March 21
Stuck with Deutschmarks

"Yes, a person is a fool to store up earthly wealth but not have a rich relationship with God."
✝ LUKE 12:21

I was excited about an upcoming trip to Germany. I would have the opportunity to speak to military spouses at a conference, reconnect with old friends, and finally spend the deutschmarks I had been holding onto for years. I kept the money, hoping I would return to Germany one day. I had already thought about the chocolate, coffee, and other treasures I would purchase. I was so disappointed when I discovered I could no longer spend the money! Germany had converted its monetary system to euros, and the date to exchange deutschmarks was long past. My money was worthless!

We hold on to many things in this life that will be worthless when we stand before God, don't we? It reminds me of the story about a man who went to heaven carrying a suitcase full of gold. When he arrived at the gate, the angel checking him in asked him why he brought street pavement to heaven with him.

Today's Scripture is part of an exchange Jesus had with a man who asked him,

"Teacher, please tell my brother to divide our father's estate with me."

Jesus replied, "Friend, who made me a judge over you to decide such things as that?" Then he said, "Beware! Guard against every kind of greed. Life is not measured by how much you own."

Then he told them a story: "A rich man had a fertile farm that produced fine crops. He said to himself, 'What should I do? I don't have room for all my crops.' Then he said, 'I know! I'll tear down my barns and build bigger ones. Then I'll have room enough to store all my wheat and other goods. And I'll sit back and say to myself, "My friend, you have enough stored away for years to come. Now take it easy! Eat, drink, and be merry!"'

"But God said to him, 'You fool! You will die this very night. Then who will get everything you worked for?'

"Yes, a person is a fool to store up earthly wealth but not have a rich relationship with God." (Luke 12:13-21)

The foolish rich man would not be able to take his wealth with him to eternity. God wants us to use what we have in this life as good stewards would, whether it is time, money, or possessions. All of these things will be worthless one day, but a rich relationship with God is priceless and eternal. 〰Brenda

✮ ✮ ✮

Father, I thank you for the blessings of life. Make me a wise and good steward of all you have given me. I pray for those who are serving the poor in war-torn countries. Provide for their needs today. ✝ Amen.

A Good Fight

May you experience the love of Christ, though it is too great to understand fully. Then you will
be made complete with all the fullness of life and power that comes from God.
✛ EPHESIANS 3:19

Each year, military members retire after a full, active life of service. They have fought the good fight, stayed the course, and served their country. How can they continue the connection and keep their finger on the pulse in order to encourage those still on active duty? Many of these families have a great desire to stay connected to their military roots, but they aren't sure how to go about it.

My husband and I chose to serve as a team during his time in the military. We rarely doubted being called into the lifestyle. We knew it was the life that was given to us to honor and cherish. We loved the travel, the experiences, and the people; many became like family to us. We weren't always thrilled about where we might be moving, but we definitely made adjustments in the long run that became yet another part of our military experience. We loved the sharing of different cultures that broadened the hometown mind-set of not only us as a couple but that of our sons.

It is up to us, who are on the outside looking in, to keep the military family at the forefront of the minds of the civilian community. I feel the retired military member has an obligation to be available to listen, to mentor, and to encourage those who are in service to our country.

Having fought the good fight and taken with you the honor of serving your country, be challenged to reconnect with those who are continuing on in their commitment to all Americans and the freedom we hold so dear. ⁓*Carol*

✯ ✯ ✯

Father God, there are many who feel cast aside when their service to our country is over. Please help me to recognize, befriend, and remember those who have served this great land. I pray today that military retirees will continue to keep the men and women who are currently serving in the forefront of their daily thoughts and prayers. Stimulate them to mentor and support in a powerful way. ✛*Amen.*

March 23
A Window Seat

Don't speak evil against each other, dear brothers and sisters. If you criticize and judge each other, then you are criticizing and judging God's law. But your job is to obey the law, not to judge whether it applies to you. God alone, who gave the law, is the Judge. He alone has the power to save or to destroy. So what right do you have to judge your neighbor? + JAMES 4:11-12

This spring, I had the opportunity to travel from Germany to Italy. I don't usually request the window seat, but because flying to Italy was a new experience, I wanted to be able to see the countryside. No one had to announce when we crossed the border. It was evident by the terrain I viewed from the sky. The fields and roads of Germany are measured and precise. The landscape is characterized by perfectly blocked-off squares and carefully designed highways. All at once, the fields were a hodgepodge of color and size, and the roads were a maze of squiggly lines. I knew I was not in Germany anymore! Now, don't get me wrong, I'm not judging Italy in a negative light. The topography observed from the airplane was indicative of an appealing and laid-back way of life.

My aerial view made me think, however, about how easy it is to make judgments about things from a distance. We judge others because their lives look like they are jumbled and out of order. We judge situations because we don't have all the facts. Isn't it interesting how things appear one way from a distance and another way when close? For instance, we may be guilty of looking down on a parent when a child has gone astray. That picture, however, looks totally different when that child is your own. We need to be careful not to follow the human tendency to make this kind of judgment.

Contrary to the song that was popular long ago, God is not One who views us "from a distance." He is not One who sits thousands of miles above the earth and judges us on the basis of what he sees. In his great plan, God sent Jesus to walk among us. He got up close and personal and chose to understand us. Jesus faced every challenge in life yet did not sin. It is because of his faithfulness that we receive mercy and grace from God instead of the condemnation we deserve. Next time you have the window seat, thank him for his mercy! ≈Brenda

* * *

Father, you are a gracious and merciful God. Forgive me for wrong judgments I have made toward others. Help me to show mercy and grace to others as you have shown it to me. I pray for national leaders today as they make decisions about world issues from a distance. Give them wisdom and clarity. + Amen.

Commitment to Serve

For even the Son of Man came not to be served but to serve others and to give his life as a ransom for many. ✚ MATTHEW 20:28

I can remember how after 9/11 my heart was filled with patriotism for this country, stronger than any other time in my life. I also remember the very first military members that I knew personally who were sent to Afghanistan and then to Iraq. I gathered boxes of requested items and encouraged Sunday school classes and community groups to join in the physical support of these men and women. One of the requests I received from a military member was for flyswatters. They needed to swat the flies that came into their desert tent area every day. I was thrilled to buy forty of them and send them out. It was one more way for me to be able to touch those who were serving our country.

The soldiers I had been corresponding with came home, thank the Lord, and I found myself just sitting back after their return. This was perhaps due to the fact that I, as most Americans, have a short memory when it comes to the terrorist attacks on our country in the last decade.

I now personally know five who are serving our country in the War on Terror in Iraq. I am back in the fight to continue to exhort, encourage, and honor these men and women, along with their families left behind. I have made a new commitment in my own heart to continue to serve them as they serve our country.

I want to invite you to put a face on the war by adopting a military family member in your community and reaching out to them with meals or phone calls or fun days.

Major Steve calls me every couple of weeks from Baghdad. He always says, "Do you have any prayer requests?" He is there not only to serve our country and serve the people of Iraq, but he is constantly thinking of how he can serve others who are back home. What an amazing example of God's purpose in our lives!

I pray we can take the lead of Major Steve and seek to serve.   ☙*Carol*

✴   ✴   ✴

Lord, instill in me a servant's heart. Help me to dig deep and know that I am blessed when I bless others. Thank you for the blessing of the military and their families as they continue to serve. ✚*Amen.*

March 25
Surprise Cold Front

But blessed are those who trust in the LORD and have made the LORD their hope and confidence. They are like trees planted along a riverbank, with roots that reach deep into the water. Such trees are not bothered by the heat or worried by long months of drought. Their leaves stay green, and they never stop producing fruit. + JEREMIAH 17:7-8

For years I heard about the spring cherry blossoms in Washington, D.C. It was hard for me to imagine that flowering trees were that special and deserving of all the press. It only took one springtime visit to convince me that trees *can* be that special. The ethereal blossoms are truly a sight to behold. This year, my husband and I celebrated the arrival of spring and enjoyed a picnic under the cherry blossoms. We walked in short sleeves with the sun shining, enjoying the unique beauty of spring at the D.C. Tidal Basin. It was beautiful!

Three days later, to everyone's surprise, a cold front moved in, and the beautiful blossoms were covered with snow. It was totally unexpected and didn't seem to make sense.

Isn't life like that sometimes? Just when we feel like we've entered a new season of warmth and encouragement, the cold wind of a surprising and unexpected challenge blows through. We find ourselves looking for cover and wondering how things could change so quickly.

Today's Scripture describes a tree that is planted in the ground so firmly and deeply that even when unexpected and surprising weather comes, it will not wither or stop yielding fruit. It states that we can be like this tree as we trust God. Even when life brings things we don't understand, we can be confident and sure. *Brenda*

Dear Lord, thank you for seasons that sometimes bring unexpected circumstances. Help me to trust you even when I don't understand. Make my roots grow deep in you, so even when challenges come, my confidence in you is sure. I ask your blessings on the children of deployed military personnel today. Help them during this time when they may not understand why they must be separated from their mom or dad. In your name I pray. +*Amen.*

Show Me the Way

When you hear a sound like marching feet in the tops of the poplar trees, go out and attack! That will be the signal that God is moving ahead of you to strike down the Philistine army.

✝ 1 CHRONICLES 14.15

David had just been anointed as king over all of Israel. The Philistines were not happy about that decision and decided to capture David. The Philistine army was a force to be reckoned with. They were powerful and numerous. When David heard they were coming to get him after he had been anointed king, he immediately went to God for instruction and his next move.

David asked God in 1 Chronicles 14:10, "Should I go out to fight the Philistines? Will you hand them over to me?" In other words, he wanted God to show him the way to victory—God's way to victory. The Lord answered David, "Yes, go ahead. I will hand them over to you."

David did not make a move until the Lord gave him the authority to move on the Philistines. So many times I hear stories from those who are serving in Iraq and other places in the world, and there is usually a time of prayer before they go into the battle or a conflict presented before them. This story is not a fairy tale. It is a part of God's living Word. And it is as much for our military today as it was for David in the Old Testament.

If you are ever at a loss as to what to pray for the military, pray 1 Chronicles 14:15 for them. Pray that God will go before them and show them the way to victory.
~*Carol*

✯ ✯ ✯

Father, I come to you to ask protection and comfort for those serving our country. Help me to remember that you are there to go before them as they deal with conflict every day. I pray for victory in this conflict. Lord, show our military the way of the battle, and show them the *way* to you. I ask these things in your Son's name. ✝ *Amen.*

March 27

Dog Races?

Give all your worries and cares to God, for he cares about you. ✢ 1 PETER 5:7

A Christian college had a marquee in front that read DOG RACES. It was a curious sight that caused some confusion. Why would the words DOG RACES be on the marquee of a Christian college? Actually the sign was to read GOD CARES, but mischievous students visited in the middle of the night and switched the letters around to present a different message.

Too often, the communication that God cares gets confused in our own lives as well. This is the message the Lord wants to speak to our hearts daily, but circumstances frequently garble the letters, and we are left with confusion rather than a message of love and hope.

I think of the catastrophes of recent years. When the winds of Katrina came, no doubt the letters spelling God's loving care appeared to be blown out of place.

When the waves of the tsunami hit the shores of Asia, the message of God's love seemed swept away by the water.

Families were misplaced and torn apart.

Lives were displaced and changed forever.

Homes were replaced with any shelter that could be found.

Storms come into our lives without the tangible winds and waves of hurricanes or tsunamis, and we have difficulty seeing God's plan and certainly have difficulty comprehending his care for us. We can, however, stand in the confidence of Scripture that states, "I will be glad and rejoice in your unfailing love, for you have seen my troubles, and you care about the anguish of my soul" (Psalm 31:7).

Just as there has been rebuilding after Katrina and restoration following the tsunami, the letters of our lives will be rearranged. We will see that we're not just part of a dog race, but that God truly cares for us. ✲*Brenda*

* * *

Dear Lord, "You clothed me with skin and flesh, and you knit my bones and sinews together. You gave me life and showed me your unfailing love. My life was preserved by your care" (Job 10:11-12). Thank you for your loving care. Help me to trust you even when the circumstances of life confuse the message. I pray today for families of deployed military personnel. Help them know your care while their loved ones are away. In Jesus' name. ✢*Amen.*

The Line Is Drawn

"But since you are like lukewarm water, neither hot nor cold, I will spit you out of my mouth!"

+ REVELATION 3:16

There was a heavy fog in the air, and the rain sent a chill through us after we stepped off the heated tour bus. Our sons were in high school at the time. My husband had wanted us to take this trip since being assigned to Yongsan, South Korea almost a year earlier. We had reached the infamous demilitarized zone—the DMZ—between North and South Korea.

A strip of land that serves as a buffer zone between the two hostile nations, the DMZ is the most heavily armed border in the world. And it gave our family an opportunity to understand just why the United States military still has a presence there.

The conflict between the two sides of Korea, one controlled by the UN and the other by the Soviets, claimed over three million lives before international intervention achieved a ceasefire. Both sides moved their troops two thousand meters from the buffer zone—but since this agreement was never followed by a peace treaty, North Korea and South Korea never did end their war.[1]

As we finished our visit that day, we were taken to the meeting place considered to be neutral when the two sides came together for talks. As we entered the large portable-style structure, we could see the North Korean soldiers watching our every move. The evidence of the line that was drawn was clear.

The United States military is there to help enforce this continued ceasefire. Our military families have and will continue to fight for the good of our country and our world. But our visit reminded me of the very real line between another set of warring entities.

A few Sundays ago our pastor referred to the spiritual line that we as Christians know in our hearts we are not supposed to cross. Unlike the DMZ, this line marks a clear division between good and evil: right choices on the one side, temptation and sin on the other. We don't want to walk on the spiritual line, teetering between good and evil; we want to make decisions and step out in faith from behind the spiritual "buffer zone." We must seek to arm ourselves spiritually and remain on the side of good. ⤚*Carol*

✫ ✫ ✫

Father God, I pray that I have the courage to draw the line in my life against evil. I pray that I continue to stand on the side of good. Show me what that is, Father, and as I see not only wars in foreign lands but also senseless acts of violence in this nation, lead me to take a bold stand against evil. + *Amen.*

---

[1] "Korean Demilitarized Zone," *Wikipedia.* http://en.wikipedia.org/wiki/Korean_Demilitarized_Zone.

March 29
May Your God Rescue You!

So at last the king gave orders for Daniel to be arrested and thrown into the den of lions. The king said to him, "May your God, whom you serve so faithfully, rescue you." + DANIEL 6:16

King Darius was truly stepping over the line. He was giving a dare to almighty God to protect one of his own. At the time of this event, Daniel had been consistently staying in touch with God through prayer and fasting. He was so close to God when he was thrown into the lions' den that I doubt he felt any fear. God had the situation covered.

The Scripture tells us, "We know how much God loves us, and we have put our trust in his love. God is love, and all who live in love live in God, and God lives in them. And as we live in God, our love grows more perfect. So we will not be afraid on the day of judgment, but we can face him with confidence because we live like Jesus here in this world. Such love has no fear, because perfect love expels all fear. If we are afraid, it is for fear of punishment, and this shows that we have not fully experienced his perfect love" (1 John 4:16-18).

Daniel had no fear because his love for God had been perfected. He was in constant communication and commitment to the Father every day. Daniel felt such love in his life from his Creator that when he was cast into the lions' den, he knew there was no need to fear what was before him.

What a challenge to us today! Our daily lives should be so filled with constant communication through prayer, that we would live a constant reflection of his love and his purpose for us. We can hold on to the fact that God will rescue us during those times. Fear cannot overtake us when we have prepared our hearts in perfect love from our Creator.   ~Carol

* * *

Father God, rescue those who are struggling with fear today. Teach them to come to you and learn the lessons of perfect love exemplified in the life of Daniel. Give strength and protection to the missionaries who go out into the world to take your hope and love to others. I pray for our military, as they are cast into the lions' den every day. May they realize the love from you, Lord, that casts out all fear. + Amen.

Courage to Stand

Be on guard. Stand firm in the faith. Be courageous. Be strong. ✛ 1 CORINTHIANS 16:13

I opened my Internet Explorer to find a news article describing the first book written by students about the tragic Virginia Tech massacre. As I read the news report, I was deeply moved by the testimony of a young woman regarding one of the slain professors. She described the professor as standing immovable in the doorway. As the bullets were fired, he continued to push the students back. She said, "He stood at the door and wouldn't move. He pushed me toward the back of the room into a corner. He himself would not move. He just stood there."[1] This young woman is convinced she and other classmates would have perished if not for this courageous man.

We never really know how we will respond in a time of crisis until it happens. I'm sure this professor did not wake up that day with a plan to stand in a doorway and risk his life to protect the lives of his students. However, when the moment of truth came, he was able to stand firm. He personified the words "Be courageous. Be strong."

When we face crisis in our lives, we may not know how we will respond. We do know that with God's help and the strength of his Spirit within us, we are able to do far more than we ever could on our own. We not only can stand firm in the time of our own need, but God can help us stand firm in the hour of crisis for those who depend on us.   ❧*Brenda*

★   ★   ★

Father, today I thank you for my life. I thank you for your protective hand that has brought me to this day. I pray for strength when I am weak. I pray for courage when I am fearful. I pray for the fortitude to stand firm in my faith when I am faced with a crisis in my life. I pray for those who have been victims of tragedy today. Comfort them and strengthen them as they look to the future. In Jesus' name. ✛ *Amen.*

---

[1] "Students Write First Book on Massacre," *ABC News.com,* July 20, 2007.

March 31
An Ugly Couch

So be truly glad. There is wonderful joy ahead, even though you have to endure many trials for a little while. ✚ 1 PETER 1:6

When my husband accepted his first pastorate, we moved our little family across the country. We were excited about this ministry opportunity and eager to find what awaited us. The deacon we corresponded with informed us that there was a home owned by the church ready for our occupancy. The people of the church were proud to provide this house, and indeed, it was a nice house for our young family.

My first impressions were positive. I was pleased with the neighborhood and happy with the curb appeal of the home. I couldn't wait to see inside. As I stepped in the front door, my eyes were riveted to the orange crushed-velvet couch, made all the more vibrant by the orange, red, and burgundy shag carpet (yes, it was the 70s). I immediately strategized: remove, recover, and replace! If that wouldn't work, maybe I could hide it in the basement. I realized quickly, however, that I was going to have to live with that couch. You see, the dear members of the church stopped by to welcome us, and one comment after the other had to do with the lovely couch that had just been recovered—especially for us!

Sometimes I'm asked to live with crushed-velvet couches that scream discomfort—my circumstances are often not my choice. How I choose to sit on that couch, however, is my choice! What circumstance do you find yourself in today? Negative circumstances can run the gamut, but the promise of today's Scripture is that they are all temporary. There is grace and mercy provided for us here on earth if we will persevere. There is an eternal home in heaven awaiting us.

Truly, "all possessions here are stained with defects and failings; still something is wanting: fair houses have sad cares flying about the gilded and ceiled roofs."[1] Our trials can be a tool God uses for discipline and training, causing us to grow in spiritual maturity. They may bring grief and pain, but through the power of the Holy Spirit we can be truly glad in the midst of them.   ❧*Brenda*

✯ ✯ ✯

Father, I choose to be grateful for the trials you allow me to experience. I pray my attitude would be one of perseverance and hope as I look forward to the day when trials on this earth will be complete. Bless those who are persevering under extremely difficult circumstances as they serve on battlefields around the world. ✚*Amen.*

---

[1] *Matthew Henry's Commentary on the Whole Bible: New Modern Edition,* Electronic Database, CD-ROM. Hendrickson Publishers, 1991.

April 1

Storm Chaser

It will be a shelter from daytime heat and a hiding place from storms and rain. ✦ ISAIAH 4:6

From the time I was a child, storms have always fascinated me. My dad would take me out on the covered side porch of our home and sit with me as a thunderstorm rolled in. The lightning would start to come and the thunder boom around us as my dad talked about it with so much fascination and excitement. He would tell me God was doing war in heaven when a storm came. He would talk about the way the clouds and the rain develop in the atmosphere. He was a chemist by trade and knew much about science. I was fascinated at the power that would come in a storm. I was taught to be wise about a storm and to always take shelter, but after that, each storm was a lesson in atmospheric activity.

Soon after our wedding, my husband and I headed to our first assignment at Fort Rucker, Alabama. Soon after getting to Alabama, we encountered a hurricane heading our way. I know this sounds so crazy, but I found myself looking forward to the event. I knew we had plenty of time for preparation so as not to be harmed.

We gathered with several of the couples and families from our apartment complex to take cover in a safe place. As the hurricane passed over us, we sat and prayed. The weather radio told us that we were now in the eye of the storm. Each of us walked out slowly to witness total calm and warm air around us. Knowing the eye was about to pass over us, we went back into the shelter and waited for the storm to pass completely, many hours later.

Immediately after the hurricane's passing, we began to put the plans in motion. As trees and debris lay all around us, several of us lit up the Coleman stoves and a couple of gas stoves in available campers nearby. We made huge pots of spaghetti the first night to serve to all who needed it. We were very thankful for the time of warning and preparation that allowed us to remain unharmed.

As life brings storms my way, I don't want to run from them or even run into them. I want to prepare for them and understand that they are a part of life as much as the calm. I want to be able to recognize the warnings as the storm heads my way. I want to be reminded that God's power and his peace are revealed through even the strongest of those storms. ✑*Carol*

✫   ✫   ✫

Father God, thank you for your almighty protection in the storms of life. Please be with those in the midst of the greatest storm in their lives, and be their peace and their calm during this time. ✦ *Amen.*

April 2
A Compass

In just a short time he will restore us, so that we may live in his presence. Oh, that we might know the LORD! Let us press on to know him. He will respond to us as surely as the arrival of dawn or the coming of rains in early spring. ✝ HOSEA 6:2-3

As Christ followers, we are to set our course on following the Lord. His Word is the compass that guides us through life. Just as a compass is a tool that shows direction by a magnetized needle on a balanced post, God's Word provides the balance we need, especially in times of storm. Just like a compass, God's Word can show us hazards that can be avoided by following its bearings.

My husband learned that reading a compass can be a life-saving skill during a fishing trip with his brother. They were fishing in an open twenty-foot aluminum fishing boat on a three-mile reef off the coast of Savannah. All of a sudden, dark clouds began to roll in, and it began to rain. They pointed the boat toward an inlet surrounded by rock. The only navigation they had was a compass, which my husband used to take note of the reading. It started to rain so hard they could not see past the end of the boat, much less see the shoreline. They kept bearing toward the opening, not making much progress against the storm, but continuing to go in the direction shown on the compass. They could have easily been overtaken by the storm and lost their way, but the compass kept them on course until they arrived safe but soaked on the shore.

There are times in our lives when storms come that make circumstances, thoughts, or the future unclear. If we "press on to know him," checking our position regularly, even when the winds of uncertainty blow, we'll make progress toward the goal. If we keep heading in the right direction through our commitment to reading and studying God's Word and doing what we know to be right, when the storm blows over, we will be closer to our goal than when we started.   ✑*Brenda*

✶   ✶   ✶

Father, "send out your light and your truth; let them guide me. Let them lead me to your holy mountain, to the place where you live" (Psalm 43:3). I pray for your protection on military pilots today as they fly missions around the world. In your name I pray. ✝*Amen.*

A Storm, a Book, and a Prayer

But Jonah got up and went in the opposite direction to get away from the LORD. He went down to the port of Joppa, where he found a ship leaving for Tarshish. He bought a ticket and went on board, hoping to escape from the LORD by sailing to Tarshish. But the LORD hurled a powerful wind over the sea, causing a violent storm that threatened to break the ship apart.

✝ JONAH 1:3-4

We experience many storms in life, but not every storm occurs because we are running away from God or because we have sinned. As seen in the case of Jonah, however, that is within the realm of possibility. Scripture says that God sent this storm, and it was indeed because of Jonah's sin of disobedience. Sin is something that brings storms and tumult to individuals and nations. It is a troubling and alarming fact that is illustrated in the circumstances Jonah encountered. While Jonah realized this, he didn't see God's complete plan. This storm was not just sent to punish him but to get him back on the right path. God sent the storm to get his attention, but it was up to Jonah to repent and admit he had disobeyed.

The Lord asked Jonah to go to preach to the people of Nineveh, and his response was to run in the opposite direction. Can you relate? I can! The comfort I find in the example of Jonah is that you don't have to be a perfect person for God to use you for a great task. Though Jonah was disobedient, even to the point of running away, there was an important job for him to do. He needed to turn around and redirect his obedience. After the storm and a detour with a large fish (see Jonah 1:17), that's exactly what Jonah did.

Something else that inspires me about Jonah is the fact that when he found himself in crisis, he prayed God's Word. His prayer in Jonah 2 has words from Psalm 42 included. Jonah had hidden God's Word in his heart, and in a crisis it made a difference. The great preacher Charles Spurgeon said it this way: "Here is a man inside a fish with a Book inside of him; and it was the Book inside of him that brought him out from the fish."[1] It's an interesting twist to crisis management, don't you think?
⤳*Brenda*

✶　✶　✶

Master of the wind and waves, "I will offer sacrifices to you with songs of praise, and I will fulfill all my vows. For my salvation comes from the LORD alone" (Jonah 2:9). Bless sailors and coastguardsmen today as they stand watch in waters around the world. In your name. ✝ *Amen.*

---

[1] Charles Spurgeon, Exposition of Jonah 2. Spurgeon's Sermons, Electronic Database CD-ROM. Copyright © 1997 by Biblesoft.

April 4
Hike Interrupted

O God, listen to my cry! Hear my prayer! From the ends of the earth, I cry to you for help when my heart is overwhelmed. Lead me to the towering rock of safety, for you are my safe refuge, a fortress where my enemies cannot reach me. ✝ PSALM 61:1-3

During an autumn weekend in the North Carolina mountains with my husband's siblings and their spouses, we decided we would hike up Grandfather Mountain, the highest peak in the Blue Ridge mountain range. Its eleven trails carry descriptions ranging from a gentle walk in the woods to a rigorous trek across rugged peaks. On the more challenging hikes, ladders and cables are the means to descend sheer cliff faces. On this particular day, the weather was perfect as we began what was to be our gentle walk in the woods.

My brother-in-law served as our guide and led us on an incline up one side of the mountain he had previously explored. He said at the top there were a few minimally steep places, but nothing challenging. After walking several miles, we reached the top of the ridge and a place where rocks replaced trees.

Suddenly, our walk in the woods had the makings of a rigorous trek. On one side of the ridge were dark clouds rushing toward the mountain, while on the other side of the ridge were clear blue skies as far as you could see. We needed to hurry off the mountain, but descent required going down a sheer rock face on a ladder attached to rock with rope. Before we could even begin negotiating the ladders, the dark clouds engulfed the ridge with gusting winds and sheets of sleet and rain.

The reality of being stuck on a mountain in the late afternoon with freezing precipitation and two jackets among six people was frightening! We found a cleft in the rock to get out of the rain. There on a mountain, where if you stood up the wind would blow you off and if you tried to walk the ice would make you slip off, we did the only sensible thing—huddled together and prayed.

Moments after we prayed, there was a break in the clouds and our opportunity to attempt a descent. Carefully, we inched across wet rocks and negotiated ladders; we made it to an easier trail before the dark clouds descended again.

We face all kinds of obstacles in life where it seems we are in a hopeless, desperate place. When it looks like there is nothing else you can do, you can pray! It's the *best* thing you can do! Call on God for help and look for a break in the clouds. Then move forward one step at a time.   ❧*Brenda*

✳   ✳   ✳

Lord, in the time of trouble hide me in your pavilion: hide me in the secret of your tabernacle and set me up upon a rock (Psalm 27:5, paraphrased). Encourage and protect our military in the midst of their difficult and dangerous work, and set them upon the rock of your truth and love. ✝ *Amen.*

Oklahoma Storm Cellar

But you are a tower of refuge to the poor, O LORD, a tower of refuge to the needy in distress. You are a refuge from the storm and a shelter from the heat. ⊣ ISAIAH 25.4

Too often we have fear of the possibility of bad things coming our way. News reports warn of potential deadly disease, share accounts of horrific accidents, and broadcast the devastation of war, and we wonder if any of those things will happen to us. None of us are immune to tragedy.

I lived a short period of my childhood in Oklahoma. I will never forget the fear I felt when I saw a storm cellar in the backyard of the house to which we had moved. It didn't help that I had just seen *The Wizard of Oz* for the first time. Oklahoma wasn't Kansas, but a storm cellar could only mean that storms of a serious nature were probable. But it didn't take me long to come to the conclusion that if Dorothy had been in a storm cellar, she wouldn't have been carried away. Instead of the cellar being a symbol of fear, it became a symbol of comfort.

There is comfort in knowing there is safe place to go if a storm comes. Scripture tells us in numerous places that God is our refuge and our help in times of trouble. Jesus himself said as he prayed to the Father, "Now I am departing from the world; they are staying in this world, but I am coming to you. Holy Father, you have given me your name; now protect them by the power of your name so that they will be united just as we are. During my time here, I protected them by the power of the name you gave me. I guarded them so that not one was lost, except the one headed for destruction, as the Scriptures foretold" (John 17:11-12).

He didn't say he would keep storms from coming our way, but he does provide a safe place in him to weather the storms.   ⁖*Brenda*

☆　☆　☆

Father, thank you for being a place of refuge from the storms of life. Help me to leave my fears of the "what ifs" of life with you, trusting you to guide me through any storm I may encounter. I pray for military families who are experiencing turbulence in their family life because of deployments or heavy work requirements. In Jesus' name I pray. +*Amen.*

Feel the Wind on My Face

We proclaim to you the one who existed from the beginning, whom we have heard and seen. We saw him with our own eyes and touched him with our own hands. He is the Word of life.
✛ 1 JOHN 1:1

Hugging is one of my favorite pastimes. I love going into meetings at the Protestant Women of the Chapel and hugging my military sisters. I love walking into our church and hugging my sweet friends I have not seen during the week. I love to hug my husband good-bye and hello during the day. When I would go to visit my father in his later years, I would go to say good-bye and hug him on the shoulders.

Whenever I am really missing our sons, I tell them that I am coming up for the day for a touch. I usually make it a day trip, and I try to get a good hug out of both of them before leaving. My mother and I are big huggers, and because we are now about the same height it really works out well.

What does any of this have to do with the wind on my face? Well, it's all about touching. Do you know how many of our men and women who are separated by deployment right now would love to have a touch from their loved ones? Do you know how many people who have lost their loved ones to war or tragedy in our country would love to have a touch from their loved ones?

Many times in my life, I need a touch. Often I need that touch specifically from God to affirm his presence in my life. I love to feel the presence of God. When I am outside on a windy day, I find such refreshment in the wind blowing through my hair and gently touching my face. I love to feel the wind blowing in before a storm—the warm air slowly becoming cooler as the storm approaches. Walking along the seashore is another favorite pastime of mine, when I can feel God's touch through the soft, salty breeze.

His touch is ever present with us. Take a moment to feel his touch this week, whether tangibly, like in the wind, or intangibly, in your spirit. Let his touch bring healing to your soul. ❧*Carol*

✶　✶　✶

Father, touch those who need to know how very much you love them today—particularly those in the military and any others who may be in harm's way. As you touch them, may they have a sense of your presence and your comfort. ✛*Amen.*

Through the Gate

Yes, I am the gate. Those who come in through me will be saved. They will come and go freely and will find good pastures. ✝ JOHN 10:9

Since 9/11, the security for military installations, as well as other government and civilian buildings, has been increased in order to keep out those who would want to attack with explosive-laden vehicles. A key element of security is a pop-up barrier system located just past entrance gates. If a car goes through the gate without authorization, a guard pushes a button, and a barrier comes up from the ground to prevent a vehicle from entering. On most installations, you must first go through a checkpoint, where your credentials are checked by a guard, before you would encounter the pop-up barrier.

We lived at one installation where it was possible to turn directly into the entrance of the army post without first going past a guard because the public road runs between the guardhouse and the entrance to the installation. Vehicles are supposed to follow directions and, once approved, proceed across the public road onto the installation. However, some people fail to see the directional signs and turn directly into the gate without approval of the guard. Several times a week, on average, the pop-up barrier stops the surprised intruder. When this occurs, the military police immediately respond and surround the vehicle to make sure it was not a deliberate attempt to encroach the protective system. Normally, it is just a red-faced visitor who failed to gain authorization to enter at the checkpoint.

This reminds me of the way we obtain permission to enter the blessings of the Lord. Jesus is the One who said, "I am the gate. Those who come in through me will be saved." We often wonder why we are not entering the blessings of the Lord. Why aren't we filled with his joy? Why don't we receive answers to prayer? Though Christians often struggle with these questions, sometimes individuals don't have access to these blessings because they have not gone through the approval through Jesus Christ to enter into God's blessings. It is through Jesus that we have access to all the righteousness, goodness, and blessing of God.

Let me encourage you today: enter through Christ and avoid the pop-up barrier to blessings in your life.   ⊱*Brenda*

✦   ✦   ✦

Father, thank you for your provision of salvation. I pray for those who do not know you and have not gained access to your blessings through your Son, Jesus. I pray for military personnel who are standing guard in dangerous areas of the world. Be their help and protection. ✝ *Amen.*

Standing for Hours

They remained standing in place for three hours while the Book of the Law of the LORD their God was read aloud to them. Then for three more hours they confessed their sins and worshiped the LORD their God. ✚ NEHEMIAH 9:3

I am the world's worst at practicing the art of patience. Just let a meeting or an event continue for more than a couple of hours and I am looking at my watch, thinking, *How can I get out of here?* I really don't know why I am thinking that. Usually, I don't have anything else that I need to do. No one is expecting me to be anywhere in the next day or so. I just think I have to leave out of pure impatience.

I wonder how it must have been for the people described in Nehemiah to remain standing for three hours to hear from the Book of the Law of the Lord. There were no microphones, so they had to tune their ears to listen intently. They did not have double-sole tennis shoes with inside arch support to make the standing easier. They were not in an air-conditioned church with soft carpet underfoot. So, it's not just the three hours part that amazes me; it's the *standing for three hours* that amazes me more.

Then, not only did they stand for three hours, but they stayed on for three more hours to complete the conference, confessing their sins and worshiping.

I came from a denominational background that conducted a worship service in one hour. That was the reading, the confessing, and the worship. We knew exactly when we would get home for dinner and could plan accordingly.

One of the wonderful experiences of being in the military was the nondenominational aspect of the chapel services. We learned that some would sing more, and others would confess more. Whatever the situation, the Lord was magnified, and we were blessed to be a part of the service.

I am challenged to stand for the Word of God. I want to stand before him, confessing my sins, worshiping, and adoring him for all he has done in my life. I want to stand on behalf of my brothers and sisters in the Lord who experience pain and conflict every day in our nation. I pray that I can be a true warrior and stand for all that is truth. ❧*Carol*

＊　＊　＊

Father, forgive me for a spirit of impatience, especially when it comes to serving others. Help me not to grow weary when standing in prayer and supporting those in harm's way. Show me ways to lovingly reach out to military families. ✚ *Amen.*

Stand Still!

"Didn't we tell you this would happen while we were still in Egypt? We said, 'Leave us alone! Let us be slaves to the Egyptians. It's better to be a slave in Egypt than a corpse in the wilderness!'" But Moses told the people, "Don't be afraid. Just stand still and watch the LORD rescue you today. The Egyptians you see today will never be seen again. The LORD himself will fight for you. Just stay calm." ✦ EXODUS 14:12-14

Not long ago, I woke up feeling like the room was spinning. It was a frightening experience. An inner-ear infection had left me feeling like I was falling. It didn't matter what position I was in; whether standing or prostrate, I was falling.

Just as the ear is the center of balance for the body, I think of faith as the center of balance for the soul. There are times when an infection in our soul throws off our balance of faith. This spiritual infection usually takes the form of fear that God is not going to help us, doubt that God's promises are true, or disobedience that makes us question whether we deserve God's help. It is hard to stand still and feel victorious when we are thrown off balance spiritually.

The faith of the children of Israel was thrown off balance as they wandered in the wilderness. Moses challenged the people to stand still and watch the Lord rescue them. The strong faith of Moses empowered him to stand firm in the midst of all the grumbling he was hearing and the promise of deliverance he as yet wasn't seeing. He knew God would provide the help needed. God spoke to Moses and indeed provided an amazing deliverance by parting the sea and allowing the people to walk across on dry land.

During my illness, I went to the doctor for medicine to remove the infection from my body. It has reminded me that during times of spiritual vertigo there is a Great Physician who stands ready to supply his help to heal our spirits, so our faith can stand strong and steady. Stand still and watch! ❧*Brenda*

✳   ✳   ✳

Great Physician of body and soul, thank you for your delivering power. Help me to stand still in prayer and devotion, not from duty but for love. Make my faith strong and steady as I trust you to work in the situations that concern me today. I pray for the faith of those who feel as if their world is spinning out of control because of circumstances brought on by the War on Terror. In your name I pray. ✦*Amen.*

April 10
God Is Not Surprised

Dear friends, don't be surprised at the fiery trials you are going through, as if something strange were happening to you. ✝ 1 PETER 4:12

I love going to lunch with my girlfriends. It is a time of fellowship and fun. I have one dear friend who likes to try the newest restaurant. We always say, "We can bring our husbands here. They will love it." Another dear friend will meet me at our standard place, where I always order one of my two favorites on the menu.

Diane blessed me with a birthday lunch recently. As we were leaving, we were discussing the amazingly hot temperatures in Alabama during the week. She shared that, having recently moved from Texas, she thought the temperatures would be cooler here. But just before she left Texas, many of her friends were saying, "Are you sure you want to go to Alabama?" Her husband was blessed in his job, and they were given the opportunity to move. She told them that she wasn't completely sure, but since God was in the middle of the decision, she definitely wanted to be a part of it.

I started thinking about what she said after I drove away. When I find myself wringing my hands over a decision to be made or worrying about a family member who is hurting or in a crisis situation, I want to always remember this: nothing in our lives is a surprise to God. So if it's not a surprise and he is in the middle of it, I don't want to miss it.

God is not surprised with all that is going on in our nation and our world. As I drive down the neighborhood streets I often think, *What hurt is behind those doors?* God sees it all and knows it all. He is right in the middle of it. He is in the middle of the conflict in our world. He is in the middle of world leaders who would seek to destroy our way of life.

Cry out to God. He is in the middle of it all and holds the answer and the comfort and the victory in his hand. He is not surprised! ❧*Carol*

✯ ✯ ✯

Father God, help me not to forget that you are in control of all things. These things that would cause me to be anxious or fearful are in the palm of your hand. Thank you for being in the midst of those who are serving our country during this time. ✝ *Amen.*

Mercy Seat

But God is so rich in mercy, and he loved us so much, that even though we were dead because of our sins, he gave us life when he raised Christ from the dead. (It is only by God's grace that you have been saved!) ✝ EPHESIANS 2:4-5

This precious verse of Scripture begins with the conjunction *but*. I have been taught that when there is a *therefore*, we need to look to see what it is there for. The same is true with this wording. The conjunction here is used to emphasize God at the beginning of the verse. In the *Bible Knowledge Commentary*, the explanation for this reads, "God is the subject of the whole passage. Great differences are suggested by the words *But God!*" The explanation continues, "In the Septuagint *mercy* translates in the Hebrew to 'loyal love.' In the New Testament the same Hebrew word means 'undeserved kindness' toward sinners."[1]

Everything revealed in studying this verse is against the world's teachings. Our loyalty in love has become a fleeting thing. When I hear the explanation of undeserved kindness, I think about the world we live in and how everyone seems to be out to get what they deserve. In other words, the world contradicts what God was trying to give to us in this passage of Scripture.

We are witnessing in our nation events that could have been resolved by accepting God's undeserved kindness. We watch as young men cry out with acts of violence, and their reasoning is simply that "no one understood me." We watch as the young "examples" in our media fall prey to bad choices and dysfunctional lifestyles because the direction they take is for the world and not the God of mercy.

We can come to the mercy seat of God the Father anytime we desire. The more we run to the things of this world, the farther we are from the mercy seat, the loyal love, and the undeserved kindness of God. He wants us to have a sense of his mercy in our lives at all times. When we are able to grasp the unconditional love that only God offers, we will come to understand that our place in this world is a place of hope and not despair.

Run to the mercy seat, and know that you are loved with an unconditional, undeserved, and loyal love! ❧*Carol*

✶ ✶ ✶

Father God, as I watch and listen to the happenings of the world around me, help me to know there is a constant in the madness of life. That constant is you! Thank you for your mercy that covers a multitude of sins. Turn the hearts and minds of those who would seek to harm and destroy, to instead seek your mercy and love for them. ✝ *Amen.*

---

[1] John F. Walvoord and Roy B. Zuck, eds. *Bible Knowledge Commentary: An Exposition of the Scriptures by Dallas Seminary Faculty* (Colorado Springs, CO: Victor Books, 1983), 623.

So Others Will Not Have To

What we do see is Jesus, who was given a position "a little lower than the angels"; and because he suffered death for us, he is now "crowned with glory and honor." Yes, by God's grace, Jesus tasted death for everyone. ✛ HEBREWS 2:9

One thing rings true for those who are serving our country right now: the reason they put on that uniform every day is for others. They are not called to serve themselves. They are called into battle and conflict on behalf of others. The same is true for those who are firefighters, policemen, security guards, teachers, pastors, and many other service professionals. They go into battle every day—whether physical, mental, or spiritual—on behalf of others.

I truly believe the battle being fought in faraway lands is keeping our country from experiencing devastating times of destruction and chaos. We hear of threat after threat that makes those who go to battle even more determined to fight on behalf of their families and countrymen.

Recently I watched an interview of a young man who had been wounded in Iraq. The interviewer asked him why he feels called to fight for our country. Looking straight into the interviewer's eyes, the young man said, "So you don't have to." Tears began to stream down the face of the interviewer, and he actually had to stand up. He went over to the young man to shake his hand and tell him how moved he was by his personal commitment to this War on Terror. That is what you do not hear on most news stories. The deep conviction to go to war so others will not have to is very real.

Jesus most certainly led by example in this area. He died so the shedding of his blood would be a covering for all our sins. He bled, died, and was resurrected so that others would not have to go through the pain of life without a way out.

God provided the Way, the Truth, and the Life for us so we would not have to go through the pain and the suffering of sin in our lives.

Thank you, Jesus, for your sacrifice for us! ✒*Carol*

✯ ✯ ✯

Father God, thank you for providing the way for us to not have to go through life without hope and without forgiveness for our sins. Thank you for those who are serving so others will not have to go through a life without hope. Thank you for their unselfish dedication to America! ✛ *Amen.*

It Belongs to the Lord

"Bring all the tithes into the storehouse so there will be enough food in my Temple. If you do," says the LORD of Heaven's Armies, "I will open the windows of heaven for you. I will pour out a blessing so great you won't have enough room to take it in! Try it! Put me to the test!"

✝ MALACHI 3:10

I have to admit the concept of tithing took a long time for me to grasp. We lived from paycheck to paycheck, and giving anything to the church did not seem possible during the early years of our marriage.

My husband did not become a Christian until about eight years into our marriage. We had not received teaching about tithing during those early years of following Christ. We always gave a small amount but never really felt convicted about tithing.

That is, not until my husband was selected for early retirement during the Clinton years. The government began downsizing the military at that time. We were suddenly cast from total security in our work and our pay to no security and only one-third of my husband's original salary.

At the time, we were attending a Baptist church, where we were exposed to teaching on tithing and the responsibility to give back what belongs to God. My husband began to realize that we were holding on to money that wasn't helping out much to begin with, and he began to tithe from the bottom line of what we had in our account. I was so scared, but during that time I saw a new countenance come over my husband. The Lord was blessing him with peace.

We were without full-time employment for about eight months after my husband left the military, but God taught me so much. As I watched my husband write the check out of obedience and pure motives each week, I knew there was a heavenly connection going on between the Lord and our family.

Our money belongs to the Lord. Our finances are to be used so that others can be blessed. If you know of someone who is struggling financially because of separation or deployment, let go and let God bless them out of your abundance. It will give you that peace that "passes all understanding." ⚓*Carol*

✷   ✷   ✷

Lord, give me a heart of giving back to you out of the resources you give to me; show me ways to bless others out of my abundance today. Give a heart of generosity and kindness to those military personnel working on my behalf on peace-keeping missions today. ✝ *Amen.*

April 14
Divine Generosity

They share freely and give generously to those in need. Their good deeds will be remembered forever. They will have influence and honor. + PSALM 112:9

The word *generosity* usually carries with it the idea of the giving of money or possessions. I wholeheartedly believe giving of our finances is a requirement for a Christ follower. I also think there is a need for generosity of spirit. From the evidence of the early church's life, we can see that they were generous with their time, talent, and treasure. The generosity of their actions was an effective testimony as they shared "with great joy and generosity" everything they had (see Acts 2:46).

A study on aging followed sixty-five-year-olds for five years. At the beginning of the study, the participants, whose prior health was taken into consideration, were asked if they had given or received emotional or practical help in the past twelve months. The outcome of the study showed a strong correlation between giving and longevity. Those who gave of themselves lived longer.[1]

Many in our culture who live by the philosophy, What's in it for me? will never know the personal satisfaction, joy, and benefits derived from helping others. This is the basic principle embedded in the teachings of Christ when he said, "Thou shalt love the Lord thy God with all thy heart, and with all thy soul, and with all thy mind. This is the first and great commandment. And the second is like unto it, Thou shalt love thy neighbor as thyself" (Matthew 22:37-39, KJV). To truly love your neighbor requires giving of your time, your talent, and your energy. If you take that to the ultimate extreme, Christ said, "Greater love hath no man than this, that a man lay down his life for his friends" (John 15:13, KJV).

God doesn't ask us to do anything he didn't model for us. He gave what he valued most when he sent his Son to bring us forgiveness of sins and eternal life with him. When people accept what Christ has done, there is great joy in heaven for what has resulted from an act of his divine generosity.

If you've been discouraged or self-absorbed lately, try practicing generosity. You may find that not only do you bless someone else, but you will be blessed as well. You might even live longer! *Brenda*

✳ ✳ ✳

Generous Father, thank you for the ultimate gift of your Son and his sacrifice on the cross for my sins. I ask for a generous spirit that would bless and encourage others. I pray for those who serve selflessly in volunteer positions as they help those who have been wounded by war. In Jesus' name I pray. + *Amen.*

---

[1] Bower Brown, "Giving Aid, Staying Alive: Elderly Helpers Have Longevity Advantage," *Science News Online,* July 26, 2003, http://www.sciencenews.org/articles/20030726/fob2.asp.

Financial Challenge

Dear friends, if we deliberately continue sinning after we have received knowledge of the truth, there is no longer any sacrifice that will cover these sins. **+** HEBREWS 10:26

My husband and I were honored to be asked to serve as facilitators for a premarriage class at our local church about seven years ago. As we were going over the book and the format of the class with the education director, we were told not to worry about leading the class on finances. One of the men at the church would be coming in to teach that section in a group setting with all the classes in attendance. We were thrilled to learn this because our finances were not where we desired them to be, and we knew we were not qualified to instruct in this area. The finance class was toward the end of the sessions, and we were eager to hear what this man would be teaching.

We arrived in the gathering room, and after a brief introduction, the gentleman began speaking with great enthusiasm. I had never heard anyone speak with such passion on the topic of finances. He shared his story, which included bankruptcy and many wrong choices that led his family into much distress. He began to talk about making a budget as soon as you get paid and spending all the money on paper before you spent a penny. We were hanging on every word. *Then* he began taking huge scissors and cutting up credit cards.

Some of you may recognize the method by now. The man speaking to us that night was Dave Ramsey.[1] I remember looking at my husband with tears rolling down my face saying, "I want this! I want what he is talking about for our family." Shortly after that, we began going through Financial Peace University to guide us through what Dave describes as a paradigm change. My father often said he had been trying to teach me this for many years and could not understand why I was listening to a perfect stranger. That always made me smile.

I thought we were there to teach a premarriage class. God had plans that would change our lives. We have received full knowledge of the truth in finances, and we are responsible. I am so thankful to be able to tell you that at this time in our lives, we are able to serve the Lord with our possessions and set an example for our sons to follow.

For those who have not set your finances in order, particularly those who are deploying, I encourage you to do so now—before you leave—by making a plan that can be followed long-distance. ∼*Carol*

✶　✶　✶

Father, thank you for teachable hearts. I ask you to instill in me a great desire to make wise financial decisions. Enable those serving our country to have wise counsel and instruction in the area of finances. **+** *Amen.*

---

[1] Dave Ramsey, *Financial Peace University*, www.daveramsey.com.

April 16
A Call to the Mailroom

But when you give to someone in need, don't let your left hand know what your right hand is doing. Give your gifts in private, and your Father, who sees everything, will reward you.
✝ MATTHEW 6:3-4

Chaplain, you need to come to the mailroom and get these boxes." My husband heard these words each day as he picked up the phone in response to a call from someone in the camp mailroom. During his deployment to Afghanistan, it became part of his daily routine to accompany his assistant to the mailroom to collect boxes that had been sent to troops from people all over America for distribution among soldiers serving far from home.

This was early in the War on Terror, and the camp for his unit was fairly austere. There was no fast food, very limited toiletries, and minimal snacks. It was a pleasant task for my husband and his assistant to distribute the boxes filled with beef jerky, chewing gum, various snacks, and personal hygiene items that were in high demand among the various units of soldiers. The recurring remark from the young men and women was, "I can't believe these people who don't even know me have sent these things." They expressed genuine appreciation. Without exception, the gifts would bring a smile to their faces, encouragement to their hearts, and sometimes even a tear of gratitude to their eyes. To them it meant they were not forgotten. It was tangible evidence that Americans cared about them and supported them.

It's hard to measure the boost in morale and the renewed determination to serve that these gifts of generosity brought to deployed soldiers so faraway from home. It had such a big impact because, though they were simple items, for the most part at that time they were unavailable. They were appreciated because they were sent not from a loving mother or thoughtful relative—although gifts from them, too, were greatly appreciated—but from unknown Americans, people whom they would probably never be able to thank in person. It's amazing the impact a small act of generosity can have on another.

On behalf of all the thousands of soldiers who over the years have been the recipient of gift boxes from generous Americans across the country, I want to say thanks for your support. You can be assured your gifts have made a difference in the heart of some soldier doing his or her best to serve our nation in a trying and difficult environment. ❧*Brenda*

★   ★   ★

Giver of all good gifts, thank you for the generosity of the American people. It has been proven time and time again. Help me take an active role in creating a culture of generosity. Provide opportunities for individuals in our nation to continue to show tangible support to those serving in the armed services. In your name I pray. ✝ *Amen.*

Give What Is Given

To those who use well what they are given, even more will be given, and they will have an abundance. But from those who do nothing, even what little they have will be taken away.
✝ MATTHEW 25:29

We know what an important part genetics plays in our makeup as human beings. God's design and creation is perfect. He knew before the beginning of time that we would have different personalities and different appearances because of our genetic makeup. Many times it even affects our health.

Years ago, researchers came to the conclusion that behavior also affects who we are and how we live our lives. We follow the example and the habits of those we live with while growing up during impressionable years.

I grew up in a time when people truly reached out to each other. Neighbors helped neighbors. Friends helped friends. My mom and dad never met a stranger and always had such love and compassion for those who were less fortunate than we were. My dad showed love for my mother all the time. He would hug her and tell her in front of us, "I love you" every day.

Some may think this is a relatively new teaching, but I watched it in action. It took hold of me as I was growing up. I don't think of people as strangers; I have a desire to help others in any way I can; I dream of ways I can make the world a better place for those I love and for those I know.

Often when we think about giving, we think about dollars. Dollars can be a great assistance in times of need. However, I was taught to give in so many other ways apart from finances. As a military family, we were always so very blessed to have people adopt us at each assignment. We loved going to dinner with them or having them take us to a new attraction in our area. The giving of themselves far outweighed any amount of money they could have offered.

I am convinced that is what is needed today. Give of yourself. Receive God's abundance for your life. Whether it is a gift of time, talent, or treasure, give generously and with a pure heart. Set the example for your family and those who are watching. Look for opportunities to give of yourself today.   ⊸*Carol*

✱   ✱   ✱

Father God, I pray that I would always be willing to teach and to practice generous living. Help me to give willingly to those who need a helping hand and be faithful in what has been given so freely to me. Thank you for the men and women who have volunteered to serve our country. ✝ *Amen.*

April 18
Times of Refreshing

Now repent of your sins and turn to God, so that your sins may be wiped away. Then times of refreshment will come from the presence of the Lord, and he will again send you Jesus, your appointed Messiah. + ACTS 3:19-20

I enjoy living in a location that allows me to experience all the seasons. Yet, in all honesty, while I appreciate all of the seasons, I do not complain if it is a short winter or summer. There is something celebratory about the first weeks of spring and fall. It's refreshment to my spirit, whether it is a much needed cool breeze after a long, hot summer, or longed-for sunshine following winter's chill.

Refreshment is a word that conjures satisfaction, energy, a boost, or a pick-me-up that is needed to revive body or spirit. In today's Scripture, the word *refreshment* means "to cool off," "a recovery of breath or revival."[1] It is an appealing promise with the requirement being repentance. Repentance and refreshment seem like strange terms to pair together, don't they?

Acts 3 is an account of Peter preaching after the healing of a crippled man. The event naturally caused a lot of attention to be turned to Peter. To his credit, he took the opportunity to turn the attention from himself and do a little preaching about Christ. His message was specifically with the Jewish nation in mind. It was a message calling for national repentance with the promise that times of refreshment would follow. His words were reminders to the Jews of the promises that had been given all through the Old Testament by the prophets as found in Isaiah 65:19: "I will rejoice over Jerusalem and delight in my people. And the sound of weeping and crying will be heard in it no more."

I'm of the opinion that we are in need of refreshment as a nation. Just as in Peter's day, though, national salvation depends upon the personal repentance and faith of individuals. Repentance is more than feeling sorrow or regret. It is a turning from sin and turning to Christ. The refreshment that follows is only something that Christ's pardoning love can accomplish.   *Brenda*

*   *   *

Father, thank you for the promise of refreshment of body and spirit. I pray that I would have clean hands and a clean heart before you. I pray your blessings on the United States of America today. I pray you would call people in our nation to personal repentance that would result in a national revival. In Jesus' name I pray. + Amen.

---

[1] *Vincent's New Testament Word Studies in the New Testament* (Biblesoft, 1997), Electronic Database. Copyright © 1997 by Biblesoft.

A Birthday Gift

And since I, your Lord and Teacher, have washed your feet, you ought to wash each other's feet. + JOHN 13:14

While stationed at Fort Lewis, Washington, I had the unique experience of enjoying some of the closest Christian relationships I have ever had. I was just coming back to the Lord, and my senses were sharpened during that time to how loving and kind these sisters of faith were.

These women came in all shapes and sizes. They were from all religious backgrounds. They were either deep in their faith or coming back to their faith at the same time I was. They were showing me Jesus like I had never seen him before. It was a time of watching people not only talk about their faith but live it out.

A special thing we did during that time was to celebrate our birthdays. There were many of us involved in this circle of spiritual sisters, and we eagerly anticipated those times together.

One of my birthday celebrations stands out in my mind. A wonderful lunch had been prepared by my dear friend Toni White. After we shared the meal together, we celebrated with a beautiful birthday cake. They knew white cake with white icing was my favorite. I then enjoyed opening the fun gifts that everyone had brought for the special day.

After the last gift was opened, we were just sitting and chatting when Toni walked out from the kitchen. She had with her a pitcher, a large bowl, and a towel. Without a word she slowly knelt down in front of me and began to remove my shoes. She looked up at me and said, "I could not think of a gift to give that would express my love for you as a Christian sister. So I decided that I wanted to wash your feet." I began shedding tears with a cry that felt almost cleansing. I honestly could not catch my breath. I have never in my life felt so humbled and so cared about as I did at that moment. After she had finished, we all spent time in prayer before leaving for the day.

That birthday has never left my memory. It has come to mind many times when I need to have a sense of humility in my life. The story of Jesus washing the disciples' feet is so vivid to me because of this experience. I pray it will cause you to think of ways to refresh others today. ~*Carol*

✶ ✶ ✶

Lord Jesus, thank you for your example of washing your disciples' feet. Your love for them by putting yourself before them is an example for me. Father, help me not to forget those who are humbling themselves every day as they serve in challenging situations on behalf of our nation. + *Amen.*

April 20
Cell Phone Joy

Some of the traveling teachers recently returned and made me very happy by telling me about your faithfulness and that you are living according to the truth. I could have no greater joy than to hear that my children are following the truth. ✛ 3 JOHN 1:3-4

Cell phones are one of the modern conveniences with which I have a love/hate relationship. How can something be so annoying and comforting at the same time? Since I became a grandparent, though, my cell phone has taken on new importance as it has brought reports of many of the firsts in the life of my grandson. I remember walking in from lunch with my husband in San Antonio. We were on the riverwalk while attending a conference when my cell phone rang. On the other end of the line, my son said quickly, "Listen, Mom." What followed was pure joy to my ears. My five-month-old grandson was laughing out loud for the first time. His cackles were music as my husband and I stood in the hotel lobby, listening to his symphony of delight.

Today we find the apostle John addressing Gaius, a young man who had sat under his ministry. The reports John received from those who had seen Gaius as they traveled through the province of Asia brought joy to his heart. Gaius was walking in truth and serving God faithfully. If it had happened today, John probably would have received a cell phone call with the news, "Brother John, just wanted you to know that Gaius is doing great. He has offered gracious hospitality to us, is growing in the things of the Lord, and you should be proud of him!"

Just as the news of Gaius walking in truth brought great joy to John, it brought great joy for my son to share the news of our grandson's development. It also brings great joy when I hear that those I have invested in are growing spiritually. I think of the joy I have had in hearing that a woman I have mentored is teaching her first Bible study, giving her testimony, or stepping into leadership for the first time. It may seem like a small thing, but it brings great joy to see spiritual growth begin to take place.

I think also of those I know who were recovering from a traumatic event. To hear news that they are able to laugh again is encouraging after they have been overcome with sorrow. Laughter signifies hope to come and is an indicator that the healing has begun.

Good news, no matter how it is communicated, is worth sharing. Share some joy with someone today! ☙*Brenda*

✷   ✷   ✷

God of joy and hope, I thank you for good news! Help me to be one who communicates the joy of your presence to others. I pray for military personnel who are separated from family today. May there be good news shared that would lift heavy spirits. ✛ *Amen.*

Dizzy, Joyful Dancing

You have turned my mourning into joyful dancing. You have taken away my clothes of mourning and clothed me with joy. ✝ PSALM 30:11

One of the greatest memories I have of being in a wonderful praise and worship service is with my dear friend Christy. My husband and I were living apart for a few months because of his job situation, and Christy and I attended different events together to keep each other company. We especially loved the midweek service at our church that included at least thirty minutes of praise, worship, and prayer. It was like a booster shot every week.

I had just celebrated a major birthday, and since my friend is so much younger than I am, she made a really big deal out of it at our workplace. Everyone at work wore black and teased me unmercifully throughout the day. Everything I did that was out of the ordinary from that day forward was blamed on my age.

Christy and I met for the midweek service and were about fifteen minutes into the praise and worship when the team began singing a song with the words, "He has turned my mourning into dancing." When that line was sung, we were instructed to turn around in a circle. Well, I did, and all of a sudden I got so dizzy that I had to sit down. Christy started laughing so hard it got me tickled, and I thought we were going to be asked to leave for sure that night. Of course, she told everyone around me my age and that I was getting too old to sing that song.

Whenever I sing that song today, I raise my hands high, stand in one place, and remember how my mourning, sadness, and loneliness from being apart from my dear husband were turned into pure joy as our laughter took over during that dizzy, joyful dancing.

If you are going through separation from a loved one at this time, find a friend who will do some dizzy, joyful dancing with you and find ways of releasing the joy in your life through moments that may seem silly, but bring health to your spirit. Choose joy today! ✲*Carol*

✶　✶　✶

Dear Father, life is heavy and hard sometimes. I need to laugh, to be joyful, and to allow your love to cover me in the times of dread or despair. Father, I pray for those who need a friend, whether in the military or in civilian life, who can share laughter and be joyful with them. ✝*Amen.*

April 22
Faith Full of Joy

But that does not mean we want to dominate you by telling you how to put your faith into practice. We want to work together with you so you will be full of joy, for it is by your own faith that you stand firm. ✦ 2 CORINTHIANS 1:24

One of the characteristics of people who truly love the Lord is their tenderness and compassion toward others. I never feel as if I am condemned or dominated by their faith. I witness how they live and how they show God's mercy to others.

When people serve the Lord with pure motives, they want to come alongside you in order to mentor or encourage you to grow in your own spiritual walk. We have many examples of those who led us in the faith in the book of Hebrews. What a joy to know there are those who still lead us into imitating their faith! The world will then see what a powerful message we send as we work together in Christ.

Many in our nation and those who are serving throughout the world understand how to work hand in hand with others. They lead each day through their character and faith. They give their lives to serve as firemen, teachers, doctors, and military service members, to name a few. Those who are of the Christian faith serve with the joy of the Lord in their hearts.

As we go through our daily lives, we can be encouraged to have a faith full of joy by working together with others. Christians need to grow in their own walk with the Lord, no matter what. True joy comes from deep within as our faith takes root and grows.

Reach out to someone full of joy, who can share your faith. Go to lunch. Share laughter together and maybe even some tears. Stand firm in your faith, and share the blessings that God has given to you. Share your full-of-joy faith with military families who need to laugh and have someone show them the love of the Lord.   ✒Carol

★   ★   ★

Dear Father, thank you for giving me the opportunity to share my faith with others and to show them a faith that is full of joy. Thank you for the joy you place in my heart through your Son, Jesus. In these times that may bring sadness, confusion, and uncertainty to military families, help me to share laughter, joy, and encouragement with them. ✦ Amen.

Joyful Morning

Weeping may last through the night, but joy comes with the morning. ✝ PSALM 30:5

I watch as the door closes behind him after we had kissed and the boys had hugged and said their last good-bye before Daddy was to leave. We had been preparing for this for several months. The preparation time for my husband's departure was always a tough time for me. I knew that my husband's mind was already mission focused.

I would find myself pretending he was already gone during the days before he was to leave for extended times. There was always that sense of peace, though, in knowing he was a phone call away. We would check off the days, and I would start asking questions like, "What do you want for your last supper before you leave?"

It always seemed that as soon as he was gone, one of the boys would get sick. I would dread the coming of night. I would ask the Lord to give me strength to get through it. Mothers understand that usually the fever or the earache or whatever it is gets worse at night. Often I would be awake all night going from my room to my sons' and trying as much as possible to catch a few winks of sleep as I comforted one of my sons in his illness.

I am known as one of those dreaded morning people. I love the mornings. I fell even more in love with mornings as a mother. It always seemed when the sun came up, I could make it. I knew we could get to a doctor or the fever would break or I could call on a friend. The morning brought so much promise to me and comfort to my heart no matter what the situation.

I know there are many who will read the words of this book and think that morning will not come for them. They are weeping through the night. *Look up*, dear one. Weeping may come in the night, but joy comes in the morning! Morning does come. It has to. It is God's way of giving us renewal not only in our physical day but in our spiritual and emotional day.

May the joy of the Lord give you strength and hope today! Remember, joy comes in the morning! ❧*Carol*

✳   ✳   ✳

Father God, you are a Lord of the light. There is no darkness in you. Help me to remember that morning will come, and you will walk me through the night. Be with those who need to be reminded of this as they are looking for morning in their lives so that their joy may be restored. ✝ *Amen.*

April 24
In His Presence

You have shown me the way of life, and you will fill me with the joy of your presence.
✝ ACTS 2:28

I have a designated quiet place that I pull away to when I am writing. I am surrounded by reference books as well as books written by many people I admire. I love this special place in our home because I can get up and walk away when I am finished in the late afternoon. I don't have to move anything from its place. It is my little corner of creativity in the world.

There is another reason I love this designated place. We have just replaced the former carpet with new frieze carpet, which is a fancy way of saying *short shag*. When I find a moment of frustration or stumble upon the dreaded writer's block, guess what I do? I plunge from the chair to the floor on my face before the Lord to just spend some talk time with him. I keep what I call a "landing strip" cleared on the right side of the desk so that I can go for it at any needed time.

This may be funny to some of you. As I write it, I feel a giggle myself. However, this is very serious to me. I want to know that at any point of distraction, frustration, or anxiety I can go facedown to spend time with my Father in heaven.

I have a favorite song that says the words I'm trying to convey. The name of the song is "*In the Presence of Jehovah*." The chorus goes like this:

> *In the presence of Jehovah*
> *God Almighty*
> *Prince of Peace.*
> *Troubles vanish, hearts are mended*
> *In the presence of the King.*[1]

Hit the floor, fall on your face, and get into his presence today. You will be refreshed, renewed, and restored by him. ⨀*Carol*

✳   ✳   ✳

Mighty Jehovah, thank you that at any time, on any floor, in any place, day or night, I can come into your presence. Father, I pray for those in harm's way, that they may come into your presence and find rest and peace as they are fighting for their country. ✝ *Amen.*

---

[1] Geron Davis and Rebecca Davis, "In the Presence of Jehovah," Meadowgreen Music Co., 1983.

Fruit-Bearing Life

"I am the true grapevine, and my Father is the gardener. He cuts off every branch of mine that doesn't produce fruit, and he prunes the branches that do bear fruit so they will produce even more. You have already been pruned and purified by the message I have given you. Remain in me, and I will remain in you. For a branch cannot produce fruit if it is severed from the vine, and you cannot be fruitful unless you remain in me." ✛ JOHN 15:1-4

I cannot tell you how many times I have read and studied John 15. Each time, I realize more and more the importance of taking a stand for Jesus. If I am not going to stand for Jesus, I may bring down someone in the process, and God is not going to let me get away with that. The only way I can grow as a Christian is to stay close by the source of my spiritual nutrition; otherwise I will die spiritually.

There are so many who want to get that ticket to heaven through salvation, but then they do their own thing in life. Countless voices tell us there are many ways to heaven. I know of only one way, and that is through Jesus Christ. As the song tells us, every day with Jesus is sweeter than the day before. Every day we are to grow and learn to love him more and more through his Word and through communication in prayer with him.

I want to stand up and have a fruit-bearing life that is pleasing in his sight. I want him to prune me but not to cut me off from the nourishment of the vine because I would no longer have a chance to bear fruit.

Challenge yourself to have a fruit-bearing life in these perilous times! ⨪*Carol*

Father, you are the vine and we are the branches. I ask that the Holy Spirit would remind me to draw nourishment from your Word and would support those in the sometimes difficult environment of the military. May others see the fruit of your love in me and through me. ✛ *Amen.*

April 26
The Wrong Can

To one person the Spirit gives the ability to give wise advice; to another the same Spirit gives a message of special knowledge. The same Spirit gives great faith to another, and to someone else the one Spirit gives the gift of healing. He gives one person the power to perform miracles, and another the ability to prophesy. He gives someone else the ability to discern whether a message is from the Spirit of God or from another spirit. Still another person is given the ability to speak in unknown languages, while another is given the ability to interpret what is being said. It is the one and only Spirit who distributes all these gifts. He alone decides which gift each person should have. ✛ 1 CORINTHIANS 12:8-11

This morning, I fixed my hair and proceeded to spray it with room freshener. The end result wasn't great for my hair, but I smelled great! As I thought about my mistake, I realized the can of room freshener did what it was supposed to do—when I pushed the button a nice smell was emitted. It wasn't the can's fault that the room freshener didn't hold my hair. I wasn't using the product for the purpose for which it was created. It was a good lesson in making sure I have the right materials to do the right job.

When it comes to the body of Christ, God has given each of us different gifts that we are to use to contribute to the good of the whole. None of us is expected to be good at everything, in the same way that room freshener is not good to hold hair in place.

There are times when I have become discouraged because I tried to do something that was not in my arena of gifting. Or worse, I have been disappointed because of my expectations for others to function in ways that may not match their gifts or abilities.

At times we all have needs, and we must look to another brother or sister in Christ for help. God has distributed his gifts of the Spirit in order that all the needs of his body can be met through us by the enablement of the Spirit. We can help each other if we are willing to do two things. First, when we are in need, we must be willing to share that need with fellow believers. And second, we must be willing to use the gifts God has given us to help others. When we all do our part, the body of Christ can have a pleasing aroma and be able to stand strong.   ✎Brenda

☆   ☆   ☆

Father, thank you for the body of Christ. I want to use the gifts you have given me to help others. Open my heart to love freely without expectation. I pray for the mental and spiritual health of those returning from deployments in National Guard and reserve units. ✛ Amen.

Cleaning Closets

"What sorrow awaits you teachers of religious law and you Pharisees. Hypocrites! For you are so careful to clean the outside of the cup and the dish, but inside you are filthy—full of greed and self-indulgence!" + MATTHEW 23:25

My husband makes fun of the way I clean closets. I have to take everything out and spread it all over the room. He says I make a bigger mess than I had before I started—and he's right. For me this is the best way to clean a closet, especially one of those that seems to just automatically collect stuff. I have to get everything out. Then I clean up the inside, throw away the junk, and put back what needs to stay.

I liken it to keeping my life with Christ in order. Over time I can collect a lot of junk. I must regularly rid myself of those things that don't belong and let the Lord cleanse me. When someone first comes to the Lord, this process can look pretty messy, but the grace of the Lord is greater than any mess in our lives. If we let the Lord do his work, he has a plan that ends up with the junk thrown away and everything else put in order.

The problem comes when people try to throw a little of God into the closet of their lives along with everything else. That just doesn't work. Before our lives can be filled with the fullness of Christ, we need to empty them out and let the Lord clean them up. Jesus condemned the Pharisees in Matthew 23:25 for cleaning the outside of the cup with self-righteous laws, while the inside of their cup was full of greed and self-indulgence. We can clean up on the outside by adopting a few Christian principles that fit our way of life, but if we want to be filled with all God has for us, we have to be cleaned from the inside out.

Is it time for some spring cleaning in your closet today? *Brenda*

✶ ✶ ✶

Dear God, thank you for your cleansing power. I pray that I would be emptied of anything that would keep me from being filled with all you have for me. Cleanse me of selfish desires and motives that would hinder your work of grace in my life. I pray for public servants today who are required to do challenging work following crisis and disaster. In your name I pray. + *Amen.*

April 28
Wallpaper Lessons

But now is the time to get rid of anger, rage, malicious behavior, slander, and dirty language. Don't lie to each other, for you have stripped off your old sinful nature and all its wicked deeds. Put on your new nature, and be renewed as you learn to know your Creator and become like him. ✛ COLOSSIANS 3:8-10

Several years ago, I decided I wanted to tear off an outdated wallpaper border in one of the bathrooms of my home. It seemed like such a simple task. At first it was simple; the initial border came down in minutes. Unfortunately, it uncovered another border that was not so cooperative. Under that border was even more wallpaper. I ripped down wallpaper, layer upon layer, for days.

Today's Scripture instructs us to strip off our old sinful nature and all its wicked deeds. The original language is describing putting off clothes, but I think my wallpaper analogy works. In my mind I can see all the things of my old nature being stripped off just as I stripped that wallpaper off the wall. Some of it came off willingly, and some of it was stubborn. There were small bits of paper that I was tempted to leave on the wall, but I knew that for a completed work it all needed to come off. When the wallpaper was finally down, I was left with a mess! There were holes in the wall from pulling off paper with too much glue. There was water damage where I overused a sponge. I had to come up with a brand-new idea to complete the task. I ended up applying a textured compound to the wall, creating a finished effect that was so much better than I ever imagined!

The stripping of my old nature is only part of the job, as well. I also need the Lord to apply the artistic touch of his grace and gifts. Even if I am scarred from the stripping of ugly things, when they are replaced with a new nature, the end result is better than I ever thought possible. He not only replaces the old with new and improved attributes but also layers his character in me. It is a restoration process that will be complete one day as "the Lord—who is the Spirit—makes us more and more like him as we are changed into his glorious image" (2 Corinthians 3:18).   ❧Brenda

✯   ✯   ✯

Great Designer, you have created the heavens, yet you are mindful of me. I thank you for the re-creation you do daily in my life as I commit my moments to you. Continue to strip me of those things that would keep me from being the best witness of your grace. I pray for military personnel who are returning from deployment. May the reunion with their families be filled with joy as relationships are renewed. ✛ Amen.

A Dead Dog

Those who live only to satisfy their own sinful nature will harvest decay and death from that sinful nature. But those who live to please the Spirit will harvest everlasting life from the Spirit.

✝ GALATIANS 6:8

My husband's first pastoral assignment provided an old house owned by the church. My strongest recollection of this parsonage is the time I was pregnant with our first child. I was teaching school and came home one day to an unpleasant odor. My husband passed it off as pregnancy-induced sensitivity. The odor persisted, however, and became stronger. We searched the house to find the source but discovered nothing. Finally, to appease me, my husband climbed under the house, where he found a dead dog—a very large dead dog. He proceeded to dispose of the remains, come into the house, quickly rid himself permanently of the clothes he was wearing, and to calmly but firmly tell me he did not want to discuss what had just happened.

Often there are things that climb under the foundation of our lives and leave an unpleasant stench. This stench could be described as sin or shortcomings that make standing with the Lord uncomfortable and often unbearable. It has to be dealt with and cleaned out when we first become aware of the presence—before the dog decays!

Sometimes the sin that we harbor results from a bad experience toward a person or toward God. Even though the dead dog was not in the main part of my house, the stench permeated every room of my home from the crawl space. We can hide sinful things in our lives that can end up pervading our entire being. It is in these times that we have to crawl on our knees and ask God to help us clean out those sins and restore our lives to a sweet aroma that brings honor to him.   ❧*Brenda*

* * *

Father, I thank you for the cleansing power of the Cross. I ask that you would "search me, O God, and know my heart; test me and know my anxious thoughts. Point out anything in me that offends you, and lead me along the path of everlasting life" (Psalm 139:23-24). I pray for those who are dealing with the effects of seeing the death caused by war. Provide comfort and help for traumatized hearts and minds. In Jesus' name I pray. ✝*Amen.*

April 30
Mine's Too Dirty

Let us go right into the presence of God with sincere hearts fully trusting him. For our guilty consciences have been sprinkled with Christ's blood to make us clean, and our bodies have been washed with pure water. ✛ HEBREWS 10:22

When my boys were teenagers, I would have liked to say that their rooms were spotless and their bathrooms immaculate. Any of you with boys know that was my own private delusion. To their credit, they did, however, keep themselves clean and well groomed. In fact, their bathroom suffered greatly from the process. I remember one day finding my youngest son brushing his teeth in my bathroom. I asked him why he was in my space, and his reply was, "I can't stand it in mine—it is too dirty!"

Living on the earth allows for things to enter our lives that stain us with filth even to the point that we don't want to be in our own skins. We would like to be someone else. We condemn ourselves for who we are. When we get to this point, we need to realize this is why Jesus came. He came to cleanse us from sin, clean up our lives, and do his transforming work. The requirement on our part is to trust in his saving grace and repent of our sins. When we do this, we can have the assurance of 1 John 1:9: "But if we confess our sins to him, he is faithful and just to forgive us our sins and to cleanse us from all wickedness."

As Christ followers, we no longer have to stand in a dirty place. Through the blood of Christ, we are free from being made to feel guilty; we stand with no doubt of our acceptance by him, and we know that our spirits are clean. ≈Brenda

Father, thank you for the cleansing blood of Jesus. Thank you for the plan of salvation. Remind me today of his sacrifice, and help me to stand firm in the joy of being guilt free, accepted, and clean in your sight. I pray for military spouses, who may feel overwhelmed by the responsibilities of caring for a home during deployment. Provide them with encouragement and hope. In Jesus' name I pray. ✛ Amen.

House Blessing

He blesses the home of the upright. ✝ PROVERBS 3:33

While stationed at Fort Leavenworth, Kansas, I met a dear woman who became a godly mentor. Jane Butler taught me many things about the Christian walk. She spent hours with me answering questions and showing me God's truth about my life as an individual, as a wife, and as a mother.

For the military family, moving to a new place is part of the package. Our family moved into houses where many other military families had lived. Through the years, we have only lived in one house where we were actually the first family to live. As my love for the Lord grew, so did my desire to honor him in my home.

One of the things Jane encouraged my husband and me to do was dedicate our new home to the Lord. We had been sent to Fort Leavenworth so my husband could attend a school. After his graduation, we remained at Fort Leavenworth, so we were then eligible for larger living quarters and began to prepare for our second move in two years.

We asked Jane and Steve if they would walk through the house with us before we moved in and ask God's blessing on it. We gathered our sons together, and the six of us began at the front door. We took olive oil and anointed the front door inside and out, asking the Lord that all who entered would be blessed and that as they departed they would go into the world, knowing God's love had been shown to them.

Room by room, we anointed and prayed specific prayers for godly conversation, godly television viewing, godly hospitality, godliness in whatever purpose a room would serve. We laughed, we cried, and we dreamed as we walked the entire house together. It was a time of truly giving back to the Lord the blessing of this home as it would be used to glorify him.

I cannot tell you how many times people have asked my husband and me to come and pray through their homes with them. I've been asked where in the Bible we are instructed to do this. There's no specific directive in Scripture that I can find for this, but I can tell you it blesses our family to know that we have dedicated our home to the Lord and are committed to serving him in and through it.   ↭*Carol*

★   ★   ★

Father, thank you for your protection in our earthly dwellings. Protect those whose homes are without a member of the family right now. Fill that void with your peace and presence. ✝ *Amen.*

May 2
Divine Colors

But you have raised a banner for those who fear you—a rallying point in the face of attack.
✝ PSALM 60:4

In response to a need to identify military units, President George Washington instituted the use of military "colors" in the Continental Army. The colors of a military unit are displayed wherever the unit is represented. The colors, or flag, are attached to a pole. Streamers, embroidered strips of cloth, are added to the pole to indicate participation in battles and achievement of awards. In essence, it is the history of the unit and a symbol of what it represents. The colors accompany the unit into combat. Stories are told of battles during the Revolutionary War and the Civil War when the colors were carried into battle and used as rallying points to motivate the troops. The soldiers' challenge was to stand up for their colors.[1]

In today's military, if the colors are not being displayed in a ceremony, they hold a place of honor in the unit's headquarters. Yet the colors can sit in the corner of a conference room and their significance not be appreciated until they are further explained. Each streamer represents sacrifice, heroism, and victory. The significance and symbolism are too often taken for granted.

For the Christ follower, the cross is our banner. It is the symbol of who Christ is and why he came to earth and the symbol of the victory we have in him. Our colors become our rallying point. Yet we, too, can take our colors for granted.

When we find ourselves engaged in the battles of this life and overwhelmed with discouragement and a sense of defeat, that is the time to do as the soldiers in the Continental Army did and rally around our divine colors—the cross! The cross reminds us that in Christ we are more than overcomers. On the cross, Christ fought the cosmic battle for the souls of humanity and defeated our enemy.

Today when you view the cross, don't look at it merely as a decoration or adornment but as an encouragement to put your faith in Jesus Christ. He is our conquering Lord!   ✎Brenda

* * *

Conquering Lord, thank you for the completed work on the cross that purchased my salvation. Forgive me for the times I choose to live in defeat and fail to remember the victory you have won. Help me today to live rejoicing in the divine "colors" of your grace. I pray for those who are working in veterans' hospitals around the country. ✝ Amen.

---

[1] Colonel Ralph R. Burr, "The Beginnings of Heraldry in the Civil War—Symbols Rally the Spirit." http://www.gmfound.com/heraldry_in_the_civil_war.htm.

Grant Us Courage

Though a mighty army surrounds me, my heart will not be afraid. Even if I am attacked, I will remain confident. ✝ PSALM 27:3

When Operation Iraqi Freedom started, my husband was the division chaplain for the 82d Airborne Division, a military unit defined by excellence, esprit de corps, and courage. I wish I could say the same for this wife of an 82d Airborne soldier. Courage was not what I was feeling as the deployment order came, and my husband left with the division. I fervently asked the Lord to help me deal with the fear and grant me courage to experience the days ahead. The day after my husband left, my devotion for the day was Psalm 27. The message was so specific that I knew God had heard my prayer. The courage to walk through the challenging days ahead would be mine if I would press into the Lord by seeking him (see Psalm 27:4, 8). The renewed courage I experienced helped me pray in confidence for my husband and his unit while they were in dangerous situations.

> Courage is fear which has said its prayers. If we are not attempting something which creates the human reaction of fear we are probably not living life as it was meant to be lived. Fear in the soul-stretching challenges of these days drives us to prayer. Eddie Rickenbacker knew what he was talking about when he said that courage is doing what you're afraid to do. There is no courage unless you're scared and are driven to your knees. Thomas Fuller, English divine and author (1608-1661), said, "Fear can keep a man out of danger, but courage can support him in it." Winston Churchill said, "Courage is the greatest virtue because it makes possible all the rest. Never give up. Never give up! Never, never give up!"[1]

In the midst of our fears, we can live in confidence that his power is real and his promises are true.   ❧*Brenda*

✶   ✶   ✶

> God of grace and God of glory,
> Set our feet on lofty places,
> Gird our lives that they may be
> Armored with all Christlike graces,
> In the fight to set men free.
> Grant us wisdom; grant us courage,
> That we fail not man nor Thee,
> That we fail not man nor Thee.[2]

✝ Amen.

---

[1] Lloyd John Ogilvie, *Praying Through the Tough Places* (Eugene, OR: Harvest House Publishers, 2005), 51.
[2] Harry Emerson Fosdick, "God of Grace and God of Glory."

May 4
The Light Still Shines

God's light came into the world, but people loved the darkness more than the light, for their actions were evil. All who do evil hate the light and refuse to go near it for fear their sins will be exposed. But those who do what is right come to the light so others can see that they are doing what God wants. + JOHN 3:19-21

As parents of two teenage sons, knowing full well that we could not possibly know everything that went on in their lives, my husband and I agreed on a prayer we would pray together. We prayed that whatever was done in the dark or in secret would be revealed in the light. We prayed for light-shining revelation. We prayed that in times of trouble, someone would be around to confront our boys or share the situation with us. The bottom line we asked for was that they would be drawn into the light for all to be exposed.

That prayer was answered many times over. We know how very much God loved them because he always brought them back into the light.

Many times in sessions of prayer for the military and their mission in the War on Terror, I pray for God to reveal that which is done in the dark by the terrorists. I pray he will reveal their plans and their locations. I pray that their night missions will be seen with God's night-vision goggles and reveal all their hiding places.

Many of us have been in dark places before. When we are there, we have a tendency to hide from God and go deeper and darker so as not to allow him to shine his light into our lives. As soon as we see the glimmer of light shining, we grasp hold of hope and promise for tomorrow.

There is victory in the light. There is victory for children whose parents stay on their faces before the Lord. There is victory in our hearts as we allow the light of Jesus to come in. The light of Christ still shines. It never goes out. Look for the *light* and let it restore your soul.   ~*Carol*

* * *

Father, teach me to stay out of those dark places in life. I ask for your light to shine with conviction and then restoration when we go there. I ask for the light to shine on those who are hiding in the dark to harm our country or who seek to harm our men and women serving in faraway lands. + *Amen.*

Fruit of War

You didn't choose me. I chose you. I appointed you to go and produce lasting fruit, so that the Father will give you whatever you ask for, using my name. + JOHN 15:16

My husband was deployed to Iraq at the onset of Operation Iraqi Freedom. He shared of the opportunity to pray with the troops before they boarded the plane taking them to their foreign destination. He asked how many of them had been told that someone was praying for them. Over 90 percent of the soldiers raised their hands. He encouraged the soldiers to believe that those prayers were going to make a difference. He wrote several times of his desire to see eternal results in the lives of those he served.

On one occasion he wrote,

> I have had many soldiers asking about chapel. I think we will have good participation for our services. When we are on a training exercise, sometimes it is hard to get a time slot. Here we get a dedicated tent. We will probably be having services every day for a while. Pray that the Lord will do a lasting work in our soldiers' lives.

Another time he wrote,

> The services were well attended Sunday (standing room only). We do have a dedicated chapel tent, so we are having a Bible study every night and three services on Sunday. Pray that the Lord will help us make an impact on the soldiers' lives while the opportunity is ripe.

As I received these messages, I began to pray the Lord would lead me to people who had become Christians during Desert Storm. I felt this would encourage my husband in knowing there were indeed foxhole decisions for Christ that were lasting. My prayers were answered as I heard testimony after testimony of lives changed as a result of war.

The great devotional writer Oswald Chambers spent time as a volunteer military chaplain to English troops in Egypt from 1915 to 1917. During that time he wrote these words: "Personally, I am more relieved than horrified that war has come, because to a large extent the hypocrisy of diplomatic veneer is removed, also the immediate result among many men is that much irresponsible pleasure seeking and frivolity is ended and real stern issues have begun. Men everywhere are more open to talk about God, the soul and final issues than heretofore."[1]   *≈Brenda*

*   *   *

Lord, thank you for your Word that goes forth even in war. I pray today for men and women who have made decisions to follow you as a result of military service. Help their commitment to remain strong. In your name I pray. + *Amen.*

---

[1] Oswald Chambers, *Leagues of Light: Diary of Oswald Chambers 1915–1917* (Louisville, KY: Operation Appreciation Ministries, Inc., 1984), 22.

May 6

Sewing Machine Warfare

For we are not fighting against flesh-and-blood enemies, but against evil rulers and authorities of the unseen world, against mighty powers in this dark world, and against evil spirits in the heavenly places. ✛ EPHESIANS 6:12

My husband's first assignment in the military was to Fort Benning, Georgia. We settled into the building divided up as a home with three other families. For several days and nights, I kept hearing what sounded like a sewing machine. I remember thinking how strange that a neighbor would sew that much! I speculated that one of the women must be a seamstress with a very successful business to keep her sewing machine running so much. I finally mentioned my observation to my husband. He laughed heartily as he explained to me that I was hearing not a sewing machine but machine-gun fire as new soldiers were training in the ranges on the installation!

In my defense, for my frame of reference the sound was just like that of a sewing machine. To know what was really going on, I needed to broaden my understanding. In the same way, when I look at circumstances through human eyes, I have found I can also wonder why difficult situations continue to occur. For instance, why don't I have more self-discipline? My frame of reference causes me to think it is because I need more personal determination. I sometimes fail to realize there is another dimension to consider. Paul points out in Ephesians 6:12 that our fight isn't against flesh and blood but against evil in an unseen world.

Now, I'm not taking the position that whenever there is failure, the devil made me do it. At the same time, it is imperative to recognize there is an enemy of my soul. God's Word instructs me to prepare myself for battle and resist his attacks. Satan is a real enemy with a real strategy to destroy the believer (see 1 Peter 5:8). He "prefers stealth strategies: the guerilla ambushes of temptation, the sporadic sniper fire of false or ungodly thoughts, a siege of distractions that causes us to neglect spiritual nourishment. Whatever his maneuvers, his objectives remain the same: to take prisoner as many people as possible and to disarm the rest."[1] The important thing to remember is that he is a defeated foe! He's lost the war, but he keeps on fighting for the minds and souls of people.

I think of those sewing-machine guns and remember the battle I'm in as a Christ follower. I must remain willing to train and enter into warfare on my knees in order to be prepared to stand victorious against the enemy of my soul.   *≈Brenda*

✶　✶　✶

Victorious Savior, thank you for canceling the record of the charges against me and taking it away by nailing it to the cross. Remind me that you disarmed the spiritual rulers and authorities and shamed them publicly by your victory over them on the cross (see Colossians 2:15). ✛ *Amen.*

---

[1] Paul Thigpen, "Our Weaponry," *Discipleship Journal*, 153 (May/June 2006).

Battle Weary

Jacob's well was there; and Jesus, tired from the long walk, sat wearily beside the well about noontime. ✝ JOHN 4:6

The word *weary* has deep connotations. It is more than just being tired or even needing rest. In *The Message* this passage of Scripture says that Jesus was worn-out from his trip. In other words, when we are weary, we have probably hit a wall and are not able to go much farther without rest or pulling away from the situation.

My dear friend Major Steve has just come home from Iraq for a couple of weeks of R & R. This time is considered to be a morale builder for families when there are periods of long deployment and separation. Although at times the second leaving is more difficult, there is always the thought that this time it is a true countdown to being together again.

The young wives, husbands, and families of these deployed men and women are weary. They are to the point of being worn-out from carrying the responsibility of so much on their shoulders during this time.

We as a body of believers are battle weary. We are at war every day for values and morals, and we have spiritual warfare coming at our families.

> *Battle weary as life goes on*
> *I often feel worn out*
> *I seek to gain my strength from You*
> *Your name I often shout.*
> *Why can't I read the Word and know*
> *The directions are quite clear?*
> *If I just seek Your presence Lord*
> *You're always very near.*
> *The arrows fly, the swords are drawn*
> *Our prayers to you I send*
> *Wondering when I can take a break from this—*
> *You say, "Have you read the end?*
> *The battle will continue*
> *Until I come back for my own*
> *Just trust in me, stay on your knees*
> *My love for you I've shown."*

When you are battle weary, look up. I say that a lot, but it is the answer in all things. Have you read the end of the book? The battle has been won, and that is our hope.
~*Carol*

✯　✯　✯

Father God, remind me that I may be weary, but I am not forsaken. As those who are in physical battle each day go out to find the enemy, give them renewed strength and a sense of peace. ✝ *Amen.*

May 8
Spiritual Eyes

"Go and find out where he is," the king commanded, "so I can send troops to seize him." And the report came back: "Elisha is at Dothan." So one night the king of Aram sent a great army with many chariots and horses to surround the city. When the servant of the man of God got up early the next morning and went outside, there were troops, horses, and chariots everywhere. "Oh, sir, what will we do now?" the young man cried to Elisha. "Don't be afraid!" Elisha told him. "For there are more on our side than on theirs!" Then Elisha prayed, "O LORD, open his eyes and let him see!" The LORD opened the young man's eyes, and when he looked up, he saw that the hillside around Elisha was filled with horses and chariots of fire.

✝ 2 KINGS 6:13-17

I remember those years of giving instruction and correction to our sons. Often they would be thinking of going outside to play, or they were ready to go out the door to school. I would say to them, "Look at my face." In other words, I wanted them to lift their eyes to my eyes so I would know they were paying attention to me.

I remember first learning and understanding about spiritual warfare that takes place in the heavenly realm. My eyes were opened after reading *This Present Darkness,* by Frank Peretti.[1] Although it is a work of fiction, the story helped me to understand that there is a spirit world where God is constantly battling for us.

When our sons left for college, I was not able to pray over them each day before they left the house. I wasn't able to touch them and to physically be with them when I prayed for them. I began to realize that my prayers were going straight to the Father in heaven, and he was watching out for them. As in the story with Elisha, it is as if I went through a time of adjustment when I had to see the unseen and open my eyes to God's working in their lives. God said to my spirit that he was out there protecting and fighting for my children even when I could not see.

We have an unseen enemy but an all-seeing God. The War on Terror has shown us that there is an enemy on this earth seeking to destroy all that is good. That enemy is difficult to identify and to destroy. But God is all-seeing in his omniscience.

Open your spiritual eyes, and know that God is there fighting your battles and pursuing warfare with the enemy of this world on your behalf.   ~*Carol*

✶   ✶   ✶

Father, thank you that at those times when I may see only defeat, you are fighting the battles for me. I pray for victory for those fighting for our country and our freedoms. ✝ *Amen.*

---

[1] Frank E. Peretti, *This Present Darkness* (Westchester, IL: Crossway Books, 1986).

The Battle Is On

The LORD says, "I will give you back what you lost to the swarming locusts, the hopping locusts, the stripping locusts, and the cutting locusts. It was I who sent this great destroying army against you. Once again you will have all the food you want, and you will praise the LORD your God, who does these miracles for you. Never again will my people be disgraced." † JOEL 2.25-26

In our Christian lives, we feel many times that parts of our lives have been stolen by the enemy. Oftentimes, he steals our joy. The enemy seeks to steal our children away from their godly upbringing by presenting a culture that is enticing in the midst of the sin that presents itself.

My husband has been teaching an adult Sunday school class for many years. He has taught many subjects that bless my heart. One of my favorites is his teaching on spiritual warfare. I especially love this teaching because he always brings his military training into the lesson.

I remember one time in particular when he was talking about how to conquer the hill that the enemy has taken. He told us that you go up and overcome the enemy and conquer that hill with military expertise. But there is more. You must then go back down the hill and conquer the territory around the hill. You see, the enemy could be hiding around the hill and capture you when you come down, and just take the hill over again. In other words, the military plan would be to conquer the territory and then fan outward to conquer the surrounding areas in order to keep the victory.

Well, you have just had the lesson of life. We are to take back from the enemy that which he has stolen from us. That could include our self-esteem or even a ministry which has been slandered. Then we are to take the surrounding territory and build up our faith and our prayer lives in order not to put ourselves in that position of defeat again.

The battle is on. Get ready for victory! ⚭*Carol*

*   *   *

Father God, thank you for restoring that which the enemy steals in the daily battles of life on earth. I pray that our men and women in the military may claim the territory on the physical battlefield overseas. + *Amen.*

May 10
Bless You

Her children stand and bless her. Her husband praises her. ✛ PROVERBS 31:28

I can remember, back in my younger days, thinking all I wanted to be when I grew up was a wife and mother. I was brought up by a stay-at-home mom, and the times of coming in the door and knowing she would be there to greet me made such an impression on me.

I also knew that if I needed her during the school day, all I had to do was call her. I knew she would be at the other end of the phone. She was committed to us young children. She was there to teach us and to encourage us and to love us.

She followed us to dance lessons, piano lessons, and expression classes. In later years, she was always at the big events in our lives, beside our dad, and always giving us smiles from the audience or bleachers.

Some of the things she loved to do as a full-time mom and homemaker were clean out closets and drawers, rearrange furniture, and cook. I remember coming back from Girl Scout camp one year to find she had rearranged my furniture. I got up that night to go out the door and ran into my wall. She felt bad about the knot on my head the next day!

She cared for us with love and kindness. I am thankful for all she did for me as a child and even now as an adult. I want to stand up today and call my mother blessed! I want to say, "Bless you for the sacrifices you made for me. My dad praised you constantly and appreciated your sacrifices for him as well."

Bless you, mothers and wives, for all that you do!   ⁓*Carol*

Father, in this fast-paced world, thank you for the mothers and wives who hold things together emotionally, physically, and spiritually in homes all over this country. I stand to call them *blessed* and thank you for their sacrifices. ✛ *Amen.*

Walk Out in Leadership

No, O people, the Lord has told you what is good, and this is what he requires of you: to do what is right, to love mercy, and to walk humbly with your God. ✛ MICAH 6:8

My favorite pastime is walking. I love to walk as fast as I can and pray with passion while I am speeding along. I feel as if it is health to my bones and my muscles and especially my heart. It is also a time of releasing stress, discussing things with my Father in heaven, and stimulating my brain for great things. I try to walk at least thirty to forty-five minutes a day. This is a commitment I have made to myself. I try to schedule everything else around that special time.

While walking the other day, I began to think about how I was aware of several things. I was very aware that my head should be held up high as I am walking. I was also very aware that my shoulders should be held back and my stomach held in.

Often as I pass others on the track, I will hear them whisper, "Look at her go! We need to keep up with her!" My step and my stature give them something to aim for. If someone passes me, I find myself attempting to catch up with them, too.

Leadership is much like exercise walking. Leaders aren't necessarily leaders just because that position has been given to them. Their stature is very much a part of their success. When they hold their heads up high and their shoulders back, they command the attention of others around them. When they seek to surpass the norm, others strive to follow them. Their sense of humility and compassion can make them outstanding leaders in their fields.

I can just imagine seeing Jesus walk into a room or even into a town square. I can imagine his head held high and shoulders back. I can imagine that others knew there was something in him that made him a leader. They wanted to be with him and be like him. They followed him wherever he went to hear more and to watch him in his daily walk.

Thank God today for those leaders who are walking with their heads held high. Be grateful and supportive of those leaders in our land who stand for what is right and seek a better world.   *Carol*

★　★　★

Father, there are so many examples of leadership in our brave men and women fighting for freedom. I thank you for their examples and ask that you bless them today with renewed strength to carry on. ✛ *Amen.*

May 12
First Chair

This same Good News that came to you is going out all over the world. It is bearing fruit everywhere by changing lives, just as it changed your lives from the day you first heard and understood the truth about God's wonderful grace. ✛ COLOSSIANS 1:6

True fulfillment in life comes when you don't just know the principles of Christianity, but when you also know the person of Christ. Many people live good lives by following Christian principles. It is the renewed man, however, who "acts upon new principles, by new rules, with new ends, and in new company. The believer is created anew; his heart is not merely set right, but a new heart is given him. He is the workmanship of God, created in Christ Jesus unto good works. Though the same as a man, he is changed in his character and conduct. These words must and do mean more than an outward reformation. The man who formerly saw no beauty in the Saviour that he should desire him, now loves him above all things."[1]

That is a difference that is evident in a life.

While attending a youth symphony, I was impressed with the beautiful sound and professionalism of the young musicians. I was especially drawn to the violin section. I noticed that most of the musicians were stiff and mechanical as they played. The sound was good, the music was lovely, but they seemed to be engrossed in playing the correct notes, resulting in a group of stiff violinists. I finally rested my eyes on the first row, first chair. Here was a young musician who was noticeably different. Her presence was subdued, but on close inspection, you could see flow and expressiveness in the way she held the bow, moved her arms, and involved even her head. It was very natural and graceful, as if the music were flowing out of her being.

I was struck by a desire for my life with Christ to be like that violinist! I long to have a life that is characterized by a relationship with Christ and naturally expressed through my whole being, rather than by the mechanical following of a doctrine or creed. Christian principles are good principles, but to know the author of those principles brings meaning to life here on earth and into eternity. ⁂Brenda

*　　*　　*

Dear Lord, I want to be fluid and graceful in my walk with you. Let there be evidence of the difference you make, not for difference's sake, but to point others to the One who is the music of my soul. ✛Amen.

---

[1] Matthew Henry's commentary on 2 Corinthians 5:15. www.biblegateway.com.

May 13
Send Me

Then I heard the Lord asking, "Whom should I send as a messenger to this people? Who will go for us?" I said, "Here I am. Send me." + ISAIAH 6:8

We are members of a mission-minded church. They instruct those who wish to serve here in our nation. They instruct those who wish to serve in other countries. Those who have given of themselves to minister in this way have been messengers for the Lord. After completing their mission work, they return with renewed hearts to share with those in our congregation how God is working in other parts of our nation and our world.

When my husband and I began to realize that we were being sent to different states and countries by God and not just by the military, our mind-set was changed. The military family has the chance to live in other areas of the country and the world. They can report what's going on as they live their lives in different places.

While stationed in one country, we had the opportunity to witness to someone who could not believe that Jesus was a real person. My husband got out the Bible to share Scripture that told of Jesus. In response, our guest began to ask more and more questions. Not only were we able to witness to her through Scripture, but since we would end up living there for five years, she could witness this Scripture as we walked it out in our lives.

While stationed in another country, I was able to answer questions of a young woman whose fiancé had started to inquire about Christianity. She had the opportunity to see my life as well as my words as we built a relationship that lasted for our two years of duty.

I don't know about you, but I always felt somewhat left out and less of a Christian because I did not have a great desire to go overseas to be a missionary. I remember the church I grew up in always welcoming those who were home on missionary furlough. As they shared their stories, I would think, *What is wrong with me? Why can't I have those opportunities to share Christ around the world?*

Well, God gave me the opportunity to be a military missionary for twenty-two years. After those years of travel around the world, I still say to him, "Lord, here I am, send me!" He may send me to a neighbor, a friend, or a young military wife. God will always send. We must be available whether we're sent within our city, our neighborhood, or the world.

Send me, Lord! ❧*Carol*

✳ ✳ ✳

Father, there is no mission too small or task too large when I lay out my life and say, "Send me!" On this day be with those who are ministering in faraway lands to those who desire freedom and peace. + *Amen.*

May 14
Let Me Be the One

For "Everyone who calls on the name of the Lord will be saved." But how can they call on him to save them unless they believe in him? And how can they believe in him if they have never heard about him? And how can they hear about him unless someone tells them?
✛ ROMANS 10:13-14

The book of Romans carries the theme that salvation is for all people. We are all in need of salvation as stated in Romans 3:23: "For everyone has sinned; we all fall short of God's glorious standard." It is the Word of God that creates faith in the heart of the hearer, but there must be those who are willing to share that Word with others. Romans 10:13-15 was written with the Jewish nation in mind, but it carries a legitimate application for every believer to carry the message of salvation to those who have not heard. "There can be no calling without belief or trust. There can be no belief or trust, without hearing. There can be no hearing without preaching."[1] "There can be no preaching unless preachers have a commission."[2]

Are we willing to share the message of salvation with a family member, friend, neighbor, coworker, stranger . . . the world?

No one is righteous, not even one
No one understands, no one seeking
*   God*
All turned away, all worth is gone
No one does good, not even one.
LET ME BE THE ONE!
Throats are open graves, tongues
*   full of deceit*
Open mouths pollute the air with
*   every lie they speak*
No one will listen, no one will hear
Racing for the honor of "sinner of
*   the year."*
Ruin, heartbreak marking their way
Never giving Jesus Christ the time of
*   their day*

Reject the Father, reject the Son
No one does good not even one.
LET ME BE THE ONE!
We all have sinned—the cost is
*   death*
We've been justified by the Son's last
*   breath*
Hung on the tree then rose from the
*   grave*
Accept the sacrifice that He willingly
*   made.*
Who will believe?
Who will be strong?
Who will do good?
LET ME BE THE ONE!

~A RESPONSE TO ROMANS 3:10-18 FROM GREGORY PACE, AGE 17[3]

❧Brenda

✳   ✳   ✳

Author of salvation for the world, let me be the one to share words of life and hope with someone who does not know you today. I pray for outreach ministries in military communities; may you refresh their love for you and their zeal for your service. ✛ *Amen.*

---

[1] NT:2784 *kerusso* (kay-roos'-so); of uncertain affinity; to herald (as a public crier). *Biblesoft's New Exhaustive Strong's Numbers and Concordance with Expanded Greek-Hebrew Dictionary* (Seattle: Biblesoft and International Bible Translators, Inc., 1994).
[2] Everett Harrison and Charles Pfeiffer, eds. *The Wycliffe Bible Commentary* (Chicago, IL: Moody Press, 1962), CD-ROM.
[3] Used by permission.

Follow His Voice

But the one who enters through the gate is the shepherd of the sheep. The gatekeeper opens the gate for him, and the sheep recognize his voice and come to him. He calls his own sheep by name and leads them out. After he has gathered his own flock, he walks ahead of them, and they follow him because they know his voice. They won't follow a stranger; they will run from him because they don't know his voice. **+** JOHN 10:2-5

My husband takes a daily morning walk around our neighborhood. It has been a wonderful way to get to know our neighbors. We live in a neighborhood that has no through streets, so it is a peaceful and quiet place to walk. This past weekend as he was rounding out the last stretch, my husband turned to see two bouncing golden retrievers catching up with him. Their energy was contagious, and considering how much he loves dogs, I am quite sure he began talking to them in his man-to-dog speaking voice.

The bad thing is that once you talk to a dog and it knows you love it, you are its friend for life. It was a very hot day, and these dogs followed him home. I looked out, and he said, "Look who found me!" Of course, we had to give them some water. They gulped it down and then enjoyed lying for a nap on our cool concrete porch.

Immediately, we began strategizing a plan to get these dogs back to their rightful owners. I started calling the neighbors and left my phone number at the Humane Society. One of the girls in the neighborhood that I consider to be an adopted daughter came to check out the situation. Rachel loves animals and will stop at nothing to help and to assist when they are in need. We drove around the neighborhood, knocking on doors and trying to find their home.

As we were pulling back into the driveway, my husband was pulling out in his truck. We came up beside him, and he said, "The owners found them!" They had been driving slowly through the neighborhood. The dogs looked up and saw their car, heard their voices—and out they ran to their owners. It was a very happy ending.

We were kind and gave them water, but their yearning was to hear their master's voice and return to their own home. In the same way, God has instilled in each of us a yearning to be with him. Follow his voice today and return to your rightful place with him.   ❧*Carol*

✫   ✫   ✫

Father, help me to always listen for your voice and look for you to pick me up and bring me back to you. Please call out to your children in the armed services—those who know you and those who do not, yet. **+***Amen.*

May 16
Words from a President, Part 1

Without wise leadership, a nation falls. ✦ PROVERBS 11:14

Religious freedom has always been a hallmark of America's existence. Our nation has found encouragement and guidance from leaders who have expressed religious concerns. Over the next few days, take time to ponder some statements from past leaders of our nation.

It is the duty of all nations to acknowledge the providence of Almighty God. **George Washington,** *first president of the United State*s

Is it not that the Declaration of Independence first organized the social compact on the Foundation of the Redeemer's mission upon earth? That it laid the cornerstone of human government upon the first precepts of Christianity? **John Adams,** *second president of the United States*

Can the liberties of a nation be thought secure when we have removed their only firm basis, a conviction in the minds of the people that their liberties are the gift of God? **Thomas Jefferson,** *third president of the United States*

Before any man can be considered as a member of Civil Society, he must be considered as a subject of the Governor of the universe. **James Madison,** *fourth president of the United States*

The first and almost the only Book deserving of universal attention is the Bible. **John Quincy Adams,** *sixth president of the United States*

The Bible is true. I have tried to conform to its spirit as near as possible. Upon that sacred volume I rest my hope for eternal salvation, through the merits and blood of our blessed Lord and Savior, Jesus Christ. **Andrew Jackson,** *seventh president of the United States*

I fervently invoke the aid of that Almighty Ruler of the Universe in whose hands are the destinies of nations. **James K. Polk,** *eleventh president of the United State*s

But for [the Bible] we could not know right from wrong. All things most desirable for men's welfare . . . are to be found portrayed in it. **Abraham Lincoln,** *sixteenth president of the United States*

Let us look forward to the time when we can take the flag of our country and nail it below the Cross, and there let it wave as it waved in the olden times, and let us gather around it and inscribe for our motto: 'Liberty and Union, one and inseparable, now and forever,' and exclaim: Christ first, our country next. **Andrew Johnson,** s*eventeenth president of the United States*[1]

❧*Brenda*

✦   ✦   ✦

Almighty God, thank you for raising up leaders of our nation who have expressed their faith and confidence in you. I pray you would guide our president with wisdom and courage to make decisions that reflect the principles ordained by you in your Word. In your name I pray. ✦ *Amen.*

---

[1] Presidential quotations on this page come from the following source: Stephen Mansfield and Sam Bartholomew, *American Destiny: God's Role in America* (Nashville, TN: American Destiny Press, 2001).

Words from a President, Part 2

Without wise leadership, a nation falls. + PROVERBS 11:14

Personal faith cannot be judged, but author John C. McCollister in his book *God and the Oval Office* concluded from his research that the majority of our presidents expressed faith in God. The following statements support this opinion.[1]

Hold fast to the Bible as the sheet-anchor of your liberties; write its precepts in your hearts and practice them in your lives. To the influence of this book we are indebted for all the progress made in true civilization and to this we must look as our guide in the future. **Ulysses S. Grant,** *eighteenth president of the United States*

I am a firm believer in the Divine teachings, perfect example, and atoning sacrifice of Jesus Christ. I believe also in the Holy Scriptures as the revealed Word of God to the world for its enlightenment and salvation. **Rutherford B. Hayes,** *nineteenth president of the United States*

In this actual world, a churchless community, a community where men have abandoned and scoffed at, or ignored their Christian duties is a community on the rapid downgrade. **Theodore Roosevelt,** *twenty-sixth president of the United States*

The Bible . . . is one supreme source of revelation of the meaning of life, the nature of God, and spiritual nature and need of men. It is the only guide of life which really leads the spirit in the way of peace and salvation. **Woodrow Wilson,** *twenty-eighth president of the United States*

It is my conviction that the fundamental trouble with the people of the United States is that they have gotten too far away from Almighty God. **Warren G. Harding,** *twenty-ninth president of the United States*

The foundations of our society and our government rest so much on the teachings of the Bible that it would be difficult to support them if faith in these teachings would cease to be practically universal in our country. **Calvin Coolidge,** *thirtieth president of the United States*

The whole inspiration of our civilization springs from the teachings of Christ and the lessons of the prophets. To read the Bible for these fundamentals is a necessity of American life. **Herbert Hoover,** *thirty-first president of the United States*

We cannot read the history of our rise and development as a nation, without reckoning with the place the Bible has occupied in shaping the advances of the Republic. . . . Where we have been the truest and most consistent in obeying its precepts, we have attained the greatest measure of contentment and prosperity. **Franklin Roosevelt,** *thirty-second president of the United States*

≈Brenda

* * *

God of all wisdom, thank you for those national leaders and military leaders who look to you for help and guidance. Look upon our nation with mercy. In your name I pray. +*Amen.*

---

[1] Presidential quotations on this page come from the following source: Stephen Mansfield and Sam Bartholomew, *American Destiny:, God's Role in America* (Nashville, TN: American Destiny Press, 2001).

May 18
Feels Like Home

The godly will rejoice in the Lord and find shelter in him. And those who do what is right will praise him. ✛ PSALM 64:10

There is nothing quite like having the President of the United States come to visit when you are stationed in a foreign country.

Upon your arrival to a foreign assignment, there is, of course, a period of adjustment. We had not been on assignment in South Korea very long when the news came that we were to get encouragement from home: President George H. W. Bush was coming to visit Yongsan. What an exciting time we had as we prepared for this special visit!

First Lady Barbara Bush would also be with him. I always loved her, because she was so witty and welcoming; I felt as if I were having a visit from my own family. The excitement built for several days. We were able to talk with our sons about President Bush's time in office and his support of the military and their families.

This was a time of feeling deep patriotism and honor while serving overseas. Just to think that the President and Mrs. Bush would take the time to visit gave everyone a much-needed boost.

We waited several hours in line to get into the American installation gymnasium. Then they walked in. They waved and smiled and quickly took their seats. After the introductions, they began to speak to us about the courage and pride they felt being in a place where so many were serving the United States of America. What an encouragement and, for a moment, what a feeling of home in that gymnasium across the ocean from our homeland.

There are two quotations from George H. W. Bush's presidency that he lived out that day in South Korea. The message he shared can be summarized by these words of his, for which his presidency is remembered:

> We are a nation of communities . . . a brilliant diversity spread like stars, like a thousand points of light in a broad and peaceful sky.

> We don't want an America that is closed to the world. What we want is a world that is open to America.[1]

✐Carol

✮   ✮   ✮

Thank you, Lord, for those in authority willing to reach out and touch families who are separated from loved ones and the country they love. As so many are stationed in foreign lands during this time, please give them a touch of home in their hearts and a knowledge that we thank God for them every day. In Jesus' name I pray, ✛ *Amen.*

---

[1] Quotations taken from www.brainyquote.com.

An Army of One

Above all, you must live as citizens of heaven, conducting yourselves in a manner worthy of the Good News about Christ. Then, whether I come and see you again or only hear about you, I will know that you are standing together with one spirit and one purpose, fighting together for the faith, which is the Good News. + PHILIPPIANS 1:27

You wouldn't expect going to see a movie at a theater on a military installation to be a patriotic and inspirational event. But it is. Instead of the fifteen-plus minutes of previews and commercials, the national anthem is played. The audience stands quietly with hand over heart as clips of historical or national significance are shown and the flag waves proudly on the screen. Each time I experience this, I feel the same emotions of surprise, gratitude for my country, and joy in being a part of such a community.

A recent report from Iraq gave an account of this happening in one of the camps. Apparently, the taped music kept stopping in the middle of the anthem. It would start and then stop again. Each time the music stopped, there was complete silence as the soldiers stood at attention. Finally, a lone voice was heard singing the words loud and strong, with more voices joining to complete the song of our nation together.

As soldiers of the gospel of Christ, we are to live our lives worthy of others' following. Just like the soldier in the theater who was willing to lead out in song, we are to live our lives for Christ with a singleness of spirit and purpose. Often it only takes one person to start singing; if it is a worthy thing, others will join in. Be that one, and sing out the notes of Good News. Be a leader in the army of the gospel of Christ. ❧*Brenda*

★ ★ ★

Dear God, thank you for the challenge of your Word to live a life worthy of my citizenship of heaven. Thank you for the promise that the battle I fight as a soldier in your army is not fought alone. I pray for confidence in the midst of my battles, knowing that you are standing beside me. I ask your protection over military personnel who are facing physical attacks on the battlefields around the globe. May the day when weapons are laid down and your Kingdom is ushered in come soon. +*Amen.*

May 20
Heroes on the Home Front

The godly people in the land are my true heroes! I take pleasure in them! ✛ PSALM 16:3

For the last four summers, I have had the privilege of spending a week in the Colorado mountains with true heroes. They are being treated to a week of ministry to refresh their weary bodies and spirits. Most of these heroes are experiencing their second or third long deployment. They are not the ones who went to Iraq or Afghanistan, but the ones who stayed behind. These are the heroes that said good-bye to their husbands once and, eight months after they returned, said good-bye again. They did not even bother to take the yellow ribbons off the trees.

Who are these women who face life with such courage and have their lives presently defined by waiting? They are your daughters, your sisters, your girlfriends with whom you went to high school or college. They are women whose emotions stay right at the surface. Yet they are women who function anyway. Each woman is characterized by the hope she has in her husband's safe return and the fear she fights in his being called away again.

I listened to their wisdom as they shared the things this war has taught them. I watched them serve one another in the spirit of true community. I heard them as they honestly spoke of their fears and frustrations. I watched as they prayed for one another and as they opened their minds and hearts to the refreshment of God's Word. I saw them care for their children with the constant prayer that they wouldn't do anything to "mess them up" while Dad was away. Oh, and I heard them laugh! It was cleansing laughter that bound our hearts even closer.

In his book *Heroes among Us*, Jim Ryun writes, "Is one born a hero, or are heroes made? I cannot help but think that one becomes a hero through consistently making small decisions that build one upon the other, fortifying one's character through a lifetime of right choices."[1]

I commend military spouses who are making right choices during a season of deployment. They are looking to God as their refuge and strength, their ever-present help in the time of trouble. They are looking to each other to build each other up and encourage each other. They are looking at creative ways to serve others.

I am better for being with them. I am proud to be a military wife alongside them. They truly are heroes on the home front.   ➳*Brenda*

✳   ✳   ✳

Father, thank you for the sustaining power you provide in times of need. Thank you for the example of faith and courage exemplified in military spouses in difficult times. I pray you would be all they need as they wait for their own military hero to return. In Jesus' name I pray. ✛ *Amen.*

---

[1] Jim Ryun, *Heroes Among Us: Deep within Each of Us Dwells the Heart of a Hero* (Shippensburg, PA: Treasure House, 2002).

Are You a Hero?

All these people earned a good reputation because of their faith, yet none of them received all that God had promised. ✝ HEBREWS 11:39

Hebrews is the book of heroes in the Bible. The lives of heroes are honored as their actions are recorded for the ages. Who would you say is your hero?

If you are a Christian, you might say Jesus Christ is your hero. A child might mention Spiderman or Underdog or whoever is on the scene at the time. Some may even say their spouse is their hero.

I've been thinking about all the wonderful people in my life who encouraged me and had a large part in forming me into the person I am today. I remember my first hero was my second-grade teacher. She knew my love of singing and set a time for me to sing onstage in front of the entire elementary school. Although I attended a public school at that time, she chose the song "Precious Lord, Take My Hand." Because she believed in me and told me that I could do it, I haven't quit singing since. She instilled in me a confidence and a love of performing and sharing music that I could not have learned from a textbook. She was a hero to me.

Then there was Mrs. Green, a third-grade teacher I worked with as a teacher's aide. I learned the patience of Job from her as she came in with such an excitement for teaching and unbelievable compassion for the children who walked through the door each day. She was a hero to me.

I think of the role models my parents were in giving an example of what it looks like to have a successful marriage. I remember the times they would encourage me to follow my husband to each assignment even when they were not easy assignments. I remember when they would give me support when I needed it but stay away when I was fine. They were heroes to me.

We have many heroes to look to today. They are our neighbors and our friends. They are in the schools and universities. They are on the battlefield of Iraq and here on our own soil. They are in the middle of the ghetto and on the outskirts of the suburbs. There are heroes all around us.

Our world has hope because of those who would choose to stand and be examples of faith and compassion. What makes a hero to you?

Are you someone's hero?   ⁓*Carol*

✳   ✳   ✳

Father God, strengthen those who would stand to be someone's hero and lead by their examples in our world today. Thank you for the heroes serving in our military. Strengthen them—and us—to be the kind of people you call us to be. ✝ *Amen.*

May 22
Share the Load

Then Jesus said, "Come to me, all of you who are weary and carry heavy burdens, and I will give you rest. Take my yoke upon you. Let me teach you, because I am humble and gentle at heart, and you will find rest for your souls. For my yoke is easy to bear, and the burden I give you is light." ✛ MATTHEW 11:28-30

This Scripture is applicable to many organizations around the world. The military member is bonded with his unit in sharing the burdens and the hardships of war. I have watched it play out many times. Recently I was watching a popular talk show that reunited many soldiers with their families for the first time since their deployments. It was very emotional. The host brought up on the screen several of those from their unit who had been wounded while serving in Iraq. The highlight of the show was the surprise of those on the screen actually being brought out on the stage. Each soldier who had been reunited with family immediately left spouse, mother, or children and ran to embrace those wounded soldiers. It was so moving to me as I watched the bond of sharing the burdens. The gratitude for the sacrifice of those wounded was evident.

I also remember watching the stories of firefighters after 9/11 and seeing how they supported each other through the chaos and heartache afterward. The stories of heroism and leadership were numerous. That was a time in which we could be so proud of the American spirit and the desire to share the burdens during great sadness and despair.

Many deployed soldiers are of the opinion that unless they come home with the whole unit, they are not coming home. They are sharing the load with incredible commitment and honor. We have also watched this as the honor guard has escorted those home who have not come home alive. They never leave their side.

What does Jesus say about sharing the burdens of life? He says that when we come to him and give him our burdens and take his yoke, we will find rest not only in our physical lives but in our souls. He says that his yoke is a perfect fit for us and that the burden will be light when we share it with him.

As you share the load of burdens with others, take up his yoke. He will give you rest. ⨳*Carol*

✷   ✷   ✷

Father, I pray for those who are home alone or being a single parent during deployment. I pray for those who are in the middle of the battle in faraway lands. Help the people of our nation to share the load by reaching out to them. Teach us all to bear one another's burdens in the name of our Lord. ✛ *Amen.*

An Elite Force

The army consisted of 307,500 men, all elite troops. They were prepared to assist the king against any enemy. ✛ 2 CHRONICLES 26:13

My first clue that something was amiss was arriving home after breakfast with a friend to find my answering machine blinking frantically. The official military-sounding voice communicating the first message caused my stomach to tie in knots: "I was just calling concerning the shooting. . . . Your husband is okay. . . . If you have questions, please call . . ." The words *shooting* and *your husband* in the same sentence were disconcerting. The next message was my husband's mother calling from another state. With concern in her voice she said, "I have felt like something is not right today. I'm calling to just check on you all—is everything okay over there?" The final message was my husband saying in a strained voice, "I guess you've heard what happened—I need you to get to the hospital as soon as possible."

Actually, I had no idea what any of this was about, but I got in my car and drove to the military-post hospital, battling fear all the way. My husband met me with a concerned look to match his voice from earlier. He explained that a disgruntled soldier opened fire on the brigade PT (physical training) formation. One officer in the brigade was killed, another officer was seriously injured, and nineteen other soldiers were shot. My husband was fifty feet away from the man who was killed. It would have been too easy for it to have been him. If not for some SF (Special Forces) soldiers, it most likely would have been. If not for the SF heroes, more would have been shot.

Reflecting on this experience, my husband says it seems like a bad movie playing in his mind. I can't comprehend that it really happened. Our nation was not at war at this time. Things like this were not supposed to happen. I thanked God for the prepared soldiers who were able to arrive on the scene and put a quick end to the chaos.

There were elite soldiers in the days of the Old Testament as proved by today's Scripture. The common link that binds them with today's elite ranks is intense preparation and organization. As Christ followers, we enter a spiritual battle every day. Snipers, often within our own ranks, will seek to destroy any spiritual ground we've gained. Be prepared to fight as one of God's elite soldiers. Continue to train each day by the study of his Word and communication through prayer. ❧*Brenda*

* * *

Mighty Warrior, I thank you for calling me to be a member of your spiritual army. Help me to arm myself for the battles that come each day. May I be prepared and ready to fight whatever comes my way through the power of your Spirit. ✛ *Amen.*

May 24
Day Is Done

For all who have entered into God's rest have rested from their labors, just as God did after creating the world. So let us do our best to enter that rest. + HEBREWS 4:10-11

The bugle call known as "Taps" is played for funerals, wreath laying ceremonies, and memorial services for the United States military. There are several different stories claiming the origin of the tune, but there is agreement about its purpose. It is a bugle call used as the last call of the day, and it serves as a summons to cease activity and extinguish lights. As residents of a military post, our family would hear the bugle play Taps at the close of each evening.

This summer I attended a traditional Marine "Sunset Parade" at the Iwo Jima Memorial. This tribute has been taking place since 1956 to honor those whose "uncommon valor was a common virtue," at the site of the United States Marine Corps War Memorial. It was an impressive ceremony with a band concert and demonstration of the marines' precision-rifle drills. The final presentation of the evening was most memorable to me. The parade concluded with a lone bugler who stood atop the memorial, playing Taps in memory of all the marines who died at Iwo Jima. As the clear tones filled the still sky, I was moved by the tribute symbolized by this haunting tune.

Taps is played at every funeral for a fallen soldier. As the notes are executed, soldiers stand at attention and render salute in honor of fallen comrades. As great as the honor we render here when these brave souls depart from this earth is, it pales in comparison to the honor God gives those who have put their faith in Christ. He welcomes those into the entry of heaven with the words, "Well done, my good and faithful servant" (Matthew 25:23).

At the end of today, take comfort in these popular verses set to Taps.[1]

> *Day is done. Gone the sun,*
> *From the lake, from the hill, from the sky.*
> *All is well, safely rest,*
> *God is nigh.*
>
> *Thanks and praise, for our days*
> *'Neath the sun, 'neath the stars, 'neath the sky.*
> *As we go, this we know:*
> *God is nigh.*

≈Brenda

✫   ✫   ✫

Dear Father, thank you for the rest you have prepared for your children. Thank you for your nearness. Help me to live today with thanks and praise in my heart and on my lips. I thank you for soldiers who have sacrificed their lives and have entered into their final rest. + *Amen.*

---

[1] There are no official words to Taps. Popular words have been created through the years. The words listed here are among the most popular.

Remember Them

Remember the days of old; consider the generations long past. Ask your father and he will tell you, your elders, and they will explain to you. ✛ DEUTERONOMY 32:7, NIV

Each year on Memorial Day, individual American flags are planted in front of each gravestone for soldiers laid to rest at Arlington National Cemetery. During the years my husband has been assigned to the Pentagon, he has had the opportunity to volunteer, along with many others, to place the flags at each headstone. He observed that when you look at the cemetery as a whole, you are overwhelmed by the number of white tombstones that dot the hillsides. But on the day he placed flags, he took time to read the name on each honored soldier's grave. He noticed the age they died and the war in which they served. For him, this experience became more than an expression of gratitude for the many who had given their lives. He made it a personal thanksgiving to each soldier.

Remembering is an important concept in Scripture. We are encouraged to remember both good and bad things of life. We are told to remember so we won't forget. Remembering keeps us from losing touch with those who have experienced pain caused by war. The headstones at Arlington and other national cemeteries around the country are reminders of lives lived with honor and sacrifice.

Memorial Day is a day of remembrance for our nation. General John Logan is credited with instituting a day of national remembrance for casualties of war. His words ring as true today as they did in 1868: "Let no vandalism of avarice or neglect, no ravages of time testify to the present or to the coming generations that we have forgotten as a people the cost of a free and undivided republic."[1]

As we read or hear of the numbers of military personnel lost during a particular war, remember these soldiers are not just a statistic. Each one had a name and a hometown. Each one was a son, daughter, mother, father, or friend.

If you have lost a loved one in a war, know that we have not forgotten. The sacrifice of those who have died in service is remembered by a grateful nation.   ❧*Brenda*

✫   ✫   ✫

Gracious Father, thank you for the lessons of remembrance throughout your Word. Help me to remember the sacrifices made for the cause of freedom. It is uncomfortable to think about war, and it is easy to forget that sacrifices are being made by individuals and families. I'm sorry for my complacency and my own desire to distance myself from events that are shaping history. Comfort families who have experienced the loss of a loved one because of war. I look forward to the day when there is an end to conflict on this earth. In Jesus' name I pray. ✛*Amen.*

---

[1] "General John A. Logan's Memorial Day Order," Harrisburg, PA: Sons of Union Veterans of the Civil War. http://www.suvcw.org/logan.htm.

May 26
Rewards to Come

Watch out that you do not lose what we have worked so hard to achieve. Be diligent so that you receive your full reward. **+** 2 JOHN 1:8

Medals are a tangible reward for a job well done. Recent stories of medals awarded to those who have performed heroic feats in battle can bring a lump to the throat and a tear to the eye. If you attend a military honors ceremony for those who have given the ultimate sacrifice, you will witness something very special indeed. The ceremony is moving and meaningful with reminders of appreciation from a grateful nation.

Scripture tells us that as members of God's family, we can look forward to the awards to come. They are going to be so much better than anything we can receive here on earth! They are eternal. Too often, that doesn't feel like enough, does it? We want the shiny medals for our job well done.

Recently, I received a call from a good friend and fellow military wife. As I picked up the phone to say hello, she said, "Hey, guess what? I just received a medal!" My friend had been honored with the "Civilian Service Medal" at a ceremony for her contributions as a military spouse to her community. We giggled for five minutes as we celebrated this tangible piece of appreciation. We were very aware that it is usually the active-duty spouse who receives the medals. It was a precious moment for both of us.

A short time ago, I gathered all my husband's awards and medals together in a display case to pass along to our sons and their families. These awards tell a great story of sacrifice, determination, and hard work. I am proud of the accomplishments these metal pieces represent, but I want them to remind me of the heavenly rewards that are to come. Those rewards will be a result of the service I offer as an overflow of my love for the Lord here on earth.   *⋞Carol*

✯   ✯   ✯

Lord, I come to you today to lay my desire for earthly rewards before you. Any recognition here on earth is nothing compared to the thought of the eternal reward that is to come. Help me to be thankful for, but not proud of, earthly rewards as I look forward to the promise of eternity with you in heaven. Protect those servicemen and women today who are doing heroic things for the cause of liberty. In Jesus' name I pray. **+** *Amen.*

Pass It On

Stand up in the presence of the elderly, and show respect for the aged. Fear your God. I am the LORD. ✛ LEVITICUS 19:32

The military is a very young culture. Upon entering the military as a young wife, I was excited to always have young couples around us who all had similar interests. It was a fun time filled with activity and functions to attend.

When my husband and I started our family, I began to realize how I missed having older people around me. My first son was born while we were stationed in Germany. Not only did we not have grandparents close by, but there were no opportunities for anyone to give me a break because all of my friends were also starting their families. We had all gotten married together, played together, and now were having children together.

We moved to Fort Rucker, Alabama, when the boys were school age. We lived in a house on a lake in the country. It was our first home off a military post, and it took some getting used to. One thing I began to notice was the presence of more mature, grandparent-type people around us.

I would visit my dear mature friends with the boys at least once a week. One of the grandfather figures would take them out to the lake as he cleaned it out and then restocked it with fish. A grandmotherly woman would take them to her garden to show them how to plant this vegetable or that flower. Often we would take some tea or Kool-Aid and just go over and visit, enjoying the stories they would share of when they had been the boys' ages.

Psalm 78:6-8 reflects the importance of passing down our faith in God from generation to generation. It says, "So the next generation might know them—even the children not yet born— and they in turn will teach their own children. So each generation should set its hope anew on God, not forgetting his glorious miracles and obeying his commands. Then they will not be like their ancestors—stubborn, rebellious, and unfaithful, refusing to give their hearts to God."

Age is something to value. Take time to appreciate older individuals in your life. Find an opportunity to get to know them and honor their years of experience.
⟡*Carol*

✭　✭　✭

Heavenly Father, help me to never forget those who have served in the military to defend our country. May their legacy of endurance and overcoming hardship be appreciated by this generation. ✛ *Amen.*

May 28
You Have No Idea What I Am Going Through

He commanded our ancestors to teach them to their children, so the next generation might know them. ✝ PSALM 78:5-6

Recently I had the honor of attending a meeting of Huntsville's Culture Club, an organization that has much history and generational influence. I was there to talk about a devotional book that I had coauthored. Many of the women in the room were retired military wives. I found myself referring to the unknowns of our current situation and the trials and struggles our young military wives are going through. I finished the brief presentation and asked if there were any questions or comments.

The women began to share with me how their lives had been as military wives. When their husbands went to war, there was no confirmation that they had arrived where they were going. There were weeks, months, and in some cases, years before they would hear from them. Many of our spouses today have the blessing of talking once a day to their loved ones, and of course, e-mail is such a blessing during deployment.

After this event with the Culture Club, I realized that I had been so caught up in the current situation that I had never even thanked my dad, who served his country in World War II. I drove to his house and said, "Dad, I want to thank you for something." I got on my knees in front of him and looked into his eyes. I said, "I have been so preoccupied with all that is going on in the world that I have never thanked you for serving our country. I love you for the sacrifice that you gave, and I love you for being a part of what America is today."

It was a moment I will never forget. About six months later, my dad passed away. I will always be grateful to those who reminded me that, yes, others do know what we are going through. Each conflict is different. The age of technology has most certainly changed everything. But we must never forget that there is a generation of those who have gone before us and set the stage for honor, integrity, and sacrifice that is carried on in our military today. ~Carol

★ ★ ★

Father, help me to be thankful for those who have gone before me, in faith or in battle. I ask you to bless them and allow them to feel the honor they deserve. Give me a heart of gratitude, and show me ways to respect, honor, and bless those valuable elders around me. ✝ Amen.

Today's Esther

When it was Esther's turn to go to the king, . . . she asked for nothing except what [the eunuch] suggested, and she was admired by everyone who saw her. ✦ ESTHER 2:15

She comes to the newcomers' coffee wondering what to expect from such a gathering with other wives. She walks in with her perky, short haircut and a butterfly tattoo on her ankle. She has just turned nineteen. She has followed the young man she loves to a place she has never been, only to find out he will be deployed in a few short weeks. She is hoping to find some semblance of understanding from others around her in similar situations. Is she prepared for this challenge? This is today's military wife.

She has just volunteered for her third community activity at the installation. She has gathered her thoughts and her facts together for this important meeting. She walks in with certainty and experience that will bring much to the table for this organization. She wants to reach out to assist the young wives. This is today's military wife.

She just found out she is on the list for a promotion at work. She is thrilled to call her husband and let him know. She dials the number, but he is not in the office. She decides to tell him when he gets home. When she enters the house, he is standing before her with papers in his hand. He tells her that he received unexpected orders, and they will be moving in three months. She puts her arms around him, knowing this is the life they have chosen. This is today's military wife.

She finds herself getting the children ready for bed. She gathers them together to read the last book for the night. "When is Daddy coming home?" She fights the emotion rising within her even though the question is asked frequently. She tells her children, "He will be home soon. Tonight we need to remember to pray for him because he misses you very much." This is today's military wife.

Esther grew into her role as queen and spokeswoman for her people. She came from humble beginnings but found herself in challenging circumstances. Scripture says that God brought her to that situation for that time in history. When the time came, she was prepared to fulfill her calling. There's no cookie-cutter or standard-issue military wife. She comes in all shapes and sizes, and represents all walks of life. If you know a military wife today, take time to tell her how very special and wonderful she is. She, too, is serving our country. She is our Esther today, "called for such a time as this." ✐*Carol*

✱   ✱   ✱

Father, thank you for these women of courage, fortitude, and compassion. As they are left behind and required to take on many roles, please surround them with people who will remind them of the amazing part they play in our military today. ✦*Amen.*

Pick Up a Stone

So Joshua called together the twelve men he had chosen—one from each of the tribes of Israel. He told them, "Go into the middle of the Jordan, in front of the Ark of the Lord your God. Each of you must pick up one stone and carry it out on your shoulder—twelve stones in all, one for each of the twelve tribes of Israel. We will use these stones to build a memorial. In the future your children will ask you, 'What do these stones mean?'" ✝ JOSHUA 4:4-6

Can you imagine the thoughts going on in the minds of the children of Israel as they crossed to the other side of the dry Jordan River? This was God's second time to dry up a body of water, and I can imagine that it was still something that could take your breath away.

The Lord wanted the people to remember this one. He told Joshua to have them go out and gather stones for a memorial. He wanted a constant reminder that God had once again protected his covenant and his people.

Have you picked up any stones lately? Do you have reminders that take you back to when God brought you through times of trials?

Not too long ago, one of our team-teaching couples taught a Sunday school class. They brought stones from a river close to their home and Magic Markers. They asked us to write on those stones a time that God had brought a victorious end to a tough time. They asked us to place the stones where we would be reminded of those times. I placed both of our stones in our flower garden. As we walk into our home every day, we see them often and stop to read them. I have had others ask what they are, and I am able to tell them why I have them there.

In the past few years, there have been many times to recall how God has brought us as a nation through great sorrow and hopelessness. We need to pick up a stone and remind ourselves that God is still in charge, and will forever be our memorial of hope and love and good both in our land and throughout the world.   ⊱*Carol*

⋆   ⋆   ⋆

Father God, help us to pass on to generations the message of your faithfulness and presence. Keep the victories at the forefront of the hearts and minds of our military families today so they may be encouraged. ✝ *Amen.*

Exercising Faith

But those who trust in the LORD will find new strength. They will soar high on wings like eagles. They will run and not grow weary. They will walk and not faint. ✢ ISAIAH 40:31

> I feel so discouraged! I have been running one to three miles several times a week. I've been able to do it, and it has felt great. The usual shin splints seem to be a thing of the past. Then yesterday I decided to run a different three-mile route. There were several small hills, but I was sure I could manage them. I was wrong. My body was not prepared for the differences. I am in great pain. To run just a short distance this morning has caused such discomfort. I'm disappointed. I thought I was beyond this kind of setback.

These words from an old journal prompted some painful memories. On several occasions in my life, I have put forth an effort to be a runner. I've wanted to enjoy it. I've wanted the endorphins to kick in so I could experience runner's high. You can ask my husband and my friends; I've given it a good shot!

My friend Shellie is a runner who patiently tried to run with me. Shellie has come up with amazing spiritual analogies about running and has shared incredible spiritual insight that came while jogging. She also wears a size two—but, more than I envy her size, I admire her discipline.

I have come to the conclusion that some people are natural-born runners. A further conclusion is that I am not one of those people. My body just doesn't seem to work that way. My husband says, however, that I am a great walker. Even though my legs are shorter, I can walk faster than him.

So this is my spiritual analogy for running: the key to spiritual fulfillment is not trying to be like someone else, but being content with the gifts and abilities God has given me, and exercising those things to the best of my ability. I still have to exercise all of the disciplines to walk. I must be willing to do the proper stretches and training that lead to victory and not make excuses as to why I can't go faster, longer, or get out and walk at all. I may not be able to run and not grow weary, but with the Lord's help, I'm going to walk and not faint. The main thing to remember is that I must exercise my faith. ❧*Brenda*

✶ ✶ ✶

LORD, you are the everlasting God, the Creator of all the earth. You never grow weak or weary. No one can measure the depths of your understanding. You give power to the weak and strength to the powerless (Isaiah 40:28-29, paraphrased). ✢ *Amen.*

June 1
With Jesus

So now there is no condemnation for those who belong to Christ Jesus. + ROMANS 8:1

In the *NLT Life Application Study Bible*, the footnote for this verse reminds us that the whole human race is on death row, justly condemned for repeatedly breaking God's holy law. Without Jesus, we would have no hope at all. But thank God! He has declared us not guilty and has offered us freedom from sin and power to do his will.

"Without Jesus" is the key to this explanation. There are so many times in my life when I remember things that have not been pleasing to the Lord. I begin to feel less like a Christian and begin to doubt that I can ever make a significant difference for the Lord on this earth. That would be without Jesus.

With Jesus there is no condemnation. He has separated my sins as far as the east is from the west. We are covered with the blood that Jesus shed on the cross for us. I belong to him. John 3:17-18 tells me that God did not send his Son into the world to condemn it, but to save it. There is no judgment awaiting those who trust him. But those who do not trust him have already been judged for not believing in the only Son of God.

Whenever I have a sense of worthlessness or even when I cry out to God to ask, "Where is my purpose?" his answer to me is, "With me there is no condemnation."

Why is this an issue we need to grasp? I am always hearing from those who are going through situations in their lives that cause them to feel discouraged, depressed, and disheartened. The enemy of our souls comes after us with a vengeance when we begin to speak about those areas in our lives. How do I know that? I have been there, done that.

We can find safety, comfort, and resolve in knowing that God has promised that when we receive Jesus' sacrifice on our behalf, we are not under condemnation. The times of difficulties will come our way, but there is a way out. Stay on your face before the Lord; he will answer your cry to him and release you from the feelings of insignificance and unworthiness.

With Jesus I can accomplish on this earth what God created me to do. ⋖*Carol*

* * *

Father God, you are my self-esteem. Having Jesus in my life gives me a sense of who I am and who I can be. In the times of loneliness and depression that come with deployment, I thank you for always being there for these families. Encourage those in the Christian community to reach out and be your hand of love and support to them. + *Amen.*

As God Protected Rahab

Before the spies went to sleep that night, Rahab went up on the roof to talk with them. "I know the LORD has given you this land," she told them. "We are all afraid of you. Everyone in the land is living in terror. . . . Now swear to me by the LORD that you will be kind to me and my family since I have helped you. Give me some guarantee." ✛ JOSHUA 2:8-9, 12

The fear of the Lord is often talked about in Christian circles. We are to stand in awe of him. It is a respectful fear, not a frightening fear. He is the almighty God.

Rahab understood the fear of God. She knew that God would protect her and her family if she would help these men who were sent to Jericho from Israel. She protected these men and allowed them to escape unharmed. They told her she must keep all her family within her quarters and put a scarlet cord in the window, so they would not mistake where she was upon their return.

This story is such a visual for me. I am a hands-on learner. I have to have things explained to me on paper or in story form. This story reminds me in pictures of many things in my life.

> Honor and fear the Lord.
> Be willing to stand up and fight for what I know to be right.
> Protect those in my family from the enemy by covering them daily with
> the scarlet cord, which I see as the blood of Jesus.

God will protect and save us from the enemy, but we have to step forward and be strong and courageous enough to grab hold of his plan for our lives. We need to step forward as Rahab did and take that promise of protection for our families. Rahab was willing to risk her life and stand courageously to face the enemy. We must take on that same posture in our world.

I often make the comment to others that I cannot understand how things got so out of control and so out of God's will so quickly. I am sure, had there been more Rahabs willing to stand strong and to protect their families, we might not be in the turmoil we are in today. ↝*Carol*

★　★　★

Father, help me to step out in faith, in fear, and in awe of your power in my life. I pray that as so many families need your protection in the current world crisis, there will be those who step forward to ask your covering on their lives. ✛ *Amen.*

June 3
Touch His Garment

For she thought, "If I can just touch his robe, I will be healed." + MATTHEW 9:21

Preparing to leave a military assignment in Germany was difficult enough. Having to leave my husband behind two months early was even more difficult. I was pregnant with our second son and could not fly after a certain time. I was preparing to head back to America with a two-year-old. My husband's tour of duty would not be completed until six weeks later. We had extended our tour for two years, and though we were in a foreign land, it had become our home.

I began feeling a bit of a pinch and shooting pain down my leg. I thought it was probably because I had been on my feet so much during that seventh month while preparing to move. The ten-hour plane ride was very restricting, and as we walked off the plane to meet my parents, the pain felt sharper than before. Our oldest son would not let me put him down to walk, and I had many men asking if they could carry him as they viewed the bulging belly in front of me. I am sure that carrying yet more weight on my already full front side did not help my physical condition.

Exactly two months later, after I was joined by my husband, our second son was born. When I came home from the hospital, I was bedridden most of the time. The condition that was causing me so much pain was a pinched sciatic nerve. My in-laws and parents came to help out because my husband was in a training school.

I remember lying in bed with tears rolling down my cheeks, saying, "Jesus, if I can just touch the hem of your garment and be healed." I could visualize the woman sneaking up behind him in the crowd and finding just a small part of his robe. She knew that anything that had to do with Jesus was enough for her to be healed. That's how I felt.

There is so much emotional healing that needs to take place in lives today. The recent tragedies on our own soil have given us a renewed sense of instability and fear.

When Jesus felt the woman touch him, the Scripture tells us his reaction: "Jesus turned around, and when he saw her he said, Daughter, be encouraged! Your faith has made you well.' And the woman was healed at that moment" (Matthew 9:22).

Reach out to touch his garment. When your emotions have taken you to a place that needs restoring or when your spiritual life is challenged, reach out to touch the One who wants to send to you the power of his healing in your life. ~Carol

* * *

Father, the world is hurting. Families who have lost loved ones or who are separated at this time are hurting. Help them to reach out and touch your garment during these times, believing for victory, protection, and healing to come. + Amen.

Batman

"Do not be afraid of them," the LORD said to Joshua, "for I have given you victory over them. Not a single one of them will be able to stand up to you." ✝ JOSHUA 10:8

One morning, I woke up to my husband jerking and flailing his arms. For several days he had endured a low-grade headache. Waking up from a sound sleep at 5 a.m., I immediately thought he was having a seizure. In actuality, a bat was flying around in our bedroom! I don't know which frightened me more! He began shouting, "A bat! A bat!" to which I responded by sticking my head under the covers until my husband shooed the intruder out the front door.

I don't know about you, but I have a fear of bats. I'm sure it has been nurtured by popular stories about the creatures. I've listened to the nature talks on why bats are our friends, but I'm not convinced. I would venture to say even those who like bats would not want them flying in their bedrooms. Having a bat in my home made me a little afraid as I thought about the possibility of being bitten by it, wondered how it entered the house, and imagined it returning with its friends.

Fear is a multifaceted emotion. For instance, someone going to war may experience the fear of being wounded, fear of being killed, fear of friends being wounded or killed, fear of losing a battle, fear of getting lost, or a fear of being captured. As a parent, I have experienced fears of what could happen to my children, fears for their safety, fears for their relationships, and fears for their choices in life. The bottom line: fear is not a simple thing.

In today's Scripture, God once again is encouraging Joshua not to be afraid. Joshua is leading the nation of Israel into an unknown land, where he will face many different enemies on unfamiliar terrain. It's possible that many different fears ran through his mind, all of them ending in catastrophic defeat. God did not reason with him through every possible fear but simply encouraged Joshua to trust in the victory that God promised he would give over all his enemies.

As Christians, we, too, have an encouragement and a promise from Jesus concerning all that we would face in this world. He simply says, "In the world you have tribulation, but take courage; I have overcome the world" (John 16:33, NASB). ✍*Brenda*

✦ ✦ ✦

Overcoming Lord, thank you for the promise of your courage in my times of fear. Help me not to be paralyzed by fear but instead trust your instructions to fear not. I pray for military spouses who are experiencing fear caused by deployment. In your name I pray. ✝ *Amen.*

June 5
Watching over Me

I look up to the mountains— does my help come from there? My help comes from the LORD, who made heaven and earth! He will not let you stumble; the one who watches over you will not slumber. Indeed, he who watches over Israel never slumbers or sleeps. The LORD himself watches over you! + PSALM 121:1-5

In times of trouble, I have stood on this promise from Psalm 121:1. I have been further comforted by what is written later in the chapter. Psalm 121:5-8 states, "The LORD stands beside you as your protective shade. The sun will not harm you by day, nor the moon at night. The LORD keeps you from all harm and watches over your life. The LORD keeps watch over you as you come and go, both now and forever." The Bible declares that God's eyes are on me.

The use of the word *keep* in this passage depicts the image of a shepherd watching and caring for sheep that cost him a great deal, or a king keeping treasures that were left to him as part of his royal inheritance. The Lord provides a hedge of protection for us, and his eyes of compassion never tire of watching over his children. His gaze of grace is on us all through the day and night.

During times of crisis when there is no visible means of help, I encourage you to look into God's eyes and see the One who truly loves you. He will help you stand firm because the foundation he provides cannot be moved or shaken.   *Brenda*

*   *   *

My helper, I look to you today for the courage to stand firm. You are my keeper and my protector. I trust that you are with me when I am afraid. Open my eyes to see that you are present. Make my footing firm and strong on your trustworthy foundation. Grant your courage to soldiers and their families who may be experiencing fear as a result of deployment. In your name I pray. + *Amen.*

Bitter Fruit

Now I will sing for the one I love a song about his vineyard: My beloved had a vineyard on a rich and fertile hill. He plowed the land, cleared its stones, and planted it with the best vines. In the middle he built a watchtower and carved a winepress in the nearby rocks. Then he waited for a harvest of sweet grapes, but the grapes that grew were bitter. ✛ ISAIAH 5.1-2

Isaiah wrote of God protecting the nation of Israel. God, through Isaiah, described them as a vineyard he had planted, and then he waited with expectation to enjoy a harvest of good fruit. He provided everything they needed to grow spiritually, yet they did not grow. As a people, they were like bitter fruit, unprofitable and offensive.

This story reminds me of the backyard of one of my childhood homes. There were several orange trees with beautiful fruit growing bountifully. When our family moved into the house, we were eager to enjoy freshly squeezed orange juice from our own trees. We picked the most luscious oranges we could find and brought them in to juice. The juice was quite pale in color, but we thought it must be a special species— hopefully, one that would be extra sweet. We all took a drink of the juice, and we scowled in unison as we tasted the bitter liquid. Our disappointment was great when we realized our trees were a variety that produced only ornamental fruit!

My family did not know the difference between a real orange tree and an ornamental orange tree. When we look at people, it is sometimes difficult to discern a true Christian from an ornamental Christian. Some people have the appearance of being believers; they attend church and claim to be Christians, but their hearts are sour. But God knows the difference between real Christ followers and those who are not.

To help us to be the spiritually fruitful people God intends us to be, he has given us his Word, preachers, teachers, and the body of Christ to cultivate Christlike characteristics. Our calling is to allow God to transform our lives through obedience and commitment. This will result in bearing sweet fruit that is pleasing to God.
❧*Brenda*

✫   ✫   ✫

Lord, thank you for the Good News that came to me and is going out all over the world. May it continue to bear fruit everywhere by changing lives, just as it changed my life from the day I first heard and understood the truth about God's wonderful grace (Colossians 1:6, paraphrased). ✛ *Amen.*

June 7
Here We Go Again

Go and walk through the land in every direction, for I am giving it to you. ✝ GENESIS 13:17

My husband and I have been married for over thirty years. We went through the dating and breaking-up years in high school and college. We committed to marriage during my senior year of college. We have traveled the world, been blessed with two sons we love deeply, dedicated our lives to Christ as a couple about ten years after we were married, and up to this point, have moved fourteen times since our wedding day.

We are at the point in our lives where we have a great desire to be close to family. We love opening our home for having family gatherings. My husband has become the one who calls our sons, sometimes twice a day. He has a great desire to be able to pick up the phone and say, "Let's go fishing today" or, "Let's go play golf." It's a guy thing, and I love that they are so close and enjoy being together as much as they do.

Wherever the military took us during my husband's active-duty days, we always met those in our community who had never left the state they lived in and often had not even left the town they'd grown up in. They were always so envious of our travels, but I often found myself being so envious of their opportunities to stay in the same place their entire lives.

The older I get, the more I understand that God knows who can do what in their lives from the beginning of time. Although my husband and I were brought up in the same hometown all our lives, we have been able to take on the lifestyle of travel and moving with great ease most of the time. We always wonder, *What does God have in store this time?*

As young men and women in the military are moved constantly during deployment, they often ask, "God, what do you have in store for me during this time?" If they come to your community, love on them. Take time to get to know them and bless them.

As life takes me through different twists and turns, I want to continue to praise God. I want to say, "Here we go again, Lord." We will take a walk in every direction and explore the new possession he will be giving us.   ❧*Carol*

✶   ✶   ✶

Father, thank you for new beginnings and times of transition led by your hand. Let us never forget you are in charge of all the transitions in our lives. I ask that those I know in our country's military service may know your peace in the midst of their many transitions. ✝ *Amen.*

A Different View

So we have stopped evaluating others from a human point of view. At one time we thought of Christ merely from a human point of view. How differently we know him now!

✝ 2 CORINTHIANS 5:16

Have you ever noticed how your attitude about things can change just by the physical view you have? For instance, one day I decided to sit and have my morning devotions at the desk in our living room rather than in my office. The desk is a French-style letter-writing desk handmade by my husband's uncle and given to us as a wedding present. It is lovely, and I use it more for décor than practicality. I sat at the desk and wondered why I had never used the wonderful space. The light was bright, the desk was not overwhelmed with piles, and the computer was not there to tempt me. It sat by a window, so I saw people who lived on the street coming out of their houses for their daily routines. I wondered what else I had missed by not taking advantage of this point of view.

When we become Christ followers, our points of view on life changes. Paul wrote to the Corinthians because they were still judging others from their old human view, void of Christian morals and values. He explained to them that as new creations in Christ, their judgments were to be from a new point of view. The old view had passed.

Paul spoke as one who had firsthand experience. Before his commitment to Christ, he had viewed things with a superior attitude. He had been proud of his Jewish heritage and his Roman citizenship. He had disdained all lower things, especially Christ followers. But his eyes had been opened, and he saw things from a different perspective. Christ became more than a teacher; he became the Son of God.

Because of Christ, we no longer view life the way we used to. We now can see people and their needs, the greatest being their need of a Savior. We see Christ as more than a baby in a manger at Christmas; he is the King of kings, sitting on a throne.

How's your point of view today?   ✺*Brenda*

✶   ✶   ✶

Father, thank you for the transforming work of your Spirit in my life. Thank you for coming in and making all things new. There are times when my viewpoint gets distorted, and I revert to judging people and situations from an earthbound standard. Forgive me for looking out the wrong window. Turn my thoughts toward your view of life. I pray for the view people in our nation have towards those serving in the armed services. May it be a view that supports and honors the sacrifice of these brave men and women. ✝ *Amen.*

June 9
Living Quarters

For this world is not our permanent home; we are looking forward to a home yet to come.
✝ HEBREWS 13:14

There are many fond memories I have of our military life as a family traveling around the world. One of the fondest, believe it or not, is our time "in quarters," which in civilian lingo is military housing. I am not sure what I loved the most about this situation. Was it the fact we did not have to worry about the monthly mortgage payments?

We were usually in a duplex and would become attached to the family next door. You could borrow something at a moment's notice, pick up each other's mail, or coordinate your flowers to match in your front beds. Our children could walk out the door and find someone to play with. There was never a lack of fellowship. If you were in the mood to visit, you'd just take your glass of tea and sit down on your front porch steps. Soon someone would be walking up to share the happenings of the day.

What wonderful memories for all of us! I remember my niece asking me as we were moving to a new assignment, "What does your new house look like?" When I told her I didn't have a clue, she was appalled that I could actually head out not knowing where I would live or what it would look like.

As military families, we travel the world knowing that we will have a home, even if we don't know what it looks like or where it will be. As Christians, we know what our heavenly home looks like, and we know that it will be prepared for us upon our arrival.

Recently, my father passed away. I often imagine that God had his heavenly home waiting for him by a heavenly lake with heavenly bass for him to catch. As the song says, "I can only imagine." ✒*Carol*

✦   ✦   ✦

Thank you, Lord, that I have living quarters in heaven awaiting my arrival. Thank you for preparing that place for me right now. Help me to live my life in preparation for my heavenly home. May those in the military have an awareness of their eternal lives to come and so live their present life in your service. ✝ *Amen.*

A Transformed Person

Don't copy the behavior and customs of this world, but let God transform you into a new person by changing the way you think. Then you will learn to know God's will for you, which is good and pleasing and perfect. ✛ ROMANS 12:2

A popular television show follows people who have been nominated by friends or family for a complete makeover. Closets are invaded and evaluations are made about what clothes, hairstyle, and makeup would maximize a person's outward potential. The results are usually amazing. An unattractive and unfashionable individual is transformed into what is described as a beautiful, stylish person. Today's Scripture warns the Christ follower not to just be transformed by following fashion and style. (I don't think it means I can't watch this show and glean fashion tips. My pointy-toed shoes are a dead giveaway!)

There is a recurring message in Scripture that says we can be transformed into a different person. This transformation manifests itself in a manner exactly opposite from the one described above. Marshall Shelly, editor of *Leadership Journal*, states that spiritual transformation "isn't about self-improvement; it's about being made brand new, inside."[1] Authentic spiritual transformation is a change that originates inside of us. This process occurs as our minds are being renewed by God's Word.

We have a choice in the transformation process. Many Christ followers are pretty good at filling their notebooks with sermon notes and teaching points on biblical truths. We often fall short in allowing those truths to impact our lives to bring genuine transformation. We are sometimes like the duck church. Every Sunday, the ducks would waddle to church, where they gathered to worship. Pastor duck would preach with enthusiasm the message, "We can fly!" The duck members would shout, "Amen! We can fly!" The service would end, and all the ducks would waddle back home.

This transformation is not one we can complete ourselves; it is a spiritual work by God. We must choose to cooperate with the Lord and watch him work. Today, meditate on the words of this old hymn as your prayer of transformation. ✺*Brenda*

✷　✷　✷

Jesus, I am resting, resting,
In the joy of what Thou art;
I am finding out the greatness
Of Thy loving heart.
Thou hast bid me gaze upon Thee,
And Thy beauty fills my soul,
For by Thy transforming power
Thou hast made me whole.

~"Jesus, I Am Resting, Resting," Jean S. Pigott

✛ *Amen.*

---

[1] Marshall Shelly, "Transformed, Not Self-Made," *Leadership Journal* (Summer 2005). www.christianitytoday.com

June 11
The Father's Will Be Done

May your Kingdom come soon. May your will be done on earth as it is in heaven.
✝ MATTHEW 6:10

There are many different types of people and personalities in this world. I'm so thankful for that! If everyone were compassionate, we would help ourselves to death. If everyone were driven and motivated to make money and be successful, I am quite sure we would destroy each other.

One of the characteristics of my personality is that I am a self-professed fixer. Do I hear an "Amen" from any of you out there? If there is a problem, I am going to find a solution. If there is a question, I am going to seek the answer.

When I am in a business environment and there is a problem, I am called a problem solver. That can be a great thing. When I am in a family situation and someone is going through a difficult time, I can try to rush that time and fix the problem. During that difficulty, I can also become too involved, so that if I step in each time and fix things, there will never be personal resolution or personal growth. That can be bad, both for the family member and for me.

How many times have we heard someone say, "Why can't God fix this?" Well, the first answer is that he can. The second answer is that we got ourselves into the mess. But he will stand with us in the midst of the situation. He may also choose to let us work it out on our own while depending on him.

I am to follow the example of our Father in heaven. I am to allow him to complete his will in his time, instead of hindering his purposes by fixing the problem through my efforts. Others will be forever changed by depending on the Father in heaven.

I want to remind those of you fixers who can totally relate to me that we have been called to higher ground during this time in history. We have been called to follow God's leading in our lives and to lead others to do the Father's will. It is a time of surrender instead of control. It is a time of prayer instead of deeds. ⁓*Carol*

*   *   *

Dear God, thy will be done on earth as it is in heaven. I pray that you, Lord, will be in the midst of those situations and those conflicts that I cannot control or fix. Father, I pray today for those who have suffered tragedy and even death because so many have turned from depending on your will for their lives. Lead me to do your will in all things! ✝ *Amen.*

Quick Change

So God has given both his promise and his oath. These two things are unchangeable because it is impossible for God to lie. Therefore, we who have fled to him for refuge can have great confidence as we hold to the hope that lies before us. ✛ HEBREWS 6:18

Wandering through a Pennsylvania antique store, I spotted a vintage pillow cover. It was purple satin with gold fringe and the words, "Lay your head upon this pillow, Mother dear, until I return home." I smiled as I thought of the son who had sent this gift to his mother during a war so many years ago. It was probably the only connection this mom had between infrequent letters that took months to arrive from across the ocean. Times have changed, haven't they?

Change is inevitable, and most progress in communication and technology has brought positive advancement. Society today has adapted to increasing rates of change and modernization. Nevertheless, personal transitions still remain a challenge. William Bridges, in his book *Transitions: Making Sense of Life's Changes*, describes the stages of a successful transition. He postulates that each transition has an ending, followed by an empty void, giving way to a new beginning. He emphasizes the importance of saying good-bye to whatever you are leaving behind, so the new beginning can come. He acknowledges that the process of letting go can be painful, but it is important.[1]

As we go through transitions, we can remain anchored in God, who does not change. His promises remain steadfast. Those who have turned to the Lord for protection and eternal sanctuary can have great confidence in facing new beginnings with hope. ⇝*Brenda*

✫　✫　✫

Unchangeable Father, thank you for the stability I have in you. Help me to trust you in the process of the transitions of life. Don't let me hold on to things in the past that are unhealthy and unholy. Give me the courage to say good-bye and to look forward to what is to come. I pray for military families who are moving from one duty station to another this summer. Grant smooth transitions to these people who dedicate their lives to service. In Jesus' name I pray. ✛*Amen.*

---

[1] William Bridges, *Transitions: Making Sense of Life's Changes* (Jackson, TN: Perseus Books, 1980).

June 13
Wedding Day

God will rejoice over you as a bridegroom rejoices over his bride. ✛ ISAIAH 62:5

It's the wedding day! Everything planned is coming together. All the bridesmaids in their altered dresses and the groomsmen in their rented tuxes are close by. The flowers are arranged in the sanctuary. The guests are making the pilgrimage to the church.

The year before was quite a year. The engagement was a bit of a surprise to everyone but the father of the bride. When the groom approached him with the request for his daughter's hand in marriage, there were many questions. After a three-hour session, the father reluctantly gave his blessing. He knew in his heart there would never be a man who could really be good enough for his daughter.

The bride-to-be had begun planning the wedding as soon as she saw the ring on her finger. Yes, she loved this man and wanted to be his wife for a lifetime, but this would be her long-awaited wedding day!

Shortly after the engagement announcement came the showers. Presents began rolling in, and the bride's family began addressing the UPS man on a first-name basis.

And so the wedding day has finally arrived! The groom is standing at the front of the church with the look of expectancy that only a groom can have. The music begins to play, and down the aisle, the bride walks arm in arm with her father, who knows in his heart this will be a wonderful union. The ceremony is very personal as the bride and groom share their thoughts of love with each other.

Those of you who are married: Do you remember that day? I have tears in my eyes remembering how precious those moments were for me. Do you know that God rejoices over you as your spouse did that day of your wedding?

In the same way, the plans you have made through your salvation in Jesus will be celebrated and filled with unimaginable love. Jesus, the bridegroom, patiently and expectantly waits for his bride, and that wedding day will be one to last throughout eternity. ⚖Carol

✱   ✱   ✱

Father God, as your bride awaits the coming of the Bridegroom, I will continue to prepare. I ask for a sense of expectancy with each day. As you have given me the gift of salvation through your Son, Jesus, may I never forget to say thank you or forget who the giver is. ✛ Amen.

A June Bride

The next day there was a wedding celebration in the village of Cana in Galilee. Jesus' mother was there, and Jesus and his disciples were also invited to the celebration. The wine supply ran out during the festivities, so Jesus' mother told him, "They have no more wine." . . . Standing nearby were six stone water jars, used for Jewish ceremonial washing. Each could hold twenty to thirty gallons. Jesus told the servants, "Fill the jars with water." When the jars had been filled, he said, "Now dip some out, and take it to the master of ceremonies." So the servants followed his instructions. When the master of ceremonies tasted the water that was now wine, not knowing where it had come from (though, of course, the servants knew), he called the bridegroom over. "A host always serves the best wine first," he said. "Then, when everyone has had a lot to drink, he brings out the less expensive wine. But you have kept the best until now!" ✛ JOHN 2:1-3, 6-10

The month of June is anniversary month for our family. It's easy to remember to send cards since my parents, my brother, and my husband and I all share the same anniversary date. Our son and his wife were married the day before.

This son's wedding service was rich in tradition and meaning. I was impressed by the pastor as he gathered the wedding party together on the night of the rehearsal and spoke to them about what was going to take place the next day. He challenged them to practice the spiritual discipline of love between that time and the wedding. He told them they were coming to a worship service with a wedding in the midst. If they were Christians, they were to come prepared to worship. If they were not Christians, they were to come prepared to respect the worship. He emphasized the wedding was more than a ceremony. It was a worship experience, and they were going to be acknowledging God and inviting him into the experience.

I have thought about the wisdom of his words for more than the wedding. A wedding is the beginning of a major transition in the lives of two people and their families. In every transition we face, we need to invite God into the experience, especially when it's something that is as life changing and as long reaching as a wedding.

Jesus' first miracle was at a wedding. No one ever expected Jesus to turn water to wine, but his presence at that wedding made a difference. It is a reminder to us that when we bring Christ into our lives, we can do things in his power that we would never expect to do on our own.   *≈Brenda*

✮   ✮   ✮

Miracle-working God, I invite you into the details of this day. Fill it with reminders of your presence as I offer you my worship. Lead your children in the military to a spirit of worshiping you, regardless of their situations or surroundings. ✛ *Amen.*

June 15
Daily Schedule

Don't brag about tomorrow, since you don't know what the day will bring. ✝ PROVERBS 27:1

I don't know about you, but it's all I can do to take one day at a time. If I think about yesterday, I am overwhelmed by the mistakes that were made and how I might have made the day better and more productive. If I think of tomorrow, I am overwhelmed by how I must make plans so as not to waste time the Lord has given me.

One of the ways I try to simplify my life is to have a schedule. I love to order my day the night before. I make a list of the most important things to accomplish and the tasks that I will try to do. I begin my morning by checking the list made the night before, and immediately I am ordered and scheduled. It helps so much not to get caught up in distractions that would deter me from accomplishment.

One of the things I know to be true is that when I have extra time on my hands or allow my day just to happen, I am more susceptible to time-wasting. By that, I mean sitting down to watch TV or spending too much time on the phone or putting off grocery shopping until it is too late in the day. I know that God expects so much more of me. He rewards me along the way with days of visiting with friends or a day of fishing with my husband. Unscheduled days become gifts to me and times of joy. I just know that if I got up every morning and thought, *What can I do today?* I would not be prepared to accomplish much.

Simple scheduling can bless your life. It will also help your family's life. When I've mentored young women, the number one concern they've had was learning how to be better homemakers. I always begin by encouraging them to make a schedule before bed each night. Write an order to your day of making beds, doing dishes, or folding clothes. Even write down times, if necessary, to keep you on track.

We live in a very chaotic world. When we begin to practice order in our homes and stand up to claim them for our families, we will bless those who enter. What can you do to make your home a safe haven for your family? ⁀*Carol*

✳   ✳   ✳

Father, there are many who witness constant conflict each day. Help me to make a plan that will bless my family and glorify you. Thank you for those who are serving our country and seeking to help others make better homes for themselves. ✝ *Amen.*

It's a Heart Thing

And I will give them singleness of heart and put a new spirit within them. I will take away their stony, stubborn heart and give them a tender, responsive heart, so they will obey my decrees and regulations. Then they will truly be my people, and I will be their God. ✛ EZEKIEL 11:19-20

One of the many fascinating things about Scripture is how extensive and complete it is on every subject. One of the most referenced words in the Scripture is *heart*.

> It broke [God's] heart. (Genesis 6:6)
>> Listen to his instructions, and store them in your heart. (Job 22:22)
>> Joyful are those who obey his laws and search for him with all their hearts. (Psalm 119:2)
>> The human heart is the most deceitful of all things, and desperately wicked. (Jeremiah 17:9)
>> Wherever your treasure is, there the desires of your heart will also be (Matthew 6:21).

The heart is the central part of the body. There is just one heartbeat between life and death. If you are a Christian, you are one heartbeat away from spending eternity with the Lord. I have learned through the years as I have dealt with high blood pressure and heartbeat irregularities, that when the heart does not beat correctly, and at the pace God designed for it, the whole body is affected.

Have you ever had your heart broken? God refers to his heart being broken in Genesis. He said he was sorry he created mankind after observing human wickedness developing. Hearts can be broken by relationships, by rebellious children, job loss, death, and divorce, to only name a few. It is as if there is no healing and resolution in these situations. It is often a time of hopelessness and crying out to God for heart healing.

What does God tell us to do? In Jeremiah 33, God instructs us to call upon his name and ask him to reveal what we do not know. He will reveal it to us. God talks about restoration and healing, prosperity and peace. God wants to heal your heart. He wants you to cry out to him for his provision.

There will be many who read this and think there will never be healing. You have lost a loved one in war or in tragedy. You have a wounded warrior who has come home, and you know life is going to be very difficult from this time on. You are still going through a time of transition from the battlefield to the home front.

The God of the universe is a God of restoration and healing. Call out to him, and seek his promise for your life. ↝*Carol*

✷　✷　✷

Father God, how each day brings with it so many challenges. When my heart is broken, give me the courage to call on you. I pray today for grace, that I, along with my brothers and sisters in the military, may serve you in wholeness and strength. ✛ *Amen.*

June 17
Simply Living

And all the believers met together in one place and shared everything they had. They sold their property and possessions and shared the money with those in need. They worshiped together at the Temple each day, met in homes for the Lord's Supper, and shared their meals with great joy and generosity—all the while praising God and enjoying the goodwill of all the people. And each day the Lord added to their fellowship those who were being saved. ✛ ACTS 2:44-47

Peter's sermon in Acts 2:38-40 is simple but powerful. "'Each of you must repent of your sins and turn to God, and be baptized in the name of Jesus Christ for the forgiveness of your sins. Then you will receive the gift of the Holy Spirit. This promise is to you, and to your children, and even to the Gentiles—all who have been called by the Lord our God.' Then Peter continued preaching for a long time, strongly urging all his listeners, 'Save yourselves from this crooked generation!'" What was the response to Peter's sermon? "Those who believed what Peter said were baptized and added to the church that day—about 3,000 in all" (Acts 2:41).

These people were the beginning of the New Testament church. As time went on, they continued in their devotion to Christ. This resulted in their devotion to one another. They shared everything: money, worship, meals, and home. They are described as doing this with great joy and generosity. The New King James Version of the Bible uses the words, "with gladness and simplicity of heart."

God has given us a simple plan of salvation that even a child can comprehend. He has provided a simple model of loving others as we would want to be loved. Living the Christian life the way God intended and the Holy Spirit guides, is not complicated when it comes to loving and serving others. Simple doesn't mean unimportant. When we master the art of New Testament simple living, we find we are doing much more than simply living. ✍*Brenda*

✳ ✳ ✳

Oh Father, give America preachers today like Peter and souls that gladly receive their words. Give us Christ followers who "continue steadfastly" in the faith resulting in life lived with "gladness and simplicity of heart, praising God and having favor with all the people"(Acts 2:46-47, NKJV). Bless those active-duty military personnel who have accepted you as their Savior during their tours of duty. Provide them with godly mentors who will disciple them and help them grow into mature Christians. ✛*Amen.*

Anthill Mentality

Our actions will show we belong to the truth, so we will be confident when we stand before God. ✛ 1 JOHN 3:19

This past summer, several youth clinics were being held for basketball and volleyball at the local community center. Above the gym floor is the community walking track, where I exercise. Every day, the kids would come in with much excitement. The coaches and supervisors would shout above the loud talking and laughing while the children were getting settled down.

As I began my walk for the day, I would find myself walking faster and faster as the noise on the gym floor got louder and louder. Basketballs and volleyballs were bouncing everywhere. The coaches would continually give instruction as the kids continued to learn different methods. During the basketball clinic, the buzzer for the timer kept going off. It seemed every time I got to that corner of the track, the buzzer would sound just below me. I was sure I was losing a couple of decibels in my hearing each time.

While these events were taking place, I would say to the others on the track that I felt as if we were walking over an anthill. I would be so excited to finish each day and walk outside to the peace and quiet.

I imagine God looking down at our lives and thinking that we look like a very active anthill. Yes, we are doing great work. We are learning new things. We are working toward a common goal just as the little ant does. Christians can do many great things and stay very busy. However, I wonder if he is also thinking at the end of our day, *Whew, I am glad that's over.*

God is a God of order. He doesn't want us running around with an anthill mentality. He wants us to be able to work without craziness and without burning ourselves out. He wants us to focus and to work in the talents He blessed us for.

There are two reactions for those who find themselves seeking to serve the Lord. One is to get involved in every activity that comes along. The other is to pray and to seek God's direction in your area of special gifting.

If you are a family member of someone who is deployed at this time, don't think you have to be so busy that you meet yourself coming and going to make the time pass. Allow yourself to work at your pace, and take time for the quiet moments to be alone with your Father, who loves you so much.   ✑*Carol*

✯   ✯   ✯

Heavenly Father, thank you for energy to do good work for you and for your Kingdom. Thank you for the gifts you've given the men and women in my country's service. Fill their hearts and minds with your love and truth, I pray. Calm my spirit, and help me to simply let you minister your peace to my heart. ✛ *Amen.*

June 19
A Little Child

Jesus called a little child to him and put the child among them. Then he said, "I tell you the truth, unless you turn from your sins and become like little children, you will never get into the Kingdom of Heaven." ✛ MATTHEW 18:2-3

Why would Jesus refer to us becoming as little children to get to heaven? We are told in other parts of Scripture that we are to grow up and not drink spiritual milk as a baby does. In this passage, he tells us to turn from sin and have hearts like a child's.

Our world now has many organizations set up to sponsor little children and to provide them with fresh water—and we have soldiers who are caring for them in the midst of their war-torn countries.

One of the men from our church who had been sent to Iraq asked that his wife send packages for the children there. She organized drop boxes with items such as toothpaste, toothbrushes, notebooks, toys, pencils, and Magic Markers; she also collected packages of new underwear and socks. Her husband knew that the children could not defend themselves in their war-torn land and that this touch of kindness would allow them to feel much-needed love and compassion. Often the soldiers will ask for bags of candy to hand out as they patrol the streets to give the children a taste of joy in the midst of strife.

When giving this example, God was saying that our hearts need to be pure and unconditional in their motives. He wanted us to come to him as our true Father, who loves us and wants to care for us.

Often when I pray on the phone with young wives whose husbands are deployed, I ask God the Father to hold them in his lap while they are alone. I want the young women to have a picture of being able to let go of their daily worries and let their Father in heaven take over. We have been taught that our concept of God sometimes rests on what our relationship was like with our father on earth. At times, that can be painful. I will tell you that this is a Father who will never leave nor forsake you. You can always run to his lap for comfort and compassion.

When life becomes too heavy, when problems overwhelm you, run to him as a simple child, and let your Father in heaven take over. ❧*Carol*

★　★　★

Father God, during these times of uncertainty in our world, help me to run to you for comfort and love. Show yourself to be ever present in the times of uncertainty and need that our military face, particularly those elements deployed to active duty. Bring relief to the children of war. ✛*Amen.*

A Word to Fathers

Fathers, do not provoke your children to anger by the way you treat them. Rather, bring them up with the discipline and instruction that comes from the Lord. ✛ EPHESIANS 6:4

I have come to the realization in the past few years that one of the reasons God gives us children is that we can have some sense of understanding what he goes through with us. How often he must say, "What was she thinking? Didn't she know that I would handle that situation?"

My husband and I have often said to our sons, "What were you thinking? Did you think through that decision?"

There is a specific word to fathers in today's verse. God knew that fathers would always want the very best for their children. God wants the very best for us. I am also quite sure that he knew we sometimes think the only way to get children to listen to us is to raise our voices and point our fingers in anger. He says to fathers, "Don't do that!" He instructs fathers to keep their cool and not anger their children into obedience. He says that discipline should come from instruction approved by him.

The world is full of angry people lacking in discipline and instruction. As a result, we have been witness to many things that we considered unimaginable. It is a time for those who know Jesus to step up to the plate as fathers and begin to discipline and give instruction as approved by the Lord. We are challenged with statistics that we cannot comprehend. The time is now. This word is to the fathers in our land. Accept the challenge, and begin to raise godly men and women who can make a difference in the world. ⁓*Carol*

✶ ✶ ✶

Father in heaven, thank you for the instruction in your Word that will bring health and life. Bless those fathers who are away from their children because of military assignments. Give them renewed commitment to raise their children by your instruction. Bless them as they must communicate long distance, and let their words be gentle and affirming. ✛*Amen.*

June 21
Father to His Children

The LORD is like a father to his children, tender and compassionate to those who fear him.
✝ PSALM 103:13

I have often heard it said
Through good times and bad
"Anyone can be a father,
But it takes someone special to be a dad."
A dad will call you on the phone
Just to say I love you.
A dad will take you out to eat
To find out all that's new.
A dad will take you fishing,
Or even to the park.
He will take you to the lake to swim,
But wants you home before it's dark.
A dad spends time in prayer for you.
He knows your every need.
And when you need some extra strength
He's there for you, indeed.
Though life may take you far away
His love is very close;
The example that he sets for you
Will help you make the choice
To choose to serve a different dad
Who goes by "Abba Father," too.
The example from your earthly dad
Is a sample of the love HE has for you.
Happy Father's Day to great dads everywhere!

⇜*Carol*

★　★　★

Father, you are my Father in heaven. You are my Creator and the Lover of my soul. Thank you for your Son, who saves me from my sins. Be a father to the fatherless during this time of world conflict. I pray for your mercy on those who have lost their fathers in faraway lands or in national tragedy. Help those fathers in America who are wayward to step up to the responsibility of supporting their families and come back to them in love and in commitment. ✝ *Amen.*

Trust the Father

How kind the LORD is! How good he is! So merciful, this God of ours! The LORD protects those of childlike faith; I was facing death, and he saved me. Let my soul be at rest again, for the LORD has been good to me. + PSALM 116:5-7

In his book *Overcoming Setbacks*, Steve Brown tells the story of a tourist bus inching its way down a steep, winding mountain road. Each curve was carefully piloted. As the bus negotiated the highway, the smell of burning brakes became evident. The bus began to pick up speed as did the fear of the passengers. Amazingly enough, a young boy slept soundly in the back of the bus, even with intermittent shrieks from a couple of the travelers.

Finally, the bus arrived safely at its destination. A passenger awakened the little boy to tell him what had happened. He asked him how he could have slept through such a dramatic journey.

The little boy responded, "It was my father who was driving the bus."

Brown adds, "Our father drives the bus too. No matter how bad the road, regardless of how worrisome it becomes, we can sleep. He's never had an accident, you know."[1]

Psalm 116 was one of the many passages that brought me great comfort during my husband's deployment to Iraq. I was reminded of the peace and assurance that comes in knowing I am God's child. I encourage you to take time to read the entire psalm and notice such verbs pertaining to God as protects, turned, and heard. These are in response to the descriptions overcome, entangled, and in great need, which pertained to me as I read. The psalmist cried out to God, "Save me," and he learned that God's nature is such that he listens, cares, is gracious, righteous, and full of compassion. He rescues those who come to him with simple, childlike trust.

You can rest today in the confidence that your heavenly Father is driving the bus. Trust him to bring you through whatever difficult journey you are on today and in the future.   ≥Brenda

★   ★   ★

Heavenly Father, thank you for hearing my cry for mercy and saving me. You have blessed my life with good things. Give me a joyful heart to serve you and testify of your faithfulness. I pray you would provide comfort to children who have been left fatherless as a result of war. In Jesus' name I pray. + Amen.

---

[1] Steve Brown, *Overcoming Setbacks* (Colorado Springs, CO: NavPress, 1992), 124–25.

June 23
Life Is a Devotional

Great is his faithfulness; his mercies begin afresh each morning. ✝ LAMENTATIONS 3:23

I am so thankful God's mercies are new every morning. I see his handiwork in all that has transpired in my life. I see the times he was protecting me in bad decisions to the times he was guiding me to make the right ones. I reflect on the times of walking away from him, thinking I could do things on my own. Because of his death in my place, my sins are "covered" with the blood of Jesus. As a Christian and a child of the almighty God, I have chosen to walk with him and ask for his guidance and his peace in my life.

Whenever I reflect on the day, I see God's hand all over it. Each day is a lesson from him in obedience. Your experiences minister to me, and my life experiences minister to you. He calls us to share our experiences and encourage each other as we go through our lives.

If you pause each day to write down how you have seen God in your day, he will always be a part of it. Each day on this earth is a testament to God's love for you or as ministry to others.

During this vacation season—whether you are able to take a vacation or not—take some leisure time with the Lord. Reflect on God's presence in your life. Write down the miracles along the way and the answers to prayer.

As you are recording these wonderful gems, I challenge you to write down some other things. Research the Scripture, and find passages that you can write down to remember to pray specifically for your family. During your time of quiet reflection, find passages that you can read as prayers for military personnel serving around the world. Find Scriptures you can pray for pastors and their families and for friends and for your own extended family.

Use the more laid-back days of summer as a time of relaxation to prepare you for what a new season is going to bring.

Life is a devotional when you stop to reflect and see how God is working in your life.
≈Carol

✳   ✳   ✳

Father God, help me pause and take time to focus on you. I pray for time to pull away and be refreshed as I spend quality time with my family. Help those in the communities experiencing deployment to reach out to the families who are left behind during these months of summer and to include them in their family activities. ✝ Amen.

The Stance of Victory

He causes wars to end throughout the earth. He breaks the bow and snaps the spear; he burns the shields with fire. "Be still, and know that I am God! I will be honored by every nation. I will be honored throughout the world." The LORD of Heaven's Armies is here among us; the God of Israel is our fortress. ⊣ PSALM 46:9-11

I am surrounded by modern conveniences created to provide me more time. Unfortunately, I seem to replace the extra time with other things. I struggle with being still, even though I believe stillness before the Lord is a key to spiritual victory. It is too easy to find something more important than taking time for quiet communion with him. The words of Calvin Miller in *A Hunger for the Holy* challenge me to make the time for communion with God: "Intimacy may not be rushed. To meet with the Son of God takes time. We have learned all too well the witless art of living fast. We gulp our meals sandwiched between pressing obligations. The table of communion with the inner Christ is not a fast-food franchise. . . . It is difficult to teach the unhurried discipline of the table to a culture brought up on frozen dinners and condensed novels."[1]

I'm not talking about getting yourself into a mind-numbing mystical condition. I'm talking about taking the time to tune out all the distractions of your life and, through God's Word and prayer, recognize the mighty power of God! Psalm 46:10 isn't suggesting we be still with an empty brain. It means we be still, filled with the awe and wonder of almighty God, and encouraged to watch him work! It follows the proclamation, "God is our refuge and strength, always ready to help in times of trouble" (Psalm 46:1). It follows the invitation, "Come, see the glorious works of the LORD: See how he brings destruction upon the world. He causes wars to end throughout the earth. He breaks the bow and snaps the spear; he burns the shields with fire" (Psalm 46:8-9).

This summer as you may be planning a vacation, think about taking time for some extended stillness with the Lord. Remind yourself of his greatness, and expect the victory that will result. ⮞*Brenda*

* * *

Mighty God, lead me beside still waters. Teach me to include leisure moments with you as part of my daily routine. Help me to enjoy the calm assurance that comes from trusting you. I pray for those who are struggling with trusting you because of tragedy or loss. May they come to know you as the one who is among them. ✝ *Amen.*

---

[1] Calvin Miller, *A Hunger for the Holy* (West Monroe, LA: Howard Publishing Company, Inc., 2003).

June 25
The Need for Quiet

Make it your goal to live a quiet life, minding your own business and working with your hands, just as we instructed you before. **+** 1 THESSALONIANS 4:11

This particular verse was written in context with other verses giving direction on how to live for Christ. We are exhorted to live a holy life in a way that pleases God. This particular verse contradicts all that we are taught as Americans. Living a quiet life is often seen as a life with no importance by today's standards.

Extroverts are wonderful people to have around. They love life, they love friends, and they lack nothing to talk about. While facilitating a group using a personality type inventory, I came to a moment of realization. Having been an extrovert all my life and going through each day at one hundred miles per hour, I was taught that this fast-paced personality needs even more quiet time. In other words, the more busyness and active involvement in life, the more rest and quiet I need.

My husband and I decided in the 1980s that buying a tent and camping with our sons would be a wonderful memory for us to share. So off we went with our newfound desire for quality family time. Upon our arrival at the campsite, we quickly set up our new gas stove and our new eight-man tent. We had the boys help gather sticks for the evening campfire. We couldn't wait to have dinner, sit and talk, and listen to the night creatures as we roasted marshmallows under the stars.

We anxiously lit the campfire to begin our quiet time in nature. We had no sooner prepared ourselves for a quiet forest evening than we heard a boom box with rock music blasting, as well as a television blaring. Soon after, the voices outside at this formerly quiet campground got louder and louder. We decided that we could not enjoy the outdoors, so we decided to retire for the night. Ultimately around 2 a.m., we made the decision to pack up and go home. It had become unbearable.

What has become of the quiet in our world? What has become of spending time just listening to nature or hearing the voice of God?

There is a need for quiet. When you can't find quiet, you understand the need for it. Seek out your quiet time. Live a life that yearns to hear God's voice. Cultivate the time for noise off and quiet within.   *~Carol*

✱ ✱ ✱

Lord God, give me a quiet place to be with you. Help those who serve our country to find a quiet place whenever they can, in order to regroup and be refreshed in your presence. **+** *Amen.*

Access Number

"There is salvation in no one else! God has given no other name under heaven by which we must be saved." ✝ ACTS 4:12

In planning for an overseas trip, I purchased a phone card to use to stay connected to my family. I made sure the card had the capacity to make international calls as I removed it from its cover and packed it in my bag. When I arrived on the other side of the ocean, I tried to place a call home, but I was unable to use my card. To my disappointment and frustration, I discovered the phone card had to have an access number for international cards. The access number for the country I was in was listed on the cover I had discarded when I was packing. The phone card was useless without an access number. I had invested in the card, but my investment was worthless without the access number. I put forth the effort to use the card, but my effort was meaningless without the access number. I had a great desire to communicate with my family, but my desire was frustrated without the access number.

As Christ followers, we never have to worry about having access to the Father. Jesus Christ is our access to him at any time. It is sad to me that so many people invest in religious activities, but they are useless in gaining eternal life without access through Jesus Christ. People put a lot of effort into doing good deeds and helping their fellow man, but it is useless in cleansing them from sin without access through Jesus. Many people have a great desire to know and communicate with God, but they are simply deceiving themselves without the connection to the Father through his only Son. Jesus himself said in John 14:6, "I am the way, the truth, and the life. No one can come to the Father except through me." We don't have access to God simply because we have a need, because we have a desire, or because we put forth an effort. We have access through Christ.   ❧*Brenda*

✴   ✴   ✴

Thank you, Lord, for providing access to you through Christ. Remind me of the price that was paid so I may have this privilege. I intercede for those who are looking to find peace in false religions or through their own goodness. I pray for communication between deployed military personnel and their families. May the times of connection be sweet and encouraging. In Jesus' name I pray. ✝*Amen.*

June 27
Bear One Another's Burdens

Bear ye one another's burdens, and so fulfil the law of Christ. ✛ GALATIANS 6:2, KJV

If you want to find out if friends are really friends, go on vacation together. The friendship is tested, and character is put to the test as you endeavor to enjoy activities that may challenge personal space. Our family had the opportunity to practice *koinonia*, a Greek term used in the New Testament (meaning having in common and sharing with one another), as we vacationed with our good friends.

We planned a weeklong canoe trip in the Boundary Waters between Minnesota and Canada with our good friends and neighbors Glen, Ruth, and their children. When the time came, we met our friends in Minnesota and began the trek to the lake country. We canoed into the national park, searched out just the right spot, and set up camp in one of the most beautiful settings I have ever seen. We had received the usual warning to be cautious about bears, but I didn't think we needed to worry about that type of invader. This was going to be a great vacation!

The second day of our trip, my husband was lounging in a hammock when my son came running up to him with the news he had spotted a bear! My husband thought this had to be a practical joke, but he became convinced to take a look, and indeed there was a bear! As the day went on, we realized this bear was not going to leave us alone. We had to think fast to come up with a plan to salvage our trip. We packed up camp, boarded the canoes, and searched for another campsite, discovering an island that had no other campers. We were amazed and surprised as we enjoyed its unique features. It was unanimous that this island was better than the first place where we had camped. We owed that bear!

This has become one of the favorite memories of our family. A frightening situation turned into an adventure as we worked together. Paul's message to the Galatians encouraged them to serve one another and share the heavy burdens of life. There are some burdens we have that we must carry ourselves, but there are other burdens that are to be shared in community. In the woods of Minnesota, a vacation shared by friends became a *koinonia* experience as we considered each other in our distress. I am thankful for an annoying bear that taught me a great lesson in "bearing" one another's burdens and, as a result, tightened the bonds of friendship. ❧*Brenda*

✭   ✭   ✭

Father, help me do my part in sharing the burdens of others. Grant me the willingness to allow others to help me when my burdens are too great to handle alone. Please provide our servicemen and women with the support and encouragement they need. ✛ *Amen.*

Northern Lights and Moose Lasagna

And all these blessings shall come upon you and overtake you, because you obey the voice of the LORD your God. + DEUTERONOMY 28:2, NKJV

I like the vivid picture painted in today's Scripture of being overtaken by a blessing. God is addressing the nation of Israel, but because of the organic nature of Scripture we are able to glean personal truths from corporate lessons. In simple terms, when we do what we are supposed to do, we will receive undeserved blessing.

What are we supposed to do? It is the same for us today, as it was for the children of Israel thousands of years ago. We are to live our lives in obedience. We must make time to listen to God in order to know his will, so we can obey.

A trip to Alaska is etched in my memory as a time I felt overtaken by a blessing. It was my third trip to the land of the last frontier. I had seen a glacier, bald eagles flying, and beautiful scenery. I'd even eaten moose lasagna! What I really wanted was to see a moose and experience the beauty of the northern lights. The purpose of my visit was to encourage and minister to women of the military chapel. Each time I visited Alaska, being with these dear women of faith and courage was blessing enough. So, even though I was disappointed to not have seen all I wanted to, I was leaving with a joyful spirit.

On the way to the airport as the car turned into the terminal, there on the side of the road was a giant moose! It was as if he were waiting to say good-bye to me. I was thrilled! I boarded my plane, and a few minutes into the flight the pilot announced, "Ladies and gentlemen, those of you with window seats on the left side of the plane are in the prime spot for an amazing show. The northern lights will be on display. Enjoy!" Well, guess who had a window seat on the left side of the plane? Me! Talk about being overtaken by a blessing. I sat in wonder for two hours as the God of the universe swirled, cascaded, tumbled, and danced lights across the sky.

I confess, there have been times when I have mistakenly tried to bargain with God for his blessings. The reality is that I have no grounds for negotiation. God overtook me with the blessing of fulfilling my desires, and it was a reminder of his goodness and mercy. He enjoys blessing us, not because we have twisted his arm, but simply because he loves us. ⮞*Brenda*

✯　　✯　　✯

Father of all blessings, thank you for your love which has overtaken my soul! May I spread that joy to others around me, and may those in the military experience the same overflow of joy whenever they encounter one of your children. + *Amen.*

June 29
Travel Light

Let us strip off every weight that slows us down, especially the sin that so easily trips us up. And let us run with endurance the race God has set before us. ✛ HEBREWS 12:1

I was an adult before I took my first flight on an airplane. That was years and hundreds of thousands of miles ago. I enjoy traveling, but flying is not the pleasure that it once was. Flight delays, lost luggage, and long waits at baggage claims have turned me into one who travels light. If it can't go into a carry-on bag, it probably won't go with me.

A trip to Turkey was the turning point for me. I was to be gone almost three weeks, so the challenge to fly without checking baggage was going to be great. I researched what to pack and how to pack it, as well as the ideal suitcase in which to pack. If it wasn't of absolute necessity, it didn't make it into the suitcase. I eliminated all unnecessary weight. It made the trip so much more enjoyable not to have to worry about excess baggage.

It is natural for us to want to get as much as we can in this life, but sometimes the results weigh us down in our ability to serve the Lord. Scripture describes this as weight that slows us down. Bible scholar F. B. Meyer asked, "Is there anything in your life which dissipates your energy from holy things, which disinclines you to the practice of prayer and Bible study, which rises before you in your best moments, and produces in you a general sense of uneasiness and disturbance? Something which others account harmless, and permit, and in which you once saw no cause for anxiety, but which you now look on with a feeling of self-condemnation? It is likely enough a weight."[1]

Perhaps you've seen those obvious tourists at an airline counter not being permitted to board a plane because their baggage is overweight. There are penalties to be paid when that happens. In order to keep moving in their travels, they have to remove something from their bags. The journey for the Christ follower needs to be moving on ahead. What are those things you may need to lay aside in order to keep traveling forward?   ☙*Brenda*

✫   ✫   ✫

Father, help me to put aside those things that rob me of joy and peace and hinder my relationship and service to you. I pray I would do my part as I yield to your Spirit to work in my life. I pray for the safety of military personnel who are traveling for duty today. ✛ *Amen.*

---

[1] F. B. Meyer, www.Bibleteacher.org.

Wake-up Call

The heavens proclaim the glory of God. The skies display his craftsmanship. + PSALM 19:1

I am a firm believer in taking vacations. I think they are worth the trouble of planning and the expense of executing. Some medical experts have gone as far as to say vacation is as important as sleep. There are businesses that are encouraging their employees to take vacations in order to enhance the quality of their work. A vacation can help ease stress and ultimately improve health.

An especially memorable vacation for our family took place following a two-year military assignment in Korea. Our airline tickets allowed us to make stops along the way back to the United States, and we took full advantage of the perk. We had an interesting few days in Japan and a leisurely week in Hawaii. Our dear friends stationed in Hawaii secured us a cottage on the north shore. We explored the beach, our boys rode the waves, and we discovered the perfection of shave ice. The cottage had an amazing view of the ocean. In fact, each morning we were awakened by the sunrise. There was no complaining about the early morning wake-up call. I wrote in my journal, "This morning something seemed to tap on the window, encouraging my eyes to open. It was the sun. Out of the window was a postcard sight. The earliest rays are peeping from the clouds and shimmering on the waves. Everything I've worried about seems insignificant to this great celebration of a new day breaking. I feel like I have box seats to the best show on earth. This is something that happens every day, and yet I feel anticipation. The clouds are silhouetted with brightness. There it is! The brilliant ball that signals time is making its appearance. God is orchestrating the beginning of a new day. The curtain is raised, and the show begins!"

Our family was in one of our many transition times. Our tired spirits and bodies were refreshed as we rested and played in a beautiful environment. The light that shone on us from that spectacular sunrise helped us see all other things with a clearer view. Some of the heaviness we were all feeling seemed lighter as we basked in the beauty of God's creation. His heavens proclaimed his greatness and reminded us of the strong God we serve.   *≈Brenda*

✶   ✶   ✶

Creator, thank you for the beauty of the earth. Your glory is displayed in the heavens and conveys your greatness. It brings thanksgiving and worship to my heart. Please bring times of rest and relaxation to military families who are weary because of lengthy duty. In your name I pray. + Amen.

July 1
A Free Heart

[God] purchased our freedom and forgave our sins. ✟ COLOSSIANS 1:14

The concept is so simple yet so difficult to grasp. The teaching has always been the same. Jesus' blood was shed freely to cover all our sins. We can rest in that fact if we have invited Jesus into our hearts. However, why does my heart not have the sense of peace and calm that it should?

Freedom has always come with a price. There is always captivity before freedom. When we are held captive to sin, our hearts are in turmoil. We can have smiles on our faces as we go about our daily schedules, but we know that there is a stirring that keeps us from the freedom that Jesus came to give us.

There are many forms of captivity today. There is pornography, adultery, abuse, and addiction. They are no different from the sins that have been in our world since the beginning of time. However, allowing God to set the captive free is something we must face every day. Sin is sin, and that has not changed. Freedom is freedom, and that has not changed.

When Jesus has come into your heart and taken hold of everything you are, the Holy Spirit convicts of sin. He will allow you to be set free forever if you will only give these secret sins to him. Proverbs 5:22 says, "An evil man is held captive by his own sins; they are ropes that catch and hold him."

Don't be deceived and bound by Satan and his tactics. Cut those ropes and be set free in your heart. Seek the Holy Spirit's conviction, and seek others to pray for you and help you. Let the Lord set you free and allow you to serve him with abandon.
≈Carol

⋆   ⋆   ⋆

Jesus, you came to set the captives free. I cannot serve or continue to minister when I am captive to sin. Anything that keeps me from serving you will hinder my witness. Give me a free heart to let the world know you are the same yesterday, today, and forever. Lord Jesus, set those who are captive to ungodly activities free by your mercy and grace. ✟ Amen.

A Righteous Nation

Godliness makes a nation great, but sin is a disgrace to any people. ✛ PROVERBS 14:34

The wording of the Mayflower Compact tells us that the earliest Americans had as their objective that America would be a righteous nation.

> Having undertaken, for the Glory of God and advancement of the Christian Faith and Honour of our King and Country, a Voyage to plant the First Colony in the Northern Parts of Virginia, do by these present solemnly and mutually in the presence of God and one of another, Covenant and Combine ourselves together into a Civil Body Politic, for our better ordering and preservation and furtherance of the ends aforesaid; and by virtue hereof to enact, constitute and frame such just and equal Laws, Ordinances, Acts, Constitutions and Offices, from time to time, as shall be thought most meet and convenient for the general good of the Colony, unto which we promise all due submission and obedience. In witness whereof we have hereunder subscribed our names at Cape Cod, the 11th of November, in the year of the reign of our Sovereign Lord King James, of England, France and Ireland the eighteenth, and of Scotland the fifty-fourth. Anno Domini 1620.[1]

I have to ask myself, as I look at our nation today, if we have held to the hopes and dreams of these Pilgrim parents. There is no doubt that as a nation we've tasted both the disgrace of sin and the blessings of doing what is right.

I am challenged by these words of the Pilgrim settlers. They came in search of a place where the advancement of Christian faith and honor would bring glory to God. I have to ask myself, *How I can help encourage that vision even today?* I conclude that as a Christ follower, I can be the salt of righteousness. I'm not naive enough to believe that even though America is still considered a Christian nation among other nations, all in our nation are Christians. I do believe, though, that it means there are enough Christian voices to encourage our government to operate under Christian principles. I know that true righteousness only comes through Jesus Christ, but even in our nation, I can be the voice of righteousness by encouraging leaders and fellow citizens to do what is right according to the principles of God's Word.   ≈*Brenda*

✶   ✶   ✶

Father, I pray for the righteousness of the leaders of the United States of America. I pray for those who will give advice to leaders. I pray for the future leadership of this nation. I pray that righteousness will be the standard for those who are caring for refugees and prisoners of war. ✛ *Amen.*

---

[1] William Bradford, *Of Plymouth Plantation, 1620–1647* (Samuel Eliot Morison, ed., 1952), 75–76.

July 3
Red, White, and Blue

Because of our faith, Christ has brought us into this place of undeserved privilege where we now stand, and we confidently and joyfully look forward to sharing God's glory. + ROMANS 5:2

The announcer said over the loudspeaker, "Our national anthem." We took our stance on the field with hand over heart. The team took off their helmets and held them over their hearts. There was a roll of quiet commotion as each man in the bleachers took his hat off and put it over his heart. The silence was loud. You could truly hear a pin drop. The national anthem was played. Every word was heard. Many sang along with the music. Many even had a tear roll down their face. That was several years ago.

Fast forward to today. The announcer says, "Our national anthem." The camera pans the crowd. Some are laughing and talking to each other. Many caps are left on. Some have their hands over the wrong side of their chest.

The national anthem can't save us from harm or even change anything going on in our lives. For me, each time it is played is a time of being thankful for those who continue to battle for freedom. It is a time to recognize that our freedom to be anywhere we want to be in America, doing anything we want to do, came with a price.

My husband and I are patriotic to the core. Among the greatest influences in our lives were our parents who taught us respect and honor for the flag and for our country. Our children learned patriotism from us as we participated in military celebrations and events that displayed America's pride.

I don't remember my dad ever hearing the national anthem without a tear rolling down his face. The fact that this song was special was ingrained in me. I want my sons to always feel that pride from the fact that their grandfathers and their father served this country with great dignity, honor, and humility.

I say, "Hooray for the Red, White, and Blue! ~*Carol*

* * *

Lord, America was founded on Christian principles by those who believed you should be a part of all that went on within this great land. Forgive us for forgetting the humility, the honor, and the pride that established the United States of America. Help me to instill in others the great patriotism of the land of the free and the home of the brave. + *Amen.*

July 4
Happy Birthday, America!

What joy for the nation whose God is the LORD, whose people he has chosen as his inheritance. ✛ PSALM 33:12

A benefit to living in the nation's capital is being a part of the great celebration that takes place on the fourth of July. It truly is a birthday party for America, topped off with an incredible fireworks display. Our first year in D.C. found us watching the fireworks on the tenth-floor balcony belonging to our good friends. It was an ideal location overlooking the National Mall.

The next year, our friends had moved out of the neighborhood, so we had to find a new observation site. We decided to walk up a few blocks to a place on the street that opened to a view of the fireworks. The view from the street was not as spectacular as that from high above the street. We were, however, able to appreciate a view on the street that we did not get on the balcony. This view was of the people we were standing with as we took in the beautiful scene. Area hotel employees and guests spilled out into the street to watch the show.

Based on the language and dress, there were people from several countries. There were young children with their parents as well as older adults. I noticed a young man in a wheelchair and even a homeless man pushing his cart. It reminded me of the words on the Statue of Liberty, "Give me your tired, your poor, your huddled masses yearning to breathe free. The wretched refuse of your teeming shore. Send these, the homeless, tempest-tossed to me. I lift my lamp beside the golden door." As I watched the sky light up behind the Washington Monument and gazed at the illuminated Capitol dome, I was proud of my country.

Many would argue that the strength of America is in its diversity and willingness to offer freedom and liberty to all. Though America was founded on godly principles, it still cannot compare to what God offers to us as part of his family and his church. Someday when we are gathered around the throne of God, there will certainly be people from all countries and all walks of life who will then be joined together, free and transformed through Christ. Now that will be a celebration!   *⋟Brenda*

✬   ✬   ✬

Lord, thank you for the privilege of being an American. I am grateful for this nation and for the principles on which it was founded and for which it stands. Protect those who are fighting for those principles, whether on a battlefield or in a courtroom. In your name I pray. ✛ *Amen.*

Our Nation's Flag

Fear of the LORD teaches wisdom; humility precedes honor. + PROVERBS 15:33

Humility does not come easy in our society. Too often, being humble is compared with being weak. The Scripture tells us that humility precedes honor. Perhaps that is why we have a hard time teaching others, especially children, to honor their elders. They see in us a pride that strives to get more and do more and to be sure that others notice.

Whenever I am around those who have fought in foreign wars, I am amazed at the humility they display. Some even begin talking in a quiet hush when they refer to past wartime experiences. They are very humble in sharing the part they played in the success of these wars. They hold our military in such high esteem, and they honor them with all their hearts. I have noticed so many times that these men and women involved directly during those times of service are never able to talk without a tear in their eye. They have great respect for our president and for all our military leaders.

It is my great joy to be able to share with veterans, and I feel as if their patriotism always makes even more of an imprint on my life each time I am with them.

I found a song sung by Avalon recently that tells of the symbolism of our nation's flag, what it stands for, and how it calls those who fight to fight for her. The words perfectly communicate what needs to be said. The last verse is as follows:

> *And somewhere beneath the stars and the sky*
> *Our flag is still standing there. She bled and she brought one land*
> *   under God*
> *Her colors still lead us there.*
> *She carried the lives of those before us*
> *She buried the bold and the brave.*
> *For freedom she holds our hopes*
> *And heads up high*
> *And for freedom she'll ever wave!*[1]

God, country, humility, and honor—a fit description of our nation's flag.   *Carol*

★　★　★

Heavenly Father, I am so very thankful for the continued influence of those who have fought for our nation. Today I ask for a renewed sense of pride for my country. I pray that the flag will become once again a symbol of honor and humility for this nation—to me, to those around me, and to those serving our country in the military. God bless the United States of America! + *Amen.*

---

[1] Matt Moran, "For Freedom," Meadowgreen Music Co., 2005.

Give Me Liberty!

It is for freedom that Christ has set us free. Stand firm, then, and do not let yourselves be burdened again by a yoke of slavery. ✚ GALATIANS 5:1, NIV

The strong stand taken by Patrick Henry in March 1775 resulted in Henry's fellow Virginians taking up arms against the tyranny of British rule. His famous and moving words spoken at St. John's Church in Richmond, where the legislature was meeting, still strike a sense of conviction in the heart of any patriot: "I know not what course others may take; but as for me, give me liberty or give me death."

The early patriots knew the value of freedom. They understood the sacrifice of freedom, and they were willing to make a commitment not only to obtain it but also to keep it.

As a Christ follower, I am not free based upon political determination but upon the victory that Christ won for me on the cross. In Galatians 5:1, Paul addresses how sad it is for those who have accepted freedom through Christ to willingly give that up by attempting to obtain their own righteousness through human effort. He states that the Christ follower is to be firm and unwavering in maintaining the great principles of Christian liberty.[1] To maintain our freedom in Christ, we have to continue to trust in him and not depend on our own ability to make ourselves righteous in the eyes of God.

The battle that we have to fight to maintain our freedom is usually a battle within ourselves. Since Christ has already won our freedom from sin, we have to fight the temptation to turn from the cross as the basis of our freedom to look to our own self-righteousness. The good news is that we have the provision of the Holy Spirit to help fight this inner battle and bring control from within and freedom instead of bondage brought on by holding to a set of legalistic rules. Stand firm in the liberty of Christ today!   *Brenda*

✶   ✶   ✶

Heavenly Father, thank you for the provision of the Holy Spirit, who helps me fight the battle to maintain my spiritual liberty. Help me to stand firm, unwavering in my devotion and commitment to you today! In Jesus' name I pray. ✚ *Amen.*

---

[1] *Barnes' Notes,* Electronic Database, CD-ROM. Biblesoft, 1997.

July 7
Proud and Thankful

Your wickedness will bring its own punishment. Your turning from me will shame you. You will see what an evil, bitter thing it is to abandon the LORD your God and not to fear him. I, the LORD, the LORD of Heaven's Armies, have spoken! + JEREMIAH 2:19

I am so very proud to be an American. I am so very thankful to wake up each morning in peace and comfort. I take great pride in posting our flag on our front porch as soon as I awaken. My husband has always had me bring it in at sunset in the evenings as a show of respect and honor. I am so thankful that as I slept during the night, there were no bombs or gunfire around me. I am very proud that our sons have the opportunity to do and be whatever they want to. I am thankful that my husband can go to work and enjoy the rewards of a hard day's work without incident.

I am not very proud that because of the freedoms we have taken so literally and out of context, God can no longer be mentioned in public schools. I am not very proud that the flag of the United States of America is publicly burned on the streets of our big cities. I am not thankful that politicians and politics are put above patriotism and honor for our military families.

Today's Scripture warns of trouble when there is no fear of sin's consequences or of God's judgment upon our land.

We can all be proud and thankful to be Americans. It is a country like no other. However, as we go farther and farther away from the central element that this country was founded on—God, the Bible, and Christian principles—we are to know that there will be punishment for turning away.

I am proud to say that I am a God-fearing, Bible-toting, and Jesus-believing American. I know and understand the history of our country. I know and understand God's warning to us as a nation. My prayer is for those in leadership to wake up and come to an understanding of God's direction for our land. My prayer is that they will be thankful for God's direction and we will not have to have our own wickedness punish us.

Stand firm today, in your place of work or sphere of influence, for truth, liberty, and justice for all.   ~Carol

*   *   *

Holy God, we are a proud nation. We are a thankful nation. I pray that you will bring conviction to the hearts of those who fear getting back to Christian principles and change their fear of man to fear of a holy God that will not be forsaken. Have mercy on our beloved United States of America. + Amen.

A Steady Process

I am certain that God, who began the good work within you, will continue his work until it is finally finished on the day when Christ Jesus returns. ✛ PHILIPPIANS 1:6

Adlai E. Stevenson Jr. is believed to have said, "Patriotism is not a short and frenzied burst of emotion but the long and steady dedication of a lifetime." This statement makes me think of the many people who are interested in marching down the street in a parade, waving a flag to celebrate America. My guess is there are more of them than there are people who are willing to walk down the sidewalk and pick up the trash to keep America clean. In other words, it is easier to be excited about anything in the celebration phase than it is in the maintaining phase.

It's fun to get in a brand-new car and drive it off the showroom floor, but for the majority of car owners, the fun is short lived when the car requires vacuuming, washing, and sitting in the waiting room while the routine maintenance is done. Think of how excited a young couple is when they get the keys to their new home and step across the threshold as proud owners. There's not as much excitement when the toilet must be scrubbed, the weeds pulled out of the flower bed, or the windows washed. An extreme example of this principle was exhibited in young college dorm mates of my husband. These young men did not want to wash their clothes, so they bought new clothes until they had a pile of clothes that needed to be washed and no more money!

Unfortunately, there are people who approach following Christ this way. They are excited about the new part but not as excited about the disciplines that are required to maintain a relationship with Christ. These disciplines may not be as fun, but they are necessary. The continuing work of God's refining process in our lives takes time. Just like Stevenson's definition of patriotism, the work of God in my life is a long and steady dedication of a lifetime. The month of July is a month of celebrating our nation's birthday. Why not make it a month of looking at where you are in the process of God's work? Then celebrate the continuation of that work! *≈Brenda*

✶　✶　✶

Thank you, Lord, for the work of grace in my life. Help me to joyfully be about your continuing work in my life. I look forward to the day the work is completed and I stand finished in your presence. May those in the military learn to work for your glory in the diverse lands in which they serve. ✛ *Amen.*

July 9
Quiet Summer Freedom

Make it your goal to live a quiet life, minding your own business and working with your hands, just as we instructed you before. ✝ 1 THESSALONIANS 4:11

The sounds of summer ring sweet and clear
Like mosquitoes buzzing 'round your ear.
The flowers with all their splendid color—
Oh, summer days are like no other.
The laughter of children playing outside
Carry sounds that the future is alive.
The pools are open, the parks are full
Thoughts are gone of work and school.
But, somewhere in a distant land
There are those with guns in hand.
Defending freedom with their lives
Having left behind parents, children, husbands, wives.
They are fighting so others will know
The sights and sounds of freedom we love so.
We hear stories of the peace and joy
They share with the children, a girl or a boy.
As we enjoy yet another summer
Of picnics, baseball, and fun with others,
Remember those who would give anything to be
A people who like us are known as free.
The price of freedom is very high
It's paid for with sacrifice you cannot buy.
As an American I enjoy good things in life
Thanks to a brave soul's labor and strife.

❧Carol

✮ ✮ ✮

Dear heavenly Father, thank you for those who have paid the cost of freedom to make it possible for me to enjoy these wonderful summer months. There is a quiet that comes during this time as I enjoy family and friends. I pray you will give a time of quiet summer freedom to those who are serving in faraway lands filled with the rumble of explosions. Bless them, Lord, for their service. ✝ *Amen.*

Sounds of Freedom

God sent him to buy freedom for us who were slaves to the law, so that he could adopt us as his very own children. And because we are his children, God has sent the Spirit of his Son into our hearts, prompting us to call out, "Abba, Father." + GALATIANS 4.5-6

The first time my husband received a military assignment to Fort Bragg, North Carolina, we purchased a home that backed up to the installation. While we were visiting the house with our real estate agent, there were artillery sounds that made the windows rattle. She commented that those were the sounds of freedom. It was an interesting point of view, and it provided a whole new spin to the potential of hearing this noise on a regular basis. If we purchased this property, I was going to be faced with a choice of annoyance or gratitude. We did purchase the home, and thankfully the artillery sounds were not something that I recall as negative. I do think of this woman's description whenever I am close to a military training ground and hear "the sounds of freedom." It's certainly not something I celebrate; rather, it is a sobering reminder of the price of freedom.

Freedom has never been without a price, from the birth of our country to those who continue to sacrifice to maintain it. I am grateful for the commitment that has resulted in the freedom I enjoy as an American citizen. I do not take for granted the personal rights I enjoy while living in the United States of America.

I also do not take my spiritual freedom for granted. As I look at Scripture, I understand the biblical definition of freedom describes more what I am saved from rather than what personal rights I have gained. Christ purchased my freedom from sin, death, and hell on the cross.

There are those who don't like the sound of the gospel that says we are sinful and deserve God's punishment. There are others who don't like the sound of salvation that says Jesus had to die for our sins. When we understand the truth of God's Word and the necessity of accepting his plan of salvation, then though the sounds of nails being driven into the hands and feet of our Lord are not pleasant, we are thankful for the eternal freedom they bring.   *Brenda*

✶　✶　✶

Father, thank you for sending your Son to buy my freedom from sin. Thank you for those who have paid the price for my freedom as a citizen of this country. Help me to be the best citizen of earth that I can be today. In Jesus' name I pray. + *Amen.*

July 11
Obedient Nation

Let us now lie down in shame and cover ourselves with dishonor, for we and our ancestors have sinned against the LORD our God. From our childhood to this day we have never obeyed him. . . . "O Israel," says the LORD, "if you wanted to return to me, you could. You could throw away your detestable idols and stray away no more. Then when you swear by my name, saying, 'As surely as the LORD lives,' you could do so with truth, justice, and righteousness. Then you would be a blessing to the nations of the world, and all people would come and praise my name." + JEREMIAH 3:25; 4:1-2

In today's Scripture, Jeremiah shares much of his disdain and sadness as Israel is going down the wrong path. He rebukes the people and tells them the truth about turning their hearts toward the one true God. God instilled in Jeremiah the wisdom and courage to condemn the sin that was taking place. There were many who had backslidden, and immorality was rampant. The people were attracted to false prophets who would say only what made the people feel good. Jeremiah 5:31 says, "The prophets give false prophecies, and the priests rule with an iron hand. Worse yet, my people like it that way! But what will you do when the end comes?"

The similarities to our nation today are mind-boggling to me. Many times when I have the honor to give talks on patriotism, I always remind the audience that God's early involvement in our nation is not merely an opinion. History reveals how our nation began. We became a nation with God at the very foundation.

In 1843, Emma Willard, author of *History of the United States*, wrote, "The government of the United States is acknowledged by the wise and good of other nations, to be the most free, impartial and righteous government of the world; but all agree that for such a government to be sustained many years, the principles of truth and righteousness, taught in the Holy Scriptures, must be practiced. The rulers must govern in the fear of God, and the people obey the laws."[1]

Being a God-fearing and obedient nation is not a new concept for America. Being one of the nations that turn their backs on God, however, is. Stand firm in obedience, and lead the way in bringing our country back to where our forefathers intended it to be. ~*Carol*

*   *   *

God, you are the Creator. You are omniscient, omnipotent, and omnipresent. You are the source of freedom of this country. Thank you for the mercy you show to our nation. Turn the hearts of people in America toward you. + *Amen.*

---

[1] Sam Bartholomew with Stephen Mansfield, *God's Role in America* (Nashville, TN: Eggman Publishing, 1996), 72.

Purple Fingers

The Lord is the Spirit, and wherever the Spirit of the Lord is, there is freedom.

✝ 2 CORINTHIANS 3:17

There can be no denying that the day of the purple finger was a high point of Operation Iraqi Freedom. While there can also be no denying the desire that a more swift and successful building of democracy would have followed, the excitement of the day of the Iraqi national election was real. Courageous Iraqis took a stand for freedom and displayed their stand by holding up purple-ink-stained fingers with pride and hope. In the midst of danger, they cast their votes. They became targets of insurgents, but that day their choice between terror and hope was clearly in view.

Iraqi voters were able to cast their votes that day because of a new level of freedom made possible by the presence of the U.S. military. As positive as this vote was, the truth is, there are limitations of man-made freedom. A strong military presence can guarantee some freedom, but there is no question that it cannot guarantee complete freedom. Even if we could guarantee political freedom, 2 Corinthians 3:17 explains there is a freedom that cannot come from any type of military presence.

The Iraqi people held up purple fingers as a symbol of freedom. The freedom sign for the Christ follower is our confession of faith in Christ. It is a freedom that has been guaranteed by the shed blood of Christ. His bloodstained body assured the freedom for each one of our souls.

> *Standing on the promises I now can see*
> *Perfect, present cleansing in the blood for me;*
> *Standing in the liberty where Christ makes free,*
> *Standing on the promises of God.*

~R. KELSO CARTER, 1848–1928

≈Brenda

✯   ✯   ✯

Lord Jesus, "May we cherish highly all the privileges that now are ours, knowing them to have been bought and paid for in the tears and toil, in the blood and sweat of many, of whom we are not worthy. O God, may Thy everlasting pity touch every trembling heart this day, and may all who are anxious find His peace as they come in simple faith to pray to God."[1] ✝ *Amen.*

---

[1] Rev. Peter J. Marshall, ed., *The Wartime Sermons of Dr. Peter Marshall* (Dallas, TX: Clarion Call Marketing, Inc., 2005), 223–224.

July 13
For Freedom We Fight

The Spirit of the Sovereign LORD is upon me, for the LORD has anointed me to bring good news to the poor. He has sent me to comfort the brokenhearted and to proclaim that captives will be released and prisoners will be freed. ✝ ISAIAH 61:1

Every conflict in the history of the world has been met with opposition. There have always been those who think they can handle things better or make better decisions about the process toward resolution. There are always those who cry out to "make peace, not war!" Some would say those who feel war is the answer are war mongers. They might even think they are looking for reasons to go to war.

Scripture talks much about the wars that were fought since the beginning of time. There are examples of battles and many who lost their lives. What I see in Scripture is that these wars happened not because people were drawn to war but because they were drawn to freedom and getting out of captivity and getting rid of the evil influence around them.

In these days of great conflict around the world I can only see that those who fight are fighting for freedom, not for love of war. The cost of freedom comes at a very high price. It also brings great rewards when the captives are set free and the brokenhearted are released and healed.

I received an e-mail from my dear friend Major Steve. They had a service remembering those who died on 9/11. He said, "We will never forget that day." That is what drives them to continue the fight. It is for freedom they fight, not just because they want to go to war. Their greatest desire is to get home to their families to live in freedom and peace after they return.

Freedom isn't free, and it comes with much more than being nice or negotiating with evil. It comes with fighting the battles on earth and in the spiritual realm.

We fight for freedom that others will know the true meaning of life without captivity. ✺*Carol*

✷　✷　✷

Jehovah Shalom, you are our peace in a troubled world. I ask that freedom would come to those who have never known it. I thank you for the brave men and women who are willing to bring the good news of freedom to those who live in turmoil. Bless them today! ✝ *Amen.*

Semper Fi

"The master said, 'Well done, my good and faithful servant. You have been faithful in handling this small amount, so now I will give you many more responsibilities. Let's celebrate together!'"

✝ MATTHEW 25:23

A story is told of a young marine who was injured during the terrorist bombing of the marine barracks in Beirut. The marine corps commandant visited the survivors while they were in the hospital. Approaching a young marine who was described as looking more like a machine than a man because of the tubes coming out of his body, the general stopped. The young man struggled to communicate his desire for a pen and paper. He struggled further to painfully write two words to pass on to the commandant: *Semper Fi*, the Latin motto of the marine corps, meaning "forever faithful."[1]

God doesn't require you to be the best mom or dad in the world. God doesn't require you to be the best husband or wife in the world. God doesn't require you to be the best soldier, sailor, airman, marine, or coastguardsman in the world. God doesn't require you to be the best doctor, lawyer, or teacher in the world. God doesn't require you to be the best _____ in the world. He requires you and me to be faithful in what he has placed before us. If your place is to stand at the church door and hand out bulletins, do it faithfully. If your place is to check water meters, do it faithfully. If your place is to prepare taxes, do it faithfully. If your place is to wait for a deployed husband, wife, son, or daughter, do it faithfully.

Semper Fi could also be the motto of the Christian. It is echoed in the words we long to hear at the end of our time here on earth: "Welcome home, good and faithful servant." ≈*Brenda*

✱ ✱ ✱

Faithful One, you have called me to live a life that honors you here on earth. Help me to follow your example of being faithful. Give me a heart that faithfully follows your Word. Show me those areas of my life where faithfulness is lacking, and give me fortitude to make necessary changes. Help me to be an example of faith to those I meet today. In your name I pray. ✝ *Amen.*

[1] James Dobson and Gary Bauer, *Children at Risk* (Dallas, TX: Word Publishing, 1990), 187–188.

July 15
Gettysburg Experience

They had gone up to Bethel and wept in the presence of the LORD until evening. They had asked the LORD, "Should we fight against our relatives from Benjamin again?" And the LORD had said, "Go out and fight against them." ✝ JUDGES 20:23

While visiting the battlefield of Gettysburg, I found myself in complete awe of the miles and miles of land where this battle had raged. I looked at every memorial along the way to view the names of soldiers and the states they came from. I looked for my mother's maiden name, my maiden name, my great-grandparents' names, as well as the names from my husband's family line. I wondered how many of those who died in this area were my ancestors. I wondered how many had to come face to face with family members on the opposing side and were killed for the sake of freedom.

There are many stories from the Civil War of brother fighting against brother to the point of death. How could a man kill his own brother? When a man is fighting for freedom, he will fight no matter what the cost. The longing to be free is built into his soul.

Why do we as a nation continue to think we can reason with our enemies? Some think we can talk them into liking us or accepting our democratic way of life. Freedom never comes on a silver platter. It doesn't come with understanding the enemy. Freedom comes with fighting him. If it isn't a freedom worth fighting for, it's not worth our time.

The price of freedom is high. No monetary amount can be applied to its cost. We are very thankful for those who serve our country and understand the cost of freedom. Our servicemen and women know they are fighting not only for their own countrymen but also for those in distant lands who want what we Americans have.

The Gettysburg experience for me was unforgettable, even life changing. The visit clarified my understanding of just what giving your all for the cost of freedom really means. *⁓Carol*

✯ ✯ ✯

Father God, thank you for those who have given their lives for the cause of freedom. I thank you for your Son, Jesus, and the shedding of his blood so I may experience spiritual freedom and have the promise of eternity. Continue to remind me of the cost of freedom, and help me to appreciate those who have paid the ultimate sacrifice. ✝ *Amen.*

Esprit de Corps

The human body has many parts, but the many parts make up one whole body. So it is with the body of Christ. Some of us are Jews, some are Gentiles, some are slaves, and some are free. But we have all been baptized into one body by one Spirit, and we all share the same Spirit. ✛ I CORINTHIANS 12:12-13

Recently my husband was visiting wounded soldiers at Walter Reed Army Medical Center. As he passed by the rooms, my husband noticed some doors that displayed huge unit crests. At first he was surprised, but soon he realized the significance of this bold visual statement. Not only were these soldiers communicating their pride and patriotism, but they were also communicating their loyalty to the unit to which they were assigned. The crest identified them with that unit and was an invitation for others who had a connection with the unit to stop and visit. It was a display of a common bond. Though some of those soldiers may never be able to actively rejoin their units in combat, they will share a strong bond with the men and women of that unit for the rest of their lives.

The same type of esprit de corps is evident on the right shoulder of my husband's military uniform, where he wears a patch with the crest of the 82d Airborne Division. This identifies him as having served in combat with that division. He changes the patch on his left shoulder when he changes military assignments, but the right patch will be worn on his uniform indefinitely. Anytime he sees someone else with that patch on the right shoulder, he feels a certain amount of affinity as a brother in arms.

As Christians, we all share this esprit de corps by being part of the body of Christ. Just as soldiers have different jobs within a unit, believers all have different roles to get God's work accomplished. An identifiable crest may not be worn on our shoulders or displayed on our doors, but we are part of the same army with Christ as our Commander. Wear that "patch" with pride! ❧*Brenda*

✯   ✯   ✯

Lord of all, thank you for your provision of the body of Christ. I pray that your body, here in America and around the world, would unite to proclaim your love through our words and actions. In your name I pray. ✛*Amen.*

July 17
Set Up for Victory

You will not even need to fight. Take your positions; then stand still and watch the LORD's victory. He is with you, O people of Judah and Jerusalem. Do not be afraid or discouraged. Go out against them tomorrow, for the LORD is with you! ✛ 2 CHRONICLES 20:17

One thing I know for sure is that God wants to set us up for victory and not defeat. Yet he wants us to endure by patiently waiting on him to lead the way. Recently I heard a young woman speak to a group of military wives, spouses of both active-duty and retired servicemen. Her words struck to the heart of what our culture communicates.

Amy Stephens, the daughter of an active-duty navy chaplain, boldly looked out into the audience and told these ladies, "You know, I could tell you, 'Come on now—get a grip and get on with it. You can do it. Get over yourself. Get on with life.'" Then she said, "If I told you that, I would be setting you up for failure. The only way you can get on with it is if you rely on the One who can change everything. If God is your source of strength and power and joy, then you can get on with it."

If these women heard and applied what Amy said, a burden would be lifted from their shoulders. Her words gave them permission to let go of the feeling that they were alone and had to survive on their own. She pointed out that, even in the midst of war, God would give them his own strength to overcome daily personal battles. God is the key to victory in our lives.

Many times, people ask me how they can pray for our military men and women stationed in distant lands. I tell them that there is always a need to pray for protection, comfort, and strength. But I have also shared lately that after studying the Bible, I have come to realize that we need to pray more for victory. We need to pray more for victory in the War on Terror. We need to switch from praying a defensive prayer, "Father protect them," to praying an offensive prayer, "Father give us victory. Go before us to lead us into victory."

Our God is a God of victory throughout the Bible. We cannot succumb to the pressure to give up because the war will never be won. God has shown his military might throughout history, and today's conflict is no exception.

Let's begin to pray for victory in this War on Terror! God wants us to be set up for victory, not defeat. He wants the spiritual and physical enemy defeated so he can reign in the hearts of those who call out his name.   ↝*Carol*

☆　　☆　　☆

God of victory, I ask today for peace, protection, and strength for all who serve our country. I come to you in boldness to ask for victory in this war. ✛ *Amen.*

Patient Endurance

Then the way you live will always honor and please the Lord, and your lives will produce every kind of good fruit. All the while, you will grow as you learn to know God better and better. We also pray that you will be strengthened with all his glorious power so you will have all the endurance and patience you need. May you be filled with joy, always thanking the Father. He has enabled you to share in the inheritance that belongs to his people, who live in the light.

✛ COLOSSIANS 1:10-12

At the beginning of Operation Iraqi Freedom in 2003, one brigade from the 82d Airborne Division was sent to Kuwait, in case their airborne skills were needed for the beginning of the war. Though the brigade did not conduct an airborne operation, they were engaged in combat from the onset of the conflict that began in March. By the time the Iraqi army was defeated and disbanded in May, there was talk among brigade's officers and soldiers of going home because they were no longer needed. The unit packed up much of their equipment and were waiting for redeployment orders when word came that they would not be going home in May or June. Instead, they would be staying for a total of twelve months. This was an emotional rollercoaster experience for not only the soldiers but also their families back home, who were looking forward to reuniting.

The soldiers were able to refocus on the mission they had and with patient endurance face the hardships of a long, hot summer in the desert of Iraq, knowing that they would miss the Thanksgiving and Christmas holidays with their families. Soldiers are trained to accept and respond to changes in mission such as the one described. They are highly disciplined in performing their duties whenever and under whatever conditions the nation calls them to serve.

As Christians, we are challenged in Colossians 1:10-12 to endure with patience. It is through the leadership and strength of the Holy Spirit and the support of other believers that we are able to face unexpected hardships with confidence in knowing that God has a purpose for our lives and we have a responsibility to be faithful to him. ≈*Brenda*

✳   ✳   ✳

Heavenly Father, may the way I live always honor and please you, and may my life produce every kind of good fruit. All the while, help me grow as I learn to know you better and better. I also pray that I will be strengthened with all your glorious power so I will have all the endurance and patience I need. May I be filled with joy, always thanking you. You have enabled me to share in the inheritance that belongs to your people, who live in the light. ✛ *Amen.*

July 19
Desperate for God

To me, living means living for Christ, and dying is even better. ✢ PHILIPPIANS 1:21

There is no other person in Scripture that could have said the above verse more profoundly than Paul. He was so desperate to be with God and all God had to give that he counted being with God even through death as better than any other life. Paul knew that he would be with God forever after his death. He did not want to ever bring shame on the Lord's name through anything else he did in his life.

This was from a man who years earlier had done nothing but bring shame on God's people. After his encounter with God, however, it was all or nothing for Paul. He knew that by living for Christ, others would come to know God.

Some definitions of the word *desperate* include "making a final, ultimate effort; giving all"; "having an urgent need, desire, etc."; and "actuated by a feeling of hopelessness."[1]

As I read through these definitions, I cannot help but think about our men and women in the military. I think of their great commitment to give up all their earthly desires to be led by an organization. There is great intensity in these young people. Oftentimes when they join a military branch of service, they are committing to a new lifestyle out of hopelessness and lack of direction in their own lives. They are desperate for a change in their lives.

These men and women are desperate to achieve. They are pushed to their limits yet stay committed. They are willing to die for their country and the freedoms we have. Those who have been called stay committed throughout their time in service. The most amazing thing is that those who are truly called into military service remain deeply patriotic and supportive of their fellow members, even upon retirement.

As a Christian, I want to remain desperate for God. I want to commit to a lifestyle of honor, hard work, and dedication so others will come to know Jesus as their personal Savior. I want to continue to bring honor to my faith and to my Lord. I want to remain so desperate for God that I can also say, "For me, living is for Christ, and dying is even better." ❧*Carol*

✱　✱　✱

Father God, give me an element of desperation in my Christian walk. I want to desire only you in my life. When other things of the world creep in, remind me to be a soldier of the cross. Thank you for the example set by our military members. ✢ *Amen.*

---

[1] www.dictionary.com

Hamburger Hill

We patiently endure troubles and hardships and calamities of every kind. We have been beaten, been put in prison, faced angry mobs, worked to exhaustion, endured sleepless nights, and gone without food. We prove ourselves by our purity, our understanding, our patience, our kindness, by the Holy Spirit within us, and by our sincere love. We faithfully preach the truth. God's power is working in us. We use the weapons of righteousness in the right hand for attack and the left hand for defense. We serve God whether people honor us or despise us, whether they slander us or praise us. We are honest, but they call us impostors. We are ignored, even though we are well known. We live close to death, but we are still alive. We have been beaten, but we have not been killed. Our hearts ache, but we always have joy. We are poor, but we give spiritual riches to others. We own nothing, and yet we have everything.

✝ 2 CORINTHIANS 6:4-10

The battle known as Hamburger Hill during the Vietnam War claimed hundreds of lives and wounded thousands. During a special television program highlighting this battle, the outcome was described like this:

"The remarkable bravery, steadfast endurance, and individual initiative of young American soldiers all contributed to the eventual victory. The 101st Airborne troopers who took Hamburger Hill persevered because they fought for each other. By the end of the fight it wasn't superior American technology or firepower that prevailed—it was, to put it bluntly: guts. This is a real chronicle of courage."[1]

I am confident that soldiers fighting to take Hamburger Hill would have preferred a peaceful march up the mountain to plant a flag of victory without a shot being fired. In war, however, battle is inevitable, and in order to be victorious, conflicts require courage and willingness to fight. In my personal life I, too, would prefer to have a Christian walk with no conflict, battles, or struggles. I read in 2 Corinthians that when I choose to follow the Lord, I must accept the inevitable fact that there will be personal challenges to face. The hope of this passage is that I don't have to face them alone and that, through it all, there will be ultimate victory through Christ. Let's climb the mountain to victory today!   ☙*Brenda*

✳   ✳   ✳

Father, thank you that I do not have to fight the battles of life alone. You have provided me with comrades in arms who fight with me and for me. You have provided your Holy Spirit, who fights on my behalf battles of which I may even be unaware. I pray for those who are struggling today with issues that cause them to feel defeated. May they know the comforting power of your presence. ✝ *Amen.*

---

[1] *War Stories Q&A; Hamburger Hill* Fox News, Saturday, August 4.

July 21
Faith to Endure

Trials will show that your faith is genuine. It is being tested as fire tests and purifies gold—though your faith is far more precious than mere gold. ✛ 1 PETER 1:7

There have been many times in my life when my faith has been tested as described in today's Scripture. I can encourage others to stay faithful and be very assured in that directive. Then just as soon as something comes my way, I worry. I have come to a point in my Christian walk that I never doubt my relationship with Jesus, but I wonder where he is at times. I think, *If only I had made that decision. If only we had gone to another place. If only, if only, if only.*

In his book *Simple Faith*, Charles Swindoll writes that the most notorious faith killer in all of life is worry. Many of us have learned the miserable art of worry from our families of origin. Charles Swindoll tells us that worry strangles the good Word of God that has been sown, rendering it ineffective and making those who once walked in simple faith unproductive people.[1]

I do not want to be rendered unproductive in my Christian walk. I have to fight the enemy when it comes to letting worry come in, and as the Scripture says, be anxious for nothing. I want a faith that endures through trials. I want a faith where Jesus shines to others when in my human effort I could shut down and shut out the world. I want a faith that can say, "I see this world and all that is going on in it, and I choose to stand with the Lord on my side and know he is in control."

How thankful I am that God holds the future. He knows the end, and he is well aware of the means to get there. As many in our world must have a faith to endure trials that are to the point of death, I pray that we remain faithful in our everyday lives and endure in prayer, in commitment, and in dedication to the cause of Christ. ⁓*Carol*

*   *   *

Father, as those who endure hardship and pain and even death in our world are keeping their faith, may that be an example to those who live in comfort and peace each day. Increase the faith of those who are struggling this day in faraway lands. ✛ *Amen.*

---

[1] Charles R. Swindoll, *Simple Faith* (Dallas, TX: Word Publishing, 1991), 173.

You'll Dance Again

We think you ought to know, dear brothers and sisters, about the trouble we went through in the province of Asia. We were crushed and overwhelmed beyond our ability to endure, and we thought we would never live through it. In fact, we expected to die. But as a result, we stopped relying on ourselves and learned to rely only on God, who raises the dead. And he did rescue us from mortal danger, and he will rescue us again. We have placed our confidence in him, and he will continue to rescue us. And you are helping us by praying for us. Then many people will give thanks because God has graciously answered so many prayers for our safety.

✛ 2 CORINTHIANS 1:8-11

A chaplain friend who serves at Walter Reed Army Medical Center relayed a story about an army sergeant and the people he inspires. This sergeant is a regular presence at the ward in the hospital that is dedicated to caring for amputees. When a new patient is brought in for his first therapy session, he is likely to find this gregarious sergeant, who asks if he may dance with the wife of the amputee. He then dances gracefully around the floor for a few moments with the surprised and probably embarrassed wife. Following the dance, he stops to look at the soldier and says, "I was right where you are eighteen months ago. If you do what these people tell you to do, you will be up and dancing with your wife yourself." The message of encouragement this sergeant consistently communicates to families facing a long road of recovery is that the struggle will be worth it.

Life is going to bring situations that cause us to feel like Paul in today's Scripture. Yet, in the midst of those times when we think we cannot endure and may even feel like we are going to die, he sends a message of hope. The dancing sergeant has chosen to make his life a testimony of encouragement. He gives other soldiers a real-life vision of how they, too, can overcome and regain many things they assume have been lost forever. There's no denying that one who has gone through a very difficult circumstance and has come out on the other side victorious can encourage others better than someone who has never had to fight those battles.

We can't really choose our battles and trials, but we can choose to be a positive voice and encouragement to others once we have come through them triumphantly. What battles have you fought that would enable you to speak a word of encouragement to someone today? ❧*Brenda*

✷ ✷ ✷

Father, I pray you would make me an instrument of blessing to others today. Thank you for the promise that I can rely on you during times when I feel overwhelmed by the circumstances of life. In Jesus' name I pray. ✛*Amen.*

Fishing Lesson

We also pray that you will be strengthened with all his glorious power so you will have all the endurance and patience you need. ✚ COLOSSIANS 1:11

We would wake up in the early morning and tiptoe out of the house so as not to awaken my sister or my mother. We would jump in the car and head off to the Blue Circle for a hearty breakfast of biscuits, gravy, sausage, and eggs. We didn't know about high cholesterol at the time. Praise the Lord for that! We just knew we needed extra energy to bring in all those fish for the day.

As we arrived at the lake, there would be a fog hanging over the water at the early hour. We would unload the life jackets and the fishing equipment into the boat, start up the motor, and off we went. It was a day of being in the presence of all creation.

Casting a fishing rod always came naturally to me. I loved it. It was with the waiting after the casting that I would become impatient. If I did not catch a fish after three or four casts, my dad would have to continually remind me that it takes a patient person to fish. It's not the technique but the patience that is important.

The most important thing about waiting for that fish is that you must have a sense of a slight *tap, tap* on the line before the fish bites. If you feel that *tap, tap*, you have to be ready to act and set the hook. It is so slight that often I would think I had even done it myself. When that fish was hooked, it was worth the wait. The joy and the excitement and the pride in my dad's face made it all worthwhile.

What an incredible lesson for our Christian life. Going after something in our lives is easy for us. Casting our desires and dreams is easy. However, when we have to wait for that gentle *tap, tap* from the Holy Spirit to confirm, it is truly worth waiting for; then we can grab hold and reel in all the blessings that go along with it. We will have a sense of the glow in our Father's face when it is from him.

And that, precious one, is your fishing lesson for the day!   *Carol*

✷   ✷   ✷

Father, teach me about patience. Allow me to share that with my children and family. I want to be able to grasp waiting for you in this world of fast food and fast answers. Give me sensitivity to the *tap, tap* of your Spirit in my life. I pray for times of recreation and relaxation for our servicemen and women. ✚ *Amen.*

This Is Not Fun!

Make every effort to respond to God's promises. Supplement your faith with a generous provision of moral excellence, and moral excellence with knowledge, and knowledge with self-control, and self-control with patient endurance, and patient endurance with godliness, and godliness with brotherly affection, and brotherly affection with love for everyone. | 2 PETER 1.5-7

As a very little boy, my youngest son, Joseph, could only be described as fun loving. The purpose of life, in his young mind, was fun. It makes me smile even now to think of his antics. The year our son was to begin kindergarten, my husband and I made the decision that I would homeschool him. I ordered the curriculum, prepared our classroom, and got ready to make school and learning fun for him.

Unfortunately, anything that had to do with learning was a test of endurance for Joseph. He was not interested in anything remotely academic. I especially remember a day when I had written his name on the wall that had been painted as a chalkboard. He was to spell his name and practice writing it. He methodically and angrily spelled out the letters, J-O-S-E-P-H and continued with marks on the board in the same methodical voice, with teeth gritted, overemphasizing each word: "I DON'T WANT TO DO THIS. THIS IS NOT FUN!"

As a young man, Joseph is still fun loving. He endured, persevered, and to appease his wife and mom, walked across the stage to receive a college diploma. Believe it or not, even after his reluctant entry into education, he is now teaching middle school.

We can endure some pretty challenging things, if it is something we want to do. For instance, people who run marathons get themselves prepared. They endure much physical duress on their bodies for training and willingly submit themselves to hours of agony on the day of the race. If it is something we do not want to do, even walking from the outer edge of the parking lot can be frustrating.

It's not realistic to go through life only doing what we want to do. There are many things that are good for us that may not be on the top of our list of fun things. But if we do these things, we will reap benefits from their accomplishment. Instead of measuring things you face by how much you want to do them, measure them by how beneficial they are. Maybe there is something today that you need an extra boost of patient endurance to make happen. It may not be fun, but it can be rewarding. ☙*Brenda*

*　*　*

Lord, I pray that you would grant me the endurance to do those things that I dread but are for my good. May I glorify you by my willingness to patiently endure challenging situations that come my way. Inspire those who are in the military on behalf of this country to endure in their circumstances, and to glorify you in their work. In your name I pray. ✝ *Amen.*

July 25
In the Midst of Them

Where two or three gather together as my followers, I am there among them. ✛ MATTHEW 18:20

Recently it was my honor to attend a women's conference and hear three well-known Christian teachers. I have always admired these women for incorporating true worship before each teaching. It is a time to focus on the Lord and the reason we gather together.

I woke up very early in the morning on the second day of the event. I had a sinus migraine or, as I like to call them, a barometric migraine. I have truly missed my calling in life. I would be a wonderful meteorologist and would not even have to go to school to get my degree. Each time I walk in for an adjustment at the chiropractor, he tells everyone there it's going to rain that day.

I was so sad to start out the day not feeling good, but I got ready and met my friends at the event. We waited in line for the doors to open and quickly headed up to the top tier to find our seats. We visited awhile with each other and heard some announcements from the stage. I sat there so frustrated that I had this nagging headache and could not enjoy the moment.

Soon the praise and worship leader came to the stage, and we began our time of praise. I had been praising the Lord and singing my heart out for at least fifteen minutes when I suddenly realized my headache was gone. I thought, *Thank you, Lord. You do inhabit the praise of your people.* I realized that as I praised him all else fell away. The weight of the world and the pain in my head were replaced with healing and joy.

We need each other. We are encouraged to fellowship and to pray together. When the weight of the world is on your shoulders, gather your Christian brothers and sisters and praise him. He is in the midst of your praise.   ❧*Carol*

✶　✶　✶

Dear heavenly Father, thank you for your presence at all times. Thank you for honoring me when I gather with other believers to praise you. I love you, Lord, and ask for your healing to come to those who are going through trials today. I ask in particular for the healing of physical and emotional wounds acquired in this country's military service all over the world. ✛ *Amen.*

July 26
Birdbath

Endure suffering along with me, as a good soldier of Christ Jesus. ✛ 2 TIMOTHY 2:3

Sometimes we take the simple things in life for granted. I learned this lesson while my husband was deployed to Iraq during the beginning of Operation Iraqi Freedom. What I took for granted proved to be a hardship he had to endure as a soldier on a regular basis. For example, taking a shower while engaged in extended combat is not possible.

On one occasion he was fortunate enough to be able to enjoy a shower in one of the most beautiful marble-tile showers imaginable. Not only that, but he was told he could use all the hot water he wanted. It was a glorious experience! Glorious until he awoke from his sleep to realize it had all been a dream!

In his words,

> I haven't had a bath for a while, so tonight, after dark, I am going to take a birdbath. Oh, the joys of soldiering. It has just started getting dark. This is a very pleasant time of day. It is cooling off, and a nice breeze is blowing. I had a dream last night that we were set up next to a chapel. I walked over to see the chaplain, and the chapel had a super nice bathroom and shower. I asked if I could take a shower and he said yes. I said I wouldn't use much hot water, and he said, "Use all you want." I was in heaven. When I woke up I thought it is pretty bad when you have fantasy dreams about getting to take a shower. I will be glad to be home.

Today's Scripture was written by the apostle Paul to the young minister Timothy. His words encouraged Timothy to persevere in his work for the Lord even through hardships. Because of Paul's imprisonment in his later years, he spent a good deal of time around soldiers. He was able to observe the hardships that come as they were often called upon to endure challenging circumstances.

As a Christ follower, I find myself enlisted as a soldier in God's army. As such, I receive the words of Paul that, as trials come, I have the need to grow stronger in my faith. The powerful message to understand here is that these trials actually work to make my faith stronger as I endure them.   *Brenda*

✶   ✶   ✶

Mighty Warrior, I thank you for your power and strength. Help me to endure the hardships that come my way without complaint but with confidence. Strengthen my resolve and fortify my faith, making me stronger in my love toward you and others. I pray for soldiers today who are enduring hardships. May they look to you for help and hope. ✛ Amen.

July 27

Waiting for Showers

Rejoice, you people of Jerusalem! Rejoice in the LORD your God! For the rain he sends demonstrates his faithfulness. Once more the autumn rains will come, as well as the rains of spring. ✛ JOEL 2:23

We wait so much for the rain showers to come in the summer. Showers are such relief not only for us but for the birds and the flowers. I watch the birds when there are long periods of drought. They go to the birdbath, yearning for water, and keep me accountable to fill it up. Taking glasses of ice water to my husband as he spends hours in the yard working is a job I take very seriously. I know that the cool water keeps him from getting a headache or even heatstroke.

Have you ever smelled rain coming? I can walk out in my yard in the summer and smell the rain that will come shortly after. I love to see the dark clouds filling the skies as the rain showers approach. I have also watched as they made a full circle around us, staying away until the rain's relief came days later.

The summer of 2007 was especially dry in Alabama. The flowers began to wilt, the tree branches drooped, and the leaves began to turn brown. But at a time when we needed water more than ever, there were watering restrictions.

One particular day, I could see the dark clouds rolling in. I began to ask God to let there be rain showers that day. I walked outside to look at the sky and could smell the rain coming. About an hour later, the skies opened up. I wanted to go out and stand in the middle of it and praise the Lord. I watched the rain come down and began to pray the prayer below.   ❧*Carol*

Father, thank you for the rain today. Thank you for the showers that are coming to water the plants and even the birds and wild animals. Thank you for the showers of blessings you give in my life. I pray right now that you shower blessings and favor on my family. I pray that you shower our military personnel with health, peace in your presence, and success in their endeavors. I pray showers of financial blessings to this nation's sons and daughters, so they can supply the needs of their families. Shower this day, Lord, with the joy of Jesus on those who are alone or having problems. May the showers of your love bring them into spiritual wellness. Thank you for this time of reflection with you and for your love in my life. ✛ *Amen.*

God Is Good?

We are pressed on every side by troubles, but we are not crushed. We are perplexed, but not driven to despair. We are hunted down, but never abandoned by God. We get knocked down, but we are not destroyed. Through suffering, our bodies continue to share in the death of Jesus so that the life of Jesus may also be seen in our bodies. Yes, we live under constant danger of death because we serve Jesus, so that the life of Jesus will be evident in our dying bodies. So we live in the face of death, but this has resulted in eternal life for you.

✛ 2 CORINTHIANS 4:8-12

The phrase "God is good" cannot be reserved for only those moments when life turns out the way we had hoped. Evangelist Leighton Ford spoke of how he wrestled with the meaning of that statement when his twenty-one-year-old son Sandy died following open-heart surgery: "Many times when someone says rather glibly, 'God answered this prayer; God did this miracle; God healed this person—isn't God good?' I've heard [my wife] say very quietly, 'Well, if God didn't heal, didn't do the miracle, is he not good?'" Of Sandy's death, he added, "I don't understand it, but God was good."[1]

To fully understand the goodness of God, we have to believe that his goodness transcends mortal, earthly living. We fall short in our faith when we believe this world is all there is and that material blessing is a demonstration of God's goodness. Who can doubt that God is good when he has prepared an eternal home that we can enjoy forever with friends and family who have also put their faith in him? The goal of the Christ follower is to keep the perspective that life in this world is a temporary existence and that we are passing through to our eternal abode, which will reveal the true goodness of God. ❧*Brenda*

* * *

Dear God, you are good. Forgive me when I doubt that goodness. Help me to trust you even when it seems you are uninterested. Don't allow me to judge your goodness on the basis of my comfort. I imagine it might be very difficult for those in harm's way, particularly in the face of battle, to be sure of your goodness, Lord, and I ask that you would mercifully give any such person the ability to trust you in spite of surrounding evil. Help me and all believers in you to hold on to your promises; make your life evident in us. In Jesus' name I pray. ✛*Amen.*

---

[1] Leighton Ford, "Yes, God is Good," *Decision Magazine*, June 1982, quoted in Stacy and Paula Rinehart, *Living in Light of Eternity* (Colorado Springs, CO: NavPress, 1986), 144.

July 29
Who Is That in the Mirror?

We never give up. Though our bodies are dying, our spirits are being renewed every day. . . . So we don't look at the troubles we can see now; rather, we fix our gaze on things that cannot be seen. For the things we see now will soon be gone, but the things we cannot see will last forever. ✝ 2 CORINTHIANS 4:16-18

I believe I will forever be young at heart. I have a good example in my mother. She and I have so much fun getting ready in the mornings when I spend the night with her. We stand side by side, trying to fix our faces and comb our hair. Often we stand there and say, "Who are those old women in the mirror?" Immediately, we crack up laughing and get back to the duty at hand. We have been told by my sister that no woman should ever go out without combing her hair or putting on earrings and lipstick. My sister was in the beauty-pageant circuit in my growing-up years, and she often won, so we take her beauty advice very seriously.

Being young on the outside and being young at heart are two very different concepts. The Bible tells us that our bodies are dying daily but our spirits are being renewed each day. We can't see our spirits being renewed by physically looking into that part of our souls, but we can trust God's Word that it is happening.

We are living in a time where many people have crushed spirits from the past or oppression in their lives. It is our responsibility to continue to strive to refresh and renew our inner spirits every day with God's holy Word and communication with him.

"All of us who have had that veil removed can see and reflect the glory of the Lord. And the Lord—who is the Spirit—makes us more and more like him as we are changed into his glorious image" (2 Corinthians 3:18). I may not always be thrilled by what I see in the mirror physically, but I can know that God knows and sees my soul. I am beautiful to him! ❧*Carol*

Father God, there are so many in the world who feel unloved and without beauty. Encourage those at home or in the military who have been beaten down by life, and let them see the beauty you can bring to their lives, even in the face of the ugliness they may be facing. ✝ *Amen.*

Battery Powered

We now have this light shining in our hearts, but we ourselves are like fragile clay jars containing this great treasure. This makes it clear that our great power is from God, not from ourselves. ✚ 2 CORINTHIANS 4:7

Have you ever noticed how many things require batteries? Just this week I have found myself frustrated because I did not have a battery for a handheld recorder I wanted to use while walking. I thought about this tiny object that provides the energy for so many things we use on a daily basis, and I came up with several spiritual applications.

A battery begins as an empty container. At the beginning stage, there is no energy and no ability to produce its own power. It is what goes into the case that produces the power. 2 Corinthians 4:7 describes us as vessels that need to be filled. I am an empty, fragile jar of clay needing to be filled with the power of God. His Spirit is what gives me any power to live a life that brings honor to him.

In order to function correctly, the contact surface of a battery must be clean. I, too, must be a clean vessel for God's power to flow through me. His desire is "to open [my] eyes, so [I] may turn from darkness to light and from the power of Satan to God. Then [I] will receive forgiveness for [my] sins and be given a place among God's people, who are set apart by faith in [him]" (Acts 26:18). It is his power that fills my heart with forgiveness and empowers me to shine a light amid the darkness.

Usually things require more than one battery: the more complicated the object, the more batteries needed, lined up in such a way that they draw on each other to bring power. That's not unlike the body of Christ.

When we are lined up together—joined as he wants us to be—his power is multiplied many times over. We can endure hardships when we stand together. Supporting one another in faith, prayer, and encouragement, we are much stronger than if we stand alone. It's an example of the basic principle Jesus taught of two or more agreeing about one thing (see Matthew 18:19). In essence, there is more power when we are linked together in the common source of God's Spirit.

I still don't have a battery to run my recorder, but I'm not frustrated anymore. Instead, I am grateful for the lesson it provided and the reminder that I need to be filled with God's power today! ❧*Brenda*

✳   ✳   ✳

God of all power, thank you for the energy of your Spirit that is available to fill me today. Make me an empty vessel, cleaned and ready for you to use. Teach me and others, particularly those in active duty, to run on your strength, not our own. In Jesus' name I pray. ✚*Amen.*

July 31
Fall Seven Times, Stand Up Eight

Just as our bodies have many parts and each part has a special function, so it is with Christ's body. We are many parts of one body, and we all belong to each other. ✛ ROMANS 12:4-5

One day last spring when I was walking to my car, I fell off the curb of the sidewalk and into the street. After looking around to see if anyone saw my blunder, I quickly walked to my car, trying not to show too much pain from the impact of my hand and knee hitting the pavement. Though I landed on my hand and knee, later that evening and into the next day the effect was felt all through my body.

I thought about this as I watched the coverage of the mining accident in West Virginia in the summer of 2007. While this tragedy happened in one state of our nation, the entire country was affected. Words of condolence and offers of help from all around the country poured in. Most of us watched helplessly as the tragic events unfolded. People in our country were hurting, and it hurt us all.

Events like this can never be viewed as positive, but there can be a positive response to such events. The right response causes us to support each other in prayer and join together in making an assessment to appreciate the good things we have.

An old Japanese proverb states, "Fall seven times, stand up eight." This is an apt description of America. It is a nation that has proved to be resilient. Undoubtedly, we will face tragedy, hardships, and difficulties, but as long as God helps us stand up one more time after a fall, we will continue to be a great and strong nation. ☙*Brenda*

Lord, I pray that America would continue to stand up after every fall. May the body of Christ take the lead in standing firm in conviction and faith. Give us leaders who will stand firm in causes that will make this nation great and strong. Comfort those in our nation who have been touched by tragedy. In your name I pray. ✛*Amen.*

A Way Out

The temptations in your life are no different from what others experience. And God is faithful. He will not allow the temptation to be more than you can stand. When you are tempted, he will show you a way out so that you can endure. ✛ 1 CORINTHIANS 10:13

When you've gone through a difficult or tempting situation, has someone ever said to you, "God will never give you more than you can bear"? Well, that is only part of the story. Scripture tells us that he will not give you more than you can handle *without providing a way out.* This part of the Scripture is the most important part. He acknowledges that we will have powerful temptations. He has known it since the beginning of time. However, when we are going through these seemingly unbearable times, he will give us a way out that will assist us in the resolve and the healing.

Let me ask you this: Do you think that Almighty God did not know that temptation would come your way when you were separated from your spouse during times of deployment? Do you think that Almighty God did not know that pornography would enable those who view it to harm the covenant relationship with his or her spouse? Do you think that Almighty God did not know that teens would stray from the values and morals of their parents and rebel when single parents were frazzled to their last nerve? Almighty God knew and knows everything that happens.

For this reason he says to us we will have temptations in our lives that we feel we cannot bear. However, when we are at that point, he will provide a way out for us. A friend may come to minister to you. It may come through counsel from someone who can help you get out of an addiction. It may even come from total forgiveness and healing.

The way out may also come when you are able to stand and say, "I need help. This temptation has turned into action, and I need help." God is there waiting to provide a way out. Call upon his name. Cry out Psalm 25:16-17: "Turn to me and have mercy, for I am alone and in deep distress. My problems go from bad to worse. Oh, save me from them all!" He is your way out! ✐*Carol*

✫   ✫   ✫

Jehovah Jireh, all I can say is *hallelujah!* I pray against temptation in the lives of precious families who are separated by conflict in our world. Give them people who will not enable them to be tempted but will lead them to you, the provider of a way out. ✛*Amen.*

August 2
A Holy Turban

Make a medallion of pure gold, and engrave it like a seal with these words: Holy to the Lord.
✝ EXODUS 28:36

The medallion described in this Scripture hung on the front of a turban worn by the priests. There are parts of the world where wearing a turban is a normal aspect of local dress, but in America it is the exception to see someone in a turban. While riding on the D.C. metro, my husband saw a young man in his early twenties wearing a turban almost the size of a basketball. He couldn't help but be drawn to the out-of-the-norm appearance.

In America wearing a turban on one's head may cause others to stare, but I've wondered if wearing a turban on my own head, as in today's Scripture, would cause me to be more holy. Would it be easier to live a holy life if the words *Holy to the Lord* were emblazoned on my head? It's like asking, Am I more likely to obey the speed limit if there is a fish on the back of my car? Now, I don't think there is anything wrong with having religious symbols to remind us to be holy. But living a pure life depends more on what I have in my heart than what I wear on my head.

Sometimes God uses hardships to develop holiness in me. It's uncomfortable, and I admit I whine and complain because things are hard. Yet these are often the very things God has allowed in order to build my character—in other words, to make me holy.

Too often the idea of holiness conjures up thoughts of the dos and don'ts of following Christ. Oswald Chambers wrote, "The destined end of man is not happiness, nor health, but holiness. Never tolerate through sympathy with yourself or with others any practice that is not in keeping with a holy God."[1] What is God using in your life today to develop his character in you?   *⮑Brenda*

*   *   *

Lord, forgive my whining and complaining. Do the work within me that allows me to stand up to the scrutiny of your holy light. May the work that goes on in our government and military be glorifying to you wherever your people are in positions of authority, I pray. ✝ *Amen.*

---

[1] Oswald Chambers, *My Utmost for His Highest* (Uhrichsville, OH: Discovery House, 1992), September 1 entry.

Because I Can

I discipline my body like an athlete, training it to do what it should. Otherwise, I fear that after preaching to others I myself might be disqualified. ✛ 1 CORINTHIANS 9:27

This Scripture is rich and challenging and applicable for today. It presents the choice to do what our bodies were created to do. That is, to take care of them as God's temple. It also presents to us the challenge to practice what we preach. Paul is actually using this example of the athlete to remind us of the privilege of serving Christ. The discipline he is speaking of is the discipline of knowing Christ and leading others to him.

I have mentioned how special my daily walking routine is to me. It is my time of prayer and reflection, and the Holy Spirit often gives me insight as I meditate on God's Word. I begin my walk with great expectations of what my time with the Lord will bring. I am excited to spend these moments with him. It is uninterrupted and intense. The more I talk and pray with him (spiritual) the faster I walk (physical).

Today I began to give him thanks for the simple fact that I can exercise daily and that I have a strong body and the energy to put one foot in front of the other. I began to thank him that I can get my heart pumping and my muscles burning. I asked him to forgive me for the times that I say, "I am not in the mood for this today."

After I thanked him for allowing me to choose to exercise every day, a young woman entered the track. I immediately noticed she was several years younger than I was. She entered with a cane and then immediately went to the inner part of the track where there is a railing. She was walking slowly with uneasiness in her step. There was a man with her on the other side, just in case she needed him.

As I passed them several times and said hello, I immediately returned to thanking God that, because I can and because he has allowed me the privilege, I am going to continue exercising (physical) and from this moment will always be thankful (spiritual).

Today, be thankful with me because you can. Today, remember those men and women who are coming home after losing limbs in war. They have to go through rehabilitation to relearn the simplest tasks. Many of us can walk out our doors anytime. So get out there today—because you can.   ⋘*Carol*

✳   ✳   ✳

Dear God, don't let me get complacent about my physical well-being. Bless those who are in rehabilitation during this time, and give them strength and healing. ✛ *Amen.*

August 4
The Bank of Trust

If you are suffering in a manner that pleases God, keep on doing what is right, and trust your lives to the God who created you, for he will never fail you. ✛ 1 PETER 4:19

A pastor calling door to door one afternoon came by chance upon two young housewives, each in the advanced stages of multiple sclerosis, that slow, terribly crippling, and usually fatal disease.

To the first, life seemed small, unjust, lonely, and senseless. She had gained some formal knowledge about God, but her limited concept of the Divine had long before become useless for her needs. Her world reached no farther than her dinner tray. Existence was without meaning.

As Pastor Baker tells it, "Five doors down the street, the second lady looked out of her window with great yearning to be up and out, participating and being involved. She asked questions about community matters, school problems, future plans, and her eyes sparkled with life even though, she acknowledged, she probably would not be around to see those fascinating projects come to completion."

"Through the suffering of the second woman there was no complaint, only thankfulness for the love and thoughtfulness of others and a profound faith in the total adequacy of the grace of God."[1]

The example in this illustration is one of trust in God. The Greek word translated "trust" in today's Scripture carries the meaning of depositing something for safekeeping. In other words, when we deposit our lives into the hands of God, he will take care of us, as exhibited by the second woman in the story. The word further communicates the value our heavenly Father places in us. Suffering will come to the Christian, but our response to suffering is our choice. Some suffering comes just because of the human condition; other suffering can be a result of sin and disobedience. The suffering addressed by Peter in 1 Peter 4:19 comes as a result of taking a stand for righteousness.

When our attitudes are of constant commitment to God, even our suffering brings glory to him. Today's Scripture points to a time when suffering will come as a fiery trial. With constant deposits made in the Bank of Trust, we will come through the fire standing firm in God's care and control.   ᴁ*Brenda*

* * *

Heavenly Father, I don't like to suffer. It makes me uncomfortable and even fearful. Help me to stand up in whatever fiery trials come my way, and to make deposits of trust that will enable me to rejoice even through pain, knowing that you are in the furnace of suffering with me. Thank you for those in the military doing difficult jobs so that I can enjoy the freedoms and comforts that they defend. Help me not to rely on this world's comforts, however, but to look forward to that glorious day after which I will suffer no more but live forever in your presence. In Jesus' name I pray. ✛*Amen.*

---

[1] W. L. Jenkins and Wesley Baker, *More Than a Man Can Take* (Philadelphia, PA: The Westminster Press, 1996), 38–39.

Choice with Discernment

Solid food is for those who are mature, who through training have the skill to recognize the difference between right and wrong. + HEBREWS 5:14

Every day we make choices. We have access to those choices at our fingertips. We can use the remote to turn on the television and then pick up the phone to order any color, size, or style of any product ever made if we are patient throughout the programming. We can also go to the computer and pull up any information on the things in life that bring us much earthly satisfaction.

Many of our choices do not have eternal consequence—but many do. In fact, sin came into the world because of a choice. When God told Eve she could eat the fruit from any of the trees in the Garden except the tree of knowledge of good and evil, she made the choice to go for the fruit after Satan tempted her to think she would be like God. God has allowed us to have choices since the beginning of time. He will not stop us from making a choice that is wrong, but there will be consequences for that decision.

This is a time when we must ask the Lord to give us discernment in making choices. Too much is at stake in our nation without this discernment. If those of us who are mature in the Lord do not stand and make decisions for moral and dignified situations, there will be no one to do so.

My husband and I take every opportunity to communicate with and admonish our elected officials when we feel something is happening that is not a choice to be made by one nation under God. We exercise our privilege as free citizens when we discern something going on that is not from the Lord.

I am thankful our God gives us choices. Each time I make a wrong choice, I find myself in a posture of repentance for days. When I make a right choice, I give thanks, recognizing growth in my decision making.

Some say we are at a crossroads as a nation. Far too many decisions have been made without discernment from the Holy Spirit. I can't be personally responsible for the decisions made on behalf of my nation, but I am responsible for the decisions that affect my sphere of influence. Each day I have an opportunity to make wise and godly decisions. If enough of us commit to doing that, we can make a difference!
⊷Carol

✳ ✳ ✳

Creator, forgive me when I have not stood up for the things I know to be right in our country. Give me a heart that seeks to serve you in every walk of life so that others will come to know you and the promise of eternity. Give our leaders and military personnel the courage to stand up for what is right. + *Amen.*

Chosen to Stand

My sons, do not neglect your duties any longer! The LORD has chosen you to stand in his presence, to minister to him, and to lead the people in worship and present offerings to him.
✝ 2 CHRONICLES 29:11

During a memorial ceremony at Arlington National Cemetery, I was drawn to observe the precise military movements of the soldier standing guard at the Tomb of the Unknown Soldier. The ritual of pacing twenty-one steps across and then back again has been done since 1948. The tomb is guarded twenty-four hours a day, 365 days a year, rain or shine. The soldiers selected as sentinels are chosen because of their outstanding military bearing and personal discipline. On the one hand, they are doing something very simple: standing guard over a tomb that honors our nation's fallen heroes. Even though these men are carefully selected, in reality, there are many soldiers who could carry out the task. What gives the tribute its distinction is not the soldier but the place and all that it represents. The place and the mission are focused on, not the soldier. For the soldier it is a great honor to be chosen to stand.

God has chosen us to stand as Christians, not because of who we are but because of who he is and what he has done. To be able to stand and proclaim the greatness of God is not a testimony to our uniqueness but an acknowledgment of God's greatness. The soldier guarding this revered tomb does his best and takes his duty seriously. We, too, must do our best and take the duty of following Christ seriously. We must never forget, though, that the primary focus is not the stance we are taking but rather the One we are representing. I'm inspired by these young patriots to be more diligent in my duty to stand for Christ today. He did not choose me to stand idle but to live my life in worship and service to him.   *⮑Brenda*

* * *

Father, it is humbling to think you have chosen me to stand before you. Help me to take that stand today with reverence, giving you the honor for which you are worthy. In Jesus' name.
✝ *Amen.*

Clapping Trees

You will live in joy and peace. The mountains and hills will burst into song, and the trees of the field will clap their hands! + ISAIAH 55:12

Don't you just love to get out of town from time to time? As you drive away, you feel your troubles getting farther and farther behind you. Recently my son was stressed-out about leaving town to go on a four-day vacation. He is in the building profession, and there is never a quitting place. When I called him the day after he got to the beach, he said, "Job, what job?" It is true we can leave our troubles behind when we get away from our normal routines.

I took a trip with my mother and sister to the lovely mountain town of Blowing Rock, North Carolina. It is a quiet, friendly place with beautiful little shops and restaurants. We enjoyed catching up with each other and spending quality girl time together.

After three days, we packed up the car and headed back home. The first couple of hours we talked of all we had experienced in Blowing Rock. We talked about the wonderful food at the local restaurant. We talked about the beautiful weather and how refreshing it was to get away from the very hot summer days.

As we got closer to home, we began to talk about situations we had left behind. We began to talk about the things we had to do that week. My sister noticed that we were on a stretch of highway that was lined on both sides with tall, thick trees. The trees were blowing back and forth in the gentle breeze. It was very obvious that this was different from the normal stretch of highway with openness on one side and a few trees on the other.

My sister said, "Just imagine these trees as all the angelic hosts and all the people who love us clapping us on in life. They are like these clapping trees encouraging us in life's journey." I will never forget that word picture. It was so powerful, and for that twenty-minute stretch of highway, the three of us just thanked the Lord for those in our lives who are cheering us on in our Christian faith.

Be a clapping tree for someone today. Encourage them in the Lord. Pick up the phone and call the spouse of a deployed military member. E-mail a soldier in Iraq or Afghanistan or one who is serving within our borders. Share some joy today with someone, and lead the way for them as their encourager and friend.   *Carol*

✴   ✴   ✴

Father God, thank you for moments of discernment in my life when I can imagine you right here with me. Inspire your children in the military to encourage those around them with the hope they have, and help me to do the same here for someone who is hurting or is lonely. +*Amen.*

Freely, Fully, Liberally

Be kind to each other, tenderhearted, forgiving one another, just as God through Christ has forgiven you. + EPHESIANS 4:32

It is a difficult thing to admit, but I am of the opinion that forgiveness is something that isn't natural to humans. Revenge is the more natural response. For instance, there are times when someone has hurt me and my reaction is to want to make them feel bad. Now, if I am honest with myself, the actual name for that desire is revenge.

Someone in ministry shared with me the advice a secular counselor gave a wife whose husband had cheated on her. The non-Christian counselor said she should deal with this by having an affair herself in order to get even. That way she wouldn't feel bad and would inflict pain back on her husband. Talk about an eye-for-an-eye mentality! The truth is, without the power of the Holy Spirit helping us, this would possibly be our natural tendency.

Today's Scripture instructs us to forgive, just as Christ has forgiven us. Forgiveness, though not natural, will set us free, but revenge will put us in personal bondage. In this life, we are going to offend others—whether we mean to or not. Our heavenly Father has made a way through Christ for us to forgive when we are offended. He provides us the help we need through the Holy Spirit to forgive others when they have offended us.

Here are some things to remember when it comes to forgiveness:

Forgive as soon as feasible following the offense. Harboring unforgiveness for a small offense may end up with you being bitter long after the offense was made.

Choose to give others the benefit of the doubt. Too often we make assumptions of others that are not true.

Recognize that forgiveness is a process. I believe God can deliver anyone from an unforgiving spirit, but I also believe the most common path of forgiveness is his bringing us to that point over time. It's also important to remember that the greater the offense, sometimes the greater the process.

Christ forgave us freely, fully, and liberally, and that is our model of how we are to forgive others.[1] Forgiveness chooses not to refer to the offense again and does not avert love or unity toward the offender. We are to treat others as Christ treats us in our offenses. ❧*Brenda*

* * *

Lord, thank you for the free, full, and liberal forgiveness you have shown me. Make me aware of unforgiveness I may be harboring in my heart. Reveal the truth of revenge that may cloak itself in passive-aggressive responses to those I love. Then help me to truly forgive others as you have forgiven me. In your name I pray. + *Amen.*

---

[1] Commentary on Ephesians 4:32, *Barnes' Notes*, Electronic Database, CD-ROM. Biblesoft, 1997.

Daily Leading

When you pray, don't babble on and on as people of other religions do. They think their prayers are answered merely by repeating their words again and again. Don't be like them, for your Father knows exactly what you need even before you ask him! + MATTHEW 6:7-8

Do you ever wonder what to say to God in your time of need? The verse above continues below with Jesus' famous words that show us how to pray. I encourage you to pray this prayer out loud today. In it is provision and direction for handling fear, choices, and temptation. In times of despair and conflict in your life, and on behalf of those who are in such need as they face this country's enemies, pray this prayer for provision, as well as for comfort and peace.   ~*Carol*

★   ★   ★

Our Father in heaven,
May your name be kept holy.
May your Kingdom come soon.
May your will be done on earth,
As it is in heaven.
Give us today the food we need,

And forgive us our sins,
As we have forgiven those who sin against us.
And don't let us yield to temptation,
But rescue us from the evil one.

MATTHEW 6:9-13

August 10
Oblivion

Love prospers when a fault is forgiven, but dwelling on it separates close friends.
✝ PROVERBS 17:9

A story is told of two unmarried sisters who had so bitter a disagreement they stopped speaking to each other. Unable or unwilling to leave their small home, they continued to use the same rooms and sleep in the same bedroom. A chalk line divided the sleeping area into two halves, separating the doorway and the fireplace, so that each could come and go and get her own meals without trespassing on her sister's domain. In the black of night each could hear the breathing of the foe. For years they coexisted in grinding silence. Neither was willing to take the first step to reconciliation.[1]

I don't know about you, but I think life is just too short to hold on to such strong negative emotions. Stories like this one are sad and so unnecessary. Proverbs 17:9 encourages us not to dwell on the faults of those we love but instead to forgive. It is easier said than done, isn't it? It's much easier to dwell on irritating habits or past offenses than it is to forget them. The true meaning of this Scripture, however, is that we are to bury those irritating things in oblivion. Oblivion!

The temptation to hold a grudge, seek revenge, or point out faults is a strong one to overcome. But the ripping of faults is the ripping out of love.[2] Whether it is a coworker, neighbor, friend, or family member, the guideline of Scripture is to get rid of those things that would separate us from loving one another. "Get rid of all bitterness, rage and anger, brawling and slander, along with every form of malice. Be kind and compassionate to one another, forgiving each other, just as in Christ God forgave you" (Ephesians 4:31-32, NIV). Let your first assumption about an irritation or annoyance be that it was an oversight or forgetfulness. And then respond with oversight and forgetfulness, allowing peace to envelop instead of irritation to separate.   ❧*Brenda*

* * *

Lord, forgive me when I am tempted to react to others with irritation and annoyance. Develop in me the habit of burying my irritations in oblivion. Protect me from wrong and unjust assumptions. Use me to be one who pulls those I love closer, not one who draws lines of separation. In this society in which tempers flare quickly, spread your spirit of peace and reconciliation. In your name I pray. ✝ *Amen.*

---

[1] Leslie B. Flynn, *Dare to Care Like Jesus* (Colorado Springs, CO: Victor Books, 1983).
[2] *Matthew Henry's Commentary on the Whole Bible: New Modern Edition,* Electronic Database, CD-ROM. Hendrickson Publishers, 1991.

Don't Fear the End

Since we are receiving a Kingdom that is unshakable, let us be thankful and please God by worshiping him with holy fear and awe. ·ŀ· HEBREWS 12.28

When my husband first came to know Jesus as his Lord and Savior in the early 1980s, there was a lot of teaching about the "end times." There were books written that gave the dates Jesus would return. Predictions were made about the new bar code stamped on products being the mark of the Beast. There was much that drew our attention from the love of God to fear of the perilous times that were to come. Unfortunately, we were making fear the focus of our spiritual understanding.

It is a good thing to study eschatology and to have an understanding of the future as God has laid it out for us in Scripture. It is good for us to study Revelation and to come to an understanding of what will happen during the Tribulation. It gives us a sense of urgency in our testimonies and in our desires that all come to know Jesus as their Lord and Savior.

When the fear of God and his Word becomes a scare tactic, however, we need to reevaluate what we are learning. When our fear in the sense of reverence and awe turns to "what is he going to do next?" we need to reevaluate. We are not to fear the future but to rest in the fact that God is in control and he wins at the end of the book!

How does this relate to our present day? We are living in a scare-tactics world. We fear the unknown. We fear different cultures. We are drawn to fear in scary movies and haunted houses. The only true fear we should have is fear of not receiving eternal life for our souls.

Americans are a strong people. Many Americans still call on the name of the Lord, asking him to protect our nation and to bless it. We know that no matter what happens to our country or our world, there is a Kingdom without end promised to us who believe in the name of Jesus.

Let us worship and adore him and replace that fear of the end with faith in the One who knows the end. We can trust him with our future! ∾*Carol*

★　★　★

Father, thank you for the assurance of the Kingdom without end. Bless those who are telling the world of your promises and leading others to a relationship with Jesus Christ as their Lord and Savior. Father, give those in the military who are standing for faith an extra measure of your grace today. ✛ *Amen.*

August 12
Prayer for Safety

In times of trouble, may the LORD answer your cry.
May the name of the God of Jacob keep you safe from all harm.
May he send you help from his sanctuary
and strengthen you from Jerusalem.
May he remember all your gifts
and look favorably on your burnt offerings.
May he grant your heart's desires
and make all your plans succeed.
May we shout for joy when we hear of your victory
and raise a victory banner in the name of our God.
May the LORD answer all your prayers.
Now I know that the LORD rescues his anointed king.
He will answer him from his holy heaven
and rescue him by his great power.
Some nations boast of their chariots and horses,
but we boast in the name of the LORD our God.
Those nations will fall down and collapse,
but we will rise up and stand firm.
Give victory to our king, O LORD! Answer our cry for help.

✝ PSALM 20

This psalm was sung before going out to war. Before the king faced the dangers and uncertainty of battle, the Israelites sang these words for safety and victory. It was a sincere prayer articulating faith and trust in a God whose power was able to keep the troops even in the midst of hazardous battle.

In today's war, the most dangerous combat operations are simply a ground convoy from one location to the next because of explosive devices along the road. The enemy intends to blow up passing vehicles. Before the convoys roll out, most of them have their chaplain present to lead them in prayer. There are stories of soldiers in the convoy not willing to leave until their chaplain is able to arrive and pray for the departure.

Whenever we are facing a difficult and challenging situation where there is uncertainty, it is always appropriate to look to the Lord in prayer. My husband and I make it a practice to pray before beginning a trip, asking for God's safety and protection as we travel. You, too, may have times when you ask God's blessings before a task or venture.

I encourage you to remember those soldiers around the world in harm's way today. Pray Psalm 20 on their behalf.   *≈Brenda*

✵   ✵   ✵

Give victory, O Lord! Answer our cry for help. ✝ *Amen.*

Dream Big

For everything there is a season, a time for every activity under heaven. ✛ ECCLESIASTES 3:1

In my Christian life, I have had the opportunity to serve in many areas of the church. I was an active participant in the chapel while a military wife. I loved being involved in the women's ministry, and as I grew as a Christian by reading the Word, I encouraged others to do so as well. I was involved in planning many of the retreats for young women to have a time of rest and study. I always wanted to give them the opportunity to have precious quiet time with the Lord.

After entering a civilian church, I was very active in teaching and leading women's Bible studies. My husband and I were involved in the youth group council and enjoyed being a part of our sons' active teen years.

Well, you say, she certainly can toot her own horn. Yes, I can. But that is not why I am sharing this with you. I am sharing this to highlight a season in my life, a season of much activity and involvement with others.

God sends us through seasons in our lives. I have been struggling to find where I am and how I can serve in this present season of my life. Each time I have felt God was leading me to do some of the things I had previously done, there has been a check in my spirit that said to me, *This isn't it.*

While spending one-on-one time with the Lord in prayer not too long ago, I was asking him what he wanted for me at this time in my life. I have been standing back and observing lately, trying not to get my hands and heart in where they did not belong. I have been letting God show me where I should be serving. I felt in my spirit something that I have not felt before. God spoke to me in my spirit, "It is time to dream big with me." I felt as if he were showing me that the service performed in my younger years was past and this was a time for a new season of service. I was so encouraged. This leading might mean several changes in my life, but I'm okay with that. I don't know if it has something to do with having lived the nomadic lifestyle of the military, but I love change.

Dream big in the seasons of your life. If you belong to a military family, pray about new volunteer service in your military community. As a citizen of this great country, dream big in your outreach to those in your civilian community. ⚜*Carol*

★ ★ ★

Father God, you are a great big God. You have no limitations. Help me to dream big with you to enhance and bless the lives of others. ✛ *Amen.*

August 14
The Flashing Light

Who will rise up for me against the wicked? Who will take a stand for me against evildoers?
✝ PSALM 94:16, NIV

There are some days when thinking of America that my theme song is the one from the old TV show *Hee-Haw*: "gloom, despair, and agony on me." My prayer is that of the psalmist as, when I look around, it appears that the wicked are the ones who triumph: "Who will take a stand for me against evildoers?" Then I read stories such as this one from the pen of the former chaplain of the Senate, Lloyd John Ogilvie:

> After opening the Senate with prayer, I attended a luncheon sponsored by Senator Mark Hatfield and Congressman Robert McEwen for a group of Washington supporters of our television ministry. The luncheon was held in Senator Hatfield's private office in the Capitol building. I noticed that the clock on the wall had several lights on it. I was told that when a vote was to be taken on the floor of the Senate, certain lights would go on at set intervals alerting Senator Hatfield to the vote. When the lights flashed, indicating only a few minutes left to vote on an important bill, the Senator excused himself and went to the Senate floor.
>
> After he left the room, Bob McEwen said, "Do you understand what the Senator is about to do? He's going to cast his vote on a very important bill. We all know he's studied, prayed, and thought about that vote, but now he must stand for what he believes is right."
>
> Then, looking intently around the luncheon table, Bob said, "We all have decisions we must make. The lights are flashing and calling for us to stand and be counted as we live out our faith." [1]

Too often I forget there are godly men and women who have been called to government service. They are watching for the flashing light to take their stand for what they believe is right. I am encouraged to think there are those who are prayerfully making decisions to keep our nation and its people strong.

Like the psalmist, I recognize there is no one that can come to the ultimate rescue of man but God. There will come a time when Christ will take the final stand for his people and take the ultimate stand against evil. Until that day I am called to support through prayer and positive action those who are making decisions on my behalf. Why not write a note of support to someone in government service today? Let them know you are praying for them as they serve.   ≫*Brenda*

★　★　★

Father, I thank you for a land that honors democracy. I pray today for elected officials who are in positions of authority to use their power to govern wisely. ✝ *Amen.*

---

[1] Lloyd John Ogilvie, *A Future and a Hope* (Nashville, TN: W Publishing Group, 1988), 86–87.

Birthdays

The LORD gave me this message: "I knew you before I formed you in your mother's womb. Before you were born I set you apart and appointed you as my prophet to the nations."

✝ JEREMIAH 1:4-5

Today is my birthday. Today is the day that God chose for me to enter the world after being formed in my mother's womb. He knew what this day held from the beginning of time. He has known me and loved me throughout all eternity.

My heavenly Father knew that I would come to love him and give my life to him. He also knew how very difficult the journey would be for me. He knew that after getting through the before-Christ journey, I would give him all the praise and honor in my life. He knew I would never turn back after that commitment. He knew there would be times of attack in my life, where the enemy would cause me to question my worth as a Christian. God also knew that I would have to search my heart and remember the truth that had been given to me at the time of my salvation. God would remind me that nothing could take away the blood of Jesus and his forgiveness.

This is my day. This is the day he gave me to come into this world. So today I want to take this time to stand and say that I recommit all my life to him. I lay myself on the altar to be a living sacrifice to him. I don't want anyone to ever meet me or spend time with me without knowing that something is different in my life. I want Jesus to shine in my eyes and through my heart.

My spiritual birthday came when I was nine years old. I can't remember the exact date, but I knew it was real. Even though I chose to go through some very difficult times in my life, God loved me through it. I was drawn back into his arms, and I have never let go of him again.

God knit me together in my mother's womb to be born on this day. I want to say to my heavenly Father, "Praise you, Lord, and thank you for your goodness and mercy in my life."

To anyone reading this today who shares this birthday, I say, "Happy birthday to you!" ❧*Carol*

✷   ✷   ✷

Creator of all mankind, thank you for the gift of life. Thank you for your unconditional love throughout my life. For others who have birthdays today, I ask you to give them a heavenly hug as they reflect on their lives. I pray that, if they have not had that second "birthday" of new life in you, today might be that day for them. Help me be a witness to those who need to be born again, and help those in the military who know you to do the same for those in need around them. ✝*Amen.*

August 16
The Unread Letter

Are we beginning to praise ourselves again? Are we like others, who need to bring you letters of recommendation, or who ask you to write such letters on their behalf? Surely not! The only letter of recommendation we need is you yourselves. Your lives are a letter written in our hearts; everyone can read it and recognize our good work among you. Clearly, you are a letter from Christ showing the result of our ministry among you. This "letter" is written not with pen and ink, but with the Spirit of the living God. It is carved not on tablets of stone, but on human hearts. ✝ 2 CORINTHIANS 3:1-3

While waiting in Kuwait to move into Iraq for combat operations, my husband did what many other soldiers through the years have done. He wrote a letter to me and our sons, to be delivered only in the event that he did not return from war. I remember him writing a note explaining, "Today I wrote a letter I hope you never have to read." I knew that he meant the letter would only be read by me if he did not survive.

In contrast to this, Paul says that we are to be a living letter read by all. Of course, he is referring to the fact that we should allow Christ to be a part of our lives in such a powerful way that when people see us they see the love of Christ, the kindness of Christ, and the mercy of Christ. In other words, through us people should see what Christ would be doing if he were here walking in human form today. There is a similarity in the two letters from my husband and Paul. For the letter of Christ to be read in us, we, too, must die. We are only a letter read by others if we die to ourselves and live for the Lord. Paul said he died daily. Of course, he was not speaking of a literal death but rather of dying to his passions and will. He was conscious each day of yielding his life to the hands of the Lord.

I'm so grateful I did not have to read the letter my husband wrote, but it is my desire and ambition to be a living letter that others can read of Christ in me. I don't want my life to be an unread letter.   ✍Brenda

*   *   *

Lord, help me to die to my passions, desires, and will today. In that death, make yourself alive in and through me. I pray others, including those in harm's way here at home and deployed all around the world in the military, would see your love, kindness, and mercy. In Jesus' name I pray. ✝Amen.

Flee!

Run from anything that stimulates youthful lusts. Instead, pursue righteous living, faithfulness, love, and peace. Enjoy the companionship of those who call on the Lord with pure hearts.

✝ 2 TIMOTHY 2:22

I had a pastor a few years ago who made a very insightful statement about the state of our country. He and his wife had just had their fifth child. Their oldest child at the time was in his early teens. He said, "You know, it has gotten so bad in our society today that I have gone past what my kids watch on videos. I don't even allow them to go into the video store to pick one out because of the lewd and disgraceful covers on the video jackets."

It is very hard work being a parent today. Yes, it always has been. However, this Scripture tells us that we must run from anything that stimulates youthful lusts. Do you know what all that encompasses? Can you watch television at all without seeing something that might be stimulating? Can you even watch a sports event without something relating to sexual enticement?

Temptation has definitely been around since the beginning of time and will always be around. Resisting it and pursuing faith, love, and peace are the toughest parts. We must take a stand in our country today. Deuteronomy 5:31 says, "Stand here with me so I can give you all my commands, decrees, and regulations. You must teach them to the people so they can obey them in the land I am giving them as their possession." We must teach our children and the present generation the evil that is in youthful lusts.

It is up to us as a nation to take a stand against all that would break down the moral fiber of our country. The way to do that, I believe, is leading through example in our own homes. Be alert and sensitive to all that is viewed on television and movies. I hear so many parents say that they don't use the computer. Well, it is time for us to learn and be knowledgeable so that we can counteract the evil that is put into the World Wide Web every day.

Be alert and be aware of the world around you today! ❧*Carol*

✱　✱　✱

Dear Lord Jesus, forgive our nation for our sin of complacency. Forgive us as a nation for overlooking so much and allowing youthful lusts to bring confusion and distraction. Give us renewed hearts of steadfast commitment to you, and bring conviction when we fall short of your standard. ✝*Amen.*

August 18
Transformation

It doesn't matter whether we have been circumcised or not. What counts is whether we have been transformed into a new creation. ✛ GALATIANS 6:15

A group of fishermen in the Highlands of Scotland were sitting around a table in a small pub, telling their "fish stories." As one of the men flung out his arms to more vividly describe the fish that got away, he accidentally hit the tray of drinks that the young barmaid was bringing to the table. The tray and the drinks sailed through the air, crash-landing against the newly whitewashed wall. As the sound of smashing glass and splashing beer permeated the room, the pub became silent, and all eyes turned to the ugly brown stain forming on the wall.

Before anyone could recover from the startling interruption, a guest who had been sitting quietly by himself in the corner jumped up, pulled a piece of charcoal from his pocket, and began quickly sketching around the ugly brown stain. To the amazement of everyone present, right before their eyes the stain was transformed into a magnificent stag with antlers outstretched, racing across a Highland meadow. Then the guest signed his impromptu work of art. His name was Sir Edwin Henry Landseer, Great Britain's foremost wildlife artist.[1]

The heavenly artist has the ability to do this very thing when we make a mess of our lives. He knows how to transform our blunders into works of art.

> *Something beautiful, something good,*
> *All my confusion, He understood.*
> *All I had to offer Him, was brokenness and strife.*
> *But He made something, beautiful of my life.*
>
> ~BILL AND GLORIA GAITHER[2]

☙*Brenda*

*   *   *

Creator, thank you for your transforming power! Help me remember that you have made something brand-new of the mess that was once me. Only your divine power can bring about this change. Thank you for the superior life I have in you! Please give your people in our military the power to transform war-torn countries from places of turmoil into places where your presence abides. ✛ *Amen.*

[1] Anne Graham Lotz, *Heaven: My Father's House* (Dallas, TX: Word Publications, 2001), 37–38.
[2] Text by Gloria Gaither; music by Bill Gaither, "Something Beautiful." Copyright 1971 by William J. Gaither. Gaither Music Company. *The Hymnal for Worship and Celebration* (Waco, TX: Word Music, 1986), 519.

How Do We Know?

"They will not need to teach their neighbors, nor will they need to teach their relatives, saying, 'You should know the LORD.' For everyone, from the least to the greatest, will know me already," says the LORD. "And I will forgive their wickedness, and I will never again remember their sins."

✝ JEREMIAH 31:34

You cannot know what God wants for you in your life until you KNOW God. You cannot KNOW God unless you KNOW his Word. I love to write in capital letters. If I could write every devotional for every day of the year in capital letters, I would. I know what it takes for me to hear from the Lord—it takes capital letters!

I know that there are so many times in my life when I made choices on my own merit and in my own desires. These choices were not because I had prayed about them or contemplated what the Lord would have me do. Jeremiah prayed in the Scripture in Jeremiah 10:23, "I know, LORD, that our lives are not our own. We are not able to plan our own course." What enables me to step out in faith and know that God will assure me of its assignment from him? How do I step out in faith and know that it is God's will and not my own plan?

I believe we have to take a step. We step out and begin the journey. It would be so wonderful to be able to live on a deserted island and have no choices to make. Just get up in the morning, sit in the sun, walk the beach, and then go to bed. However, even on a deserted island there would be choices.

I remember an episode of *The Andy Griffith Show* where Howard was getting so stressed-out in his job that he decided he would give everything up to live in a beach shack on an island. The excitement was overwhelming when he got there. Each day became a little less exciting, until finally he just turned into a blob on the beach. There was no structure and no reason for him to exist except to get up in the morning. He realized that his job allowed him the privilege of having a meaningful life.

God does not want us to live our lives without meaning. We've each been given a purpose, ultimately to glorify God and help others come to know him. Take a step in sharing him with someone today. That is a step in the right direction! ⟵*Carol*

★ ★ ★

Lord Jesus, you are the Way, the Truth, and the Life. Thank you for the direction you will provide as I take a step of faith toward you. Today there are many who have taken steps of great sacrifice and commitment to serve their country. I pray your blessings and protection upon them today. ✝*Amen.*

August 20
Where's the Fruit?

Jesus told this story: "A man planted a fig tree in his garden and came again and again to see if there was any fruit on it, but he was always disappointed. Finally, he said to his gardener, 'I've waited three years, and there hasn't been a single fig! Cut it down. It's just taking up space in the garden.'

"The gardener answered, 'Sir, give it one more chance. Leave it another year, and I'll give it special attention and plenty of fertilizer. If we get figs next year, fine. If not, then you can cut it down.'" ✛ LUKE 13:6-9

Our rented home in Germany was a lovely row house complete with cherry trees in the backyard. We looked forward to enjoying the fruit from the trees during the time we made this place home. The first year, the trees were picked by the landlord before we moved in. He was kind enough to give us a small basket of cherries with the promise that next year they would all be ours. The second year, we waited with anticipation to enjoy the luscious fruit. We watched the cherries grow and kept our boys from picking the fruit until it was fully ripe. Finally, the day came when the fruit was ready. We designated the afternoon following our errands for harvesting. Our errands completed, we returned home with the anticipation of sweet cherries to enjoy. We surveyed our trees from top to bottom and could not believe that where there had been branches abundant with fruit that morning, now there was not enough to fill a quart jar!

The next year when the cherries were coming in, we were determined to keep our eyes on them. We did not go away when they were close to being harvested, only to be met with disappointment again. Because of an excessive amount of rain and moisture that year, the cherries burst open before ripening and were inedible. During our entire time of living in that house with the cherry trees, we were never able to enjoy the fruit.

God expects fruit from our lives as taught in this parable from the book of Luke. If year after year my life resulted in no productivity for whatever reason, I can't help but think the Lord would be disappointed in me. His purpose for me is to bear fruit. I know the disappointment of a fruitless tree! I don't want to just take up space; I want to produce the fruit of godliness, accomplishing the purpose God intended for my life. *≈Brenda*

✳   ✳   ✳

Great Gardener, cultivate in me the fruit of your Spirit. Accomplish your purpose in my life and use me to do all the good I can as I serve you. Plant your truth in the hearts of others, in my immediate surroundings and in the places where your military work, to hear and heed your voice. In your name I pray. ✛ *Amen.*

Huge Crowd of Witnesses

Since we are surrounded by such a huge crowd of witnesses to the life of faith, let us strip off every weight that slows us down, especially the sin that so easily trips us up. And let us run with endurance the race God has set before us. ✛ HEBREWS 12:1

Have you ever felt a sense of need to pray for someone about a specific thing at a specific time? I had just that need the other day. I began praying for our youngest son. He will finish college by the end of the year, and after being out of school for five years, it has been a huge challenge. I began praying for employment and for creativity for him to be able to make a wonderful living financially after receiving his degree. I prayed for a young woman to come along that will love him and be his wife for a lifetime. I began to thank the Lord for all the blessings he has brought to us as parents. I began to praise the Lord for the laughter and joy and adventurous spirit he has always brought into our lives. I gave God thanks that our son tells others of the love of Jesus.

All of a sudden, this passage in Hebrews came to my mind. I envisioned all of those people of faith that are mentioned in Hebrews standing around our son and cheering him on in his life and his ambitions here on this earth. I imagined the people of faith who have gone before us wanting young people who love Jesus to make it in this carnal world. My son is surrounded by this huge crowd of witnesses and those who have fought the hard fight of this earth and have come out victoriously.

I suddenly felt so encouraged by this huge heavenly crowd of witnesses and realized that, through my prayers and the prayers of others, our son will continually be strengthened in his spirit, which will also make him stronger in his goals in life.

We do this by keeping our eyes on Jesus, on whom our faith depends from start to finish. *⋘Carol*

✶   ✶   ✶

Father, thank you for loving my children even more than I can. I pray your encouragement for those who are single, deployed parents today. Let them know that you are sufficient to care for their needs and those of their children. ✛ *Amen.*

August 22
A Perfectly Good Airplane

By his divine power, God has given us everything we need for living a godly life. We have received all of this by coming to know him, the one who called us to himself by means of his marvelous glory and excellence. + 2 PETER 1:3

Second Peter 1:3 is one of my favorite verses of Scripture. I am encouraged to think that all I need to live a godly life is available as I come to know Christ. It is important to understand that Peter is talking about experiential knowledge, rather than a database of knowledge about the Lord. I can attend Bible study after Bible study and know about Christ but still not really know Christ.

The difference can be illustrated when I think about my husband and his experience of jumping out of airplanes. Prior to actually jumping out of a perfectly good airplane, he gained a great deal of knowledge of what it would be like. The instructors at his airborne school gave him the technical information about the speed of the plane, the tensile strength of the parachute, and the fact that he would feel the prop blast from the engines. This prop blast would open the parachute when he exited the plane.

In anticipation of jumping out of a perfectly good airplane, he also interviewed others who had been through airborne school. He heard their personal stories—some good and some bad—describing in vivid detail what they thought he should know about jumping. Even though he gathered a lot of data and information, and even though he could almost see himself making a jump, he still did not know personally what it was like to jump out of an airplane until he actually did it for himself. One is the knowledge of facts; the other is knowledge gained by personal experience.

Of course we need to know the facts about God, but more importantly, we need to know him as our personal Lord and Savior. It is through knowing him in this way that we gain the strength we need in order to face whatever life brings us. ✒*Brenda*

✴ ✴ ✴

Savior, thank you for your provision in giving me all I need to live a godly life as I wait for your return. Help me to continue to grow in my experiential knowledge of you. Give me the wisdom and strength to make every effort to respond to your promises. Help me to supplement my faith with a generous provision of moral excellence, and moral excellence with knowledge, and knowledge with self-control, and self-control with patient endurance, and patient endurance with godliness, and godliness with brotherly affection, and brotherly affection with love for everyone (2 Peter 1:5-7, paraphrased). In your name I pray. + *Amen.*

In the Pit of My Stomach

The Holy Spirit helps us in our weakness. For example, we don't know what God wants us to pray for. But the Holy Spirit prays for us with groanings that cannot be expressed in words.

✝ ROMANS 8:26

Have you ever been to the point when all you could do was groan to the Lord without words as you physically ached?

I can tell something wrong going on in my world—and by that I mean in my family and with my friends—when I feel pain in the pit of my stomach. When I have received calls of marriage problems or relationships breaking up, my stomach has actually stirred. When I am listening to someone talk of an illness that has overcome a loved one, I can feel that sorrow physically. The ache in my stomach is like my measurement of my surroundings.

This certain groaning or depth of feeling is for me a way of knowing just what I should lift up to the Lord in prayer. I know that as soon as I feel that sense of hurt in the pit of my stomach, it is time to fall on my face before him and lift those cares to him.

There are good and bad things about being a compassionate, caring person. The good thing is that you are a compassionate, caring person. The bad thing is that when you take on the situations of people around you, you can get physically down.

With so many crisis situations in the world, there is constant groaning within our culture. It seems that just as we get past one crisis situation, another one is around the corner. I am so thankful we have a God who manages and takes care of all those things that come along. Does that mean we should just say, "Let God take care of it"? No, I don't think that is the right response. Our response to a world that is hurting is to pray and ask the Lord whatever the Holy Spirit leads in our hearts. He will take over from there. What a blessing to know that!

Today, if you have a feeling in the pit of your stomach that you just cannot explain, take those things that are bothering you to the Lord. The Holy Spirit will pray for you without words as you release it in your heart.   ☙*Carol*

✫   ✫   ✫

Father, on this day I release the sense of uneasiness and discomfort in the pit of my stomach. As the world is in conflict around me, I thank you for being in control and knowing all the answers. You are almighty God! ✝ *Amen.*

August 24
Playing in the Dark

I pray for you constantly, asking God, the glorious Father of our Lord Jesus Christ, to give you spiritual wisdom and insight so that you might grow in your knowledge of God. I pray that your hearts will be flooded with light so that you can understand the confident hope he has given to those he called—his holy people who are his rich and glorious inheritance. ✛ EPHESIANS 1:16-18

In their book *Living in Light of Eternity*, Stacy and Paula Rinehart relate this story:

> Once when the Cleveland Symphony was performing *The Magic Flute* by Mozart, an electrical storm caused the lights to go out. Undaunted by the difficulties, the members of the orchestra knew the music so well that they completed the performance in the dark. At the end of the performance, the audience burst into thunderous applause, and a stagehand illuminated the orchestra and conductor with a flashlight so that they could take their bows.[1]

The music was in the minds of these musicians even when their eyes could not see the notes on the paper. Paul communicates his desire to have the hearts of his readers flooded with light. His challenge to us today is to know God and his Word so well that even when we are seemingly surrounded by darkness, the light of God's Word and love in our hearts will lead us in the way we should go until the lights return.

I'm not referring to pursuing some inner light that is deep within; instead, we should ask God to transform us by shining his divine light into our hearts. That transformation will allow us to understand the hope that is ours. It is a hope that describes an absolute certainty of future good. When we understand this, we can walk through any dark time this life brings.   ❧*Brenda*

*   *   *

Dear God, I pray today for spiritual wisdom and insight so that I may grow in my knowledge of you. Flood my heart with light so that I can understand the confident hope you have given me. I acknowledge your calling on my life as your holy child who is your "rich and glorious inheritance." Make that calling known to those in my life and to those in the military who do not yet know you, I ask. ✛ *Amen.*

---

[1] Stacy and Paula Rinehart, *Living in Light of Eternity* (Colorado Springs, CO: NavPress, 1986), 30.

No Fear in Love

Such love has no fear, because perfect love expels all fear. If we are afraid, it is for fear of punishment, and this shows that we have not fully experienced his perfect love. **+** 1 JOHN 4:18

While our family was stationed at Fort Lewis, Washington, my dear sister in the Lord always read from her *Amplified Bible* during studies. Sometimes it was exhausting for there to be so many words in one reading. Before I knew it, though, I found myself looking forward to this interpretation. I am an extrovert—a great quantity of words doesn't usually make me uncomfortable!—and I got used to the translation.

The Amplified Bible quotes 1 John 4:18 in this way: "There is no fear in love [dread does not exist], but full-grown [complete, perfect] love turns fear out of doors and expels every trace of terror! For fear brings with it the thought of punishment, and [so] he who is afraid has not reached the full maturity of love [is not yet grown into love's complete perfection]."

What an appropriate word for today! The Scripture is a perfect representative of the Living Word. On this August day, do not miss this teaching. When I know I am loved, I feel confident and can conquer the world. I reflected to my husband the other day that when we are together on decisions, all is well. When we are not on the same page, we are miserable. We have come to depend on the love and direction from each other in our married life.

God's love, which is the only perfect love, can turn fear out the door and expel terror! As our brave men and women go into countries that have never been without fear of punishment, separation from families, or even death, they are taking with them the promise of love. It is a promise of life without fear.

We have heard story after story of young children beginning to trust our American presence in faraway lands as fear is replaced with love. Often the soldiers request candy and school supplies to hand out as they walk through the cities and meet the families. The smiles on the faces of these young children are evidence of knowing someone cares for them.

There is no fear in perfect love. Together with the Lord, we are loved and we are good. When we are not on the path of righteousness and separated from the Lord, we are miserable, and fear abides.

As Americans, we seek to offer the love we experience in this country to those who live daily in fear. We honor those who take that challenge in this life.   *≈Carol*

★   ★   ★

Jehovah God, you are perfect love. I ask your protection on those in faraway lands who live in constant fear for their very lives. I pray that the love of Jesus continues to be spread throughout the world. **+** *Amen.*

August 26
The Message of Scars

From now on, don't let anyone trouble me with these things. For I bear on my body the scars that show I belong to Jesus. ✛ GALATIANS 6:17

The New Testament describes the scourging received by the apostle Paul during his arrests and imprisonments. There was no doubt he carried physical scars from the beatings he endured because of his testimony and witness of Christ. How do scars fit into your theology? I have encountered people who cannot accept a theology that allows such pain. Yet when I look through Scripture, I find that God never promises we won't be wounded or suffer injury in this life.

Like Paul, many of us carry some scars that are reminders of past experiences. Paul used his scars as a journal of the power of God helping him to overcome, even to the point of death. Like Paul, the wounds and scars that we have can be a positive reminder of what God has brought us through.

I think of soldiers who have been wounded on the battlefield. There are times, when a soldier is wounded with shrapnel, that the doctor leaves a portion of the foreign substance in the body and the body heals around it. There is no doubt that the remaining scar and the residual shrapnel are reminders of the battle that this soldier survived.

For many soldiers, scars are shown with pride as a proof of their allegiance to their country. General Lafayette, one of the French volunteers to the cause of the American Revolution, said, when struck in the foot by a musket ball, "I prize this wound as among the most valued of my honors."[1] This is the same type of pride Paul speaks of when addressing his scars. They were an identifier of his life in Christ.

Paul's scars were physical, but for many the scars carried are unseen. For the Christ follower, these scars are a symbol of the healing power of God. God can use them to help us identify with others and give opportunities to share the message that Christ is the Healer.   ☙*Brenda*

✶   ✶   ✶

Almighty Healer, I ask for your healing power to shine through the scars of my life. Give me an opportunity to share your message of healing and hope today. In your name I pray. ✛*Amen.*

---

[1] Commentary on Galatians 6:17, *Barnes' Notes,* Electronic Database, CD-ROM. Biblesoft, 1997.

Shall We Dance?

Since we are living by the Spirit, let us follow the Spirit's leading in every part of our lives.
✝ GALATIANS 5:25

Let's think of something really fun today. Let's think of dancing. When the man and woman pair up as dance partners, it is the man's responsibility to lead in this activity. He is taught to place his hand on the woman's back in such a way as to guide her steps across the floor. The strongest dancer of the two should be the man. If the man does not know what he is doing with the particular dance step, the woman will most often step all over his feet, and they will go in different directions. He is the element of stability in the routine.

As a wife, I often find myself trying to lead in my relationship with my husband in the marriage dance. I state my case, and I whine a lot. Sometimes even the silent treatment comes. But I am miserable. I am stepping all over myself and going in different directions when I try to put myself into this lead position.

When I come back to my husband, let him put his hand just where it needs to be in the situation, and step in time with him, I feel such a sense of peace. I did not become a wife to lead my husband. My heart's desire is to follow his direction as the spiritual head of our house. As I minister to young women, teaching them about their relationships with their husbands, I must be that example of following my husband's leading from the Lord. I can't talk it and teach it if I don't live it.

The Holy Spirit wants to lead in every dance of life. He is waiting for us to come to him and allow him to take us in his arms of love and compassion so that we will not stumble as we dance our way through life. When the Holy Spirit leads us, we will follow our husbands, and we will follow the leading of a beautiful dance in spiritual unity.

Stand up to the world and rest in the arms of the spiritual leader. Don't try to dance on your own or out of step with God's music. He has set the tempo and the direction before you. Dance with conviction and strength with him.   ❧*Carol*

✷   ✷   ✷

Father, help me to keep in step with you. When I begin to be drawn into the world's dance, pull me back in and lead me in your ways. As families, particularly those separated by military duty, are struggling with the lack of conviction for a godly marriage, give them a renewed sense of your leading in this holy covenant. ✝ *Amen.*

August 28
Grace to Stand

He gives us even more grace to stand against such evil desires. As the Scriptures say, "God opposes the proud but favors the humble." So humble yourselves before God. Resist the devil, and he will flee from you. ✛ JAMES 4:6-7

I recall a story told of a young army specialist guarding a nuclear munitions depot in Germany during the days of the Cold War. A general wanted to gain entrance into the depot. The young soldier standing guard responded with respect, "Sir, I will have to see your ID." The incredulous general outranked the specialist in appearance and power, yet he had to submit to the request of this underranking soldier. The soldier had been given the orders to guard this place, and he was going to stand on those orders no matter how many stars were on the general's uniform.

The young soldier had the grace to stand without intimidation because he was standing on the authority of his orders. He showed respect to the general, but he did not allow him to pass without proper identification.

I am not comparing this general to the devil, but like the general attempting to gain access to the munitions depot, the enemy of our soul tries on a regular basis to gain access to our lives. Just like this young man stood on the authority of his orders, we are to stand on the authority of God's Word. When we stand our ground and challenge the enemy, not in our own authority and power but in the power of God, we will win the battle. This is the humility to which James refers—knowing we are standing our ground through the power of the Holy Spirit and not on our own. The enemy of our soul can wrestle us, but when we stand using the authority of God's Word, he must flee. ✍Brenda

⋆　⋆　⋆

Thank you, Lord, for the power of your Word! Help me to stand on the power and authority of your Word, not being intimidated by the enemy of my soul. Help me to recognize his strategy and let my trust in fighting him be in you and not in my own ability. In your name I pray. ✛ Amen.

Tempted by the World

One day Jesus said to his disciples, "There will always be temptations to sin, but what sorrow awaits the person who does the tempting!" + LUKE 17:1

Well, that's a relief. Jesus says there will always be temptation to sin. We can take a deep breath and know that temptation will come and that temptation in itself does not make us bad. From the beginning of time, in the Garden of Eden, there has been temptation. The temptation to sin presents itself each day, whether it holds out that second piece of pie or comes in the dark of a quiet room with just you and the computer.

Jesus also shows us the other side of that temptation. He tells us the person who tempts someone to the point of sin will pay a price. He says in Luke 17:2, "It would be better to be thrown into the sea with a millstone hung around your neck than to cause one of these little ones to fall into sin." This tells me that if I am the one being tempted in my Christian life, that is normal. If I set up someone else to be tempted, I am held accountable to a higher punishment.

How can we stand and look sin in the face and not be tempted to follow through when our minds have initiated the process? By allowing God to take over what our hearts and minds in their weakness might give in to. When we are tempted to dwell on past sin, we can trust in the forgiveness provided by the cross of Christ and know that confessed sin is forgotten and we have been covered with the blood of Jesus.

When we are tempted by others, we can physically turn and walk away. Young people are put in the middle of compromising situations every day. They can walk away and show there is another way by their actions. It is a proclamation that they are not going to give in—there is another way, and that way is God's way.

> *When life just seems to suck you in*
> *When all around you fall into sin*
> *When life's great trials wear you out*
> *Sometimes you just want to scream and shout.*
> *There is a way, the Lord would say*
> *To turn and simply walk away*
> *You can stand for what is good and right*
> *And not be tempted by the night.*

≈ *Carol*

* * *

O Lord God, temptation to do what is not right in your eyes is in front of me every day. I pray a special blessing on the youth of today. Give them deep conviction and strength. Help them to stand up to temptation and to say no when they need to. Fill the young men and women in our military with moral conviction, that those representing our country's interests may be honorable and good in all they do. + *Amen.*

August 30
Do-or-Die Courage

In your strength I can crush an army; with my God I can scale any wall. ✛ PSALM 18:29

Sergeant Alvin C. York is a favored World War I hero from Tennessee. Living in the hills of Tennessee provided ample opportunity for him to become an expert marksman. Despite his religious convictions, York eventually accepted his duty to serve his country when he was drafted and subsequently sent overseas. On October 8, 1918, York and sixteen other soldiers mistakenly found themselves behind enemy lines.

That day in the Argonne Forest of France, then–Corporal York became an American hero. Substantiated reports from his fellow 82d Division comrades stated that he captured 132 Germans and personally silenced the deadly machine gun of a superior German military unit.[1] Reading the diary of Alvin York, it is evident he didn't set out to be a hero. The opportunity to be a hero came from his unit being lost and finding themselves in a do-or-die circumstance.

Just as York didn't go looking for ways to test his courage, we don't need to go looking for ways to test our faith. When we find ourselves in a situation that seems to be overwhelming, that is the time to look to God for help, strength, courage, and guidance. He has promised over and over to help us when we are overwhelmed. In his strength we can step out to do those things that, when we look back, we're amazed by what we were able to do. We can know it wasn't anything we did on our own but rather the grace of God that was at work in and through us. God can help us win battles that seem insurmountable. ☙*Brenda*

Oh, Lord, quicken in me the spirit of courage. Help me to walk boldly into this day, fortified by the hope I have in you. May I face whatever comes my way with the courage that comes from the power of your Holy Spirit. In your name I pray. ✛ *Amen.*

---

[1] Dr. Michael Birdwell. "Legends and Traditions of the Great War: Sergeant Alvin York." http://worldwar1.com/heritage/sgtayork.htm.

Hanging over Me

We must quickly carry out the tasks assigned us by the one who sent us. The night is coming, and then no one can work. + JOHN 9:4

Procrastination has often been a cause of spiritual defeat in my life. There are things I allow to hang over my head until I end up wearing them like an awning. An awning is usually something that brings protection and shade, but the canopy that suspends above me does not protect me—it weighs me down. It carries the weight of guilt, laziness, fear, and inadequacy. I find every excuse in the book to convince myself why it is okay not to complete whatever task it is that needs my attention. Too often I find myself exemplifying the words of Mark Twain, "Never put off tomorrow what you can do the day after tomorrow."

Why do we procrastinate? Psychologists have described procrastinators as people who sabotage themselves out of the fear of failure. Others say it comes from a lack of discipline or laziness. Apparently famous people such as Neville Chamberlain, Agatha Christie, St. Augustine, and Leonardo da Vinci all struggled with chronic procrastination.[1]

Whatever the reason for procrastination, if allowed to continue, it can lead to a cycle of spiritual defeat for the Christ follower. There are some things in life that are not impacted by procrastination, but the habit of allowing distractions to veer me off course can plummet me into a cycle that is difficult to rise above. You see, when I procrastinate, I end up standing still instead of moving forward in the purpose God has for me to accomplish. Jesus modeled moving forward in today's Scripture when he explained there was coming a time when it would not be possible for us to do God's work.

What about you today? Is there something you've been putting off? Whether it is cleaning a room, working on a relationship, or taking the next step to grow in your spiritual life, make today a day of moving forward. ≈*Brenda*

✶   ✶   ✶

Lord, help me to get moving! Don't let me become stagnant and defeated because I refuse to do my part in participating in your plan for me. Don't let me miss the opportunity to accomplish today those things that would honor you. Help our country to accomplish much good this year. +*Amen.*

---

[1] Piers Steel, Procrastination Study. http://webapps2.ucalgary.ca/~steel//Procrastinus/casestudies.php.

September 1
This Time of Year

May the glory of the LORD continue forever! The LORD takes pleasure in all he has made!
+ PSALM 104:31

As we begin today, I would like to ask you to take a moment and read all of Psalm 104 from your Bible. The psalmist proclaims God's creation and how very much he cares for it.

I hear people say, "I love this time of year." Or they say, "I have been waiting all summer for this time of year." Or they might even say, "I love when football comes back around this time of year." For many people, autumn is their favorite season, and there are so many reasons. It brings order to our schedules for the new school year, a type of recreation that has not been enjoyed during the hot summer months, exciting new colors, and a crisp in the air as the calendar leads on toward the holidays and winter.

I remember when my husband and I decided on a wedding date. It was in September, and it just happened to be the evening of a big hometown football game. Everyone asked us to change it because it would interfere with that game. We decided that we didn't care if we were the only people in attendance—we were sticking to our original date. I am so thankful we did. It was mid-September, and we love that time of year. It was my dad's birthday and a special time every year of remembering him along with our anniversary.

I can imagine what this time of year brought to many of our forefathers throughout the centuries. It was a time of refreshment after hot summer months but also a great time of preparation in getting ready for the long winter ahead. It was a time to bring in the harvest and store up for whatever hardship was to come.

As we reflect today on this time of year, perhaps we can be challenged to reach out to those in our lives who need Jesus. We can reach out to those who need refreshment after times of troubles and disappointment in their lives. We can share a word with those who are just on the edge of changing their lives for Jesus. We never know if we are to lead them to Christ.

Psalm 104:30 says, "When you give them your breath, life is created, and you renew the face of the earth." Enjoy this time of year with a renewed heart to lead others to eternal salvation.   *Carol*

* * *

Father God, Creator, Giver of Life, you are the Creator of all seasons on this earth. You are the Creator of the seasons of life. As I enjoy this new season today, bring to my mind someone who needs refreshment in you and help me to reach out in your love. Please comfort those who are in the season of family separation because of military deployment. + Amen.

A Heart for Learning

It is senseless to pay tuition to educate a fool, since he has no heart for learning.

✛ PROVERBS 17:16

Someone who embodied a heart for learning was the late A. W. Tozer. During his lifetime he was not only a pastor but also the editor of his denominational magazine and author of more than forty books. Two of these books, *The Pursuit of God* and *The Knowledge of the Holy*, are considered Christian classics. He is one of the most quoted theologians, and yet Tozer never received a formal theological education. His thirst for knowledge of God sent him to his knees, and there with his Bible he asked the Holy Spirit to be his teacher.[1]

I am drawn to the concept of having a heart for learning. One of the things I long to cultivate throughout my life is a teachable heart. I value education, but I recognize that having a heart for learning means more than enrolling in school. There are times when I've been forced to learn some things I didn't necessarily want to learn, but I found myself in the position where it was a necessity. When my husband was deployed to Afghanistan, I recognized my need to become educated in areas I didn't previously know much about concerning our financial plan, our computer system, and other details usually covered by my husband. These things weren't my natural bent, and learning about them was a stretching experience. More than learning these details, though, I wanted to be open to learning the spiritual lessons I knew would certainly accompany this challenging time.

Today's Scripture speaks of one who has been given an opportunity to learn but has no will or desire for the lesson. Instead, the heart is set on other things, and the opportunity is missed. Learning any lesson takes some desire. As this season of yellow buses and school supplies begins, I am challenged anew to remember that the foundation of any sound knowledge and learning is to know Jesus Christ. What about you? ≈*Brenda*

✳ ✳ ✳

Lord, you are my teacher. Make my heart teachable and help me to learn the lessons you give me the opportunity to learn. In your name I pray. ✛*Amen.*

---

[1] A. W. Tozer, *The Knowledge of the Holy: The Attributes of God: Their Meaning in the Christian Life* (New York: HarperOne, 1998).

September 3
Enjoy the Moment

Young people, it's wonderful to be young! Enjoy every minute of it. Do everything you want to do; take it all in. But remember that you must give an account to God for everything you do.
✝ ECCLESIASTES 11:9

PRESENT TENSE
It was spring
But it was summer I wanted,
The warm days,
And the great outdoors.
It was summer,
But it was fall I wanted,
The colorful leaves,
And the cool, dry air.
It was fall,
But it was winter I wanted,
The beautiful snow,
And the joy of the holiday season.
It was winter,
But it was spring I wanted,
The warmth
And the blossoming of nature.
I was a child,
But it was adulthood I wanted.
The freedom,
And the respect.
I was 20,
But it was 30 I wanted,
To be mature,
And sophisticated.
I was middle-aged,
But it was 20 I wanted,
The youth,
And the free spirit.
I was retired,
But it was middle-age I wanted,
The presence of mind,
Without limitations.
My life was over.
But I never got what I wanted.
~JASON LEHMAN, 14 YEARS OLD[1]

Enjoy the moment of today!   ~*Carol*

✶   ✶   ✶

Father, thank you for the power in these words reminding me that each moment is a gift from you. Thank you for the gift of freedom in our United States of America. ✝ *Amen.*

---

[1] Jason Lehman "Present Tense," quoted in Charles Swindoll, *Simple Faith* (Dallas, TX: Word Publishing, 1991), 175–176.

School Zone

Don't bother correcting mockers; they will only hate you. But correct the wise, and they will love you. Instruct the wise, and they will be even wiser. Teach the righteous, and they will learn even more. Fear of the LORD is the foundation of wisdom. Knowledge of the Holy One results in good judgment. ✦ PROVERBS 9:8-10

Fond memories are associated with the month of September and the first day of school. As a child, my favorite thing was to pretend I was a teacher. My dad would bring home leftover worksheets from the school in which he served as principal, and I would hold my little brother hostage to my teaching. Eventually I became a real teacher with a real classroom. Today, I still enjoy hearing from some of my former students. I also enjoy listening to my daughter-in-law talk about her kindergarten class. She cares deeply for the children and is committed to making school and learning a positive experience. I'm blessed by her dedication and am grateful the children in her class have a teacher who is devoted to them.

Whether they are teaching at home, in a church school, or in public schools around our nation, teachers are heroes. The value of a good teacher who is committed not just to teaching facts but to developing citizens is priceless. As this new school year begins, pray for teachers who are dedicated and devoted to providing a positive learning environment and experience for children.

There are numerous references throughout Scripture to the importance of gaining knowledge. These references are usually couched in the admonition that with knowledge is also the need for understanding. As this new school year begins, pray for educators who are not content with presenting facts but willing to guide students into understanding.

Prayer Zone Partners is a ministry that encourages prayer for schools.[1] The challenge to make each school zone a prayer zone is one I am accepting this year. This is how it works: When entering a school zone, take the time as you slow your car to a lower speed to pray for the teachers, administrators, and students who attend school there. Whether you have school-aged children or not, this type of prayer is an investment in the future of our nation. I think it is a great idea! ↷*Brenda*

✭　✭　✭

Father, as this new school year begins, I pray for teachers with godly values who will use their power to influence and bless their students. I ask you to allow them to see the opportunity they have to touch lives for eternity. I pray for safety and protection for the schools of our nation, including the military academies, which teach our future leaders, soldiers, and officers. ✦*Amen.*

---

[1] For more information on Prayer Zone Partners, go to www.youthalive.ag.org/pzp.

Listen to Wisdom

These are the proverbs of Solomon, David's son, king of Israel. Their purpose is to teach people wisdom and discipline, to help them understand the insights of the wise. Their purpose is to teach people to live disciplined and successful lives, to help them do what is right, just, and fair. These proverbs will give insight to the simple, knowledge and discernment to the young. ✛ PROVERBS 1:1-4

While I've been writing these devotionals, it has sometimes been very difficult to stop when quoting a biblical reference. If there were enough space on this page, I would want to write out the entire book of Proverbs. In the *NLT Life Application Study Bible*, the introduction for Proverbs 1:1–9:18 says it is "Wisdom for Young People." In the footnotes we are told that Proverbs begins with a clear statement of wanting to impart wisdom for godly living. It was originally directed to young people; however, people of any age can benefit from its teachings.

Proverbs 2:3 says, "Cry out for insight, and ask for understanding." God tells us that when we can ask for wisdom, he will give it to us. However, there are times that we must truly seek wisdom and cry out for it in our lives. God also tells us in the book of Proverbs that oftentimes when he corrected us in wisdom and tried to show us the correct way to go, we rejected him. Therefore, we have to take the consequences.

Whenever I have a chance to give a Bible as a gift to a young person who is graduating from high school or college, I write from the words of Proverbs 3:5-6, which says, "Trust in the Lord with all your heart; do not depend on your own understanding. Seek his will in all you do, and he will show you which path to take."

As adults, and especially as those who are mature in the Lord, we must take the time and the effort to teach our children and the young people in our spheres of influence. They need to know there will never come a time when they are smart enough or knowledgeable enough to match the wisdom of the Lord. They must seek his wisdom and keep him close to their hearts.

The world says Christians are needy and have to depend on Jesus. I agree. We *are* needy and have to depend on Jesus. There is no other way in this nation to understand the things around us than to fear the Lord and listen to his wisdom.

Stand and listen! Stand and trust! Stand in truth and learn wisdom from above!
⮑*Carol*

✱ ✱ ✱

Heavenly Father, you are Truth. You are Wisdom. You are Holy. You are Love. You are everything I need. I pray for wisdom in and protection of the lives of the young people in this nation. ✛ *Amen.*

Man on the Street

Hear the word of the LORD, O people of Israel! The LORD has brought charges against you, saying: "There is no faithfulness, no kindness, no knowledge of God in your land." ✛ HOSEA 4:1

I am often discouraged by the opinions I hear concerning Christianity. During a recent church service, a video was shown with someone interviewing people on the street with the question, "What comes to mind when you hear the word *Christian*?" The responses were such things as "Crazy . . . Scary . . . Fanatic . . . You don't want to know." Yeah, pretty negative opinions. On the one hand I thought, *Scripture doesn't say that Christians are going to be well thought of or praised.* On the other hand I thought, *What kind of witness has been shared that these low opinions would be the norm?*

Reading today's Scripture, I get the impression if there had been technology in Hosea's day, the same type of opinion would be shared in a man-on-the-street video. The description of "no faithfulness, no kindness, no knowledge of God in your land" is sobering. I'm challenged as a Christ follower to do my part to change the minds of people. Is that crazy? Is that wrong?

George Buttrick, former chaplain at Harvard, recalls that students would come into his office and say, "I don't believe in God." Buttrick would then reply, "Sit down and tell me what kind of God you don't believe in. I probably don't believe in that God either."[1]

The goal of Christianity is not to gain the approval of the world, but we can't ignore the admonition of Jesus: "By this all men will know that you are my disciples, if you love one another" (John 13:35, NIV). The focus of the message Hosea received in Hosea 4:1 was on having a right attitude and mind-set toward God. *Hmm,* now that I think about it, when we have the right attitude and mind-set toward God, there may be people in this world who see the better side of what God wants us to be as Christians. It's not about how well I am thought of; it's how well I am representing him. As a Christ follower, I am not going to win a popularity contest, but I can grow in my knowledge of him and my love for him in order to share that love with others. ☙*Brenda*

✶　✶　✶

Lord, give me the grace to fulfill your command to love others. Convict me of the sinful attitudes and actions that keep me from reflecting your love, so that in obedience I may love others and bring glory to your name and hope to those around me. In your name I pray. ✛ *Amen.*

---

[1] Philip Yancey, *The Jesus I Never Knew* (Grand Rapids, MI: Zondervan, 1995), 264, quoted in James Emery White, *A Search for the Spiritual* (Grand Rapids, MI: Zondervan, 1996), 35.

September 7
Vain Labor

Anything I wanted, I would take. I denied myself no pleasure. I even found great pleasure in hard work, a reward for all my labors. But as I looked at everything I had worked so hard to accomplish, it was all so meaningless—like chasing the wind. There was nothing really worthwhile anywhere. + ECCLESIASTES 2:10-11

Labor is another word for hard work. It means much more than just doing a job—it really means sweat and calluses and true dedication to your specific endeavor. So many today are involved in hard labor most of their lives. Some in other countries must tend to rice fields while standing in knee-deep water with heavy baskets strapped over their shoulders. We witnessed this while stationed in South Korea. Many countries in Europe still plow the fields by hand as they get the land ready for harvest.

Americans also labor in the fields and have much to show for their accomplishments in farming and land management. Our thoughts have turned to the coal-mining industry in recent years because of the tragic mine accidents that have occurred. We have become very aware of the hard labor and health problems that are involved for these workers.

There is another type of labor that many Americans pursue—labor for such things as fine cars, mansions, and jewels. It is a labor that Scripture tells us is in vain. We have many examples daily on the covers of magazines that entice us to want to labor more for material things than to be rewarded in our hearts for hard work. We are drawn to what our neighbors have and what Hollywood communicates is important.

Labor is not in vain when it is done as unto the Lord. No matter what your profession in life, whether it be coal miner, administrative assistant, teacher's aide, or gas station attendant, do not labor in vain. For the Christ follower, labor done for God will be rewarded one day in heaven. I often say to friends who give their lives for others, "Your crown is getting full of jewels in heaven right now." Consider your hard work on this earth as preparation for your heavenly rewards.   ~*Carol*

*   *   *

God in heaven, help me to exert my energy today in those things that have eternal value. Thank you for those unselfishly serving our country by laboring for freedom in other lands. + *Amen.*

Do What Comes Up

You know that Stephanas and his household were the first of the harvest of believers in Greece, and they are spending their lives in service to God's people. I urge you, dear brothers and sisters, to submit to them and others like them who serve with such devotion.

✝ 1 CORINTHIANS 16:15-16

When I think of people with a servant's heart, I think of my friends John and Cheryl, who were both military officers when I first met them. Cheryl was a full-time student at the Army War College, and John worked in Washington, D.C., for the National Guard. Both John and Cheryl make it a practice to volunteer above the call of duty in a variety of programs. For example, while a full-time student at the Army's senior-level college, not only was Cheryl very successful as a student but she also volunteered to serve as the chapel choir director and organist. She was involved in other programs including a senior citizens tea, raising funds for college scholarships, and even spearheading the creation of a U.S. Army War College anthem. Currently, Cheryl is involved in volunteer outreaches that serve both local and national causes.

I recently attended John's retirement ceremony, where the citation of his volunteer service outside of his military duties was impressive. Among a list of activities mentioned was his ongoing donation of blood platelets for use at Walter Reed Army Medical Center. While living in the D.C. area, both John and Cheryl volunteered for several years, serving military service members at the USO. Retirement was something John looked forward to so he could devote even more time volunteering in his community.

When asked why they serve, Cheryl's response was, "Focusing on others is far more valuable and interesting than focusing on yourself. I hope to be remembered as someone who put others first and worked selflessly for God."

Psalm 100:2 charges us to "serve the LORD with gladness" (Psalm 100:2 KJV). This is the example given by Stephanas and his household and commended by Paul in today's Scripture. It is the example I see in my friends John and Cheryl. The word *devotion* in this Scripture means they "appointed themselves" whenever they saw a need to work to meet it. Cheryl described it this way: "It's about doing what comes up." I like that! ❧*Brenda*

✧　✧　✧

Lord, you lived your life in service to others, and that is what I am to do as well. I pray your blessings on those who are willing to give of themselves beyond their required responsibilities. You did this for me, suffering through no fault of your own, not only in giving your life for my salvation but also in providing a model to follow as I serve others. I pray for a willingness to do what comes up in service to others today. ✝*Amen.*

September 9
Take a Breath

God said, "Let the land sprout with vegetation—every sort of seed-bearing plant, and trees that grow seed-bearing fruit. These seeds will then produce the kinds of plants and trees from which they came." + GENESIS 1:11

What a glorious time to take in all of creation. I love the fall season of the year. Today I felt as if I could actually breathe outside after the hot, muggy summer. It is a time of wanting to sit on the porch and go for long walks and enjoy the beauty of an autumn-colored world.

I asked someone the other day why I had not heard from her daughter-in-law days after I had e-mailed her. She said, "Oh, she is just so busy." I asked another young woman if I could come to take her out to lunch, and she was just too busy for the day. Recently, I wanted to walk the local botanical gardens with a young friend and her precious children. They had to go to the grocery store. Do I take this personally? No, not really. I just feel sad that people are too busy to take in a breath of God's majesty. Our priorities are so out of sorts, and instead of taking a breath, we can't seem to catch our breath.

Fall is a wonderful time of year to enjoy. Whether at the local high school football game or a walk in the park on the weekends, it is a time to enjoy creation. The crisp air and the beautiful colors show us that we have a very creative God. His majesty is shown, and his glory is all around us during this time.

What a blessing to live in a country where people take pride in the creation around them. Many people plant beautiful fall flowers and decorate with the signs of harvest on their porches. We take so much of this for granted, and that is why we need to take a breath this time of year in thankfulness to our God and our country.

Enjoy the day! ⋖Carol

⋆　⋆　⋆

Father, thank you for the crisp, cool air and beautiful colors that signify autumn. Be with those who are in service to our country and not able to be in their beloved America this time of year. Keep us from being so busy that we cannot enjoy what you have given us on this earth. + Amen.

Soul Rest

Take my yoke upon you. Let me teach you, because I am humble and gentle at heart, and you will find rest for your souls. ✝ MATTHEW 11:29

In his book *Praying to the God You Can Trust*, Leith Anderson tells a story of Americans who contracted Africans to transport provisions on a lengthy and arduous trail. "Each day the Americans pressed the laborers to walk faster, work longer and travel farther. Finally the entire crew sat down and refused to continue. They explained that they had to wait for their souls to catch up."[1]

I thought of this story after communicating with my dear friend Patti concerning her experience during her husband's deployment. She wrote, "My greatest challenge was taking time for myself—especially the first deployment when the children were younger (ages 2, 4, 11, and 13). I didn't get to bed until really late yet had to get up super early. For some reason, I could hardly get in bed before midnight no matter what. I got very little sleep, ate chocolate, drank coffee, and was wiped out."

Patti went on to say that she finally "got a grip." She says, "I started going to the gym, doing a Bible study with the lieutenants' wives, put my son in preschool, and turned off the news. That helped." In retrospect she says, "For me, I needed rest more than anything. Physical rest, but every other kind of rest there is. I was striving, striving, striving. I was mentally, physically, and spiritually exhausted." She feels very strongly that one of the greatest challenges for deployed spouses is learning to deal with the ongoing nature of wartime domestic stress. She states that the self-care that she finally incorporated into her routine is something she now sees as a responsibility and not a luxury.

Patti is describing the need to let our souls catch up to the results of the push we too often place on our bodies. Matthew 11:29 describes a weight much like the one Patti was allowing herself to carry. The picture is of one with a heavy load placed on him. Each step makes the load heavier and more overwhelming. A godly mentor gave Patti a word of encouragement during this time that mirrors the message emphasized in this passage: "Everybody says to you, 'Be strong.' But Jesus says to you, 'I know you are spent, you are tired, you are weary. Just rest—rest in me.'" That's soul rest!   ⋟*Brenda*

✭   ✭   ✭

Jesus, help me to take your yoke today and learn of you, finding rest for my soul. I pray for families who are struggling with the ongoing stress of war. In your name I pray. ✝*Amen.*

---

[1] Leith Anderson, *Praying to the God You Can Trust* (Minneapolis, MN: Bethany House Publishers, 1996), 39.

September 11
The Day in September

I have heard all about you, LORD. I am filled with awe by your amazing works. In this time of our deep need, help us again as you did in years gone by. And in your anger, remember your mercy. ✛ HABAKKUK 3:2

The year is not really what matters. The day will be forever etched in the memories of all Americans. Today as I watch early morning television, many of the stations have the audio of the names of those who lost their lives being read aloud. That in itself is very sobering. We need to remember their names. We need to be able to realize it was not just buildings that were destroyed. Individuals, families, and communities were destroyed as well.

What a day this is to be thankful. We can be thankful that we as a nation have survived. We will never look at our freedom the same way again. We are free to express opinions even against our government and our president. We are free to pursue our lives' ambitions and dreams.

The evidence of God's healing on so many of the families who lost loved ones during that day is such a testimony. I am so thankful that the Christians come forward and say, "We could not have made it without our faith. God has brought us through." You can see the peace on their faces as their eyes glisten with tears.

My pastor shared a story from the day in September 2001. He said that a woman who had lost her husband was devastated because he had not called her. So many other workers in his office had called their wives as they were fleeing the towers, but she couldn't understand why she had not received a call. A few weeks after the day, a coworker's wife called her and asked if she had ever heard from her husband. She shared the news that the reason he had not called was because he was leading a group in prayer. During that day in September he was spending his last moments sharing Christ with others.   ❧*Carol*

* * *

Father God, remind me that each day is a gift from you. Give me a heavenly mind-set that thinks more of others and their eternal security than my earthly comfort. Bless those families who were left behind after September 11, 2001, and give them peace that many of their family members were doing Kingdom work that day in the midst of tragedy around them. ✛ *Amen.*

20/20 Vision

O our God, won't you stop them? We are powerless against this mighty army that is about to attack us. We do not know what to do, but we are looking to you for help. + 2 CHRONICLES 20:12

I prided myself for many years on the fact that I had 20/20 vision. Many of my friends wore bifocals while I was enjoying a spectacle-free life. Then for several months I noticed that my eyes were blurry in the morning. Silly me—I thought it was the overnight eye cream I was using that was causing the fuzzy vision. I can't remember what it was that jolted me into the reality that I needed to begin to wear reading glasses. During this same time, I was studying the passage of Scripture in Hebrews 12:1-2 that held the challenge to keep my eyes on Jesus.

As a Christ follower, I am continually faced with distractions and challenges that pull my attention away from my desired focal point. Soon after September 11, 2001, I was reading in 2 Chronicles and was reminded of King Jehoshaphat. I found great comfort in his example. Interestingly, Jehoshaphat's kingdom was attacked by surprise, and he was amazed at the intelligence of the enemy! It sounded pretty familiar. His first reaction was fear, which he quickly turned into a godly fear as he directed the people of his kingdom through a time of prayer and fasting. In 2 Chronicles 20:12, we find a beautiful Old Testament example of Hebrews 12:1-2 as King Jehoshaphat closes his prayer by saying, "O our God, won't you stop them? We are powerless against this mighty army that is about to attack us. We do not know what to do, but we are looking to you for help."

What a powerful example for us today! Whether it is how we are to look at a national crisis or how we are to raise our children, there are times when we must say, "We do not know what to do!" The key to victory is in the example set by King Jehoshaphat when he follows that statement with the words "but we are looking to you for help." ≈*Brenda*

* * *

Father, I thank you for examples in Scripture that comfort and challenge me today. I pray that I would look to you in times of crisis, no matter how great or small. I thank you for providing the help I need when I do not know what to do. I pray for those who are struggling to deal with the effects of war and terror. Help them to look to you for comfort and guidance. In Jesus' name I pray. + *Amen.*

September 13
Wisdom from Above

We have not stopped praying for you since we first heard about you. We ask God to give you complete knowledge of his will and to give you spiritual wisdom. **+** COLOSSIANS 1:9

It always amazes me that we can go to school and know that, if we don't open the textbook and study, we are not going to learn the subject. We will study for hours for a test. We will get together with others to confirm our learning. We will grow in great knowledge of the subject. When the test is given, we are prepared to make a grade to be proud of. Yet we can't seem to see it the same way for our spiritual lives.

Why is it so different? Why is it that we cannot grasp the concept of the spiritual textbook sitting on the table every day?

There is much knowledge and deep understanding to come from studying God's Word. We can learn about those who have gone before us and the trials, tribulations, and victories they had. As you go through the Scriptures, you will find an example of someone who has gone through any situation that you encounter in your life.

We're told in Scripture not to forsake the fellowship of other believers. We're encouraged to discuss and confirm our faith with each other.

However, today's Scripture tells us that there is more. Studying for our life lessons and for the tests that come in our lives every day is important. Studying the Scriptures also leads us to spiritual wisdom, which is the key to victory in our lives on this earth. Many times you have heard people say the wisdom of the world says, "I can do this on my own." God wants us to depend on him for spiritual wisdom.

On this day ask the Lord to give you spiritual wisdom. Pick up that text and begin to study, seeking his direction for your life.

"Listen as Wisdom calls out" (Proverbs 8:1).   *Carol*

* * *

Father God, instruct me today in your wisdom from above. Help me not to look at the wisdom of the world but to wisdom that is everlasting. I ask for wisdom for the ones in charge of our nation. I ask you to give the president and military leaders wisdom from above. **+** *Amen.*

Defying Gravity

We have been greatly encouraged in the midst of our troubles and suffering, dear brothers and sisters, because you have remained strong in your faith. It gives us new life to know that you are standing firm in the Lord. ✝ 1 THESSALONIANS 3:7-8

My young friend Megan spent her junior high and high school years participating in competitive cheerleading. On several occasions I had the privilege of watching her practice, and it was always a jaw-dropping experience. She would seem to defy gravity as she flipped, twisted, and turned with her jumps and tumbles, always ending up standing on her feet. It was obvious Megan had to have a good sense of balance, as well as the sense to know when to stop in order to make her descent. Somehow she consistently maintained an awareness of the placement of the ground.

No matter what kind of flips, twists, and turns life brings, we need to learn how to land with our feet on the ground. The members of the Thessalonian church were not shaken when false teachers attempted to throw them off balance by declaring that the second coming of Christ had already occurred. The fact that they kept their balance was a comfort to the apostle Paul. Paul had grounded this church in biblical truth and prayer, which produced a church that stood firm even when false doctrine could have turned it upside down.

I can think of many things that can throw us off balance besides false doctrine. Whatever those things may be, the Christians in Thessalonica are a great example to us today. Like them, we can have faith even when the circumstances of life cause us to flip and twist. We can know that, when all is said and done, God will help us land, standing firm on the solid foundation of Christ.   ✐*Brenda*

☆   ☆   ☆

Lord, keep me balanced and grounded in you and the principles of your Word. Help me to stand firm even when I am faced with things that may challenge my faith. Amid the twists and turns of daily life, or hardship, or even battle, keep your children secure in you, Jesus. In your name I pray. ✝*Amen.*

September 15
Go Dawgs

[Jesus] replied, "If they kept quiet, the stones along the road would burst into cheers!"
✝ LUKE 19:40

My husband has been a football fan since he could walk. He was an athlete from a very early age. He received accolades along the way and developed into a very good player by the time he reached junior high. Not only did my husband play football in junior high and high school, but he went to college on a double scholarship for baseball and football. After his freshman year, they told him he had to choose which sport he wanted to play, and he became the college quarterback. My football hero!

Our oldest son graduated from the University of Georgia. He will forever appreciate me after I write this particular story. I got involved in Georgia football as soon as he started at the university. Each week, we set aside that time on Saturday to root for our team. During the games, I'd scream, jump around, and pace a lot—especially if they were losing. I have to admit I would even pray that they'd win when the game got really close.

I love the role as cheerleader for my favorite team. I also love the role as cheerleader for my husband and my sons. I scream for their accomplishments. I pace when things are going on in their lives that are not so pleasant. I pray for them, especially when there is a trial or a decision to be made in their lives.

The Scripture for today tells us that as Jesus was riding into Jerusalem on a donkey, the people began to praise him as he came by. They said, "Blessings on the King who comes in the name of the Lord! Peace in heaven, and glory in highest heaven!" (Luke 19:38). Some Pharisees told Jesus to make the people quit cheering. He said to them that if he asked his followers to stay quiet, the stones would start cheering. In other words, when God is present, there is praise. When we are cheering for our families, our leaders, and our country, it is honoring the God of all blessings. When he presents a win to us, if we don't praise and honor him, creation will.

Cheer for your family and pray that God will honor them in their faithfulness to him.   ~*Carol*

✳   ✳   ✳

Father God, you are in the midst of victory throughout Scripture and in the world today. Lord, I pray today for victory in the War on Terror. I pray for victory in the hearts and lives of those who have been in bondage to tyranny so they might have victory in their hearts and come to know Jesus as their Lord. Praise you, Lord! ✝ *Amen.*

Complaints

Then the people complained and turned against Moses. ✛ EXODUS 15:24

In an Asian monastery, there were very strict rules. The most unusual restriction was that each monk could only speak two words every ten years. After Brother Barney had been a resident for ten years, he was brought in to his superior to speak his two words. "All right, Brother Barney, what are your two words?" asked the superior. Brother Barney sheepishly said, "Food bad!" At the end of twenty years, Brother Barney was called in for his two-word interview. "What do you have to say for yourself?" Brother Barney meekly murmured, "Bed, hard!" Now after thirty years, Brother Barney was called in for his third interview. This time Brother Barney angrily blurted out, "I quit!" His superior quickly responded, "Well, I'm not surprised. All you've done for thirty years is complain!"[1]

We may roll our eyes at this old story, but it illustrates the propensity many of us have to complain. We're not alone in this tendency—just go through the book of Exodus and read of the grumbling from the children of Israel after they were miraculously delivered from slavery.

Are there any benefits that come from complaining? Is there a right way to complain?

I actually think there is benefit that can come when we pursue change in the areas that cause us to complain. An example comes from my own experience as a military spouse. The Army has set up what is called the Army Family Action Plan, where soldiers and families gather together to recommend changes they think will improve military life. These constructive complaints in the form of recommendations for change are raised to the senior leadership of the Army. Over the years, helpful changes have resulted in these complaints being dealt with in a positive forum.

Unfortunately, complaining done by the Israelites in the desert is the type of complaining in which I more often engage. It was the automatic reaction then and continues to be the most automatic reaction in the face of difficulty or discomfort. Philippians 2:14 admonishes us to "do everything without complaining and arguing." The Greek word used for complaining here is the same word used to describe the rebellious children of Israel in Exodus 15:24. It is the type of complaining that is useless and wastes words and energy. Herein lies the choice when I am faced with discomfort—useless, wasted words or the pursuit of positive change? ❧*Brenda*

✶　✶　✶

Father, forgive me when I complain just for the purpose of voicing my displeasure or discomfort. Help me to rise above my personal comfort to use challenges as an opportunity to make improvements. ✛*Amen.*

---

[1] Tim Timmons, *Loneliness Is Not a Disease* (New York: Ballantine Books, 1983), 86.

September 17
Life Is Hard

Is not all human life a struggle? Our lives are like that of a hired hand. + JOB 7:1

If anyone knew how hard life could be, it would be Job. At the beginning of the Bible's account, Job is set for life. He has land, livestock, wealth, and a large family. His wife loves him. He has trusted the Lord for all he has and is very thankful to him. Life is good.

Then comes Satan the accuser. He says the only reason Job trusts in God and honors him is the fact that life is good and there is no testing. God gives Satan permission to go after Job in a big way. The story remains for all of time, showing us that Job never gave up his faith in the Lord at any time. Even his own wife told him to curse God, but Job did not.

In our land today, there are many who have achieved great wealth. When I was growing up, anyone making one hundred thousand a year was rich. Now, making a million dollars a year is becoming common. There are more and more people with wealth.

There are also those in our great country who continue to struggle financially and work very hard for a living. They will not know the pleasures of possessions and fame. Yet they continue to work hard and labor faithfully so that many are blessed by their commitment.

We are told in Matthew 11:30, "My yoke is easy to bear, and the burden I give you is light." Jesus knew the weight of the world would be heavy. He knew that burdens would weigh us down and that we would be challenged in every aspect of our lives. He had no intention for us to carry those burdens throughout our lives but to hand them to him in exchange for his love and his redemption.

When I find myself crying out to God over situations that I cannot control, I speak out loud, "Lord, help me to give these burdens to you. My heart is weighed down and my soul is in conflict. Life is hard but you are good."

Whether your heart is weighed down with politics, war, family strife, or marriage issues, God is standing by to hand you his perfectly fitting yoke. He will only give you a burden that is light because he takes the remainder of the cares with him.

Stand up today and let him place the yoke of peace, grace, and mercy on you!
∕Carol

✴   ✴   ✴

Father God, your yoke fits perfectly, and your burden is light! Help me to release and give all my cares to you. Bless those in harm's way who are holding fear and uncertainty in their hearts. Enable them to pray and release those cares to you today. + *Amen.*

Loving Discipline

Have you forgotten the encouraging words God spoke to you as his children? He said, "My child, don't make light of the LORD's discipline, and don't give up when he corrects you. For the LORD disciplines those he loves, and he punishes each one he accepts as his child."

✝ HEBREWS 12:5-6

In this passage, the writer of Hebrews quotes from Proverbs 3:11-12 in order to remind his readers of God's paternal love toward them. The recipients of the letter were tempted to go back to their old way of life. They were living in a time when the stability of the world as they had known it was in question. They had forgotten how much better their new life in Christ was compared to the system of rules and legalities they held before. Persecution and difficulty caused them to question the reality of their faith.

As our Father, God does not send discipline to us in order to simply inflict pain. The enemy of our soul makes it his purpose to convince us that any trouble we experience means that God does not love us. The reality is that our loving Father wants to see us become mature in our faith. Often that maturity comes through difficulties. Discipline from God is not the same as punishment for wrongdoing, but rather as part of developing our character. Christ faced difficult situations, and we sometimes do as well. We should not view these as punitive actions from the Lord, but rather opportunities for improvement.

The story is told of a surgeon who, due to unusual circumstances, found himself having to operate on his own son. As the son was receiving anesthesia, he said to his father, "You won't hurt me, will you, Dad?" Fighting back the tears, the father responded, "Son, I may have to hurt you, but I will never harm you."[1] Life on this side of heaven will bring its share of hurts, but don't yield to the temptation of thinking it is because God does not love you. Allow the Lord to use difficult circumstances to train you to become a mature child of God.   *≈Brenda*

✳ ✳ ✳

Heavenly Father, you discipline me for my good so that I may share in your holiness. I admit it does not seem pleasant at the time. As a result, I trust you will produce a harvest of righteousness and peace in my life. Therefore, strengthen my feeble arms and weak knees, encouraged by the knowledge that your "chastening hand is controlled by your loving heart."[2] Please do the same for those who may be weary of their work in the military. In Jesus' name I pray. ✝ *Amen.*

---

[1] Leith Anderson, *Praying to the God You Can Trust* (Minneapolis, MN: Bethany House Publishers, 1996), 129.
[2] Warren Wiersbe, *Be Confident* (Wheaton, IL: Victor Books, 1983), 139.

September 19

My Life, His Purpose

"Now my soul is deeply troubled. Should I pray, 'Father, save me from this hour'? But this is the very reason I came! Father, bring glory to your name." ✛ JOHN 12:27-28

The Purpose Driven Life has been such a powerful tool used of the Lord.[1] It has given both believers and nonbelievers reason for considering what our purpose is on this earth. I love the fact that it has bridged past being a book read only by Christians to challenge those in the world to search their hearts and lives for true meaning and purpose.

My husband and I were married shortly after my college graduation. He had been in the military for a year after he completed his college degree. Marriage really "fit" me. I loved being a wife. I loved keeping the house straight and having dinner on the table for my man when he came home at night. I loved planning weekend activities together and just being together as a married couple.

Then came motherhood, and I was quite sure that nothing in all the world could compare. I felt so much purpose in my life in taking care of this little one. I was usually exhausted from the challenge but at the same time very fulfilled. I continued with my commitment to my husband and being the wife he had known by keeping the house in order and meals that he enjoyed on the table. It was my heart's desire to be the very best wife and mother that I could possibly be. I would tell people that I was definitely created to be a wife and mother. I felt this was God's calling on my life.

As time went on and I began to grow in the Lord, I also came to realize that God had called me to another purpose, and that was to lead others to Jesus. This did not mean that I should give up the role of wife and mother that I was committed to, but it meant that I was to look at the world with eternity in mind. The things on earth would be accomplished by dedication and hard work. The things of the spiritual world would come through God's wisdom in my life and the sharing of his love.

On this wonderful day of your life, be encouraged that God has called you to a purpose on this earth. Whether you are a military man or woman or a corporate chief executive, God has a calling for you to fulfill. Look to him for your purpose and ask for wisdom to discern the earthly from the heavenly. He will stand with you to show you a purpose that will last a lifetime and into eternity.   *⋗Carol*

✯ ✯ ✯

Lord, help me fulfill your purpose for me today. May I bring glory to you through all that I do and say. In your name I pray. ✛ *Amen.*

---

[1] Rick Warren, *The Purpose Driven Life: What on Earth Am I Here For?* (Grand Rapids, MI: Zondervan, 2007).

A Word from Our Sponsor

All around him was a glowing halo, like a rainbow shining in the clouds on a rainy day. This is what the glory of the LORD looked like to me. When I saw it, I fell face down on the ground, and I heard someone's voice speaking to me. ✛ EZEKIEL 1:28

Alaska is a place where the glory of the Lord is evident through the beauty of nature. On each of my visits, I've had a memorable experience. On my most recent visit I spoke at a conference on the topic of heaven. One side of the room was banked with picture windows that held the view of a sparkling lake, golden autumn trees, and majestic mountains topped with the first snow of the season. It was a sight to behold. And despite this tempting view, the attendees blessed me with their attention. That is, until the last night.

After my introduction, I noticed people turning their heads toward the window. It was evident they were trying hard to keep their attention focused on me and the message I was attempting to share. There was a murmur in the audience, and I finally turned my head to see what was causing the distraction. What I saw totally arrested me!

The sun was glimmering on the lake and causing the leaves and snow to sparkle. But that wasn't what caught us all off guard. Out of the center of all this was the most brilliant rainbow I have ever seen. As a speaker, I did the only thing I could think of: I shut my mouth and led everyone outside. There we saw that the rainbow completely surrounded us. Basking in the beauty of the moment, we spontaneously sang the chorus of Chris Tomlin's "How Great Is Our God."[1]

The military spouses in attendance were far from home, many of them experiencing the fatigue that accompanies a long-term deployment. We had gathered for a time of encouragement and had been discussing the hope of heaven. It was as if the Lord said, "We interrupt our regularly scheduled programming for a word from our sponsor." The display of majesty was confirmation of the gracious promise that God's covenant with us remains true.

Today's Scripture references Ezekiel's vision of the throne of God. It is the same as John's vision in Revelation 4:3 and holds the promise for us as Christ followers that one day we will view his throne surrounded with a rainbow. What I saw in Alaska is only a taste of the beauty we will behold in heaven! It can't come soon enough! ❧*Brenda*

★　★　★

Lord, as I view the beauty of creation, open my eyes to see your hand in all your works and help me to serve you with joy and gladness. Reveal your deep beauty to those who are in desolate, war-torn places. ✛*Amen.*

---

[1] Chris Tomlin, "How Great Is Our God." Alletrope Music, 2004.

September 21
Why Do We Pray?

Never stop praying. ✛ 1 THESSALONIANS 5:17

Why do we pray? If you were asked by someone why you pray, what would your answer be? Would it be that you want to stay in communication with God throughout the day? Would it be that you find yourself feeling helpless to do anything for yourself and others so prayer is a way to reach out in those situations? Would it be that when the world seems to be against you, prayer helps you sense God's presence?

These are all reasons for me to pray. I have such a desire to stay in complete communication with God throughout my day. One of the life lessons that came my way as my sons were on their own was realizing the only way I could touch their lives was to pray for them. I could pray God would grant them wisdom, mercy, and grace in their lives.

I take the words "pray without ceasing" in 1 Thessalonians 5:17 (NKJV) seriously. I want to remain in an attitude of prayer throughout the day. In computer terms, I don't want to be shut down at any point.

Several years ago I realized that I was in a habit of saying, "I will pray for you." Whenever someone came up to me or called with a need, I would let them tell me the whole story and then say, "I will pray for you." Sometimes I did pray for them, and sometimes I did not.

I made a commitment to myself that if anyone shared a request with me, whether in person in the hallways at church, in the grocery-store line, or even on the phone, we were going to pray right there. My mother and I were recently leaving a parking lot after enjoying a latte together. I said, "Mother, look. She is praying over that girl." Sure enough, there was a lady with her hand on a young pregnant woman's tummy, and they were praying together in the middle of the parking lot. We both got teary and said, "That's what living in an attitude of prayer is all about."

It's not just about giving thanks at the table or asking for help during a crisis—it is about a relationship with our holy God the Father who invites us to "come boldly to the throne of our gracious God. There we will receive his mercy, and we will find grace to help us when we need it" (Hebrews 4:16). ⚭*Carol*

☆　☆　☆

Precious Father, thank you for allowing me to be in constant communication with you. Help me to continue to look to you, asking for grace and mercy for those who are serving our country at home and abroad. ✛ *Amen.*

Answers Will Come

I will answer them before they even call to me. While they are still talking about their needs,
I will go ahead and answer their prayers! ✚ ISAIAH 65:24

Look at this verse closely. Read it out loud one time. Did you get it? God knows exactly what we are going to pray before we even speak the requests or needs. So why do you think that he wants us to continue in prayer?

It is all about seeking his face. It is all about depending on him. Because our minds are finite and his mind is infinite, we do not know the answers. We must ask him to direct us to his will in our lives.

Not only does he give much instruction about prayer in the Scriptures, but he also promises to give answers to prayer. I want to list some of those references for you today:

> Keep on asking, and you will receive what you ask for. Keep on seeking, and you will find. Keep on knocking, and the door will be opened to you. For everyone who asks, receives. Everyone who seeks, finds. And to everyone who knocks, the door will be opened. (Matthew 7:7-8)
>
> You can pray for anything, and if you have faith, you will receive it. (Matthew 21:22)
>
> I also tell you this: If two of you agree here on earth concerning anything you ask, my Father in heaven will do it for you. For where two or three gather together as my followers, I am there among them. (Matthew 18:19-20)
>
> When they call on me, I will answer; I will be with them in trouble. I will rescue and honor them. (Psalm 91:15)
>
> Let us come boldly to the throne of our gracious God. There we will receive his mercy, and we will find grace to help us when we need it. (Hebrews 4:16)

So, dear ones, that is why we pray. Answers will come. God will see to that. As we all know, the answer can come in many forms, such as yes, no, maybe, or wait. God desires our communication with him, and he honors the prayers of the righteous.

Pray today for peace in our nation. Yes, in our nation. We think so much about the peace around the world, but we often forget the turmoil and spiritual battles in our own country. Pray this day for victory in the War on Terror. Pray for safety and supernatural strength and wisdom for those who are serving our country. Pray this day for families left behind and for those in our communities to surround them during this challenging time.

Answers will come! ∾*Carol*

✶   ✶   ✶

Father, today I pray for an army of people willing to stand in prayer on behalf of America. Bless the president and those who lead America. Bless those in the military as they serve this beloved country. ✚ *Amen.*

Continue Believing

My dear brothers and sisters, if someone among you wanders away from the truth and is brought back, you can be sure that whoever brings the sinner back will save that person from death and bring about the forgiveness of many sins. ✝ JAMES 5:19-20

These words are very dear to my heart. I spent years of wandering away from the truth. I spent years of knowing in my heart what was right and godly and still doing what I knew not to do.

I had the Word of God hidden in my heart, which brought deep conviction along with many tears and much inner turmoil. I can remember going forward to rededicate my life almost every time I heard the hymn "Just As I Am without One Plea." I can also remember feeling very alone during those times of wandering and thinking that I didn't even know who I was anymore.

Have you had those times in your life? Are you going through those same situations right now? The truth is in you and the truth is real, but you find yourself wandering away from all that you know to be true.

I will tell you that there were many people who invested in my life during this time of wandering. They believed in me and prayed diligently that I would be brought back to the truth. They consistently showed God's love to me.

My grandmother never quit praying for me. My mother and father never quit praying for me. They stood in the gap for me during that time in my life and continued to believe that I would return to God and commit my life to him.

I am very thankful for those who did not give up on me and trusted that God had a plan for my life. God honored their diligence and their desire to help this sinner come home. I want to stand for others who are wandering and to bring those back who could be forgiven and saved from death.

I continue to believe in those whom God has called unto himself and who have become so entrapped in sin that they cannot see the way. He is the Way. Continue to believe in that, and you will be a blessed follower of the Lord.   ❦*Carol*

✳   ✳   ✳

Father God, thank you for those who prayed for me over the years. Use me to stand in the gap and lift up those who feel unable to pray for themselves. I think today particularly of those in the military who know you—strengthen them and increase their faith; as well as those who do not know you—mercifully come to them, Lord. ✝ *Amen.*

September 24
Prayer of Praise

Great is the LORD! He is most worthy of praise! No one can measure his greatness.

✛ PSALM 145:3

Great is the Lord! We need to praise him for all his goodness and faithfulness. His unconditional love and mercy in our lives are beyond anything the human mind can comprehend. He weaves the details of our lives into service and honor for him. When our hearts belong to him, there is nothing in our lives that comes without his direction and purpose.

Why not take some time today to write down the things for which you can praise the Lord? I find that when I see things on paper, it becomes more real to me. Take this day to write out a prayer of praise after you list these revelations about your God.

God inhabits the praise of his people, and he will be there with you as you are praising his name today. What a beautiful month to praise him. Look around you at creation and feel the coolness in the air. Give him praise that you got up today and that you can sit to thank him for the wonderful things in your life.

This can be a day of praise that a loved one has been protected as they have served in military service. It can be a day of praise that your son or daughter was protected in school after a scare of someone calling in a threat. This can be a day of praise that your family member has just gotten through a surgery in the hospital.

We have so many things to give him praise for in our lives. Oftentimes we don't take the time to do so, but today I am challenging you to create your own personal praise report to God.

Hold on to your prayer of praise from today. When times may take you to a place of hopelessness or despair, read your prayer of praise out loud to remind you of God's goodness in your life.

Great is the Lord! He is most worthy of praise!   ⁓*Carol*

✶   ✶   ✶

I praise you, Lord! I honor your faithfulness to your people who call upon your name. May a prayer of praise remain on my lips through all my days. ✛ *Amen.*

September 25
Dog Tags

Never let loyalty and kindness leave you! Tie them around your neck as a reminder. Write them deep within your heart. ✛ PROVERBS 3:3

A common trick for remembering something is a string tied around a finger. The idea that something tangible will trigger the desired memory has proven successful. My husband wanted to provide a tangible tool for his soldiers to be reminded of God's available presence as they prepared for deployment to Afghanistan in the summer of 2002. Because they were soldiers, he placed an order for dog tags. These weren't your ordinary military-issue dog tags. On one side of the tag was the American flag, and on the other side was the Scripture "Be strong and courageous . . . for the LORD your God will be with you wherever you go" (Joshua 1:9, NIV). Hundreds of soldiers took a tag and placed it on the chain around his or her neck along with the official tag. These tags served as a tangible reminder that God would sustain them through the trying time ahead. My husband recalls one soldier asking if he could have an extra one to give to his wife, who was staying behind, to remind her that she, too, could be sustained by God while her husband was away.

There was no magic power in the dog tag my husband handed out, but God's Word on the tag was a reminder that God's power is a very real comfort in times of crisis. There are many promises that communicate this message throughout Scripture:

> He will never leave you nor forsake you. (Deuteronomy 31:6, NIV)
> The temptations in your life are no different from what others experience. And God is faithful. He will not allow the temptation to be more than you can stand. When you are tempted, he will show you a way out so that you can endure. (1 Corinthians 10:13)
> Don't be dejected and sad, for the joy of the LORD is your strength! (Nehemiah 8:10)
> I will ask the Father, and he will give you another Advocate, who will never leave you. (John 14:16)

These are examples of biblical truths we can depend on to sustain us through whatever comes our way. Whether you wear a promise around your neck or not, these promises can be depended upon as we carry them in our hearts.   *≫Brenda*

✦   ✦   ✦

Lord, I thank you for your Word, which is a comfort, help, and encouragement to me, not only in times of trouble, but every day. I pray for those who need to experience your comfort today. Provide a word that will give them the courage to face this day. In your name I pray. ✛ *Amen.*

Sustained

LORD, sustain me as you promised, that I may live! Do not let my hope be crushed.
✛ PSALM 119:116

I remember, one day during my husband's deployment to Iraq, thinking about the word *sustain*. I had never focused any attention on this particular word. It seemed a rather old-fashioned biblical word. My greatest understanding of the term came from long-ago piano lessons as I recalled the use of the sustain pedal. Pushing the sustain pedal would hold a note and carry it in a more melodic, less abrupt manner. Why would this be a word I was thinking of at this time? I quickly looked up the word and found that the synonyms included *maintain, continue, carry on, keep up, keep going, uphold, nourish, support, feed, help, aid,* and *assist.* I realized this was what I was experiencing as I was being buoyed upon the prayers of others during my husband's absence.

I have since thought more about this concept of being sustained. To me it represents not only an element of future hope that things will be better but also a present strength that comes from within through the support of prayers from others and especially from the Holy Spirit. The original language for the word *sustain* in Psalm 119:116 provides a wonderful word picture of being propped up and can be translated "give me thyself to lean upon." My friend Maria expressed this same type of experience during her husband's deployment. She says it was a time of "leaning into God and having his strength make the stance firm." The crises that come into our lives provide opportunities for us to experience God's sustaining power. I'm so grateful for the invitation to lean into him and the knowledge that I will be sustained.

The story is told of the missionary to Africa, David Livingstone, who walked over twenty-nine thousand miles facing much opposition from his own countrymen as he fulfilled the call of God on his life. Enduring the death of his wife early in their ministry and health issues that left him half-blind, he still penned these words in his journal: "Send me anywhere, only go with me. Lay any burden on me, only sustain me. Sever me from any tie but the tie that binds me to your service and to your heart."[1] ❧*Brenda*

✭ ✭ ✭

Father, I stand no longer than you hold me and go no further than you carry me.[2] Thank you for the arms that will sustain me as I lean on you. Bless those who are in need of your sustaining grace as they experience challenging situations. In your name I pray. ✛ *Amen.*

---

[1] Joseph Stowell, *Through the Fire* (Wheaton, IL: Victor Books, 1988), 150.
[2] *Matthew Henry's Commentary on the Whole Bible: New Modern Edition,* Electronic Database, CD-ROM. Hendrickson Publishers, 1991.

September 27
A Metal Cover

Every word of God proves true. He is a shield to all who come to him for protection.
✛ PROVERBS 30:5

Deployed soldiers receive care packages from people all over the country. Often the packages contain Bibles. During his deployment, my husband received a pocket-size New Testament and Psalms with a zipper. The unique thing about this particular Bible was the thin piece of metal placed on the covers. During each war, these metal-covered Bibles have been very popular. And during each war there are stories of lives being saved by Bibles carried in the pocket of soldiers. Just recently, an Orlando, Florida, news station carried a report from the Iraq War of a soldier who was protected from more serious injury because of the Bible in his pocket.[1]

I have no doubt the story reported from Orlando is true. There are pictures and video to substantiate the story, along with words from the soldier thanking those who were praying for him during his deployment. However, with all the body armor soldiers wear today, the norm is that their hearts are protected by a half inch of steel, as opposed to a paper-thin piece of tin on a Bible. Sometimes people have a superstitious element of faith that even though they may not serve God, they put a Bible in their pockets to protect from a stray bullet just in case. The chances of a Bible with a metal cover saving a life may be incalculable; however, the confidence that the God revealed in Scripture can protect our souls in any situation is 100 percent guaranteed.

My husband encouraged soldiers not to trust in the metal cover of a book but to put their trust in the Person revealed in the pages of that book. Interestingly enough, the original word for "true" in today's Scripture is a word used for refining metal. It points to the fact that whatever trials we encounter, God's Word can be trusted. It will be like a shield to protect us. That's a metal cover we can depend upon! ✒Brenda

Father, you are my rock, my fortress, and my savior; my God, you are my rock, in whom I find protection. You are my shield, the power that saves me, and my place of safety (Psalm 18:2, paraphrased). ✛ Amen.

---

[1] "Bible in U.S. Soldier's Pocket Stops Sniper Bullet," posted August 14, 2007, updated August 15, 2007, www.local6.com/news.

Filled with His Glory

Then the cloud covered the Tabernacle, and the glory of the LORD filled the Tabernacle.

✝ EXODUS 40:34

The glory of God can be defined as the personal presence of God. We read in Exodus 40:34 that God's glory and presence were so powerful Moses could not even enter the Tabernacle. It is interesting to me that the Tabernacle was not a particularly beautiful, elaborate, or magnificent structure. It was basically made of tarps and poles, like a big tent, so it could be moved when the Israelites moved. But when the glory of the Lord descended on the Tabernacle, it became the most important structure in the world. For us, this passage can be a reminder that this same glory of God lives within the humble home of our earthly bodies. We can be filled with this glory!

The word *glory* carries the meaning of something weighty, not as in a burden, but as in having value and worth. As a Christ follower, I don't want my life to be characterized by meaningless fluff; rather, I desire my life to be characterized by meaningful depth. I cannot deny that it has been the challenges and struggles of life that have brought any depth of character I may possess. It's a process of consistent emptying and filling.

When we allow God to fill us with his glory, he empties our hearts of sin and fills them with his righteousness. He drains out all of our selfish pride and replaces it with his spirit of humility. He pours out all our anger and bitterness and pours in his compassion and love. He pumps out all our anxiety and fear and exchanges it with a powerful faith in him. He cleanses us of our immorality and fills us with his holiness. If this is the result, I say, "Empty me and then fill me to overflowing!" *≈Brenda*

✫   ✫   ✫

Father, empty me of those things that are meaningless to make room for those things that carry eternal weight. Don't allow me to be cowardly toward any difficulty today may hold. Safeguard me from those things that would fill me with anything other than the fullness of your Spirit. In Jesus' name I pray. ✝ *Amen.*

September 29
Intended for Good

You intended to harm me, but God intended it all for good. He brought me to this position so I could save the lives of many people. ✛ GENESIS 50:20

Salvation Army Commissioner Samuel Logan Brengle was almost killed by a brick thrown at him during a street meeting. During his eighteen-month recuperation, he began to write for the ministry's *War Cry* magazine. His articles on holy living were so helpful and popular that they later were printed in the book *Helps to Holiness*, which has continued to bless others throughout the years.

When Brengle finally recovered, his wife presented him with the brick that had almost caused his death. Engraved upon it were the words from today's Scripture, "As for you, ye thought evil against me; but God meant it unto good to save much people alive" (KJV).[1]

One of the greatest challenges we have as Christ followers is to really believe that when something bad happens to us, it can actually be a part of God's plan to bring about something great. It is somewhat of a mystery on our part how something that seems to be an evil act can actually be part of a good plan in the mind of God. That is why he is God and we are not!

In the case of Joseph, his brothers did an evil thing to sell him into Egyptian slavery. I doubt Joseph thought it was a great plan at the time. Afterwards, however, he was able to look back with understanding to see that this act of evil by his brothers was part of a greater plan God had for his life. Let's be careful not to limit the power of God at work in our lives and to hold tight to the truth that God knows how to work *all* things together for good (see Romans 8:28). *Brenda*

✳   ✳   ✳

Lord, I pray for a heart to trust your good work in my life. Even when I cannot see the good, give me confidence to know you have not forsaken me. In your name I pray. ✛ *Amen.*

---

[1] W. T. Purkiser, *When You Get to the End of Yourself* (Grand Rapids, MI: Baker Book House, 1970), 27.

Oasis in a Box

They will neither hunger nor thirst. The searing sun will not reach them anymore. For the LORD in his mercy will lead them; he will lead them beside cool waters. ✚ ISAIAH 49:10

The heat of the desert in Central Asia can be brutal. My husband's unit was set up in the middle of the desert. There were no buildings or trees, and the beaming sun was creating temperatures of well over one hundred degrees. It was impossible to get cool. On one hot day, my husband was making his pastoral rounds, visiting various people in the compound. As the sweat drenched his body, he remembered the guys in the communication truck.

The communication truck was the size of a pickup truck with a camper on the back. Since the equipment had to be kept cool, there was air-conditioning in the truck. As he visited and encouraged the soldiers there in these cramped quarters, he was able to have a brief—yes, it was brief—retreat from the heat of the day.

The respite my husband received in that air-conditioned box was just enough cool refreshment to get him through the rest of the day. As he was refreshing others with words of encouragement and blessing, he was also being refreshed (see Proverbs 11:25).

The Lord knows how to restore our souls even when we can't see any shelter from the heat of our circumstances. There may be no visible shelter or shade, but he can provide an oasis—even in a box. This is the promise of the words of Isaiah 49:10—God will enable us to withstand the heat of the day. It carries the picture of a shepherd leading his sheep to a cool, refreshing stream to protect them from the burning sand. Allow the Great Shepherd to lead you to a place of rest from the pressure and heat of this day. *⁊Brenda*

*   *   *

My Shepherd, thank you for the promise of refreshment when the heat of this life gets overwhelming. I pray for your enablement to endure the issues that cause me to feel burdened. In your name I pray. ✚ *Amen.*

October 1
It Will Fit

The LORD directs our steps, so why try to understand everything along the way?
✝ PROVERBS 20:24

"To the child of God, there is no such thing as accident. He travels an appointed way. The path he treads was chosen for him when as yet he was not, when as yet he had existence only in the mind of God."[1]

A desire of my heart has been to travel the world. As a military spouse, I have not only had the privilege to do this but I have had the chance to live in both Europe and Asia. There have been countless miles logged over the years as God has provided opportunities to share a word of encouragement with others throughout the world. The stamps in my passport are treasured reminders of these gifts.

I've had to travel alone enough to appreciate the times I've had a traveling companion. My friend Victoria and I journeyed many miles together during a term of leadership for the military chapel women's ministry Protestant Women of the Chapel (PWOC). Each time we are together, something reminds us of one of our many expeditions, and we find ourselves laughing as we relive a special time.

In preparing to return home, we always ended up having much more to pack than when we started, and the concern would be if it would all fit. Our catchphrase and declaration was, It will fit! Many times we realized that there were some things we could leave as a gift for the hotel housekeeper or our host. But someway, somehow those things that were most important always did fit into the suitcase.

"It will fit" continues to be our catchphrase today as Victoria and I compare notes on things other than literal packing of a suitcase. Now we discuss our schedules and the ministry goals and dreams the Lord allows us to have, and we encourage each other that if something truly is God's appointed way, it will fit.

We have to be cautious that we don't crowd our lives with so many things that we become too busy to enjoy the gift of life God has given us. God does have an appointed way for each of us to travel. If we find that doing what God wants doesn't seem to fit, then maybe that is the time we should consider removing something that is unnecessary.   *Brenda*

* * *

Lord, thank you for the promise of your direction through life. Keep me ever mindful of the priorities that are pleasing to you. As I begin this new day, I place all of the choices of how I can spend this day before you. Help me to complete the things that truly fit and to remove the things that are extra weight. In your name I pray. ✝ *Amen.*

---

[1] A.W. Tozer, *We Travel an Appointed Way* (Camp Hill, PA: Wingspread Publishers, 1988), 1.

October 2
Fire Truck Prayer

Dear brothers and sisters, honor those who are your leaders in the Lord's work. They work hard among you and give you spiritual guidance. Show them great respect and wholehearted love because of their work. And live peacefully with each other. + 1 THESSALONIANS 5:12-13

My husband was working in his office in Arlington, Virginia, when he was distracted by a loud crash coming from the street below. He looked out the window and saw something he had never seen before. A fire truck had flipped over on its side while rounding a sharp curve on an entrance ramp to the highway. From his twelfth-floor office all my husband could immediately do to help was call 911. As he was overlooking the scene, he saw that in a matter of a few seconds those who were passing by stopped their vehicles and ran to the fire truck to offer assistance. The nonprofessional rescuers climbed onto the overturned truck to help the trapped firemen get safely out of the truck. It was only minutes before several other fire trucks and rescue vehicles arrived on the scene, but it was ordinary citizens who were the first responders to assist the professional rescuers.

It was unusual to see the professional rescuers in need of being rescued themselves by untrained civilians. Yet at the same time, it was encouraging to see how many civilians quickly responded to the professionals when they were in need.

As I reflected on this event, I thought what a great example it was for those of us who are Christ followers in relation to those who serve us in professional ministry. Men and women who have dedicated their lives to helping us in our time of need sometimes find themselves turned upside down. There are ways we as laypeople can respond when our professional clergy are in need of help because of a crisis in their lives. Instead of sitting back and waiting to see if they can rescue themselves, we can be available to offer encouragement and to pray for them.

The month of October has been designated as Clergy Appreciation Month. Why not create an opportunity to bless those who serve you as pastors, chaplains, and other professional clergy? 1 Timothy 5:17 advises, "Elders who do their work well should be respected and paid well, especially those who work hard at both preaching and teaching." This appreciation is appropriate throughout the year, and the challenges faced by these servants of God are very real. Our prayers and support will make a difference! *Brenda*

✻   ✻   ✻

Father, thank you for those who have answered your call to proclaim the truth of your Word. Strengthen them spiritually, emotionally, and physically as they spend their lives in selfless service. Protect their families. Make me willing to help by taking my place in the body of Christ. Protect also those who have answered the call of country, strengthening them to work ably and well on our behalf. + Amen.

October 3
Airport Reflections

It was by faith that Abraham obeyed when God called him to leave home and go to another land that God would give him as his inheritance. He went without knowing where he was going. + HEBREWS 11:8

I found myself sitting in a Japanese airport, not sure how to proceed. Usually when traveling to speak at a conference, I am prepared and have all of my traveling ducks in a row. But this particular time it dawned on me that I did not have any information concerning who, if anyone, was coming to meet me. I had no plan as to where to meet or if I was to look for someone specific. I did not feel anxious about this, even though I was in unfamiliar territory. I had faith that somehow, some way, someone would arrive to take me to where I was supposed to go.

Today's Scripture refers to the Lord telling Abraham to leave his homeland. The amazing thing about this is that Abraham did it even though he didn't know where he was going. He didn't know the route he was going to take. It was a journey of faith. Abraham knew God had a purpose. God had called him. He was not on a spiritual journey of his own making. God had not revealed every step of his journey nor those people the Lord would bring across his path to assist him in settling into the land the Lord promised.

As I reflected on my airport experience, I thought about my own faith journey. In this case, I had been invited to come to Japan. I felt confident someone would eventually come to find me, which they did. There was a plan and a purpose; I just did not know all the details. As a Christ follower, I don't discover God's plan and purpose for me by creating my own spiritual journey or my own spiritual plan. God has a very specific plan. He sent his Son to die for me. My role is to be obedient and take the next step in which he leads. Just like Abraham, I am to step out in faith, believing the Lord will lead me through this journey with a plan that is full of his promises here in this life, but more importantly, for a promised land that is eternal. If we are obedient, we will find at the end of the journey we are exactly where God wants us to be. *≈Brenda*

*   *   *

Father, help me to trust your plan and purpose for my life. Calm me down when I get anxious to know the next step, and remind me that you are leading me exactly where you want me to be. Give to those who are deployed and to their families your abiding peace in the midst of so much upheaval. + *Amen.*

Cleansing Tears

You keep track of all my sorrows. You have collected all my tears in your bottle. You have recorded each one in your book. ✝ PSALM 56:8

Tears have always been a ready part of my emotions. I often find myself crying at the card shop. I love the card shop commercials. I look forward to the holiday commercials the most because they are so heartfelt. I cry when the houses are being built on television for people who need them so desperately. I cry over movies whether or not I've seen them before.

When people are dealing with a loss in their lives, you will hear them say, "I just can't stop crying!" You see, I believe that is a gift to us from our Father in heaven. He gave us the ability to release our emotions through tears. Tears are very cleansing in the sense that they enable us to not hold on and become physically ill with emotions stored up inside.

When my husband and I were growing up, the thought was that boys shouldn't cry because it made them look less manly. That is something that has softened through the years, but many were left from that time with ulcers and frustration from being taught not to show their emotions.

There is a need for emotion in our lives—especially when we are going through the loss of a loved one or a close friend. Even if you need to go into a private room or place where you can be alone, it is very important that you are able to let your emotions flow. God cares so much about your sorrows that we are told he has collected all your tears in a bottle.

David's crying out to God over and over in the Psalms gives me an example to follow. I will many times go to my living room and cry out to God when life becomes more than I can handle. When someone I love is going through times of conflict and trial, I will cry out to God and not be ashamed to let the cleansing tears flow.

Remember on this day that God is our Creator. He knew we would need to cry, or he would not have created tear ducts for our bodies. Cry out to God and let the cleansing tears take the sadness and grief from your heart. He will collect them for you in his heavenly bottle. ⮞*Carol*

★   ★   ★

Father God, on this day there are many in our nation who are crying out to you. There are daily reports of tragedy and crisis in America. I am often confused and disheartened by those who want to harm my fellow citizens. Keep me on my face, Lord, crying out to you for your direction, and let me not be ashamed to cry tears of compassion for my world. ✝ *Amen.*

October 5
Enter into the Iron

They bruised his feet with fetters and placed his neck in an iron collar. + PSALM 105:18

The beloved missionary Amy Carmichael sensed God's call on her life at an early age, when she began helping the children of millworkers in her home country of Ireland. A debilitating pain would leave her bedridden for weeks at a time, yet her passion to carry God's love to the world was so great that she lived as a missionary to India, staying there without furlough for thirty-five years.

At one point Amy prayed, "Lord, teach me how to conquer pain to the uttermost henceforth, and grant this my earnest request. When my day's work is done, take me straight Home. Do not let me be ill and a burden or anxiety to anyone. O let me finish my course with joy and not with grief. Thou knowest there could be no joy if I knew I were tiring those whom I love best, or taking them from the children. Let me die of a battle-wound, O my Lord, not a lingering illness."

Amy was bedridden for almost twenty years of her life. She never fully recovered from a crippling fall and lived her later years in much pain and completely dependent on others. Yet this great woman of God did not become bitter because of her seemingly unanswered prayer. During these years of confinement, she wrote prolific volumes testifying to the depth of God as a loving Father, her hiding place into whom she would "tuck" herself as a little child and trust to carry her through.

Writing of her pain, she refers to Psalm 105:18, which points to Joseph and the pain caused by the iron fetters on his feet when he was taken into slavery in Egypt. She writes of discovering a translation of this Scripture as, "Joseph's soul entered into iron—entered, whole and entire in its resolve to obey God, into the cruel torture." She writes that it was not her soul that was in cruel torture, but merely her body. "And as I lay there, unable to move it came to me that what was asked of Joseph, in a far greater degree, was asked of me now. Would I merely endure it, praying for the grace not to make too much over my poor circumstances? Or would my soul willingly enter into the iron of this new and difficult experience?"[1]

You probably have not chosen your own "irons," but with God's grace you can find meaning in the midst of your difficulties. Ask God to help you enter into the iron in a way that brings glory to him and fulfillment to you.   ❧*Brenda*

✱   ✱   ✱

Father, I ask for your grace to glorify you through the difficulties of life—for myself here at home, and for my country's soldiers, all over the world. Make those things that look to us like chains become the iron that melds our lives to yours. + *Amen.*

---

[1] Amy Carmichael, *You Are My Hiding Place* (Minneapolis, MN: Bethany House Publishers, 1991), 93.

Remembering

Now stand here quietly before the LORD as I remind you of all the great things the LORD has done for you and your ancestors. ✛ 1 SAMUEL 12:7

This passage of Scripture today takes us to Samuel's farewell address to his people. Samuel was reviewing his time with the Israelites so that they would remember how they had gotten to this point. He was reminding them of all God had done for them.

As I stood over the hospital bed my dad was lying in, I began to remember those wonderful times I had spent with him. I remembered the boat and fishing with him. I remembered him smiling and winking at me when I most needed his love and encouragement. I remembered the times of holding hands with family and friends and asking God's blessing on our holiday celebrations. He would close the prayer by saying, "Amen and dig in." What an amazing and blessed life to remember with my dad. There were many hard times and times that each of us would have gone back to do over, but at that point I was flooded with the positive memories.

In finding this verse for today's thoughts, I began to reflect on all God had done for me in my life. It's not just the *doings* but the *beings* I have experienced with him as my God. The most amazing thing is that he has been with me completely along life's road, even when I was not with him. That is so powerful.

As we pray for God to give or answer something for us, should we think first to remember all that he has been to us in our lives? Before we criticize our great nation, our president, or our commanders in the military, should we take time to remember that we live in freedom every day of our lives? Should we remember the goodness and mercy God has shown to our country?

When you are going through the loss of a loved one, remember the good things that came with that person. If the relationship was difficult on this earth, begin to journal the good things you remember about your loved one. Thank God for those times when you are ready to do so. Allow yourself time to heal, and then remember all the great things the Lord has done for you and your ancestors. ❧*Carol*

★　★　★

Dear heavenly Father, you are the giver of life. Remind me of your tender mercy and grace. Help those who are serving our country to remember the great things in their lives that are blessings bestowed on them and their families. ✛ *Amen.*

October 7
Gold Star Moms

When Jesus arrived at Bethany, he was told that Lazarus had already been in his grave for four days. Bethany was only a few miles down the road from Jerusalem, and many of the people had come to console Martha and Mary in their loss. ✛ JOHN 11:17-19

Up and down the streets of American towns today, small, rectangular flags hanging in the windows of homes is a common sight. The white flag, trimmed with red banners, will hold either blue or gold stars. These stars indicate that someone in the family is serving in the military (blue) or has died in service to their country (gold).

This small tribute to military personnel traces its roots to a British mother who lost her son in World War I. Recognizing that "self-contained grief was self-destructive," this mother set out to organize a group of women who like her had lost children in military service.[1] Their purpose was to provide comfort to one another, but also to supply TLC to veterans who were hospitalized. These women became known as Gold Star Moms, and their mission of loving service spread across the ocean and is alive and well today.

There were no gold stars in the window of Mary and Martha's home from today's Scripture, but it was evident they were grieving. Theirs was not a self-contained grief, as manifest by the many people who were present. In Jewish life, it was customary for a group to gather to help others grieve, so much so that often people were hired for this purpose.

In the midst of grieving, the sisters individually confronted Jesus to ask why this had happened. Why didn't God intervene? The normal thoughts and questions of why, and if only, were extensive. The example of today's Scripture communicates that not only is it healthy to share our grief with others, but it is healthy to share our grief with the Lord as well. In this case, when Christ arrived, he raised Lazarus from the dead (although not to have him permanently live on earth, for he died again). He was raised as a demonstration of Christ's power, showing that one day we will all be raised to live with him forever.

Immediate help in our grief comes from the Lord through his Spirit. But a permanent answer when we have lost a loved one who is a Christ follower is the eternal life we'll share together in the Resurrection. ➽Brenda

✶　✶　✶

Lord, you knew sorrows and were acquainted with grief. Help me in times of sorrow not to shy away from those who would benefit from my support. Remind me that they don't need me to tell them I understand, or that their grief will pass, or they are being tested, or any other platitude. Instead, help me to be willing to be a friend who will share in their sorrow and extend your grace. In your name I pray. ✛ Amen.

---

[1] American Gold Star Mothers, www.goldstarmoms.com, 2128 Leroy Place, NW, Washington, DC 20008.

All That Is Left

Because of the privilege and authority God has given me, I give each of you this warning:
Don't think you are better than you really are. Be honest in your evaluation of yourselves,
measuring yourselves by the faith God has given us. ✛ ROMANS 12:3

In the military, the anticipation of promotion and selection lists that come out each year weighs heavily on the minds of those on active duty. The military member waits for acceptance into the next school or the possibility of changing the branch of service, as well as being promoted to the next level of leadership. It is very important to keep striving to be the best you can be and continue to go forward.

Often this striving is associated with one's self-worth. As with executives and corporate America, climbing the ladder of success can take the place of true security and confidence within one's life.

When the military began downsizing in the early nineties, my husband and I realized exactly where we placed our confidence. We were cast into the civilian world quickly and without preparation. We suddenly did not have a promotion list to wait for or a uniform to prepare. Our identity with the world we had known for twenty-two years was stripped from us.

Within a month we knew that we had to dig much deeper to understand and to go forward in this situation. We realized as the days passed that all that was left was our love for each other and God's love for us. It became more and more reassuring to us that those two things were all that mattered.

Life changes are regular and normal. When we have given our hearts to Jesus Christ, there is so much more than a life waiting on the next promotion or job opportunity. When all that is left is your love for your family and God's love for you, you can know that your life is blessed.

Stand before your heavenly Father today and thank him for the security and peace you have in knowing that when all is taken away, Jesus is all you need. You can look to the future with excitement and anticipation in knowing he will show you the way. ✑*Carol*

✦ ✦ ✦

Father God, I ask for your strength for those who serve our country today. I ask that your Holy Spirit will instill in them inner peace and the knowledge that comes from the security of salvation. Thank you for their service to our country. I stand and honor them today. ✛ *Amen.*

October 9
Prepared

I can do everything through Christ, who gives me strength. ✛ PHILIPPIANS 4:13

The story is told of a young man who flunked out of college and was too frightened to return home to share the news with his father. In anticipation of his father's reaction, he sent a message to his father's best friend. The message read: "Flunked out. Be home tomorrow. Prepare Dad."

A response was quickly returned: "Dad prepared. Prepare yourself!"[1]

I understood this need for preparation when my husband deployed to Afghanistan. I watched him and the unit he was serving prepare rigorously for the experience. The preparation included such things as physical training, a first aid refresher, land mine awareness, and staff operational planning.

I realized there was a certain type of preparation that I needed to do as well in order to deal with what was ahead. During my quiet time one day, I jotted down some thoughts on the topic of being prepared. I recognized my need to

> **P**lan to carry out
> **R**esponsibilities normally not mine.
> **E**ducate myself and believe in the
> **P**ossibilities of what can be done.
> **A**ccept the
> **R**eality that the worst can happen.
> **E**liminate all
> **D**oubts that with God's help I can do what is required!

In retrospect, I see that I was attempting to approach the fear of Richard's deployment with a sense of realism and trust in God. Today, long after the deployment was completed, I recognize these thoughts on being prepared are applicable to not only deployment but everyday life.

Paul, in making his declaration of being able to "do everything through Christ," was not being vainly boastful. He knew the supernatural strength that was available to him through Christ. J. B. Phillips translated Philippians 4:13 this way: "I am ready for anything through the strength of the One who lives within me."

Paul reached this level of preparedness over many years of seeing God at work in his life through good times and bad. He had learned that regardless of what came his way, with God's help he would be able to face it. We may not be as prepared as Paul to face the challenges before us; however, there is no better time than today to begin to prepare for what will come tomorrow. We do this by learning to trust God with everything that comes our way, believing his hand is at work even when we can't see it.   ≈*Brenda*

✶   ✶   ✶

Father, I am confident of all this because of my great trust in you through Christ. It is not that I think I am qualified to do anything on my own. My qualification comes from you (2 Corinthians 3:4-5, paraphrased). ✛*Amen.*

---

[1] Norm Lewis, *Priority One* (Orange County, CA: Promise Publishing, 1988), 63.

Different Grief

Confess your sins to each other and pray for each other so that you may be healed. The earnest prayer of a righteous person has great power and produces wonderful results.

✝ JAMES 5:16

One of the most important life lessons I've learned was about grief—not the stages of grief I'd been instructed to identify but the different kinds of grief. A dear friend of mine was deserted by her husband for another woman. I went to visit her one day soon after she had found out the news. I pulled into her driveway and saw all the curtains were pulled. As I walked into her home, I saw she was sitting in her bathrobe, and I realized she was definitely headed into depression.

I immediately opened the curtains, helped her to her feet, and asked what I could do. She said, "You know, if my husband had died, everyone in the church would be here surrounding me with food, fellowship, and prayer. He left me for another woman, and I am grieving the death of our relationship, and you are the first person to even come to see me."

For this woman, grieving the loss of the man she loved had begun. Even though he was still alive, she could no longer be with him. People struggle with how to deal with someone who is grieving in circumstances such as divorce, an empty nest, elderly parents, or even retirement. Don't be afraid to approach and support friends who are experiencing these challenges in their lives.

As today's Scripture tells, we are to pray for each other so that we may be healed. There are so many different kinds of grief. There may be someone in your church or neighborhood who has just sent a son or daughter to war. Encourage your neighbor and recognize that he or she is grieving.

Hold on to this teaching today, and know that the earnest prayer of a righteous person has great power and wonderful results.   ～*Carol*

✷ ✷ ✷

Heavenly Father, help me to recognize the different types of grief and trust you to help me through. Help me to be open and available to others during their difficult times. ✝ *Amen.*

October 11
Korean Heaven

If our hope in Christ is only for this life, we are more to be pitied than anyone in the world.
✝ 1 CORINTHIANS 15:19

While living in Korea, I became acquainted with two lovely Korean women. I was blessed to have them visit my home on numerous occasions. Mrs. Hwang was Buddhist, and Mrs. Kim was Catholic. One of their visits came soon after the death of Mrs. Kim's mother. Some friends had told her about a woman whose husband's departed spirit kept coming into the home. She became so afraid her mother's spirit would come to her that she could not sleep.

Mrs. Hwang shared her Buddhist belief that the soul must often come back to complete a good deed in order to go to a better place. The women asked what I thought about this concept. I shared that my eternal life was not based on good works but on what Christ did on the cross for me. I went on to say that I have no question I would be in heaven with Christ when I die and that this hope not only gives me confidence of eternal life but enhances my life here on earth.

Before my friends left, Mrs. Kim asked me to pray for her. She said she'd never done that before, but she felt I was a special person and God would hear my prayers. I told her God heard our prayers not because we are special but because he is. I prayed for him to take away Mrs. Kim's fears, replace them with his peace, and allow her to rest and trust him. As these two dear women left my home, I continued to pray for the bondage of fear that came as a result of superstitions to be broken.

Heaven and hell are two topics that frequently come up in conversation, most often in a lighthearted, uncertain, no-way-you-can-know kind of way. Many people don't think you can have a concrete understanding of heaven, much less the certainty of going there. But the whole point of the Bible is that there is certainty about this fact. Though Christ was a great teacher and example of how to live a godly life, his primary purpose for us was not only to have a complete life here on earth but to have certainty of life with him in heaven forever. The basis of that certainty is in our full faith and trust in Christ as our personal Savior.

It was a joy for me to pray a simple prayer with Mrs. Kim that day in Korea. If you are reading this devotional today and are not certain about the hope of heaven, I invite you to pray this simple prayer of salvation with me: *Brenda*

✳   ✳   ✳

Father, I confess my sin and ask for your forgiveness. Be the Lord of my life, and help me to live with the hope of heaven in sight. ✝ *Amen.*

A Grieving Heart

God heard their groaning, and he remembered his covenant promise to
Abraham, Isaac, and Jacob. ✛ EXODUS 2:24

My heart grieves over what could have been. I grieve for the foundational truths, with God at their core, that originated in our land. I grieve as I read through the statements made by our forefathers, who established this great nation in honesty and conviction. I believe our forefathers worked on behalf of those they served. They were thinking not only of their present day but the days long after they'd be gone. We can read the facts in history books and see that the original intent for our great land cannot be questioned.

My heart grieves because what was once determined as wrong is now accepted as right. My heart truly grieves because at the click of a mouse, pornography can enter the home of anyone with Internet access. It can enter the hearts of our young people and cause marriages to crumble.

My heart grieves for the political atmosphere of our nation as we seek to be politically correct instead of remaining strong with deep conviction for right and wrong.

I pray that as the present generation grows up in our land, there will be leaders stepping forward who are not afraid to stand up for the values that founded our nation. I pray that as we fight the battles in the heavenly realm, as well as those on earth, we will seek truth in a new way.

A grieving heart cannot be healed by continuing in the way it is going. It must change direction. As a nation we have gained so much knowledge and education in the past fifty years that can be used to reach out and touch the lives of those around us. So many times it is used for destruction or confusion.

The young people of our country have so much for which to be thankful. They have all the amenities of life, along with technology at every turn. I would challenge them to step up and stand for purity and those things which are eternal. I would challenge them to be that one person who turns the tide of our country back to what our forefathers intended.

Let's change our grieving hearts for our country to a heart of joy and gladness.
⤳*Carol*

✦   ✦   ✦

Dear heavenly Father, as my country suffers more and more tragedy and falls deeper into the trap of sin and despair, I pray for conviction to return to the heart of America. Remind the people of our nation of the foundational values that this great land was built upon. ✛ *Amen.*

October 13
Place of Tears

When they walk through the Valley of Weeping, it will become a place of refreshing springs. The autumn rains will clothe it with blessings. ✝ PSALM 84:6

A few years ago, I was attending a women's luncheon at a church conference. The speaker was an older woman who was known for her close walk with God. She was from the South and had an endearing way of communicating. The woman used many charming colloquial expressions that brought a smile to my face. One of the things she said made such a deep impression on me that I don't think I will ever forget it.

This speaker shared her heart concerning a difficult time in her life. She described her response like this: "I went to crying, and then I went to praying." I had never thought of tears or prayer as a place.

It is interesting that in today's Scripture, crying and praying are indeed described as a place. The Valley of Weeping, or the Valley of Baca, is thought to refer to a dry and rocky valley on the Israelites' way to their place of worship in Jerusalem. The valley was filled with crevices in the rocks that were normally dry and offered no refreshment to the traveler because of the harsh conditions. When the heavens opened and poured out rain, however, the Valley of Weeping would suddenly become a place of multiple pools of water, each pool offering refreshment. The weary travelers could then go from pool to pool, dipping in the water to refresh their fatigued bodies.

In a spiritual sense, a valley is a place of dryness and spiritual defeat. It is there that we cry out to God. When God hears our prayers and opens the windows of heaven, somehow he turns the dry and arid place into one filled with pools of blessing.

This was the message I heard from this dear saint of God. She knew where to take her sorrow—to the place of prayer. She clearly acknowledged that her prayer then took her from a place of defeat to a place of victory. "They go from strength to strength, till each appears before God in Zion" (Psalm 84:7, NIV). That's a place I want to go! ❧Brenda

★   ★   ★

Father, I have set my heart on a pilgrimage toward heaven. I recognize there will be valleys of tears that I must pass through. Thank you for the promise of your refreshment along the way! I look forward to the day I stand before you in the place where there will be no more tears. Encourage weary hearts today, particularly those separated from loved ones through deployment. Use me to bring refreshment to others. In Jesus' name I pray. ✝ Amen.

Don't Send Me Back

LORD, look down from heaven; look from your holy, glorious home, and see us. **✛** ISAIAH 63:15

Because we chose to send our sons to a private Christian school, the drive to school took about an hour when our sons were elementary students. It was a wonderful time in the car as we traveled back and forth each day. We listened to tapes of children's songs, and they knew every word. Someone told us about a new singer named Carman. We bought a tape and listened each day to his intense and entertaining music. The boys just loved one song describing Jesus calling Lazarus from the grave.

Another song on that particular recording was a song about a man dying and going to heaven. Upon entering heaven, the man turned around and saw the face of God in all his glory. God spoke to him and said he was going to send the man back because his family was praying for his healing on earth and he was going to honor those prayers. The man stood in front of God, the Father, Creator, and King, and said, "Please don't send me back." At that moment the man realized that heaven was a beautiful and perfect place where God our heavenly Father resides, and he did not want to return to earth.

When people say things like "Come quickly, Lord Jesus!" as they reflect on the world's situation, I always feel their hearts are right with God. My husband and I look up from the newspaper every day, thinking, *Will this be the day?* It is a time in history when I am ready to be rescued from the sin and strife of the world.

Today as you stand before the Lord and talk to him about your daily life, talk to him with an eternal perspective. We don't know how long we have to serve him on this earth. We don't know whom he will put in our paths. We must stay in the Word and in prayer with him each day. In a heartbeat we can be with our Father in heaven, and we will be saying, "Don't send me back." Live with eternal perspective, knowing that we are here for the purpose of spreading the gospel.   *◈Carol*

✳   ✳   ✳

Heavenly Father, give me eternal perspective and an eternity mind-set as I go through this day. Grant those who are in harm's way renewed joy in knowing we are just passing through this world. Thank you for preparing a heavenly home without war and without pain that is waiting for us. ✛ *Amen.*

October 15
One Moment

Jesus turned around, and when he saw her he said, "Daughter, be encouraged! Your faith has made you well." And the woman was healed at that moment. + MATTHEW 9:22

One moment . . .

Life can change for the good or the bad in an instant. This fact was brought out in a powerful way as I was attending a women's conference hosted by a military women's ministry. I was honored to hear the testimony of a young woman whose husband was killed in Iraq. This bright and lovely young mother of four stood and addressed a room full of women associated with the military and testified of God's faithfulness in the midst of tragedy. I will never forget her words as she held up her hand, with her palm facing outward, said, "In one moment my life changed 100 percent," then rotated her hand palm inward. One moment . . .

I left the conference to travel home with my friend. We arrived to the news that someone very close to my friend had lost her husband. In one moment, life for a young wife, small children, friends who loved him, and a community who respected this man was changed 100 percent. One moment . . .

There is no way to be completely prepared for such life-changing tragedy. We can't live our lives fearful that tragedy will occur, and yet if it occurs to us or to someone we know, we must be ready to respond. I am thankful for those trained professionals, pastors, counselors, and others who are available to assist in times of crisis. Their help in time of confusion and loss is invaluable. But I am also thankful for those friends and neighbors who offer ready comfort and practical help. In the case of my friend, at a moment's notice, people were there with caring and useful help. One moment . . .

In the immediate moments after our world has collapsed, we may be at a complete loss about the next step. However, as others come alongside to help us get through the hours and days following, we can get to the point where we work through the crisis. The young woman who shared her story at the conference was able to stand and proclaim that with God's help life can go on. Life can change in one moment, but moment by moment, the healing process can eventually produce restoration. One moment . . .   ❧*Brenda*

★　★　★

Lord, this life is measured in moments. One moment can bring tragedy; another moment, triumph. I give you the moments of this day. Help me to respond in loving support to those who may need a moment of my time, recognizing the precious gift it is. Communicate your love to those who are grieving today and take them one step further in their process of restoration. + *Amen.*

Unconditional Grief

As all the people heard of the king's deep grief for his son, the joy of that day's victory was turned into deep sadness. ✛ 2 SAMUEL 19:2

My grandmother knew an unconditional grief. Three of her children preceded her in death. One of her daughters died with a kidney disease. One of her sons was a military man serving in World War II. He stepped on a land mine and died instantly. The third of her children who preceded her in death was only forty-eight when he died with an aneurism while walking off the tennis court. He was a minister and performed the marriage ceremony for my husband and me.

I am sure these children were not perfect. I am quite sure there were times of rebellion or difficulty in watching them grow up. As parents we have those times of crying ourselves to sleep, wondering how we can lead our children into better circumstances.

King David knew the pain of losing just such a child. Though Absalom had been a rebellious son, when David was told that Absalom had been violently murdered, he wished he himself had been killed instead. Celebration over the simultaneous demise of David's enemies was overshadowed by the murder of his son.

It doesn't take much news-watching to see that all over the world people grieve over their children, over the drugs in their schools and crime in their communities, over the loss of their youth in faraway battles. Even in situations of a child's guilt, time after time I have seen a parent on the news express shock that their child, a "good boy," would ever do such a thing. And they are always deeply grieved.

We have a Father in heaven that is always on our side, regardless of our circumstances or what we have done. He wants to reach out to us with his unconditional love. In times of grief—whether over something that has been done to us or something that a loved one has done to others—he will give us unconditional support and the promise of eternity. May the Lord bless you this day if you are experiencing the unconditional grief that comes with loving someone so much.   ⤴*Carol*

✶   ✶   ✶

Lord Jesus, thank you for being my Advocate in life. Thank you for being the example of how to react toward those I love. Thank you for allowing me to forgive and move forward as I experience grief and loss. Comfort those at home and abroad who mourn this day. ✛ *Amen.*

Walking from the Bus Stop

LORD, you know the hopes of the helpless. Surely you will hear their cries and comfort them.
✝ PSALM 10:17

I was told there is a woman on my street dying of cancer. Apparently, several weeks ago she received a hopeful report from her doctor. Within days, however, the situation changed, and she was sent home with no hope.

I remember seeing her walk her very large dog. Her head was wrapped in a scarf, but there was always a pleasant look on her face. She and the dog would accompany her little boy to the bus stop.

This morning I glanced out my window, and my eye spotted a man with head low, steps heavy, walking from the bus stop. A very large dog was by his side.

I recorded these words in my journal several years ago. I remember feeling helpless in wanting to reach out and help this woman and her family. Helplessness is a natural emotion in situations such as this. We often feel helpless whether it is someone we know or someone we don't know. In my case, I struggle with not wanting to impose on the grief. I have found, however, that most people are receptive to concern, comfort, and prayers. What I have had to remember is that people are not looking to me for a solution. They just need me to show up. I can pray and ask God to sustain them. I can throw myself on the grace of God on their behalf, looking to him to help others when I feel helpless.

Scripture tells us that the Lord is our ever-present help in times of need (see Psalm 46:1). He can help sustain us beyond the capability of others. His help is ours to receive and to share. ❧*Brenda*

✱   ✱   ✱

Father, help me to show up and offer help today. Don't allow me to stand by and wallow in my feelings of helplessness. Propel me into meaningful acts of care and concern, even if that means just showing up. You who are the helper of the helpless, use me to convey your presence of comfort today. In Jesus' name I pray. ✝ *Amen.*

One Heartbeat

God has made everything beautiful for its own time. He has planted eternity in the human heart, but even so, people cannot see the whole scope of God's work from beginning to end.
✝ ECCLESIASTES 3:11

This verse is so cool! God planted eternity in the human heart. He put it there so that we would be drawn to it for our entire lives. That is the void in our hearts that seeks to know him.

More than once in this earthly body of mine, I have been what I would say is a heartbeat away from crossing into eternity. Since my early forties, I have had problems with high blood pressure and atrial fibulation. When you can feel your heart beating in your ears, it is a very uneasy feeling. When you lie down to go to sleep and you think your heart is going to jump out of your chest, you really start thinking about eternity.

I remember one day as we were touring in Asia, our family was on a huge bus. As we were leaving one of the tour sites, rain began to fall in sheets. The bus driver decided to go back the exact muddy route from which we'd come. As the rain came down, the bus began to slide back and forth on the muddy roadway. We looked over to our left and saw a mountain wall. We looked to our right and saw a sheer drop that would certainly cause great injury and possibly death to those of us in the bus. I grabbed one of the boys very tightly, closed my eyes, and began to pray. My husband did the same with our second son. I always keep my eyes closed on any park rides to alleviate the fear of knowing I may be in danger. I knew that if I didn't open my eyes during this sliding and slipping, I would not be able to realize how dangerous this situation was.

Needless to say, we made it that day, and I have never been so thankful to get back on concrete in my entire life. I have often thought about how God will hold me tightly in his arms when the time comes for me to go to my eternal home. There will be no fear and no question of where I will be going. When I am one heartbeat away, he will be holding me close to his heart.   ⁓*Carol*

✱   ✱   ✱

Father, on this day I pray for those who are a heartbeat away from you every day of their lives. They are on the battlefields with danger all around and the thought of eternity very close. Hold them near to your heart, and give them the peace that passes all understanding. ✝ *Amen.*

Missing Man Formation

Then David said to Joab and all those who were with him, "Tear your clothes and put on burlap. Mourn for Abner." And King David himself walked behind the procession to the grave.
✛ 2 SAMUEL 3:31

One of the most recent additions to the landscape of Washington, D.C., is the new Air Force Memorial. The design of the memorial includes three stainless-steel spires soaring upward to depict the vapor trails of an Air Force jet in its bomb burst maneuver. It is quite a striking sight, especially when it is illuminated at night.

Each time I view it, I am reminded of a ceremony I attended that included a flyover by military jets. These jets were not doing their bomb burst maneuver; rather they were flying in the missing-man formation. The missing-man formation is a solemn aerial memorial said to have begun in World War I with the British Royal Air Force. To privately symbolize the loss of life following a military mission, the crew would alert the troops below by leaving a hole in the usually tight formation. Today this public ceremony is a visual reminder of someone who is lost or dead. Whether it is displayed by three out of four planes flying—one pulls off and three keep going, or the consistent hole in formation—this ritual is a moving tribute to fallen heroes.

What do the missing-man formation and our Scripture for today have in common? 2 Samuel 3:1-35 is an account of the death of Abner, a man who had served the king faithfully. In this passage, we see King David giving public expression to his grief in honor of this man's service. Jewish customs during Old Testament times used rituals such as weeping, wearing sackcloth, cutting one's hair, fasting, and throwing ashes on oneself as signs of deep mourning. These rituals engaged a community in the grieving process, showing how we all share in the sorrow of those who die in a time of usefulness.

Performing rituals is an important step in the grieving process. It has been said, "When words are inadequate, have a ritual." The symbolic acknowledgement that someone is gone and things will be different is a healthy validation of a celebrated life. In the case of the missing-man formation, the three airplanes that are left also symbolize that the mission will go on. The hole is felt and the loss is real, but we can find comfort in remembering that the purpose of those who have passed will continue. *≈Brenda*

✶   ✶   ✶

God of all comfort, your Word promises that you will bless those who mourn and comfort them in their grieving. Send your hope today. Remind those who grieve of precious memories. Surround them with those who will love and help. In Jesus' name I pray. ✛ *Amen.*

Once to Die

Just as each person is destined to die once and after that comes judgment, so also Christ died once for all time as a sacrifice to take away the sins of many people. + HEBREWS 9:27-28

This I know to be true: Death is final. There is no going back. There is no more time for those on earth to forgive or to spend time with that person. There are no more phone calls or e-mails or cards to send. The life on this earth is over, and Scripture tells us after that comes judgment.

This realization has been very difficult for me to grasp. I am a person who loves spending time with my friends and family. When I have an opportunity to spend even a few hours with those who are special to me, I will make every effort to do so. Often I go overboard to be with people and will drive several hours for an hour of fellowship with them. When I have lost those whom I have spent much time with, I spend time soul-searching.

I ask myself some questions:

1. Did I spend quality time with this person?

2. Did I correspond with him regularly to let him know how much I cared about him?

3. Did I show forgiveness to her?

4. Did I tell her I loved her?

When a dear friend of mine lost her son, I immediately wanted to call and hear her voice. I wanted to tell them I loved them and cared about them.

Many times we hear of those in combat who have sent letters home to their parents, telling them how much they love them for all they have done. We often learn that the letter is just the thing that gets parents through after hearing of the death of their loved one.

Today's Scripture tells us that each person dies only once and after that comes judgment. If we die only once, that must mean we live only once (on this earth anyway). Take this life and spend time with those you love. Do not let there be any regrets in your time spent with others, so that when they are gone you may have perfect peace in their absence. ⁓*Carol*

✳   ✳   ✳

Father God, in this world of fast-paced schedules and feelings of being overwhelmed, lay on my heart the need to stay in touch with those I love. Give me opportunity today to say, "I love you" to those dear to me. + *Amen.*

October 21
Termination Snow

Do your best to get here before winter. ✛ 2 TIMOTHY 4:21

While visiting Alaska one autumn, I witnessed the excitement that came with the first snow on the mountain peaks. This snow is so significant that it even has a name. Termination Snow signals the end of summer and serves as the sign indicating winter is coming.

This wasn't the only hint that the season was changing. I also had the privilege of staying in a beautiful B & B that was complete with Alaskan ambience. When it was time for me to leave, I wanted to thank the owner for the lovely and hospitable accommodations, but she could not be found. I was told she was in the garden taking advantage of the light because the time for being able to garden was coming to an end.

In this case, fall signaled a time of preparation before the winter came and prevented such activities. "Come before winter" was Paul's request to Timothy in 2 Timothy 4:21. He knew that when winter came, Timothy would not be able to travel. He requested Timothy's presence, as well as the coat he had left and some parchments that were very important. This simple request from a man near the end of his life also admonishes us to make sure we do those things we plan to do someday before it is too late.

The parchments most likely were portions of the written Word of God. When I think of the Word of God, I think of how God has given it in order that we may understand and relate to him. It reminds me that there are those who plan at some point to have a right relationship with the Lord. "Come before winter" is a reminder of the need to have that right relationship before it is too late.

In my library is a very little book entitled *The Do It Did It Handbook*. The purpose of the book is to help one "capture the goals, dreams, ideas, and fleeting thoughts"[1] of life. Most of the listings are fun and trivial, but I'm drawn to the intentionality of the authors. The few words of today's Scripture are words of intentionality as well. They have caused me to think of those things that I need to do before winter.

As you read this, you may be reminded of something you intend to do someday. It may be something in regard to a friend or family member. Perhaps it's a conversation that needs to take place or a disagreement that needs to be resolved. If it is something of significant importance, let me encourage you not to wait until winter comes—take advantage of the opportunity given to you today! ❧*Brenda*

☆　☆　☆

Lord, thank you for the opportunity of today. Don't let me miss it! Please fill with your purpose and peace the spouses of deployed military personnel. ✛*Amen.*

---

[1] Debra P. Raisner, David H. Raisner, and Glenn S. Klausner, *The Do It Did It Handbook* (Riverside, NJ: Andrews McMeel Publishing, 1996).

Glory Gain

What do you benefit if you gain the whole world but lose your own soul? Is anything worth more than your soul? + MATTHEW 16:26

The stories in Scripture give us glimpses of the lives of those who have strived to gain all they could on this earth. In Bible days, palaces, gardens, land, servants, and even the number of wives were all measures of great power and wealth for men such as Solomon and David.

In America today it is very similar. The bigger the house and cars, the more important a person's worth seems to be. We see lists of highest paychecks per movie or most money made in one year by those who are at the top of the ladder in their professions. We often find ourselves striving harder because of those who have made it in our country. That can be a good thing.

Being all that you can be and striving to achieve and use your gifts and talents are great. Blessing your family with a wonderful home and times away together is also good. And many wealthy people in our land reach out to those less fortunate than themselves. They are using what God has blessed them with to bless others.

The thing that must always be remembered is that material wealth is temporary. When you give your heart to Jesus Christ and ask him to come in as Lord and Savior of your life, you gain an eternity in heaven. It is a place that many forget as they strive for worldly gain. It is a place often not thought about when life is good and going your way. There is no amount of money, fame, or fortune that will ever allow us to live forever on this earth. We will be passing on to eternity with our last breath. The promise of heaven to those who know Jesus is one of great peace. The promise of eternal damnation is not.

Today's is a very simple theme, but I will tell you that many are thinking daily of their eternal home. As you read this, many, particularly those in combat situations, are putting their lives on the line and realizing that they are a heartbeat away from eternity. Choose today where you will spend your eternity. The moment you ask the Lord to be your Lord and Savior, you gain a place in the Lord's kingdom of glory, and you will never look back. *Carol*

✦ ✦ ✦

Father, turn my heart toward the thought of heaven with you today. As those in our nation put their lives on the line every day as soldiers, firefighters, police officers, and even teachers, give them a desire to know where they will spend eternity. + *Amen.*

October 23
Celebration of Life

Who can win this battle against the world? Only those who believe that Jesus is the Son of God. ✛ 1 JOHN 5:5

The verse above really is what life's all about, isn't it? Life is about winning the battle against this world. If we stand strong in our faith and fight the good fight, there will be a celebration when our days on earth are over. I know you have been there. You go into a funeral or memorial service, and there is a spirit of joy resting there. People are smiling and even laughing, and you begin to think you have come to the wrong place. Then you realize that this person was most definitely a Christian. This person won the battle against the world and is now resting in the arms of our heavenly Father.

The time of remembering a loved one or a friend is very different when there is doubt or concern about where they are spending eternity. The service perhaps is a bit more somber and reflective.

The Christian service is one of a life well lived and a life of helping others in times of need. When I have been a part of this type of celebration, I am reminded of how I want it to be when I pass on from this world. I want there to be great celebration and affirmation that I loved Jesus during my time on earth. I want people to know that I made mistakes but that God held my hand through every turn.

Have you ever thought about whether your death would be a celebration or a question to others? Have you ever thought at the point of taking your last breath where you would be when you reached eternity? I think this is one of the most difficult concepts for people to grasp. This is especially difficult for younger people because to them death seems so far away.

Today is the day. Do not wait another day to seal your eternal security. Make your plans today for a celebration of your life when you are gone. Think of the family and friends left behind and how peaceful they will be to know where you are and with whom you are spending eternity. Then know with confidence you will stand before the Father and say, "I am home and ready for my eternal celebration." ⁓*Carol*

✭   ✭   ✭

Father God, I want my passing from this earth to be a celebration for others. I want to know where I am going and that I will spend eternity with you. So today I recognize Jesus as the Son of God. I recognize his sacrifice on the cross for me. I want to ask Jesus into my heart and my life today so that I am sealed in eternity with heavenly security. ✛ *Amen.*

Will I See Her in Heaven?

Dear brothers and sisters, we can boldly enter heaven's Most Holy Place because of the blood of Jesus. ✛ HEBREWS 10:19

My husband had the awesome experience of leading his mother to the Lord one Easter Sunday. She had run out of her heart medication while visiting us in Georgia. Thinking she could go without it for a few days, she woke up one day unable to catch her breath. Immediately we rushed her to the hospital. They got to the problem quickly and said she needed to rest in the hospital a few hours.

We were getting ready for Easter service the following Sunday when my husband came in. He started putting on his suit and getting ready to go with us. I said, "Oh, honey, I know it is Easter Sunday, but your mother needs you." She had been discharged from the hospital, but I didn't want us to leave her alone.

"The boys and I will go on, and we will be praying that as you spend time with her, you will have the opportunity to share the reason for Easter Sunday with her."

As we pulled into the driveway after church that morning, my mother-in-law came out of the house and, with the biggest smile I have ever seen, said, "I accepted the Lord today!" Oh, my goodness; what a way to celebrate Easter.

About six months after that Easter, my mother-in-law passed away. She had sealed her heart eternally, and we knew where she was. During those six months, she began going to church, and her husband went with her. When she died, he continued to go.

After going to the church on his own for almost ten years, my father-in-law began asking the pastor questions about eternity. One of the most poignant questions was, "Will I see her in heaven if I accept the Lord?" The pastor quickly told him yes, we would all be in heaven together. Six months before his own death, my father-in-law accepted Jesus as his Lord and Savior.

Have you ever noticed the difference between a Christian and one who is not when they've lost a loved one? In recent years, tragedies such as 9/11, Columbine, Virginia Tech, Enterprise High School, and the War on Terror have brought untimely death to so many. What peace and comfort come when we are able to say *yes* to those who ask, "Will I see them in heaven?" *Carol*

✴ ✴ ✴

Lord, I pray for those who do not know you. I pray they will come to the realization of your grace through your Son, Jesus. Whether it be six months before they pass on to eternity or six years or six minutes, thank you, God, for preparing a heavenly home for our reunion with you and with each other. Give comfort to those who have lost loved ones in recent tragedies. ✛ Amen.

October 25
He Knows We're Coming

In my Father's house are many rooms; if it were not so, I would have told you. I am going there to prepare a place for you. ✛ JOHN 14:2, NIV

In the book *When God Prays*, Skip Heitzig shares the story of a little boy who accompanied his father to the Empire State Building. They entered the elevator to make the long ascent. As they began to make the climb upward, the boy's eyes widened as he watched the numbers flashing to indicate the many floors. Rising higher and higher to floors fifty, sixty, and seventy, the little boy nervously tugged at his father's hand and said, "Daddy! Does God know we're coming?"[1]

When talking about heaven, Jesus used familiar images to help his disciples understand the message. For instance, in Jewish culture when a young man and woman became engaged, the young man would begin to prepare for his bride to join his family. A common Jewish home would be built around a courtyard with different rooms surrounding it. Grandparents, parents, and uncles and aunts would all have rooms that faced the courtyard. The newly engaged young man would go to his father's house to add another room to the family home. When the room was complete and his father gave the word, the young man would finally go to bring his new bride to the home they would enjoy together.

Scripture likens Christ to a bridegroom coming for his bride. We are in the time of preparation as the bride of Christ. He is now in heaven preparing the place where we will spend eternity with him. He knows we're coming, and he's making all things ready! ≈*Brenda*

* * *

> Sing the wondrous love of Jesus,
> Sing His mercy and His grace.
> In the mansions bright and blessed
> He'll prepare for us a place.
> When we all get to Heaven,
> What a day of rejoicing that will be!
> When we all see Jesus,
> We'll sing and shout the victory![2]

✛*Amen!*

---

[1] Skip Heitzig, *When God Prays* (Carol Stream, IL: Tyndale House Publishers, 2003), 175.
[2] Eliza E. Hewitt, William Kirkpatrick, and Henry Gilmour, "When We All Get to Heaven" (public domain).

A Wonderful Place

They were looking for a better place, a heavenly homeland. That is why God is not ashamed to be called their God, for he has prepared a city for them. ✛ HEBREWS 11:16

There is so much excitement when you look through the eyes of a child. They have such creativity because their minds have not been clouded by reality and the downside of life. Often children help us see the brighter side of a situation.

My understanding of what a wonderful place heaven is has come through many different avenues. One of our pastors taught a series about heaven. I got so excited about getting to heaven, I had to remind myself that my time on earth was not finished. It was very important for me to concentrate on God's purpose for me here until he was ready to take me home. As the pastor took us through the Scriptures, I began to understand just how much God loves us in order to prepare all of eternity for us to be with him.

My mom and dad moved from Florida to live in Nashville the last two years of my dad's life. They lived in my sister's guesthouse, and we were able to visit with them often. Their great-grandchildren living in Nashville would also visit them from time to time. My dad always had a story to tell them, or my mom would read them a book. It was a sweet time of fellowship. The children loved it.

After my dad passed away, my mom remained in the little house for a couple of months. We continued to visit Mom frequently while she was there. The children would come in and ask, "Where's Opa?" We would always tell them he is in heaven. One day after giving our standard answer that Opa is in heaven, Mary Gabriel broke into loud song and sang these words:

> *Heaven is a wonderful plaaaaaaaaaaaaaaaaaaaace*
> *Filled with glory and graaaaaaaaaaaaaaaaaaaaaace*
> *I want to see my Savior's face*
> *'Cause heaven is a wonderful place!*[1]

We must fulfill our purpose on this earth. God has created us for great purpose. However, we have a home waiting for all those who know Jesus as their Lord and Savior, and it is a wonderful place.   ❧*Carol*

✶　✶　✶

Father God, as I look around each day and see our nation and our world in such turmoil, remind me that I have heaven to look forward to. I pray that I will lead others to you, Lord Jesus. I pray that those who are serving here or abroad in our military family will understand the hope of eternity as they give their very lives for the cause of freedom. ✛ *Amen.*

---

[1] Wolfgang Koperski, "Heaven is a Wonderful Place," published Tonos (German Import), 2001.

October 27
Visible God

Ever since the world was created, people have seen the earth and sky. Through everything God made, they can clearly see his invisible qualities—his eternal power and divine nature. So they have no excuse for not knowing God. ✛ ROMANS 1:20

My current favorite author is Francine Rivers. She makes the Scripture come alive to me through her fiction. I feel as if I have experienced the story from Scripture and have new excitement about it after completing one of her books. Just now I am reading *The Priest*, her story about Aaron and his role with Moses in leading the Israelites out of captivity.[1]

Each time God instructed Moses to go before Pharaoh with signs and wonders, Pharaoh would taunt him by asking why he should be afraid of an invisible God when he had visible gods all around him. What astonishes me is being reminded of just how they believed there was a god for everything and how, if they needed another one, they would just build and name it!

After completing a chapter of *The Priest* one morning, I sat in my comfy reading chair and thought to myself, *If ever there was a visible God, it is my God!* I began to thank him for his presence in my life. I began to praise him for the times he has stayed with me until I've come back to him. I began to thank him for the evidence of who he is in creation through the beautiful leaves and the coolness of the climate of fall and winter.

I thought of family members and friends I know who shine with the light of Jesus in their lives. The evidence of trusting God is in their very countenance.

Recently I had a conversation with a young military wife whose husband is deployed and whose tour has just been extended for three months. He was scheduled to come home the week before the holidays. She loves the Lord with all her heart and knows the evidence of that so-called invisible God in her life by the peace that is in her heart during this most difficult time.

If people ask you how you can trust and believe in an invisible God, give them the Scripture from Hebrews 11:27 that reads, "It was by faith that Moses left the land of Egypt, not fearing the king's anger. He kept right on going because he kept his eyes on the one who is invisible."

Seek him, stand before him, and praise him for his presence in your life! ✎*Carol*

✦ ✦ ✦

God, thank you for being there with every breath and every step I take. I ask for your presence and protection for military members and their families today. Surround them with your presence, and give your angels charge over them. ✛ *Amen.*

---

[1] Francine Rivers, *The Priest* (Carol Stream, IL: Tyndale House Publishers, 2004).

Perfect Peace

You will keep in perfect peace all who trust in you, all whose thoughts are fixed on you!
✝ ISAIAH 26:3

I have just returned from my daily walk to the mailbox at the end of our driveway. I always get so excited to see a real card addressed to me. I enjoy e-mail, but I still love receiving snail mail that I can hold in my hands as I read it. I immediately looked to see the return name and address. It was a card from my dear friend Sue.

Immediately I felt a peace in my heart because she cared enough to send me a card. I also knew that it would be a blessing to my day and to my life. Sue and I have this connection as if we truly know each other's heart. Some of you may have a brother or sister in the Lord like that. I knew that this card was going to hit the chord of what I was experiencing during this week.

I opened the envelope to first see the beautiful pink card with pink roses that said, "Thinking of You." I opened the card, smiling to myself, and saw how personalized it was by her. She wrote, "Carol, I am reminded of how wonderfully and uniquely God created you to be just who you are . . . a dear and special friend!" As I stood in the driveway before walking on to the house, I realized that she knew because God knew how very much I would need this blessing today. She is truly led by the Spirit, and we are tied together by the Spirit of a living God.

This perfect peace released me from the cares of the day and enabled me to stop and think that one day I will spend eternity with my dear sister Sue. I envision that she and I will remember the times we thought of each other and called or sent a card.

Aren't we always looking for a bit of heaven on earth? Some may say that's their favorite vacation spot. Others may say it is their favorite restaurant. I say that today Sue showed the perfect peace of heaven through her thoughtful communication.

Find someone to whom you can send perfect peace for just a moment. Sit down today and write or e-mail someone serving in our military. Send a card to the pastor or his wife. Perhaps sending a love note to your own spouse or another family member would be your gesture. Bless someone today, so that they may take a quiet breath and praise him for that moment of perfect peace. *Carol*

✳ ✳ ✳

Father, thank you for the perfect peace that comes from knowing that you love me through others. Give me the opportunity today to be your love to someone else today. Please give your peace, which transcends all understanding, to the men and women in harm's way across the globe. Shalom. ✝ *Amen.*

October 29
The Harvest of Souls

[Jesus said,] "You know the saying, 'Four months between planting and harvest.' But I say, wake up and look around. The fields are already ripe for harvest. The harvesters are paid good wages, and the fruit they harvest is people brought to eternal life. What joy awaits both the planter and the harvester alike! You know the saying, 'One plants and another harvests.' And it's true. I sent you to harvest where you didn't plant; others had already done the work, and now you will get to gather the harvest." + JOHN 4:35-38

This is the season of harvest. We live in the South, and the crops of peanuts and cotton are getting ready for picking. There is no way to stop the growth or the ripening except a very severe drought. Once the seed is planted, the work of God's plan for nature takes over.

During this month of the year, many organizations have harvest festivals with games and goodies in place of the Halloween activities. Scarecrows, colored leaves, pumpkins, and magnificently shaped gourds are among some of the most familiar symbols of this season.

Just before today's Scripture, Jesus had spoken with the woman at the well. The disciples found him there and were very surprised he had been talking to her. Jesus began to share today's Scripture with them. He told them of the spiritual harvest that awaits them. Jesus made it very clear that the nourishment he really needed came from doing God's will.

In today's world, we must never miss a chance to be a planter or a harvester of souls. We are living in a world where tragedy and crisis are daily events. I often say I feel as if we are spiraling downward in our nation right now. The growing numbers of school shootings, sexual teacher/student encounters, and other things that are not supposed to happen to our children have spurred me on to believe that I cannot miss even one encounter if God sends someone my way.

When God brings someone to mind, I try to immediately get in touch with her, to let her know she is on my mind and in my heart that day. Among my acquaintants, I try especially to be tender towards the leading of God to military members and their families, as they are often desperate for a word of encouragement.

As you look into the beautiful fields of earthly crops this month, remember the harvest of souls God has laid before you, and be ready to gather them up and receive your nourishment for all eternity.   ∼Carol

★   ★   ★

Father, I am often overwhelmed with the number of people who need to know you. Help me to do my part to gather the harvest on your behalf, one soul at a time. Thank you for those in other lands who are risking their lives to plant hope and peace in the lives of others. + Amen.

Moonless Night

Even in darkness I cannot hide from you. To you the night shines as bright as day. Darkness and light are the same to you. ✛ PSALM 139:12

My husband recalls a time while on military maneuvers in Germany when he became so disoriented from the darkness, he had a hard time returning to his own tent. The commander of his unit had strongly emphasized the practice of light discipline. Soldiers were to operate in the dark in order to conceal their position from the enemy. In the evening, my husband would frequently go from tent to tent, making pastoral visits with soldiers. On one particular winter occasion, forgetting how early darkness would come, he went into a tent around dusk. After visiting for about an hour, he walked out of the tent and into a moonless night. He found himself in pitch black, the darkness emphasized by the thick canopy of tall evergreen trees. He could not even see his hand twelve inches in front of his face.

As he attempted to get his bearings, he noted that it was so dark he wasn't even sure which way to go back to his own tent. He had a flashlight, but to maintain complete light discipline as instructed, he didn't have the freedom to utilize it. Later he observed that when there's light, it is so easy to move around the camp area, avoiding the obstacles of ropes, stakes, or things such as fallen trees. In complete darkness, however, there is a sense of disorientation that brings with it great caution. Nothing in the camp had changed; he just couldn't see it.

There are times in life when it seems we've stepped into a moonless night. We can't see which way to go or where to place our next steps. A sort of spiritual disorientation sets in. It may occur at the death of a loved one. Or it can come through something like the loss of a job in the prime of life, when it seems too late to begin a new career and you're just not sure what step to take.

It's in these times of disorientation that we must remind ourselves that even when we step into a moonless night, God has not changed. The permanent markers of his love, his Word, and his will are all in place. These are the times to pause and ask God to help us regain our orientation and use the light of prayer and his Word to shine on the path before us. We can then take one step at a time until the dawn of God's plan brightens our surroundings. *✎Brenda*

✦   ✦   ✦

Lord of light, in whom there is no darkness, shine the light of your truth on my path today. May I trust you for each step, knowing that you do not change. Though darkness hides you, I say with confidence: you are there! ✛ *Amen.*

October 31
Nocturnal Animals

I will give you treasures hidden in the darkness—secret riches. I will do this so you may know that I am the LORD, the God of Israel, the one who calls you by name. ✛ ISAIAH 45:3

Several years ago, my husband and I were traveling to visit with our son and his young family. Because we were going to be later than we had originally thought, we called to give our new estimated time of arrival. Our three-year-old (at the time) granddaughter answered the phone. She told us with great animation in her voice that she had been watching and watching for us to come and now it was getting dark and to please be careful of all the nocturnal animals! We chuckled at her use of such a sophisticated term, but to her, the fear was very real. She didn't want us to be out among the things that lurked in the darkness.

There is a fear that can come from literal, physical darkness. Of late, however, I have been reminded of the fear that can accompany the darkness of not knowing the future. I'm referring to those times of darkness when we cannot see the outcome and cannot see what might be ahead to bring harm.

One of my dearest friends has just been told she has an aggressive cancer. While those of us who know and love this precious woman are devastated by the news, we are all being blessed by her testimony of God's faithfulness in her life. She is continually sharing the hidden treasures she is discovering in this dark place in which she finds herself. Everything in me screams to tell her to beware of the nocturnal animals, but I know that it is often in the darkest of places that God reveals the greatest treasures.

Today's Scripture speaks of treasures that can only be found in darkness. In the time of Isaiah, treasures were buried in vaults deep below the earth. In this passage, God is speaking through the prophet Isaiah with the promise to King Cyrus that he will give him these secret treasures for his obedience.

When we find ourselves surrounded by darkness, we need to remind ourselves of who is still in control. As we turn to the Lord in faith and confidence, we can rest assured that he will protect us in the midst of our darkness, and we can know that hidden just outside our natural vision are blessings waiting for us if we continue to trust in him. ✦Brenda

✫   ✫   ✫

Lord of grace and mercy, thank you for the lessons you kindly provide in the dark places of life. I pray for my friend and others like her who face the unknown outcomes—diagnoses, relationships, deployments—of daily life. I thank you for examples of obedience—people who are willing to step into the darkness with a faith that says you are enough. Give me that same willingness today. ✛ Amen.

Me and Rosie

God has not given us a spirit of fear and timidity, but of power, love, and self-discipline.

✝ 2 TIMOTHY 1:7

I was staying overnight at a friend's house when, because of an unexpected obligation of my friend's, I found myself alone in the house with Rosie, the family dog. The friend left early in the morning while I was still in my room. I could hear the dog barking and whining as if agitated. After a while I needed to leave my room, but I didn't want to face the dog by myself. I had never been in my friend's home alone with their dog. I wasn't sure how she would react. Would she growl at me? attack me? try to bite me?

Finally, out of necessity I decided I would attempt a dash down the hallway to another room. Moving quickly down the hall, I suddenly realized the dog was closed up in the master bedroom. My fear and uncomfortable delay were all for naught. I released the dog from her captivity, and instantly I was her best friend. I thought how throughout life we try to stay where we think it is safe because of a perceived threat. Sometimes those fears are genuine, but often we make them into something worse than they are. Just as I was uncomfortable staying shut up in the guest room, we often suffer unnecessarily by locking ourselves into a safe place to protect ourselves from our fears. This leads us to only later discover the truth in the words of President Franklin D. Roosevelt, "The only thing we have to fear is fear itself."[1]

I believe this is what Paul may have been referring to when he wrote, "God has not given us a spirit of fear." The spirit of fear can be debilitating. It will certainly rob us of joy. It can prevent us from stepping out of our safe places. It will cause us to endure unnecessary discomfort. Sometimes we just have to open the door and face our fear. When we do, we may find that what we feared was not nearly as frightening as we thought. We can be confident of this one thing: we do not have to face our fears alone. God is always right there with us.

"When I am afraid, I will put my trust in you. I praise God for what he has promised. I trust in God, so why should I be afraid? What can mere mortals do to me? . . . My enemies will retreat when I call to you for help. This I know: God is on my side!" (Psalm 56:3-4, 9). *≈Brenda*

✫   ✫   ✫

Lord, you are my Savior, and I know that the fears I experience do not come from your hand. Grant me peace in you, Lord, as I turn over to you the things that grip me with fear. Release me to serve you and those around me with freedom. ✝ *Amen.*

---

[1] Franklin D. Roosevelt, Inaugural Address, March 4, 1933.

November 2
It Begins with One

We know that there is only one God, the Father, who created everything, and we live for him. And there is only one Lord, Jesus Christ, through whom God made everything and through whom we have been given life. + 1 CORINTHIANS 8:6

What comfort the Scripture for today brings! This verse written by Paul, who was one of Jesus' apostles, was intended to help believers know that their faith was real.

Through the years, we have watched in many different situations in our culture how one person can change the direction of many—for good or bad. One person began the crusade to get prayer taken out of public schools. One person was responsible for Roe vs. Wade and the legalization of abortion. One person had the concept of a galaxy faraway, and now Star Wars is a household topic. Recently a sixteen-year-old young man changed a congressional order to have "God and Country" remain in a certificate honoring his grandfather.

There are so many different situations in our country today that overwhelm us in thinking there is no way we can make a difference. Past experience shows that not to be true. One person, one event, one action can change the world.

God has set our days before us. He knows our deepest thoughts, desires, and dreams. He knows how we can affect the world around us if we allow ourselves to be emptied out and let his love and salvation flow to others.

While traveling around the world as a military wife, I found one thing to be true: the world got smaller. I remember on our first visit to the shopping area in Seoul, South Korea, we ran into a man who had graduated from the same college as my husband. We had never met him before, but my husband happened to be wearing a T-shirt with the logo of the school.

Being a military wife taught me to be assertive and not fearful of the what ifs. I love pursuing dreams and seeking out people of influence. I love to glean the experiences in their lives and apply them to mine. My husband always encouraged me as a military wife to speak up when I saw that things were not as they should be. He reminded me that God had given me a personality to communicate, and he loved that I would always fight for the cause.

Don't wait until someone else takes the lead. Life's adventures begin with one thought, one person, or one action. Stand and be that one to change the world. *≈Carol*

* * *

One and only God, be with all of those who are taking a stand in order to make the world a better place. Give them courage and fortitude as they fight battles on behalf of others. Make me a change agent for you today. + *Amen.*

The Vacuum Cleaner

Your Father knows exactly what you need even before you ask him! ✝ MATTHEW 6:8

My grandson is fascinated with vacuum cleaners. It's been comical and endearing to see him interact with the cleaning machine. Vacuum cleaners actually have a place in the faith story of our family. In the early years of our ministry, my husband was the associate pastor for a church in Calhoun, Georgia. I was teaching school, and while teacher pay is not what it should be today, it really was below par at that time. We had purchased a vacuum cleaner at a yard sale for fifteen dollars. That was big bucks for us in those days. We used it for at least two years until it finally bit the dust (groan).

Our budget did not include the purchase of a new vacuum cleaner. One day my husband had to go into an electronic store for something related to the church. He noticed at the checkout counter that there was a shiny new vacuum cleaner with many little stickers all over it. A contest was being held, and the grand prize was this lovely machine. The person who guessed the closest amount of stickers that had been placed on the machine would be the winner. My husband began filling out the form. When he placed the number for his guess in the blank the employee said, "If you put a 1 in front of that you would be closer." My husband had nothing to lose, so he followed the advice. Several days later it was announced on the radio that the vacuum cleaner was ours!

God provided for us beyond our own ability to provide for ourselves. The original guess my husband gave was not a good guess. The employee that offered the advice did not know my husband. He had never seen him before. He did not know our great need for a vacuum cleaner. Yet God used him not only to provide a practical need but to build our faith and confidence in a personally involved God.

Often our prayers consist of a laundry list of needs that we want to make sure God knows. Today's Scripture reminds us that God knows our needs even before we ask. I can't remember putting the vacuum cleaner on our prayer list, but God knew we needed it and met that need before we could ask. I'm thankful we serve a God who cares about all of our needs, and though Scripture encourages us to make our needs known to him in prayer, he often enjoys blessing us even before we ask.
≈*Brenda*

✶ ✶ ✶

Father, thank you for your blessings. Thank you for your provision. Thank you for your loving care. ✝ *Amen.*

November 4
A Campaign Button

Select from all the people some capable, honest men who fear God and hate bribes. Appoint them as leaders over groups of one thousand, one hundred, fifty, and ten. ✛ EXODUS 18:21

While rummaging through some memorabilia, I came across an old presidential campaign button I wore during the first campaign in which I could vote. For me, the opportunity to vote was, like getting a driver's license, one of those major passages to adulthood. Standing there in the small curtain-partitioned booth, I was nervous about making sure I pushed the right buttons. Though I only had one vote, I wanted to make sure it counted for the candidate I thought should be the next president.

Today's Scripture is an early reference of the need to select individuals to assume responsibility for leadership in the newly forming nation of Israel. Leaders are selected in every nation in one way or another, but I am thankful that in America all citizens have the freedom to express their desires for those who lead.

We see the need to select individuals who want to lead for the right reasons and possess the right qualities. This is true within the church as well as the government. When the need arose for leaders to take care of administrative issues in the newly formed Christian church, the apostles gave the guidance to choose those who were "full of the Spirit and wisdom" (Acts 6:3-4).

Though serving in the church is not the same as serving in the government, selecting godly men and women who are full of wisdom is crucial regardless of where they are serving. As citizens we have the responsibility both to do our part in electing those whom we believe are godly leaders and to support them as they labor to be servants of others.

The act of voting in an election is a responsibility to be taken seriously. The opportunity for each of us to exercise this duty has been bought by people who have taken a stand for democracy throughout the history of our nation. I encourage you to become informed about candidates and their political positions and to pray about how you are to cast your ballot. Then stand and have your vote count!   ≈Brenda

✶   ✶   ✶

God of individuals and nations, thank you for the opportunity to live in a free society. I pray that you would direct me to use my vote appropriately. I pray you would help those who will seek social justice and increase human rights to be elected. May your will be done and your sovereignty rule over the plans that are made by men. In Jesus' name I pray. ✛ Amen.

Those Were the Days

Lord, you alone are my inheritance, my cup of blessing. You guard all that is mine. The land you have given me is a pleasant land. What a wonderful inheritance! ✝ PSALM 16:5-6

The Scripture for today tells us of the joys of a life lived with God. He is our inheritance, and that is such wonderful hope. We have as our inheritance a perfect God who will unconditionally love us and want the best for us throughout our lives on this earth.

The beginning of the holiday season always brings memories flooding in to my heart and mind. I think of my inheritance through the blessing of a family who loved each other and fought to stay on the side of truth and freedom. I have a legacy of great-grandparents and grandparents whose lives were difficult. They were very poor and lived with no running water or electricity. Most of them did not attend school past the second grade because they had to begin working at a very early age to help out the family. Both sides of grandparents were involved in the coal-mining industry, and my mother's dad died after a mining accident.

So why does it seem that we always say those were the "good ole" days? We have so many comforts of life in the present day. We have electric washing machines and dryers, which would have been considered true luxuries in the days of my grandparents. We have bathrooms in our homes. We have not only one but often three or four bathrooms in our homes. Such a luxury could not have been imagined in those days.

The inheritance we have from those days is much more than events or comfort items. I have an inheritance of hard work and determination.

Most importantly, I have an inheritance of faith in God. I remember my grandparents and their commitment to prayer and service to others. My parents had a firm foundation of faith from their parents, and I had a firm foundation of faith from my parents.

We do not have to struggle physically as much as those who went before us in the good ole days, but the spiritual struggles are great in our country today. Be strong in your commitment to pass on a legacy of faith in God to your children and grandchildren. Give them an inheritance of a faith that does not waver or cower. Someday they will say of your times in their lives, "Those were the days." ∼*Carol*

★ ★ ★

Father God, I pray that my days on earth are not wasted. I pray that I leave an inheritance of your Kingdom work on earth. Thank you for those who are standing for freedom in order to make it a legacy that can be passed on to the children of generations to come. ✝ *Amen.*

November 6
The Messenger

"Look! I am sending my messenger, and he will prepare the way before me. Then the Lord you are seeking will suddenly come to his Temple. The messenger of the covenant, whom you look for so eagerly, is surely coming," says the LORD. ✛ MALACHI 3:1

Messengers were very important to the spreading of the gospel in biblical days. John the Baptist was one of the most well-known messengers in the New Testament. This verse is in part referring to John the Baptist. Just as we have become accustomed to daily news alerts, people back then were used to the appearance of a messenger to deliver a word from the Lord.

Our family decided several years ago that since we had heard many of the old stories from the past, it would be a wonderful idea to have the messenger record it for all posterity. My sister bought a tape player with a microphone and asked my dad to begin talking into it and telling stories of his life growing up. Our mother said he would sit for hours reliving his life and sharing stories that only he as the messenger could share. The final product was hours of wonderful stories for our children and grandchildren.

The message of Christ and the legacy of our faith have been passed on throughout the Scripture. It is the history of our faith.

During this wonderful holiday season, make a commitment to spend time at the feet of a messenger in your family. Take your children to hear stories from times gone by. If you can possibly find a veteran in your family who has fought in wars defending our country, encourage that person to share his or her stories. The messenger who understands and knows the facts is the one who can give life lessons. Take time to remember how living in this wonderful country is a blessing. Listen to the messenger.   ⚘Carol

✭　✭　✭

Lord Jesus, you came to this earth to give the message of salvation. Thank you for those who have shared the message of your love throughout history. I ask that the message of hope and freedom will be given to those in faraway lands who have never known that message as part of their lives. Thank you for those in the military who are giving their lives for these families. ✛ Amen.

The Family Line

Tell your children about it in the years to come, and let your children tell their children. Pass the story down from generation to generation. ✛ JOEL 1:3

A genealogical study on the Pace family led us to discover that my husband's ancestors were carpenters and woodworkers. This was especially interesting since his grandfather actually was a furniture maker who passed the business to my husband's uncle, who then passed the family business to his son. My husband himself has always enjoyed working with wood and has built several lovely pieces of cherished furniture that stand in our home. This same pleasure for building and working with his hands is seen in our youngest son. It is fascinating to study these genealogical threads of talent as gifts and interests are passed from generation to generation.

There are some tangible things I hope will pass from generation to generation in our family. I don't have any valuable family heirlooms, but I hope the pieces of furniture built by Pace hands will continue to be treasured when my husband and I are gone. I also hope the journals I have kept over the years and the Bibles my husband has read and written in will be read and valued by my children. My prayer is that they will see the inner thoughts of an authentic faith. I pray that as they read the words behind the actions, they will see the doubts, the fears, and the imperfections, but also the confirmation of what they saw us live—that God was always the center of our lives.

A cherished memory for me is walking by my father's bedroom and seeing him on his knees beside his bed. As a child and teenager in my father's home, I knew it wasn't a show on my behalf. It was an action of his authentic faith that helped attract me to making that faith my own.

In a spiritual sense, I can pass on a legacy of faith to my children. I can pass down stories of God answering prayers for our family. I can pass down values based on biblical principles. I can pass down traditions that illuminate our beliefs. The faith that is so important in the lives of me and my husband, however, must be individually accepted by my children and their children. May it be from generation to generation! *≈Brenda*

✶　✶　✶

Father, be glorified in my home today. Help me to communicate a genuine faith that will live on long after I am gone. Remind me that I am not responsible for the salvation of others, but I am responsible to live a life that is built on your saving grace. May our family line continue to have the thread of grace flowing through. ✛ *Amen.*

November 8
The Christian Family

Never speak harshly to an older man, but appeal to him respectfully as you would to your own father. Talk to younger men as you would to your own brothers. Treat older women as you would your mother, and treat younger women with all purity as you would your own sisters.
✝ 1 TIMOTHY 5:1-2

Today is a new day. Today is the beginning of "all things new." The Scripture today is an *aha* moment for me.

First of all, God's perfect intent for our lives is for us to have a commitment to Christ in our hearts. We are invited to ask Jesus to be Lord of our hearts and Lord of our lives. We are also told not to be unequally yoked with those we marry (see 2 Corinthians 6:14). When Christians marry Christians, they have children and seek to bring those children up to love and serve Christ. Christian parents are to teach their children about respect and honor and instill in them pure morals and values for their lives. As the Christian family learns together, they also worship together, learning commitment to growth through God's Word.

Today's Scripture communicates that after our own personal family is established, God asks us to go a step further. It says that we should treat all as our fathers and brothers, mothers and sisters. What if we were to do that in our country today?

I daresay divorce statistics would drastically go down, in Christian families but perhaps also in families that do not know God, as we speak his truth into their lives. We would never look at another woman's husband, or another man's wife as anything but a brother or sister. We would never look at a mentor who is guiding and helping me as anything other than a father.

We would also reach out to all as part of our family in times of need. Often when people ask how they can reach out to the military members and their families, I begin to think that if they thought of them as their brothers and sisters, mothers and fathers, there would be no doubt on their part.

Take some time to evaluate your family to make sure you are growing in respect and love for others.   ≈*Carol*

* * *

Father God, as I stand before you today and reevaluate the design and plan you have for me, I recommit my family to you. I ask for your strength to support those Christian families who are separated through mission or deployment. ✝ *Amen.*

A Warrior Heart

All Israel and Judah loved David because he was so successful at leading his troops into battle.

✙ 1 SAMUEL 18:16

During her son's deployment to Iraq, my friend Diane wrote these words:

> My son Patrick is a soldier in Iraq and has been there for over a year and will be there for a while more. God has been so merciful in blessing me with a faith to trust in HIM and be at peace about Pat being at war. There have been moments when my heart was not at rest, but those times have been few and far between. Today is one of those days when I have to press into my Savior and God, praying extra hard for my son. I pray for my faith to increase.
>
> My mother's heart is sad that my son has to endure the rigors of war and all that it entails. Yet, I KNOW that God is sovereign in all things—in war and in my son's life both physical and spiritual.
>
> I have been thinking about King David. He was a mighty warrior! He was a soldier's soldier! YET, he was a man after God's heart. What a precious picture that is to me of this manly man, this soldier in battle with a tender, surrendered heart to God. I pray that this is how God will work in my son.
>
> I know there are soldiers who return from war with their hearts hardened by what they have seen and experienced in battle. The example of David can indeed provide great hope as we see the way he was able to keep a tender heart before the Lord. In David's time, war was traumatic and gory with thousands of soldiers on each side battling in close combat with swords and spears. The fact that David could survive these experiences of war and not be hardened in his heart can assure us that by the grace of God our soldiers can also return from battle to assume normalcy in their lives.[1]

I'm happy to report that Diane's son Patrick made it safely home from Iraq. At the time of this writing, he is preparing to marry a lovely young woman who faithfully awaited his return. Welcome home, Pat! ≈*Brenda*

✶ ✶ ✶

Father, I pray today for veterans who have served their country. I pray for healing for those who have returned wounded in body and spirit. I pray that your peace will comfort them, your hope will strengthen them, and your grace will affirm them. In Jesus' name I pray. ✙ *Amen.*

---

[1] Thanks to Diane Boucher for her heartfelt words concerning her son's deployment. Used with permission.

November 10
Honor Their Lives

True humility and fear of the LORD lead to riches, honor, and long life. ✦ PROVERBS 22:4

There is no greater compliment or sense of purpose than to be honored. We watch as "Hail to the Chief" is played to honor the president as he enters a room. We watch the honor given to the queen of England in all of her royal attire as she presides over ceremonies. If you have ever been to a graduation ceremony and seen the sea of caps and gowns and heard the applause bestowed on the graduates when they crossed the platform for their diplomas, you will get a sense of what it means to be honored.

Have you noticed that authentic honor does not usually come when the person or group seems to expect to be honored or toots their own horn? There are many who provide service or assistance just to receive honor or recognition. Many times they are the ones that are up front on every scene and very visible when any special situation occurs.

I have worked for employers who would take credit for all that was done in the company. I have also worked for employers that never receive accolades without acknowledging that everyone within the company had something to do with its success. Today's Scripture makes it very clear that true honor and humility are intertwined.

In the preface of our book *Medals above My Heart*, there is an explanation of humility and honor concerning the military wife. It reads

> There are no military service medals that are handed out to military wives for their bravery, gallantry, heroism, or exceptional service. The rewards, however, are greater than any medal could display. The life of the military wife is one that reaps exceptional benefits through personal character and leadership development, adventure, relationships, and opportunities for service.[1]

The purest form of honor comes with service that is done out of the goodness of love in a relationship. This is the military wife. She serves alongside her military husband unselfishly, and we honor her life as well as that of her military husband.

We honor the lives of those today who are serving this great country. ～*Carol*

✶   ✶   ✶

God, I come to you to ask that you honor those who are serving the United States of America and place your favor upon them. Bless them as they serve in humility, seeking to bring to others freedom and peace. ✦*Amen.*

---

[1] Brenda Pace and Carol McGlothlin, *Medals above My Heart: The Rewards of Being a Military Wife* (Nashville, TN: Broadman & Holman, 2004), 9.

Selfless Service

There is no greater love than to lay down one's life for one's friends. ✚ JOHN 15:13

On Veterans Day weekend 2007, my husband prayed an invocation for an award ceremony at the Pentagon. First Lieutenant Walter B. Jackson received the Distinguished Service Cross, which is the second-highest medal our nation gives for heroism, second only to the Medal of Honor. He is the seventh soldier since the end of the Vietnam War to receive this award.

Lieutenant Jackson received the medal for "selfless courage under extreme enemy fire." Specifically, Lieutenant Jackson's unit came under fire from Iraqi insurgents. He was shot while attempting to administer first aid to a wounded comrade. The brave army officer returned fire while continuing to tend to the injured soldier. He was shot again but did not stop providing help to the wounded to the point of refusing medical care for himself until his fellow soldier could be treated.

In presenting the award, Lt. Colonel Thomas C. Graves, the task force commander at the time of the incident, made the statement, "All the leadership schools, classes, and years of experience never really prepare you for the time when you are standing among heroes who have given their all, where their first concerns still remain with their fellow soldiers. It reinforces duty and commitment unlike any other experience."[1]

Lieutenant Jackson's actions are not only heroic, but also selfless. Even while wounded, he put himself at further risk to rescue another who had been wounded worse than himself. This putting others before oneself is not only an attitude of the core army values but a Christian virtue that the Christ follower should strive to hold.

Often we are encouraged to serve one another, which doesn't mean only when it is convenient or without cost. For the Christ follower, the underlying motive for selfless service, like Lieutenant Jackson, is not to receive recognition for our acts. What should drive us to selfless service for our fellow man is the love of God flowing through us. Christ himself declared the power of God's love when he stated, "There is no greater love than to lay down one's life for one's friends" (John 15:13). Rarely will we be called upon to pay the ultimate sacrifice on behalf of another, but as Christians we are to pursue knowing and loving God so that selfless service guides our actions.
≈*Brenda*

✴   ✴   ✴

Lord, thank you for heroes who continue to stand in our midst. Thank you for those who live lives characterized by selfless service. I pray your love would flow through me and guide my actions today. In your name I pray. ✚*Amen.*

---

[1] J. D. Leipold, "Lieutenant Awarded Distinguished Service Cross," www.army.mil/news, November 2, 2007.

November 12
Six Generations

I remember your genuine faith, for you share the faith that first filled your grandmother Lois and your mother, Eunice. And I know that same faith continues strong in you. ✝ 2 TIMOTHY 1:5

Dining in the home of a friend, my husband and I learned a very interesting family legacy of service to our nation. We knew our friend was a graduate of West Point and had committed twenty-plus years of his life in service to our nation. What we didn't know was the family legacy of service he represented. Hanging on the wall of the dining room was a picture of six generations of West Point graduates dating back to 1823. It is believed that Dwight's family represents the longest unbroken chain of West Point graduates in our military.

Our nation is built upon the values that we hold dearly as established in our Constitution, passed from one generation to the next. These values include such things as our freedom of worship and freedom of speech, as well as the right to pursue life, liberty, and happiness. I believe these national values, though not held by every citizen, make up the core reason of why America is a strong nation today.

Likewise, the Christian church is built upon the eternal values given to us by God and demonstrated in the life of Jesus Christ. In our Scripture today, we read that Paul acknowledged the legacy of faith in Timothy's life that was passed on to him from his grandmother Lois and his mother, Eunice. We have a legacy of faith that has been recorded for us in the Word of God and lived out for us in the lives of those who have gone before us. I'm thankful for the legacy of faith passed on to me by my parents. My husband and I have worked hard to pass on a legacy of Christian faith to our sons. We have entrusted to them to pass it on to our grandchildren.

Not all Christians receive their faith from their families of origin. Although we cannot all look back to a legacy of faith in our families, we can all look forward with a commitment to establish a legacy of faith for our children and their children that will endure until the Lord comes.   *≈Brenda*

* * *

Father, thank you for the opportunity to establish a legacy of faith that can be passed down to my children and grandchildren. So often I fail in my desire to live a life that I want my children to emulate. I ask you to make the attraction of living life for you strong and firm despite my weaknesses. I am grateful for the occasion to pursue happiness in this nation, but protect me from making it appear that is the primary goal of life. May my children see that the primary goal of life is to know and love you. ✝ *Amen.*

A Name above My Pocket

Whatever you do or say, do it as a representative of the Lord Jesus, giving thanks through him to God the Father. + COLOSSIANS 3:17

What does it mean to be a representative of the Lord Jesus Christ? Members of the military have their branch of service emblazoned on their uniforms. As a soldier in the Army, my husband has the words *US ARMY* embroidered over his pocket, communicating that he represents the United States of America. Military personnel like my husband have a code of conduct to follow, which includes a list of things they do and a list of things they don't do. There are skills they are expected to possess in order to be a soldier, sailor, airman, or marine of the United States of America. They must train regularly so that they will be able to fulfill the requirements of their duty. They not only represent the United States, but when deployed, they are functioning in the authority of the United States and are backed by all the resources of the United States.

In like manner, as a member of the army of the Lord, I am to live my life as though I were wearing the name of Jesus above my pocket. I represent Jesus with my actions, words, and attitudes. The degree of effort that I put into my daily tasks reflects Jesus as well. How well I train to be a soldier of the cross determines my success in the spiritual realm. I ask myself, *Would Jesus be delighted to have his name affixed above my pocket as I go about my day?* In a practical sense, I think this is what it means to do things in his name.

Thankfully, I am not left to rely on my own wisdom to live up to this mission. I have his Word, which teaches me the way to go, and his Spirit, who encourages me and guides me. There is great confidence in knowing not only do I represent Jesus and his name, but I am backed by all the authority of God himself![1] *≈Brenda*

✷   ✷   ✷

Father, I thank you for the power that is in your name. I ask you to enable me to live a life worthy of your call. Give me the power to accomplish all the good things my faith prompts me to do. May the name of my Lord Jesus be honored because of the way I live (2 Thessalonians 1:11-12, paraphrased). + *Amen.*

---

[1] Thanks to Jacquline Grose for the inspiration and most of the words of this devotional thought. Used with permission.

Legacy of Honor

You younger men must accept the authority of the elders. And all of you, serve each other in humility, for "God opposes the proud but favors the humble." ✦ 1 PETER 5:5

I think we have missed this in our nation. As a nation, we have fallen away from honoring our elders, and this is reflected in a lack of respect for parents, teachers, and others in authority. I believe it is all interrelated and a part of the breakdown of national values.

One of the things I will remember most about living in foreign countries as a military family was the structure of the family. In Europe and Asia, parents and grandparents were very much a part of the core family and often remained in the same household throughout their lives. Grandparents mentored and were available to nurture and care for the children in the home.

One of the activities I love is interacting with older adults. I enjoy spending time with those who have been strong in their lives and faith and have wisdom to share. I have had the opportunity to minister in testimony and song several times to different senior communities. I come away being the one who is truly blessed. Their tears of remembering and heartfelt emotions always give me such a peace about life. Their hugs and words of encouragement are pure and meaningful.

My husband and I gave a devotional and song recently to a group of wonderful seniors. Afterwards, the comments were genuine, and my husband was so blessed by their words. He said two of the men came up and thanked him for his service in the military. They understand the concept of God and country. For these warriors of the past, the two go together.

If you do not have a senior friend in your life, you are missing an amazing opportunity for lessons in honor, humility, patriotism, and history. In our great United States of America, we have been through much and are actually still a young country. We need to sit at the feet of those who have established this great land. Find someone to bless your life and teach you the legacy of honor.   ⚘*Carol*

✦   ✦   ✦

Father God, on this day I ask that you bless those who are seniors in our country. Help others to reach out to encourage and uplift them during this season of life. I pray, Lord, that they in turn will be willing to share their stories, in order to pass on the wisdom learned from lives well lived. ✦ *Amen.*

Responsible Legacy

"Look! I am creating new heavens and a new earth, and no one will even think about the old ones anymore." + ISAIAH 65:17

Today's Scripture passage is talking about the eternal new heavens and new earth. It is a very good parallel to our new lives in Christ. When we accept the Lord and begin our new lives with him, we should not even think about our old lives on this earth. We have been made new at that point in our faith.

One commonly held belief in today's culture is that anything that is wrong in our lives can be blamed on someone else. If we overeat, it is our parents' fault. If we can't stay in a relationship, it is our parents' fault. If we can't keep a job, it is our siblings' fault for always fighting with us and not resolving issues. The list goes on and on. We are not taking responsibility for actions in our lives.

When we become new creatures in Christ, he is our measurement of the newness in our lives. He is our legacy and our reason for all that we do in this life on earth. We can only compare ourselves to his goodness and his glory when we make mistakes or falter in our daily routines.

I love having Christ as my measuring stick. He gives me Holy Spirit eyes that see the world with renewed passion and renewed commitment to reach out and pray or serve when an opportunity arises.

John Adams, one of our founding fathers, wrote, "Our Constitution was made only for a moral and religious people. It is wholly inadequate to the government of any other."[1]

The same is true of our Bible. It is written for morality and for directions in this life. Scripture directs the reader to God the Father, Son, and Holy Spirit. We have our salvation and the Holy Bible to direct us into newness of life. It is time for blame to stop and responsibility to take its place. We must stand for our faith and our new lives through Jesus Christ. My prayer is that we take responsibility for our faith and develop it in a way that would be pleasing to God. *Carol*

* * *

Lord, thank you for those who founded our nation on Christian principles and morals. Forgive our nation for straying from this origin. Thank you for those who are fighting for truth and living for honor. + *Amen.*

---

[1] Sam Bartholomew with Stephen Mansfield, *God's Role in America* (Nashville, TN: Eggman Publishing, 1996), 43.

Just One More

[Jesus] replied, "The Father alone has the authority to set those dates and times, and they are not for you to know." + ACTS 1:7

Thanksgiving always brings a time of thinking of family in a loving way for me. I get so excited planning the meal and even planning the table setting for those who will be in our home to celebrate the day.

I was arranging some special decorations the other day specifically for Thanksgiving, and I thought how I would love to have just one more Thanksgiving dinner with my dad. I would love to say thank you this time of year just one more time for all he gave me. I would love to hear him say, "I love you today!" just one more time. I would love to hear him fuss at my mom and tell her that he will have another piece of pumpkin pie if he wants to. I would love to hear him tease the boys just one more time.

Is there someone in your life that you wish you had just one more time of fellowship with? There is no one who can fill the void for that person, but happy memories and thoughts bring much comfort.

The disciples were worried that they were going to be alone when Jesus left them. Jesus told them and us in John 14:16, "I will ask the Father, and he will give you another Advocate, who will never leave you." Jesus provided the Holy Spirit to remain with us and through the Spirit, he is with us always and will be with us until we meet him in eternity.

This year as you gather with family during the Thanksgiving season, think of the wonderful opportunity you have to say what you want to say to them. Think of ways to make memories that will last forever. I know from talking with many who are serving in our military in faraway lands that those memories keep them together during this time of year. They are thankful that they can think of those who love them at home and have a sense of family in their hearts.

This year, make just one more memory while you are together, and thank the Lord for all those who have gone before you.   *Carol*

* * *

Father, thank you for the blessings of memories, those made and those yet to be made. Thank you for the sacrifice of military families. Bless them today. + *Amen.*

Bring Them In

Don't lord it over the people assigned to your care, but lead them by your own good example.
✝ 1 PETER 5:3

I love teenagers. (That's right; I said it.) They bring such excitement and drama to life. They are always looking for something exciting to do or someplace exciting to go. They laugh and they cry without reserve. When they are passionate about life and things that give them purpose, they will put all they have into making it a part of who they are.

My husband says that he walks into a room full of teenagers and immediately turns and runs. When I walk into a room of teenagers, I run to the middle and sit down. They energize me and remind me that life is worth living.

While living in Georgia, we were blessed to move into a lovely home with a swimming pool. Our family was coming from an overseas assignment, and we were moving into a place where our boys knew only two people in the entire city. We felt that having a pool would bring young people to our house, which would not only give them a place of fun to hang out but give us an opportunity to know their new friends. I always made sure there was popcorn on hand, and I would often make cookies or order pizza.

My husband and I tried to get to sleep at least by ten at night, but we often had to yell down the stairs for everyone to hold down the laughter. "Hold down the laughter"—isn't that wonderful?

What we did not realize was that as we were giving these kids a safe place by bringing them into our home to hang out, we were also building trust with them. As the years progressed and the situations in their lives became more serious, many of these young people would come by just to talk, ask advice, or allow me to pray for them. What a gift that was as we reached out to them.

Many times we speak of the military wife or husband and often forget the military child. If you have a child who can reach out and be there for these military children during deployment or separation times, it will bless you and your family to be able to be a part of their lives. Young people from military families need those willing to bring them into their homes for fellowship and laughter.

During this family time of year, be willing to reach out and make a difference in a young person's life. ⚬*Carol*

✳   ✳   ✳

Father, I thank you for the young people in our country today. Help me to extend a hand and allow them to have a safe place to laugh and know the excitement of youth. Bless those children of military families, who often long to be with their moms and dads serving our country. ✝ *Amen.*

Fly Away

When you go through deep waters, I will be with you. When you go through rivers of difficulty, you will not drown. When you walk through the fire of oppression, you will not be burned up; the flames will not consume you. + ISAIAH 43:2

A very dear friend of mine once shared incredible wisdom with me. She told me that when your children are old enough to leave home on their own, you must think of them as birds leaving the nest. You cannot hold on to their tail feathers and say, "Fly away." You must let go. When you do let go, you let go with an open hand that they can return to anytime they need to.

At the time she shared this with me, our sons were in grade school. I heard her but truly did not understand the full meaning. I would one day, long afterward.

It's that middle-of-the-night call that is the most unsettling when your children are grown. My husband answered just such a call one night, and the voice on the other end said, "He's been shot!"

WHAT?

The words were repeated. I actually heard them, because the room was so quiet and the hour so late. A friend of our son's said that Alex had been shot at close range by a thief in the neighborhood but had survived.

"You should have seen it," he said. "We just knew he was dead. When the gun went off, he went straight to the ground, hard as a rock. The man stood over him, waiting to see if he would get up, and he did not. Then the man ran away."

At that moment, I knew that only the presence of God Almighty had saved Alex's life. I immediately envisioned his angel smacking him to the ground in order to keep him still until the man ran away. He turned out to have merely a graze from the bullet, running from the outer part of his eye to his ear. It looked like a skid mark. I told those who were with him to go immediately to our older son's house for the night after they finished with the police. The next morning in the very early hours, I stopped to get biscuits for the fifteen or so friends who had spent the night there and headed over to be with them.

There have been many times since that day when, in the midst of my daily routine or hearing of another parent's heartache, I have thanked God for protecting Alex. God's protection, after all, is far superior to any that I can give.

Let your children fly away, and be ready to open your hand and your heart on their behalf.   ∞*Carol*

* * *

Father God, I pray that my children and those of military parents may leave the nest and become mighty warriors for your Kingdom on this earth. + *Amen.*

Simple Thanks

Giving thanks is a sacrifice that truly honors me. ✝ PSALM 50:23

This is the season of Thanksgiving. Giving thanks is a sacrifice to God. Giving him thanks is very important to him, and this verse tells us that it honors him.

Why is it that as humans, we have a tendency to let the negative completely override the positive in our lives? When I am going through trauma or difficulty, I can find myself thinking, *What do I have to be thankful for?* There are other times when I begin comparing my life to others, and I find myself thinking how thankful I would be if I had what they had.

As my mind is refocused on today's Scripture and the importance of being thankful, I can begin to think of all those things for which I am thankful. First of all, how very thankful I am that Jesus is my Lord and Savior. That is the constant in my life that enables me to continue each day.

Secondly, I am so very thankful for my husband. My husband has always been the head of our household. He and I have known each other since our teen years. He accepts my extrovert personality, and we have venting sessions from time to time. I will tell you, however, that I always look to him for the final decision. I am so thankful he is the strength on this earth for me. I am so thankful that he has always been the provider for our family and has assumed the role with much commitment.

I am thankful that our family is centered on love for one another. There are so many families that don't have love in their relationships. Often they just exist with each other. I am very thankful for the love that is felt between our family members. We pray for each other and always desire the best for each other.

There are times when I walk around the house and thank God for our home and for the beautiful birds and butterflies that reside in our yard. How wonderful to realize my praise is a sacrifice to God and that I honor him when I thank him for creation.

If you are going through a negative time in your life, set aside a moment for offering a sacrifice of praise and give simple thanks to God. If you are going through a time of separation because of deployment or extended military service, give simple thanks to God for his love and protection. If you have lost a loved one this year, give thanks for the life of that one who has passed on and thank God for all they meant to you.

God is honored by your times of thanksgiving.   *⚘Carol*

✶　✶　✶

Father, I thank you! Fill the men and women in military service, and their families, with thankfulness for your sovereignty and love. ✝ *Amen.*

November 20
Almighty Provision

Abraham named the place Yahweh-Yireh (which means "the Lord will provide"). To this day, people still use that name as a proverb: "On the mountain of the Lord it will be provided."
✝ GENESIS 22:14

The story of Abraham and Isaac is beyond comprehension to me. When I think of obeying God to the point of walking my son to his death, I can't even find a thought that would prepare me. I want so much to be obedient to God as a Christian and always obey his words to me. I feel so inadequate, however, when I compare my life as a Christian to those who have gone before me as godly examples of obedience.

I do know the bottom line of this story is to show us just how confident we can be to know that God will provide. He will provide to us exactly what is needed for each situation in which we find ourselves.

During this wonderful Thanksgiving season, I remember so much of God's provisions for our family through the years. Thanksgiving was an anxious time for me as a young wife and mother. It always seemed to come too long after midmonth pay and too soon before end-of-the-month pay. It was difficult to buy all the things for a wonderful celebratory meal with the military pay my husband received at the time.

Provision always came, however, through wonderful friends who were usually older than we were. They would allow us to come and enjoy their delicious meals, beautiful homes, and loving fellowship. It meant so much to us as a family to share in those traditional times with others. My heart was always thinking that someday I would be that person to invite young families to come for a Thanksgiving celebration.

Every year since then, I have tried to keep a lookout for those who would also be blessed to spend a day and share a meal with someone who could provide for them. Americans have such a wonderful opportunity during this time to look for those families who need tender, loving care this year because of deployment. Oftentimes even the parents of those who have been sent overseas would love to spend the day with someone in their home.

Aside from providing physical needs through a place to visit and the sharing of a meal, you can also share provision with them through your spiritual encouragement. God's almighty provision is waiting for any who would have him come into their lives. Share your home this season, share a meal, and allow his almighty provision to come to bless those in your care. ❧*Carol*

* * *

Father, thank you for showing me through Scripture that you will provide. You care for me and love me more than I could ever imagine. Father, give me Holy Spirit eyes for those who need extra care this holiday season. ✝ *Amen.*

Blessed Be Your Name

Blessed be the name of the LORD now and forever. ✛ PSALM 113:2

Matt Redman has written a modern-day hymn of praise entitled "Blessed Be Your Name." The words are powerful and uplifting in any setting and at any time. I experienced one of the most meaningful renditions of this song during a visit to Fort Campbell, Kentucky, in the spring of 2006.

My son accompanied me on this trip with the goal of gathering videotape footage of the weekly chapel women's ministry. This footage would be used to produce an information video for the international PWOC (Protestant Women of the Chapel) ministry.

At this time, Fort Campbell was experiencing many combat casualties. Most of the women in attendance had husbands in Iraq. Memorial services were part of the weekly schedule, and all of these women had been touched in one way or another by loss. I observed the women as they came in, asking about one another. They did not shy away from the issues they were facing, but it was obvious their purpose for coming was not for a complaining session.

The program began, and the women prayed for one another. They shared testimonies of praise of how God was empowering them to make it through difficult times. Then they began to sing, and oh, how they sang! "Blessed Be Your Name" was among the selections for that morning. The women began singing the words of the last chorus, "You give and take away. My heart will choose to say, Lord, blessed be your name!"[1] These words spoken so many years ago by Job, declaring the sovereignty of God in the midst of pain and brokenness, took on a modern-day voice (see Job 1:21).

As Gregory and I witnessed these women singing, it was a very intense moment. We watched them submit themselves to the hands of the Lord in worship. These women were singing this song with every ounce of faith they could muster. They weren't just singing to fill up time before a speaker or Bible study. They weren't singing just to be entertained. Through their song they were connecting with God, and it was evident his Spirit was strengthening their souls in the process.

That day at Fort Campbell, Kentucky, I caught a glimpse of sacrificial worship. In dark and challenging moments, these women were choosing to trust God. I choose to say with them today, "Blessed be your name!"   ❧*Brenda*

✳   ✳   ✳

Father God, help me to choose to sing your praise even in the tough moments of life. I want to bless you and trust your sovereign will for me even when I am afraid, discouraged, or bereaved. I say with all my heart—blessed be the name of the Lord now and forever! ✛ *Amen.*

---

[1] Matt and Beth Redman, "Blessed Be Your Name," Kingsway's Thank You Music, 2002.

November 22
Beyond Words

Yes, they knew God, but they wouldn't worship him as God or even give him thanks. And they began to think up foolish ideas of what God was like. As a result, their minds became dark and confused. ✛ ROMANS 1:21

Thankfulness is just like anything else in our daily lives—if we aren't careful, we might miss it. Each day is filled with so many things for which to be thankful. Often we don't even realize the blessings we have until they are gone.

In my morning prayers, I thank God, my Creator, for allowing me the privilege to take a breath and get out of bed that day. I am aware that every day is a miracle and a blessing from the Lord. If you think you might not have anything to be truly thankful for in your life, examine your heart.

Did you sleep in a soft, cushy bed last night? Were you able to adjust the temperature just right in order to cuddle up under the covers? Was there an actual roof over your head? Did you have a shower and freshen up before you dressed for bed?

Did you wake up this morning and go straight to get your first cup of coffee? Were you able to turn on the television to catch up on the news and weather? Were you then able to have choices for what you would eat for breakfast?

Those questions only get us from bedtime through the first hour or two of our morning, and already we have so much for which to be thankful. Imagine those who are serving in foreign lands. Most of them cannot answer yes to any of those questions. There are those serving who get up in the morning and give thanks for God allowing them to be alive and fighting for a cause in their lives.

I want to be thankful for the time I have on this earth. I want to spend time with family and friends and be thankful that every memory we make together will last a lifetime, even for generations to come.

On this November day, I am grateful beyond any words that I could put on paper for the continued sacrifice and commitment of our military members and their families. It is beyond words what they experience and how they live from day to day in service to America. I want to say thank you to all those who have chosen to be a part of the military lifestyle. Your service will be a legacy to all who come after you.
↝*Carol*

✳   ✳   ✳

Father God, on this day I am grateful to you as my Creator and my Savior. I ask your blessing on those who are less fortunate than me and my fellow Americans. I ask that you grant peace and safety to those fighting in other countries today. ✛ *Amen.*

Company's Coming!

Be dressed for service and keep your lamps burning, as though you were waiting for your master to return from the wedding feast. Then you will be ready to open the door and let him in the moment he arrives and knocks. ✦ LUKE 12:35-36

As I'm writing this, I am sitting in the passenger seat of a vehicle on Interstate 81 the evening before Thanksgiving. The traffic is an issue because people are headed the same direction I am to spend the holiday with loved ones. Preparations are being made at someone's house for the family gathering.

Getting a house ready for guests reminds me of being first married. My husband and I were both very busy attending school and working. On one particular occasion, our little apartment was a huge mess. There were dishes piled in the sink. Dirty clothes were strewn all over the floor. Books and papers from school projects were everywhere. It was evident the last thing we expected was guests.

A knock at the door put me in a panic. Standing at our front door were my husband's beloved uncle and aunt. We were thrilled to see them, but my heart sank as I realized these two favored relatives were going to view my unkempt home. If I'd only known they were coming!

As Christ followers, we've already been notified that Jesus is coming again. He's given us indicators of the conditions of the world at the time of his coming so we will not be caught off guard and not have our spiritual house in order.

Unfortunately, there will be many who will be surprised at Christ's return, just like I was when my uncle and aunt came to visit. This is often the case when we are too focused and engaged simply in improving our quality of life here on earth.

As a Christ follower, I am to be looking for his return with anticipation. I need to frequently ask myself, *What do I need to do if Christ were coming today? Is there someone with whom I need to make amends? Is there something that needs to be removed from my life? Is there anything I need to do to make my inner life clean and prepared for the coming of the Lord?*

When my aunt and uncle knocked on the door, I couldn't say, "Can you come back in two hours so I can clean up my house?" When Christ comes he will not say, "I'll come back in a few hours if this is an inconvenient time." I must be ready. ✺*Brenda*

✧   ✧   ✧

Lord, I want to have my spiritual house clean and ready for your coming. Remind me of anything that needs to be put in order in preparation for that great day! ✦*Amen.*

Song of Thanksgiving

He has given me a new song to sing, a hymn of praise to our God. Many will see what he has done and be amazed. They will put their trust in the LORD. ✚ PSALM 40:3

When I think of my salvation in Jesus Christ, I realize how thankful I am for this gift. In remembering all that I have to thank God for this time of the year, I am reminded that my faith in Jesus Christ is the thing that matters most. Although family and friends and anything of this earth might be taken from me, no one can ever take Jesus from my heart.

Isaiah 12 gives us a song of praise for our salvation. It can be something we read out loud today to remind us to get on our knees to thank God for such a blessing:

> In that day you will sing: "I will praise you, O LORD! You were angry with me, but not any more. Now you comfort me. See, God has come to save me. I will trust in him and not be afraid. The LORD GOD is my strength and my song; he has given me victory." With joy you will drink deeply from the fountain of salvation! In that wonderful day you will sing: "Thank the LORD! Praise his name! Tell the nations what he has done. Let them know how mighty he is! Sing to the LORD, for he has done wonderful things. Make known his praise around the world. Let all the people of Jerusalem shout his praise with joy! For great is the Holy One of Israel who lives among you."

Stand in front of the Lord today and read this out loud to thank him for salvation. Commit to telling the world of all he has done and making his praise known to those who need the hope of Jesus.

As you are standing before him today, pray for those in your neighborhood and your community. Pray that God would prepare you to be a friend and a helper to any who need to be loved and cared for. Ask him to bring to mind those to whom he would have you minister.

Stand on this day and pray for those who need to come to know him as their Lord and Savior. Pray for those who are in harm's way and standing at the brink of life and death. Pray for peace for their families as they are celebrating Thanksgiving an ocean away.

Sing a song of thanksgiving today so the world may know the joy of Jesus that is in your life.   ❧*Carol*

✫   ✫   ✫

Father, thank you for your salvation. I ask for protection and boldness on behalf of those who go without fear to fight the fight for freedom. ✚ *Amen.*

My Heart Is Full

The LORD is my strength and shield. I trust him with all my heart. He helps me, and my heart is filled with joy. I burst out in songs of thanksgiving. ✛ PSALM 28:7

We often find ourselves pushing away from the table after a big meal and making a comment about being full. Our youngest son often makes a very "gentle" comment when he says, "I feel like I am going to be sick." Okay, that's when you are really full. We do have a tendency in this country to eat until we could burst. There are many places that have unlimited buffets or huge portions that would feed a small family of four. It is commonplace in America.

This time of year always brings the thought of meal planning and overdoing it for the Thanksgiving dinner. Many times we have not just one potato dish, but we have mashed potatoes, sweet potatoes, and possibly a hash-brown casserole. There is always dressing or stuffing that is made with bread or cornbread. Just the ingredients could keep you going for days.

While sitting on the porch this morning with my coffee and feeling the coolness in the air, I realized how full my heart is this time of year. My heart is full of excitement in planning menus for the four or five extra people coming in for the long weekend. My heart is filled with anticipation as I change the sheets and prepare the guest rooms. My heart is full with love as I know my mother and my son's fiancée will be here with us. My heart is full in knowing that this year we will be able to afford to have the meal and the plans that we desire. My heart is full as I look over our backyard, thinking about our sons playing football on Thanksgiving Day.

I am full of thanksgiving as I remember our military days. It was an exciting time of new beginnings and new relationships. We were blessed by each new assignment through the years.

Take this time of year to think more about the fullness of your heart than the fullness of your stomach. It will bring much to be thankful for as you celebrate. ∼*Carol*

✳ ✳ ✳

Lord, I pray for those who will be spending this Thanksgiving Day away from their loved ones. Give them fullness of heart, knowing that you love them. ✛ *Amen.*

The Mess Hall

I will thank you, LORD, among all the people. I will sing your praises among the nations.
✛ PSALM 108:3

One of the favored traditions of this military family has been celebrating Thanksgiving with the soldiers my husband has served. For my husband, that meant wearing his dress uniform to preach at the chapel Thanksgiving Day service. Following the service, our family would head to the dining facility, otherwise known as the mess hall, for a Thanksgiving feast.

The Thanksgiving Day meal for a military dining facility has been described as the Super Bowl for military cooks. They go all out with decorations and create a feast in the truest sense of the word. From the printed menus to the ice sculptures for ambience, from shrimp cocktail to pumpkin pie, it is special. Oftentimes my husband and other officers would go behind the chow line to serve the soldiers, giving them opportunity by way of a symbolic gesture to show their appreciation for these young troops.

It was during a time of war that President Abraham Lincoln proclaimed an official day of thanksgiving to be observed on the third Thursday in November of every year in America, making this a national holiday. And it was President Woodrow Wilson who during World War I declared Thanksgiving a special day for those in military service. On military installations, this day was to be complete with a church service and full dinner in order to acknowledge "the great blessings God has bestowed upon us."

Even in faraway lands in the midst of combat zones, on Thanksgiving Day a chaplain will be flying to forward operating bases to conduct a Thanksgiving service for troops. Along with the chaplain will be freshly cooked turkey and all the trimmings.

As you enjoy this Thanksgiving holiday and all the traditions that accompany it for you, won't you join me in praying for military personnel serving around the world? Consider the attitude and thoughts of the originator of America's Thanksgiving Day, President Abraham Lincoln, as he instructed a nation to thank almighty God.

> I recommend to them that, while offering up the ascriptions justly due to him for such singular deliverances and blessings, they do also, with humble penitence for our national perverseness and disobedience, commend to his tender care all those who have become widows, orphans, mourners, or sufferers in the lamentable civil strife in which we are unavoidably engaged, and fervently implore the imposition of the almighty hand to heal the wounds of the nation, and to restore it, as soon as may be consistent with the Divine purposes, to the full enjoyment of peace, harmony, tranquility, and union.
> —President Abraham Lincoln, Washington, D.C., October 3, 1863.[1]

≈Brenda

---

[1] National Park Service, *Historical Handbook*, "Abraham Lincoln's Thanksgiving Proclamation," http://www.cr.nps.gov/history/online_books/source/sb2/sb2w.htm.

Gleaning the Fields

Ruth gathered barley there all day, and when she beat out the grain that evening,
it filled an entire basket. ✛ RUTH 2:17

A trip to Turkey has been one of the highlights of my life thus far. I experienced a Communion service in the caves of Cappadocia where early Christians worshiped to escape persecution. I walked the roads that Paul walked in Ephesus. I heard the words of the apostle John read in the locations of the seven churches of Revelation. I listened as Turkish Christian women shared their love of Christ in their own language. I didn't understand their words, and they did not understand mine, but there was no doubt we understood each other's hearts.

I also spent some time with lovely American women at the Incirlik Air Force Base in Adana, Turkey. Amy, Deb, Aulene, and others made me feel at home. One evening, Aulene invited me for dinner. The meal was delicious, the fellowship was sweet, and the conversation was uplifting. She told me later that the meal was a true surprise because she didn't have the ingredients for any recipes she wanted to prepare and the commissary was closed, so she couldn't go shopping. As a resourceful military wife, Aulene began going door-to-door, asking her neighbors if they had this ingredient or that ingredient. She ended up with everything she needed and more to make a delicious meal. It was just like Ruth gleaning the fields!

In today's Scripture passage, Ruth was able to glean in the field because of the generosity of Boaz—even to the point that he instructed his field hands to leave a little extra grain behind for Ruth. This same generosity of spirit is often shared in a military community that is based overseas, where there is a sense of knowing you can depend on your neighbor whenever you are in need.

The first Thanksgiving, the struggling pilgrims learned that in order to survive in this new land, they had to depend upon the support of one another. They even learned that their newfound friends, the Indians, were willing to generously assist them in learning some of the finer points of survival. As they joined together for that first Thanksgiving meal, each bringing their contribution, as well as their thanks for the goodness of God, bounty of the land, and support for one another, they created a tradition that long endures in our nation. Family and friends go to great lengths to show their gratitude to God and to one another.

Is it too corny to say I learned a Thanksgiving lesson in a land called Turkey?
✍*Brenda*

✶　✶　✶

Gracious Lord, thank you for every blessing that is mine. May my life express my gratitude for your bountiful provision. Whenever I have the opportunity, let me be an encouragement to those who help to ensure the blessing of my freedom in this nation. ✛ *Amen.*

November 28
Black Friday

Let me say this, dear brothers and sisters: The time that remains is very short. So from now on, those with wives should not focus only on their marriage. Those who weep or who rejoice or who buy things should not be absorbed by their weeping or their joy or their possessions. Those who use the things of the world should not become attached to them. For this world as we know it will soon pass away. ✛ 1 CORINTHIANS 7:29-31

I must be insane!" These words were e-mailed to me the day after Thanksgiving from my husband's BlackBerry. He was in an electronics store, standing in an enormous line before dawn in order to be one of the few early shoppers to get a hot item as a Christmas gift for one of our sons.

What would make people be willing to demonstrate such a sense of urgency before daylight? In the case of Black Friday, there are opportunities in the way of bargains offered by merchants for a few hours. As a Christ follower, Scripture implies I am to live my life with a sense of urgency. I don't think this means that I am to live life in a hurry, but rather I am to be watchful in order not to miss opportunities the Lord would place before me as a faithful servant. I am to live my life to influence others to become part of the family of God while the opportunity is still available.

Thanksgiving is a season of counting the blessings of life. I sometimes think I am so blessed that the sense of urgency in living my life for Christ gets diminished. The world urgently needs to see Christians living authentic lives of hope and faith in Christ. I don't want to lose the sense of living my life with godly passion and urgency in order to fulfill his will and purpose.   ☙Brenda

★   ★   ★

Lord, thank you for each blessing in my life. Protect me from viewing urgency in terms other than sharing the life I have in you with others. Open my eyes to see the opportunities to stand for you today. In your name I pray. ✛ Amen.

November Praise

Praise the LORD! Praise God in his sanctuary; praise him in his mighty heaven! + PSALM 150:1

I've been pleasantly surprised this fall to notice that even in late November, the leaves of the Northern Virginia trees are still brilliant and beautiful. Walking through the city or driving in the suburbs, I've being awed by the red of the maple, dogwood, and sumac trees, the yellow of the poplar, hickory, and beech trees, and the orange of the mighty oaks. The splashes of color have brightened the landscape of D.C. in abundance.

This past weekend as I was sitting in chapel at Fort Myer, I was drawn to the clear glass window above the altar area. Revealed there was the beauty of tall trees that made their home on the edge of Arlington National Cemetery, displaying their yellow and orange autumn brilliance. The bright, colorful leaves brought the handiwork of the Father right into the Sunday morning worship.

As the congregation stood to sing the doxology, I was moved by the glory of God demonstrated in the beauty of his creation.

> *Praise God, from Whom all blessings flow;*
> *Praise Him, all creatures here below;*
> *Praise Him above, ye heavenly host;*
> *Praise Father, Son, and Holy Ghost!*[1]

It is far too easy for me to overlook the blessings God has given me. Whether it be the beauty of an autumn tree as I drive my car through an urban neighborhood or the overladen closet in my apartment, I take so much for granted. A call-in guest on a radio talk show I was listening to today commented that we live in a nation so blessed that as Americans, compared to most of the world, we live with an abundance of material things. In all honesty, I must admit that instead of giving thanks for my abundance, I'm often guilty of thinking how I can add to it.

I don't understand God's blessing, just like I don't understand how temperature affects the sugars in trees to produce autumnal works of art. It is so comforting to know I don't have to understand these things to appreciate them—or to enjoy them! ❧*Brenda*

☆　☆　☆

Father God, as you have blessed me, may I learn to enjoy your blessings and acknowledge your favor. All good gifts flow from your hand. Thank you for the beauty of the earth and the beauty of my life. May I see your blessings in the unexpected places of today. + *Amen.*

---

[1] Thomas Ken, *Manual of Prayers for the Use of the Scholars of Winchester College*, 1674 (Public Domain).

November 30
Awake, My Soul!

Awake, my soul! Awake, harp and lyre! I will awaken the dawn. ✝ PSALM 57:8, NIV

While researching the doxology for yesterday's devotional thought, I came across the history of the song. I was amazed to find that this popular refrain sung through the ages was written in the 1600s. It is actually the very last stanza of a much longer hymn. The song was written at a time when the church believed hymns should only be Scripture sung to music—anything else was considered blasphemous. The author, Thomas Ken, was a professor at Winchester College and wrote the song with strict instructions to the young men at the school to only sing it in their rooms.

The style is far from modern, but the message is a powerful charge to begin the day as the psalmist David did in Psalm 57 with praise and thanksgiving to a faithful God! Let it be your hymn of prayer and praise today.

Awake My Soul

Awake, my soul, and with the sun
Thy daily stage of duty run;
Shake off dull sloth, and joyful rise,
To pay thy morning sacrifice.
Thy precious time misspent, redeem,
Each present day thy last esteem,
Improve thy talent with due care;
For the great day thyself prepare.
By influence of the Light divine
Let thy own light to others shine.
Reflect all Heaven's propitious ways
In ardent love, and cheerful praise.
In conversation be sincere;
Keep conscience as the noontide clear;
Think how all seeing God thy ways
And all thy secret thoughts surveys.
Wake, and lift up thyself, my heart,
And with the angels bear thy part,
Who all night long unwearied sing
High praise to the eternal King.
All praise to Thee, who safe has kept
And hast refreshed me while I slept
Grant, Lord, when I from death shall
*   wake*

I may of endless light partake.
Heav'n is, dear Lord, where'er Thou art,
O never then from me depart;
For to my soul 'tis hell to be
But for one moment void of Thee.
Lord, I my vows to Thee renew;
Disperse my sins as morning dew.
Guard my first springs of thought and
*   will,*
And with Thyself my spirit fill.
Direct, control, suggest, this day,
All I design, or do, or say,
That all my powers, with all their
*   might,*
In Thy sole glory may unite.
I would not wake nor rise again
And Heaven itself I would disdain,
Wert Thou not there to be enjoyed,
And I in hymns to be employed.
Praise God, from Whom all blessings
*   flow;*
Praise Him, all creatures here below;
Praise Him above, ye heavenly host;
Praise Father, Son, and Holy Ghost![1]

❧Brenda

---

[1] Thomas Ken, *Manual of Prayers for the Use of the Scholars of Winchester College,* 1674 (Public Domain).

December 1
A No-Fault Ministry

We live in such a way that no one will stumble because of us, and no one will find fault with our ministry. In everything we do, we show that we are true ministers of God. We patiently endure troubles and hardships and calamities of every kind. ✛ 2 CORINTHIANS 6:3-4

There has always been a price to pay for peace. Paul tells us of his hardships while trying to spread the gospel of peace to others. If you have a chance, read through verse thirteen in 2 Corinthians 6 as Paul tells of all his trials while preaching the truth of God to others. Today we see many who seek to destroy innocent lives for the sake of what they believe to be peace. They murder and deceive to try to establish what they believe to be truth.

This season of the year is when we concentrate on the birth of Jesus, who came to bring everlasting peace to our world. He came so we would have hearts of love and understanding. Because of his gift, we can live in such a way that others would follow him, too, by our example.

Jesus walked this earth in a no-fault ministry. His standards and his teachings were things we can follow and emulate without regret. His love for others and the way he always found the time or the strength to minister when there was a need serve as a model for us to follow.

Recently our pastor dressed in jeans and a tattered jacket. He put on dark glasses and wrapped his hand in what appeared to be a bloody cloth. He put on a hat to cover his head, and then he sat outside a construction trailer on the grounds of the church during the Sunday school hour. He waited for someone to come to ask him if he needed help. No one did. One woman who saw him went in and asked one of the men in the church to please go to check on him. His point was to challenge us to minister to those who are different from us. He then taught about the Good Samaritan and showed how easy it would be to pass someone by.

I pray that I can stand before the Lord and witness to him that I did the very best I could to have a no-fault ministry on this earth. Peace comes with a cost, as does living with the heart and mind of Christ, standing ready to minister to the world around us. ❧*Carol*

✳   ✳   ✳

Lord, thank you for allowing me through your Holy Spirit to minister to a hurting world. Help me to be prepared every day. Thank you for those who are paying the price for peace as they serve in the military. ✛ *Amen.*

December 2
Public Praise

I stand on solid ground, and I will publicly praise the LORD. ✛ PSALM 26:12

The Christmas celebration has become a subject of debate in our nation. There are those who feel that celebrating the birth of Christ should not have so much press. There are those who feel that the Nativity scene should not be a part of the Christmas experience in the United States. Christmas carols have come under attack for being too religious.

I am more and more convinced that Christmas needs to celebrate the birth of Christ. That's the reason the holiday began. We would have never had Christmas to celebrate had Jesus not been born. It is a celebration of a birth so miraculous and so holy that even the stars led the way to his manger.

If we did not display the Nativity during the Christmas season, it would be the same as not displaying the flag on the Fourth of July. We sing songs of worship all year, but "Silent Night, Holy Night" was written to tell of the birth of Jesus Christ. "O Holy Night" was written in recognition of that holy night when Christ was born.

As time goes on, I become more and more steadfast in standing up to the naysayer who would attempt to take Christ out of Christmas. I stand on solid ground, as the Scripture says, to let others know in public praise. Christmas Day is a Christian celebration not to be taken from me.

There are many in the military stationed in places far from their immediate families, whether that is in the United States or in foreign countries. I can tell you, after living as a military family overseas for seven of the twenty-two years of service, that Christmas was a time that gave us a sense of homecoming. It was our time as Christians to decorate and celebrate this holiday celebrated around the world in different ways. Often it was a time to publicly praise the Lord through explaining what Christmas is all about.

I know there are many this Christmas season who will not be with their families and families of those who have given the ultimate sacrifice of their lives who will never be with their loved one again. I pray on their behalf that I can continue to publicly praise the Lord and keep Christ in the Christmas celebration.   ✺*Carol*

* * *

Father, thank you for this wonderful time to celebrate the birth of your Son, Jesus. Help me not to waver in my commitment to keep this time of year holy and to remember the true meaning of what this season is all about. Bless those who serve this country and need an extra measure of your peace and joy during their times of separation or deployment. ✛ *Amen.*

Reach Out and Touch

On that day, says the LORD of Heaven's Armies, each of you will invite your neighbor to sit with you peacefully under your own grapevine and fig tree. + ZECHARIAH 3:10

Bev Brandenburg influenced my life in so many ways as a military wife. I have shared before about her influence in teaching me to be hospitable and to invite people into my home for fellowship. She taught me different ways of entertaining and fun ways to make my guests feel special. More than anything, she always taught me to be myself in every endeavor.

My husband retired from the military twelve years ago, but Bev is still influencing my life in a positive way. I want to pass along a holiday suggestion. It is the most wonderful way to have a sense of peace during the year, knowing you have touched your neighbors at this holiday season. Bev invited me to her home for a cookie exchange. She explained to me that she began this tradition many years ago with about five people. The one I attended had approximately sixty in attendance. Everyone brought three dozen home-baked Christmas cookies. As Bev served hot cider to her guests, they sampled the cookies set around the tables. This was a joyous event and, I knew, something I wanted to begin.

I began the next year delivering invitations to about ten ladies in the neighborhood. We had approximately five in attendance that year. Only two of us had ever sat down and spent time talking to each other. We had so much fun and learned about our families and favorite pastimes.

Last year we had the fourth annual Christmas cookie exchange, with twenty-five women in attendance. What a wonderful celebration of getting to know new neighbors and touching base with those whom we had not been able to see throughout the year.

Reach out and touch your neighbors this year. Be thankful for the home God has given you to share with others. The cookies you have left over can be taken to the closest National Guard and Reserve units or even boxed up and sent overseas to bless those in harm's way. Perhaps you know a military family close by with children that you could take the extras to. Take a stand and be a leader in your community in fellowship and in fun. *Carol*

★   ★   ★

Lord, I love that you give us times of pure fun and fellowship. Help me to reach out and touch my neighbors and friends and to extend that hand to our military members and their families during this holiday season. + *Amen.*

December 4
Plans of His Heart

God blesses those whose hearts are pure, for they will see God. ✛ MATTHEW 5:8

Planning for a trip or an event is one of my favorite things to do. I may get a bit stressed when it comes to what to wear for those activities, but the rest is so much fun. I love to lay out dreams and expectations of what is to come. I love to get out the paper and begin to brainstorm about what we will do or where we will go. I make a list of possibilities and a list for contacts to be made in order to make things happen. Calling ahead for reservations and assuring we can proceed on the selected date or dates are always a must.

Planning for Christmas usually begins the first week of December for me. Thanksgiving is my favorite time of year, so I don't want to miss that day with plans of Christmas. The Saturday after Thanksgiving, we put up the tree and decorate the whole house for the Christmas holidays. I begin the lists of things to do from that point until Christmas Day arrives.

There are so many opportunities to celebrate the Christmas season. This time of year we usually get in at least one tour of homes in the historic district of town. We also have a couple of designated company get-togethers and church-class celebrations.

In early grade school, our sons were old enough to begin memorizing, and we had them memorize the Christmas story from Luke 2. On Christmas Eve each year they would gather their Star Wars figures and act out the Nativity scene while reciting the Christmas story verbatim. It was a precious time. If we had company, the guests were thrilled to see this activity. It gave them a hands-on lesson each year in understanding just why we celebrate Christmas.

Our plans are not always God's plan, and our ways are not his ways. Take time this year to add "celebrate Jesus!" to your to-do list. Spend time with God, asking what his plans are for you this beautiful season of his birth. Approach God with a pure heart, seeking his plans for your season of celebration.   ❧*Carol*

☆　☆　☆

Lord God Emmanuel, I am excited to begin planning the celebration of your birth. Instill in my heart a desire to spend time with you, reflecting on the meaning of this glorious season. I ask your favor and your joy for those who will not be with their families this year. I ask for an extra measure of outreach from the community to surround them with love and care. ✛ *Amen.*

New Traditions

This is a gift from God, who brought us back to himself through Christ. And God has given us this task of reconciling people to him. ✝ 2 CORINTHIANS 5:18

My dear friend and fellow military wife Cheri Rogers leads a grief recovery class at our church.[1] The impact of this class in the community has been amazing. Many who are not even members of the church attend. People come to know that there are others who understand and have gone through similar situations. Every person's grief is different, but the pain felt is something with which others can identify.

With the holidays here, there are specific directions and ideas that can help someone to get through this time of year. Many of us have had family traditions going since childhood that included everyone within our families. When one of those members is no longer a part of the family unit, situations often need to be altered.

Cheri gives several ideas in her class. One of the things she suggests is to possibly plan an out-of-town celebration, especially the first few years. If you have always cooked a Christmas Day meal and the same things for that meal, you might want to consider going to a restaurant the first year. Cheri shared with the group one evening that her son, Scott, always loved cheesecake. She said that, since his death five years ago, she still cannot make a cheesecake. Each time she begins one, she ends up throwing everything away and having a good cry.

Christmas is a celebration of the birth of Jesus. Start new traditions that focus on family and faith. In a recent article Cheri wrote for our church magazine, *Faith and Family Matters*, she says,

> Focusing on the true meaning of the holiday can remind you that your loved one took part in celebrating, but the holiday was not about him or her. Thanksgiving is about giving thanks to God for the blessings of the past and those that remain. List your blessings and share your appreciation with those who make the list. Christmas is the birthday of Jesus. He is the only reason you will ever see your loved one again. Honor Jesus by at least setting out the nativity or giving a "Happy Birthday, Jesus" cake. All the decorations, gifts, food, parties, and activities would have never evolved if God had not sent His son to make a way for you and those you love to spend eternity with Him. So let us grieve as those who have hope. Let that hope fan the tiny spark that is still deep within you. As you keep your eyes on Jesus, you will cry, but you will not drown in a pit of despair.[2]

~Carol

* * *

Father God, thank you for traditions that focus on you. Lord, I ask that during this time of year you will be with those who have lost loved ones. ✝ *Amen.*

---

[1] Cheri Rogers has granted permission to reference her story.
[2] Cheri Rogers, "Getting through the Holidays," *Faith and Family Matters* (December 2007).

Overwhelmed

Because I am righteous, I will see you. When I awake, I will see you face to face and be satisfied. ✛ PSALM 17:15

One October day, I went to Lowe's with my husband; I thought I would buy some pansies to plant for our warmer climate's winter months.

Darkness had come for the evening as we drove up to the store. Shining through the windows in the garden center were Christmas trees all lit up. It wasn't even the end of October! I told myself I would not be tempted by the beauty of their displays. I grabbed a cart and began selecting my pansies. After deciding on eight dollars' worth of flowers, I peeked through the Christmas section that led into the main store to see if my husband was returning. I walked around the pansies a while longer and even exchanged a few for healthier-looking ones.

Five minutes turned into fifteen, and I thought I would just go into the store to see if I could find him. However, once the doors opened into the Christmas section, I was overwhelmed—and hooked. Immediately I began thinking that I really needed to spiff up some older decorations. I put one item into my cart, and then another. I kept peeking towards the door, actually hoping that my husband would come through so I could stop this madness. I was thankful not to have a regular cart but only a flower cart so it was harder to cram in so many items.

Fifteen minutes turned to twenty, and we were heading into the thirty-minute time frame. Suddenly, I began putting back on the shelves everything I had gathered, aside from the pansies. I thought, *It's not even the end of October!* I began to feel the stress releasing from my neck and shoulders. My eight dollars' worth of flowers would have turned into about fifty dollars' worth of being overwhelmed with Christmas decorations.

When my husband walked through the door, I was patiently waiting in the pansy section. I smiled and said, "Are you ready to go?"

Isn't that so much the way life is, especially this time of year? We become overwhelmed with all the stuff we can buy. Step back and remember those who need a kind word, a hug, or a lunch with a friend just to talk while their families are separated as their spouses, sons, and daughters are serving our country.

Be fully satisfied in service to others and have a merry Christmas.   ⟿*Carol*

☆   ☆   ☆

Lord, thank you for showing me in my times of weakness to buy and have more just how very important life and service to others are. Bring to my heart and mind today someone who needs a touch from you. May I bring true holiday spirit to others in their time of need. ✛ *Amen.*

Waiting for a Redeemer

Praise the Lord, the God of Israel, because he has visited and redeemed his people.

✝ LUKE 1:68

The Christmas season was always a special time in my church. However, observing each Sunday of Advent was something I first became acquainted with when my husband became a military chaplain. I found it to be something that was rich with meaning. Using the Advent wreath to celebrate the season became a special family tradition that we continue to practice in our home. It signifies the four Sundays prior to Christmas as a time of preparation and anticipation for Christ's coming.

I am drawn to the reminders of Advent. Maybe it's because I am a visual learner and the symbolism of the wreath communicates the message to my mind and heart. The candles remind me that Christ is the Light of the World—the victor over darkness. As they are lit each week, I am reminded that Christ came to redeem the world, and that he is returning again! Each candle reminds me of an important aspect of the process of waiting for my Savior.

> The first candle represents *hope:*
> "All nations will come to your light; mighty kings will come to see your radiance." (Isaiah 60:3)

> The second candle represents *peace:*
> "For a child is born to us, a son is given to us. The government will rest on his shoulders. . . . His government and its peace will never end" (Isaiah 9:6-7).

> The third candle represents *joy:*
> "Sorrow and mourning will disappear, and they will be filled with joy and gladness" (Isaiah 35:10).

> The fourth candle represents *love:*
> "God showed how much he loved us by sending his one and only Son into the world so that we might have eternal life through him" (1 John 4:9).

> Finally, the white center candle represents *Christ:*
> "Suddenly, the angel was joined by a vast host of others—the armies of heaven—praising God and saying, 'Glory to God in highest heaven, and peace on earth to those with whom God is pleased.' When the angels had returned to heaven, the shepherds said to each other, 'Let's go to Bethlehem! Let's see this thing that has happened, which the Lord has told us about. ' They hurried to the village and found Mary and Joseph. And there was the baby, lying in the manger" (Luke 2:13-16).

In a culture where Christmas décor is merchandised in October, I need the reminder of my simple Advent wreath. It is the profound reminder that I am waiting for my Redeemer. ⮞*Brenda*

✶ ✶ ✶

Emmanuel, thank you for leaving your throne and coming to dwell among us. In the challenges of each day, remind me of your coming. Help me to prepare my heart today in anticipation. ✝*Amen.*

Lights Out

I am come that they might have life, and that they might have it more abundantly.

✝ JOHN 10:10, KJV

My son and his wife have a Christmas tree that has the lights already attached. It is supposed to make things easier, and for the past several years they haven't had to bother with stringing lights on their tree. This year however, when they put up the tree and plugged it in, there were bright shining lights on the top and bright shining lights on the bottom, but nothing in the middle.

We sometimes are like my son's Christmas tree. Too often we live in the partial fullness of what God wants and has planned for us. He came so that we might have life, and not just life, but abundant life! He wants us to live a complete and whole life in him.

My son's tree can still be pretty if it is decorated, but it will not be complete without all of the lights sparkling. It needs more than just the top and the bottom; it needs the abundance of all the lights for the full effect. The word *abundance* in today's Scripture means something that is not absolutely necessary, but is an overflow or surplus. You see, the Lord could have just come to earth to keep us from hell, but he came for so much more! He came to give us peace, joy, hope, and love that will help us in this life, as well as tastes of eternal blessings to come.

John 10:10 describes Jesus as the shepherd giving his sheep a rich and satisfying life. He leads the sheep to the best places for fulfillment and nourishment. He doesn't just want his sheep to survive, but he wants them to thrive. We live in a fallen world, and there is going to be suffering, but God is sovereign, and he allows our suffering to work in the process of abundant life. The Good Shepherd has come to lead each of us to his complete, full, and eternal life. ↝*Brenda*

*　*　*

Lord, you are the God who made the world and everything in it. You do not live in man-made temples, and human hands can't serve your needs—for you have no needs. You give life and breath to everything, and you satisfy every need. From one man you created all the nations throughout the whole earth. You decided beforehand when they should rise and fall, and you determined their boundaries. Your purpose was for the nations to seek after you and perhaps feel their way toward you and find you—though you are not far from any one of us. For in you I live and move and exist (Acts 17:24-28, paraphrased). ✝*Amen.*

Decorations

A voice said, "Shout!" I asked, "What should I shout?" "Shout that people are like the grass. Their beauty fades as quickly as the flowers in a field. The grass withers and the flowers fade beneath the breath of the LORD. And so it is with people. The grass withers and the flowers fade, but the word of our God stands forever." + ISAIAH 40:6-8

When we were stationed overseas, Christmas was usually a time of year when we needed to be flexible. Often we were not near enough to family to attempt to get together, so we drew close to each other and to other military families during those years. It was so much fun to learn about different traditions. We often spent our Christmas with persons of different cultures while we were stationed in foreign lands.

Our youngest son was six months old when we decided to actually go home for the holidays. We were closer to our hometown than we had been in many years. My husband and I decided we would place the presents from Santa under our tree before we left. When our oldest son, who was then three years old, came in after our trip, he would be excited to see the gifts.

My husband took the boys out to the car, and I placed the beautiful packages under the tree before leaving for the week.

Upon our return, we were excited to let our oldest son run into the house first and view the wonderful display of Santa gifts. We watched as he ran to the living room and stopped suddenly. As we turned the corner, we saw the presents completely covered up with pine needles from the very dry, live Christmas tree. It was a depressing sight. The beauty I had prepared had faded quickly during our time away. We got our son out of the room, and I cleaned everything up and took the presents outside to brush off the pine needles. He finally could see his presents—but the presentation had lost its glamour.

I thought about that Christmas morning the other day. I thought of how it could have ruined Christmas for our family. Instead, we brushed the needles away, as the beauty of the tree had faded, and we enjoyed the rest of the day.

After vacuuming pine needles for a while that memorable day, I realized that Christmas is in the heart. This year there will be many who will not spend Christmas with family, and their "home for the holidays" could be with a Charlie Brown tree or even a computer screen as they watch their families open presents from across the ocean.

Decorations fade—and sometimes aren't even possible because of our circumstances—but the Word of God, the message of his Son born that Christmas day, stands forever. ~*Carol*

★   ★   ★

Jesus, help me to keep Christmas in my heart. Please fill the hearts of those serving in lands far away from home. + *Amen.*

Focused on Peace

Pursue righteous living, faithfulness, love, and peace. Enjoy the companionship of those who call on the Lord with pure hearts. ✚ 2 TIMOTHY 2:22

We talk so much about peace during this time of the year. In a perfect world, there would be an end to all crime and wars for at least a week so that all could focus on what peace really is. When we talk of peace, it is usually in reference to the activities going on around us. Let's focus today on the peace in our hearts.

Scripture tells us that God came to this earth to bring peace. He sent his Son as the Prince of Peace. Did wars, conflict, and strife end at that time? No, they did not. Jesus dealt with tragedy, demonic activity, sickness, conflict, and resolution of conflict every day that he walked on this earth during his time of ministry. So what is the peace he was supposed to bring?

The peace focus that will change your life forever is the peace within your heart. From the beginning of Christ's life on earth, that peace was available to all who would invite him to come in as Lord of their lives.

Peace is a fruit of God's Spirit when we have him in our lives. The word we use often when describing a place or an event of rest is *peace*. It is something we strive for in the busyness of our days. As mothers, we seek a moment's peace when the children are napping. As military spouses, we seek the peace of knowing our loved ones are safe.

Those who serve in our military look for the peace that comes in knowing they are doing a job with passion, commitment, and purpose.

2 Timothy 2:22 tells us to pursue faith and love and peace. When our focus is on the things of the world and the worries therein, we lose sight of the peace God wants us to have. Keep your focus on peace this holiday season and pray that those who are in turmoil, conflict, and wars will be blessed with God's perfect peace during this Christmas season. ⚘*Carol*

✦ ✦ ✦

Father, thank you for the peace you gave through your Son, Jesus Christ. Let there be a peace focus in the hearts of those who reside in turmoil and conflict every day. ✚ *Amen.*

A Gift from Bavaria

The LORD has given them special skills as engravers, designers, embroiderers in blue, purple, and scarlet thread on fine linen cloth, and weavers. They excel as craftsmen and as designers.

✝ EXODUS 35:35

Half-timbered houses line the streets of the Bavarian town of Oberammergau. Beautiful fresco paintings cover the walls of many of the buildings, giving witness to the religious beliefs or occupation of the resident. This charming German town is the home to some of the most gifted woodcarvers in the world. Dating back to the Middle Ages, this art form has been passed down from generation to generation.

This year, a small carving of the holy family will find a special place of honor in my home as I decorate for Christmas. It was carefully purchased during a visit to Oberammergau this summer. My husband and I found a shop off the beaten path, where we were warmly greeted by the owners. They told us the story of their shop and proudly showed us pictures of their son, who was also a woodcarver, and his family. Gaining a glimpse of this humble man and his wife makes my wooden treasure even more valuable.

We were impressed as we walked through the town and viewed the carvings. The beautiful crèches depicting the Nativity were intricately detailed. There is no question these artisans are truly gifted in woodcarving, and their talent is inspiring.

God has given us all unique gifts to use to glorify him and bless others. Christmas is about gifts. I'm not talking about the material ones we purchase for each other but rather the gifts of love, hope, and peace. Your gifts may not be like those crafted by the woodcarvers of Oberammergau, but they are your gifts that God has given you to share with others. Our heavenly Father gave the basis of all gifts—his only Son to save the world. Today's Scripture states that God gave special skills to the artisans who were to design the Tabernacle. It leads me to believe that skills, whether they are in art or administration, are indeed gifts of God given to us to honor him. This Christmas give the gifts that God has given you.   ❧*Brenda*

✷   ✷   ✷

Lord of all good gifts, thank you for the gift of your Son, the Savior of the world and Savior of my soul. Help me today to use the gifts you have given me to bless others and honor you. Thank you for the gifts you've given those in military service; may they use them for the good of the world. In your name I pray. ✝*Amen.*

December 12
Passion Play

I will fulfill my vows to the LORD in the presence of all his people—in the house of the LORD in the heart of Jerusalem. ✛ PSALM 116:18-19

Woodcarvers are not the only reason the small town of Oberammergau has become famous. In 1632, in the middle of the Thirty Years War, the town was being ravaged by the Black Plague. Despondent and bereaved, the inhabitants of the town made a vow to God. If he would stop the plague, they would stage a play to illustrate the death and resurrection of Jesus Christ for as long as the town existed. Amazingly, there were no more deaths, and the people of the town have kept their promise. The first play was in 1634, and every ten years another play is produced by the volunteers of this remarkable town. All of the actors and the set and costume designers come from this small town of approximately five thousand people. Their offering and fulfillment of their vow to the Lord is viewed by over one million people who come from all over the world each decade.[1]

It is remarkable to consider this type of commitment to God. It is not unlike what David describes in Psalm 116. This song of thanksgiving is for deliverance from trouble and sickness. David desires to give a tangible demonstration of his gratitude for God's help. When he wrote this psalm, he desired to fulfill his vow to the Lord in a timely manner. He wasn't ashamed to publicly display his love and trust in God; in fact, he hoped others would join him.

Fulfilling commitments can be a challenging thing involving sacrifice and will. The ultimate symbol of commitment is the focus of the play in Oberammergau—the cross of Christ. The cross is the symbol of the Father's commitment to us. He sent his Son as a commitment to forgive our sins, accept us into his family, and take us to heaven. Even when we fail in our commitments to him, God does not fail to keep his commitment to the world. ☙Brenda

✫　✫　✫

What can I offer you, Lord, for all you have done for me? I will lift up the cup of salvation and praise your name for saving me. I will keep my promises to you in the presence of all your people (Psalm 116:12-14, paraphrased). ✛Amen.

---

[1] "The Oberammergau Passion Play," http://www.oberammergau.de/ot_e/passionplay/.

Peace I Give

I am leaving you with a gift—peace of mind and heart. And the peace I give is a gift the world cannot give. So don't be troubled or afraid. ✛ JOHN 14:27

We hear so often about peace treaties, peace accords, or peace conferences in the news.

The reason these continue is that peace on earth is very tentative. Peace on earth comes for only a short time. At any moment, a person or an event may come along causing more conflict, and you begin at square one. How often have we watched as the first shot is fired to break the treaty or the agreement?

The Scripture tells us that there will always be wars and rumors of wars. We learn from God's Word that as long as the earth goes on in its present state, there will be no lasting peace.

Christmas often brings thoughts of peace around the world. We pray that others will have a sense of quiet and a sense of worth as they struggle in the conflict of their daily lives. We sing songs that recite "sleep in heavenly peace" or "let there be peace on earth."

We desire that those in harm's way who are fighting for freedom in other countries will be able to have a moment or even hours of peace during this time of year. The military families separated during this time of year long for peace. They seek peace of mind and heart and also pray for peace to come in the midst of conflict.

There is a lasting peace. It is the only lasting peace to hold on to on this earth. Jesus spoke to give us reassurance that the peace he left with us would be peace of mind and heart. There is nothing that can take that away from us. There is no shot fired or person in disagreement to remove that peace from our hearts and our minds.

As we celebrate the Christmas holidays, let's remind each other of that true and lasting peace as the busyness begins to take over, lest the presents become more important than the Gift. Peace will come when we reach out to others, and our focus will stay on Jesus and his peace and not the ever-changing peace of the world.

"I am leaving you with a gift—peace of mind and heart" (John 14:27). ⁓*Carol*

* * *

Lord, thank you for your gift of peace. Bless those experiencing internal as well as external turmoil and conflict today with your peace of mind and heart. ✛ *Amen.*

December 14
Prepare and Renew

No one puts new wine into old wineskins. For the old skins would burst from the pressure, spilling the wine and ruining the skins. New wine is stored in new wineskins so that both are preserved. ✝ MATTHEW 9:17

Everyone needs a new beginning at some point in their lives. Perhaps it is a new beginning with a broken relationship. We may need a new beginning when it comes to starting a new job and having to learn new skills. We take time to prepare ourselves and go into these new beginnings with renewed commitment to succeed.

In our travels as a military family, we looked forward to new beginnings. Some transitions were more difficult than others, but the new experiences were always waiting for us. I enjoyed seeking out new ways to serve in the community or church. We looked for new activities for our sons. My husband looked for the closest golf course and lake to fish in. These were all preparations for our daily life in the place we would live for several years before moving on. These newfound activities gave us a foundation and secured us in our place in the move.

The *NLT Life Application Study Bible* has a footnote for today's Scripture that I think is so powerful in the New Living Translation. It reads, "The Good News did not fit into the old rigid legalistic system of religion. It needed a fresh start. The message will always remain 'new' because it must be accepted and applied in every generation. When we follow Christ, we must be prepared for new ways to live, new ways to look at people, and new ways to serve."[1]

What a challenge for us during this Christmas season.

The Christmas story happened when Christ was born over two thousand years ago. Yet each year for so many it is brand new. As the story is told and people hear it for the very first time as Christians, it takes on new meaning. God makes the wineskin new every year so that the freshness of the age-old story will be contained.

Let us be as those new wineskins, ready to be made new through the birth and blood of Jesus Christ. Let the new wine flow from your heart to others in your community and in your place of work so the Christmas story will live on in the hearts of those who hear it.   ❧*Carol*

☆   ☆   ☆

Jesus, you create newness in my heart each year if I allow you to do so. Give me a heart that will hear and speak the gospel to others. Bless the missionaries taking the gospel to faraway lands and those who are serving our country. Give me new ways to live and serve others. ✝ *Amen.*

---

[1] Tyndale's New Living Translation Bible (Wheaton, IL: Tyndale House Publishers, 1996), 1423.

Puzzled

He will be called: Wonderful Counselor, Mighty God, Everlasting Father, Prince of Peace.
✛ ISAIAH 9:6

Each year my father-in-law is presented a new puzzle for Christmas. The whole fam-ily usually joins together to help in the process of completing the project. We have been known to put together a 1,500-piece puzzle in one evening. While stationed in Germany, unable to return home for the Christmas holiday, we actually found a five thousand-piece puzzle to send back home. There were so many pieces that they had to be placed on one 4x8 sheet of plywood and the puzzle assembled on another 4x8 sheet of plywood. Instead of the quick, one-night puzzle marathon, the puzzle took many days. With the family gone following the Christmas gathering, it took my father-in-law even longer to complete the large cardboard riddle.

Solving a jigsaw puzzle as a family is a great illustration of how families can work together. Puzzles by their very nature are problems, yet as family members work together, there is great joy in seeing the picture become clear. It is not uncommon for the holidays to bring family conflict of some sort. As I prepare for family gatherings, it helps me to remember I am responsible for my attitude and actions and to recog-nize the need to keep my expectations in balance. It is a gift in itself for our family to enjoy being together. When I remember that no one can meet my deepest emotional and spiritual needs but God, I release my family members from the responsibility to meet those needs.

Sometimes the holidays can bring conflict in families, but we can do everything possible to make it a time of sharing, supporting, encouraging, and uniting. God established the unique responsibility to work toward good family relationships by establishing the principle of honoring our father and mother as one of the Ten Com-mandments. He knew the importance of working together as a family to solve the problems of life, but he also knew that sometimes it is a challenge to have harmony in the home. So he commands children to honor their parents. The Bible also gives instruction for husbands to love their wives and for wives to respect their husbands. Strong families are a God-given blessing. We honor God—and help ourselves—when we do our part to fill our families with love.   ❧*Brenda*

✫   ✫   ✫

Thank you, Father, for the gift of family. Help me do my part in honoring those I love. In Jesus' name I pray. ✛ *Amen.*

December 16
Angels Stand

The highest angelic powers stand in awe of God. He is far more awesome than all who surround his throne. + PSALM 89:7

Angels stand in awe of God. Although our God is with us at all times, he is not to be considered just our problem solver. He is an almighty God who is omniscient and omnipotent. He is the King, the Ruler, and the Giver of life. He is the Alpha and Omega, the beginning and the end. He knows the future and covers the past with the blood of his Son, Jesus. God is with us in temptation, trial, and victory. He is in the midst of our praying when two or more are gathered. He is there with us when we lift our voices to him in the still of the night or the early morning. He gives mercy, grace, and everlasting life to those who will call upon his name.

During this Christmas season, stand in awe of God with the angels. They understand his holiness and his amazing love. Stand today and lift your hands to thank him for this past year and for the year to come. Thank him for his coming in human form at the Virgin Birth. Praise him for your family and friends during this season and pray that they may come to know him personally as Lord and Savior.

Recently I called my mother and told her that I was just completely overwhelmed by how God is intimately involved with everything in life. I told her that I had been struggling to call a dear friend I had not seen or heard from for several years. This precious one had just lost her son. All day, I struggled with the thoughts of wondering if it was the right time to call. I had talked myself into just sending a card and letting her know I was thinking of her. I had gone out to the back porch, and the urge to call her became overwhelming. I picked up the phone and called. She answered and said to me, "I needed you to call at this second. I was desperate for someone to talk to just at this very moment." I stood that day in awe of God.

December is a time that is not always easy to get through, especially when your life has taken a turn the year before. God cares so very much for you. Stand in awe of him and allow him to come in and give you peace and comfort. ⮑*Carol*

*   *   *

Father, Son, and Holy Spirit, thank you for your tender care every day. Help me to act upon your promptings to bless others. Encourage others to reach out to the families and parents of those serving our country by picking up the phone, sending a card, or providing an invitation to share a meal. +*Amen.*

Hope to Share

Even if you suffer for doing what is right, God will reward you for it. So don't worry or be afraid of their threats. Instead, you must worship Christ as Lord of your life. And if someone asks about your Christian hope, always be ready to explain it. ✛ 1 PETER 3:14-15

There is hope in the Christian faith. There is hope for the future and hope for today. As Christians, our faith should be deepening every day. There is to be a longing to know God more intimately through his Word and through communication in prayer.

As we go through our daily lives, there are many times we are captivated by interesting conversation. These conversations may include political, social, or even religious opinions. When it comes to something that we know to be a form of sin, should we be politically correct and sit back and just listen? Or should we take the directive of today's Scripture and suffer for doing what is right and speak out on God's behalf and the hope we have in Jesus Christ?

The month of December always brings much opportunity to share your faith with others. You may have the opportunity to share your salvation experience or why you believe in the Virgin Birth that is celebrated at Christmas time.

Stay in God's Word during this season, and be ready to share the hope that is within you when the opportunity presents itself. Many of our soldiers are walking the streets in distant lands this month. Many are sharing the goodies sent from home with the children who greet them as they pass by. They are showing love and hope to these children. These courageous men and women are sharing smiles and even gestures of kindness in shaking hands and talking to those who have suffered so much. The Christmas season is all about giving hope to our world.

Psalm 71:5 says, "O Lord, you alone are my hope." That says it all for a hurting world. Keep the hope of Jesus in your heart, and be ready to share that hope with others this Christmas.   ⌐*Carol*

✳   ✳   ✳

Lord, the hope in my heart is you. The hope in this world is you. Thank you for those who are sacrificing the time spent with their own families, churches, and communities to give hope to others who are hurting. ✛*Amen.*

December 18

A Christmas Journey

Because Joseph was a descendant of King David, he had to go to Bethlehem in Judea, David's ancient home. He traveled there from the village of Nazareth in Galilee. **+** LUKE 2:4

Gerald Horton Bath recounted the experience of a small African boy who listened carefully as the teacher explained why Christians give presents to each other on Christmas Day. "The gift is an expression of our joy over the birth of Jesus and our friendship for each other," she said.

When Christmas Day came, the boy brought to the teacher a seashell of lustrous beauty. "Where did you ever find such a beautiful shell?" the teacher asked as she gently fingered the gift.

The youth told her that there was only one spot where such extraordinary shells could be found. When he named the place, a certain bay several miles away, the teacher was left speechless.

"Why . . . why, it's gorgeous . . . wonderful, but you shouldn't have gone all that way to get a gift for me."

His eyes brightening, the boy answered, "Long walk part of gift."[1]

For many of us, traveling is part of the holiday season. Traveling to be with family and friends during the holidays gives us a destination that is secure in a world where security is not a premium. Indeed, long trips are tiring and require an extra effort to be with family over the holidays. Making the journey is a part of the gift.

The account of Christ's birth is full of stories about journeys. The gospel of Luke tells the birth of Christ and carries the stories of several journeys: the journey of Joseph and Mary from Nazareth to Bethlehem, the angelic journey from heaven to the shepherds' field, and the journey of the shepherds to the stable.

The greatest journey was the one of God's own Son coming down from his heavenly home to dwell among us. Indeed, his long journey was an important part of the gift! *Brenda*

*   *   *

Thank you, Lord, for leaving your home in heaven to bring salvation to a fallen world. When I become weary from my journey here on this earth, remind me of the journey you took to bring me eternal life. In your name I pray. +*Amen.*

---

[1] Gerald Horton Bath, "Long Walk Part of Gift," in *The Greatest Christmas Ever: A Treasury of Inspirational Ideas and Insights for an Unforgettable Christmas* (Tulsa, OK: Honor Books, 1995), 69.

Christmas behind the Iron Curtain

God blesses those who are persecuted for doing right, for the Kingdom of Heaven is theirs.

✝ MATTHEW 5:10

I received a note from a young military wife stationed in Germany, updating me on her life there. The last line of the note said, "Wish you were here to go with me to the Christmas markets." I wished I were too! With just the mention of Kristkindlmarkt, I can envision the sights, sounds, and smells of this lovely German tradition.

Imagine rows and rows of stalls with a variety of treats and wares. The smell of freshly baked lebkuchen or gingerbread, sweet speculass cookies, and hot mulled cider floats through the air. In the crisp winter evenings of Advent, tiny white lights beckon you to the center of town to celebrate this unique Christmas tradition. It was always interesting to me that this market did not seem commercialized. I marveled at the emphasis on religious symbols from the name translated "Christ Child Market" to the white lights that symbolize his purity.

Our family lived in Germany when the Berlin wall was still in place. We were surprised to learn there was a Christmas market in East Berlin. Our curiosity was aroused, so we decided to take a Christmas journey to check out what it would be like to attend such a market in an atheist country. We drove all night, passing through the various Communist checkpoints. The next evening, we made our way to the market. Instead of the celebratory and joyous markets of then–West Germany, we found this market to be rather gray and solemn. The tents were all uniform. Somber classical music was piped in over an audio system. It was rather sad.

Yet there was still Christmas. From the time of Christ, there have been governments that have attempted to eradicate the Christian faith. But even where worshiping Christ is illegal, Christ followers have continued to risk their very lives to honor our Lord. I was glad to be able to peek behind the Iron Curtain to find some public symbol of the holiday honoring the birth of Christ.

It is too easy to forget the persecuted church in other lands when in America I can take my pick of not only which church building but which worship style I prefer. This Christmas season, remember Christians where there are no open symbols of Christ. Pray Matthew 5:10 on their behalf.   *Brenda*

✫   ✫   ✫

Lord, I thank you for the faithful witness of those who are being persecuted because they follow you. I ask you to provide strength to those who face hardship because of hatred and fear. I pray for courage for those who are imprisoned or in peril. Grant hope for their families. Awaken the church in America to stand firm against persecution and stand in the gap in prayer. In your name I pray. ✝ *Amen.*

Thank You, Jesus

These are written so that you may continue to believe that Jesus is the Messiah, the Son of God, and that by believing in him you will have life. + JOHN 20:31

On this day in December, I want to encourage you to write a note of thanks to Jesus for his birth. I encourage you to think of the things that have come from him in your life this year. Try this unique exercise to give him worship and honor. This is my thank-you note to Jesus:

> Dear Jesus,
>
> Often I get too busy to stop and consider just how very much you have meant to me in my life. I remember the day I walked the aisle of my church and made a public profession of faith to you. My parents, the pastor, and congregation were so proud and so blessed at this decision. I also remember having a sense of your presence in my life in my younger years. I remember always taking time out to thank you for your birth and your coming to this earth to save us from our sins so we would have the promise of eternity. I remember in the midst of presents, food, and fellowship, our family always read the Christmas story from the book of Luke. The true meaning of Christmas was always in my heart. I also remember those times of walking away from you in my life and the times that I cried out to you, knowing you were always there with me even in those times of conflict and despair.
>
> This Christmas I want to reflect and remember your goodness, mercy, and grace in my life. I want to sincerely say, "Thank You, Jesus, for who you are and what you mean to me every day."
>
> Merry Christmas, Jesus!

&*Carol*

✶   ✶   ✶

Thank you, Jesus, for the opportunities you give me to share your love with others. Thank you for those who reach out to people less fortunate and for the blessing they bestow on those who receive. I ask for safety and protection for those who are in the midst of battle on this earth whether it is physical or spiritual. + *Amen.*

Heavens of Brass

Are you also confused? Is our champion helpless to save us? You are right here among us, LORD. We are known as your people. Please don't abandon us now! ✛ JEREMIAH 14:9

The Message articulates Jeremiah 14:9 with these words: "Why do you just stand there and stare, like someone who doesn't know what to do in a crisis? But God, you are, in fact, here, here with us! You know who we are—you named us! Don't leave us in the lurch."

Wow! It seems a little bold to speak to God in that way, but the prophet Jeremiah was lamenting on behalf of a nation in crisis. There was a terrible drought, and as he prayed he felt as if the heavens were made of brass. I feel that way sometimes, don't you? It is easy to become fearful in the midst of a crisis like the one described and believe that God does not care.

Crisis is one of those words that have been diluted because of overuse. We say we're having a crisis for such trivial things as when our hair won't go right or when we fail to set the alarm clock. It is used at times when we cannot control a situation. But there are very real crises going on every day. During the time of this writing, the people of Atlanta have just gathered on the capitol steps to pray for rain. The water supply is quickly running out, and they are looking to God for help. Their city is in a state of crisis. While there is a drought in Georgia, there are out-of-control fires in California that have created a crisis.

The crisis events we hear about on the news may not mean much to us because we don't have a personal connection to them. They sadden us, but they don't affect our well-being. When crisis does affect us, we can be confident that God knows and cares. During these times, don't be embarrassed to seek out professional help if needed. God has gifted counselors who are able to provide meaningful assistance. Most importantly, take your crisis to God in prayer. Like Jeremiah, you may feel like the heavens are brass, but cry out to God anyway!

The word for *crisis* in the Greek means "decision" or "judgment." It can be described as a turning point when we come to a critical moment in time. Times of crisis truly can become opportunities for positive change if we allow God to take them and use them to glorify himself. You see, God has not abandoned us in our times of need. He knows the crisis, of whatever magnitude, you face today.   ☙*Brenda*

✳   ✳   ✳

Today I cry to you, Lord! Hear my prayer on behalf of those who are experiencing times of crisis, whether in domestic or military life. Come to their aid, mighty Father. ✛*Amen.*

December 22
On the Wall

I placed armed guards behind the lowest parts of the wall in the exposed areas. I stationed the people to stand guard by families, armed with swords, spears, and bows. + NEHEMIAH 4:13

This verse was revealed to me in a new and exciting way while attending Midtown Fellowship in Nashville, Tennessee. Pastor Randy began talking about the importance of standing with each other as Christian brothers and sisters. He said that we all need to be able to stand together in this life and then explained the reasons.

He referred to the story of the rebuilding and defending of the wall in the Old Testament book of Nehemiah. The reason for the guards to be arranged by family is that Nehemiah knew their love for their families was greater than their fear of the enemy. He said the nature of great courage is great love. When we know what we will die for (because of great love), it becomes very easy to know what we will live for.

Deployed military personnel will be quick to tell you that the best thing you can do for them while they are away is to care for their families. It is very important for them to know that people are providing them with encouragement and care. When they rest assured in this, they can fight the battle and face the enemy with confidence and without reserve.

Pastor Randy also pointed out that Jesus was the first to stand with us hand in hand and that we now keep going in that standing together as life goes on. Without the support and love from our brothers and sisters in the Lord, we are alone in standing against the enemy of our faith and in facing situations in the physical world.

In this Christmas season, find someone to stand with who will give you courage and love in order to cast out fear in your heart. This is a scriptural principle and the way God meant it to be. Stand in love with your family as you put the enemy on notice that he cannot come near your family to steal and destroy.

The defense of that wall so long ago is still a necessity. May we continue with courage and passion to defend our faith—together. ~Carol

* * *

Father, you are the reason I can fight the enemy with conviction. You are my victory. I pray for victory for those who are in harm's way today. May your people stand with them and with their families in prayer and in hope for their quick return. + Amen.

Shining Lights

You are the light of the world—like a city on a hilltop that cannot be hidden. No one lights a lamp and then puts it under a basket. Instead, a lamp is placed on a stand, where it gives light to everyone in the house. ✛ MATTHEW 5:14-15

There is something about the displaying of Christmas lights. They can light up the darkest and dreariest home. They can make the shopping centers seem new and vibrant. One of the most magnificent displays of Christmas lights is at the Opryland Hotel in Nashville, Tennessee. Every year, lights are strung all around the hotel, and thousands of poinsettias are planted. It is truly a winter wonderland.

Hanging the lights across our front porch and turning them on for the first time makes my heart happy. I love getting up very early the morning after we have decorated the tree, turning on just the Christmas tree lights, and drinking my first cup of coffee. Memories flood my mind and heart during those times.

When I was a young girl, colored lights were very popular. Gradually the trend has been for all white. Whatever the color, the brightness is what warms the heart.

Do you know where I am going with this today? Do you happen to know anyone right now who is possibly sitting in the dark, guarding a tent or an outpost in some faraway land? Do you know someone who can only have a string or two of lights hanging in the mess hall? Could there possibly be someone in your downtown area who has no lights at all, unable to afford the electric bill?

Is there someone you know whose heart has been darkened by a broken relationship or their decision to leave church because of hurt from a church member?

Darkness is all around us, but guess what? Today the light is brighter than ever before. The more darkness that surrounds us, the brighter the light becomes. We have been given instruction in God's Word from the mouth of Jesus to be the light of the world. We are to be that shining light that brightens the room, the heart, or the situation when we are around. We have Jesus in our hearts, and he cannot be put out by the darkness that surrounds us.

As the Christmas lights shine this year, so let the light of Jesus shine to others through you.   ⮑*Carol*

✶   ✶   ✶

Father, I pray at this Christmas season your light will shine in the hidden places. I pray that evil will be revealed and destroyed. Be with those who are sitting in dark places today whether physically or spiritually. Shine your light in their hearts. ✛ *Amen.*

December 24
The Right Time

When the right time came, God sent his Son, born of a woman, subject to the law.
✛ GALATIANS 4:4

Conventional wisdom would say that the King of kings and Lord of lords being born in a stable was all wrong. Surely something had gone haywire in the cosmic timetable. Give or take another day, and there might have been room in the inn. But Scripture says when the right time came, the fullness of time—God's appointed time—Christ was born. It implies that it did not happen by accident or chance. God was shaping the world for the right conditions in which to send his Son. There was basically one government that had brought peace to much of the world. There was one language known across various cultures. The Romans had connected a road system that facilitated the dispersion of the church and the spread of the gospel. There was a chronological sequence of events that was part of God's timetable for Jesus to be born in a stable in Bethlehem.

God had a timetable for the first Advent that was perfectly calculated. The timetable is still in effect, and there is a time calculated for the second Advent as well. Take hope today in knowing that his time will be fulfilled, in our world and in your life.

> *Now are the days fulfilled,*
> *God's Son is manifested,*
> *Now His great majesty*
> *In human flesh is vested.*
> *Behold the mighty God,*
> *By Whom all wrath is stilled,*
> *The woman's promised Seed—*
> *Now are the days fulfilled.*
> *Now are the days fulfilled,*
> *Lo, Jacob's Star is shining;*
> *The gloomy night has fled*
> *Wherein the world lay pining.*
>
> *Now, Israel, look on Him*
> *Who long thy heart hath thrilled;*
> *Hear Zion's watchmen cry:*
> *Now are the days fulfilled.*
> *Now are the days fulfilled,*
> *The child of God rejoices;*
> *No bondage of the Law,*
> *No curses that it voices,*
> *Can fill our hearts with fear;*
> *On Christ our hope we build.*
> *Behold the Prince of Peace—*
> *Now are the days fulfilled.*
>
> ~AUTHOR UNKNOWN[1]

☙Brenda

✶ ✶ ✶

Savior of the world, you came at the right time. You will come again at the right time. I wait expectantly for you today. ✛ *Amen.*

---

[1] "Now Are the Days Fulfilled," author unknown, 1746; translated by Frederick W. Herzberger; Text from *The Handbook to The Lutheran Hymnal* (St. Louis: Concordia Publishing House, 1941), 81. Prepared for Public Domain by Project Wittenberg.

Hey, unto You a Child Is Born!

A child is born to us, a son is given to us. ✛ ISAIAH 9:6

For many years, one of our family Christmas traditions was to read aloud Barbara Robinson's *Best Christmas Pageant Ever*. The endearing story of children described as the "awful, cigar smoking (even the girls) Herdmans" is a tender but humorous tale of the true meaning of Christmas.[1]

The terrorizing Herdman family, led by wild-eyed Imogene, shows up at Sunday school one morning because they heard there were refreshments. The announcement is made about the Christmas pageant, and they all decide they will participate. It doesn't matter to them that this was the first time they had set foot in a church. The brazen Imogene ends up playing the unlikely part of Mary, and the other five Herdmans overtake the rest of the major roles. They end up putting their own spin on the story, like bringing the baby Jesus a ham and beating up Herod because he was mean. It all makes sense to them, and in a strange and honest way, it makes sense to me.

The Herdmans are the unlovable people of the world, but they represent all of us who need a Savior. They give the best gifts they have to offer. And in the end, they discover the true meaning of Christmas. They are changed as they encounter the truth of the love of God born as a baby at Christmas. The church is changed as well, as it is reminded of what its purpose and mission really is.

One of my favorite parts of the book is when Gladys, who plays the angel, runs down the aisle of the church shouting, "Hey, unto YOU a child is born!" I had never thought of it quite that way before, but it is oh so true. Unto me, and you, and every person who ever lived—a child is born!   *↬Brenda*

✶   ✶   ✶

Loving Savior, you came to bring a personal message of love and hope to individuals like me, my neighbors, and my fellow Americans serving the country in the military. Thank you for your personal presence and involvement in my life. Your coming changed the world, and your coming changed me. Help me never to lose the child-like wonder as I stand to praise you! Bring that same wonder to those servicemen and women who do not yet know you. ✛ *Amen.*

---

[1] Barbara Robinson, *The Best Christmas Pageant Ever* (New York: HarperTrophy, 2005).

December 26
Going for the Glory

Jesus was born in Bethlehem in Judea, during the reign of King Herod. About that time some wise men from eastern lands arrived in Jerusalem, asking, "Where is the newborn king of the Jews? We saw his star as it rose, and we have come to worship him." + MATTHEW 2:1-2

When the wise men first saw the glorious star, they committed themselves to finding the person for whom it shone. They were going for the glory.

It was a long, grueling trip, probably taking at least three months by horseback. Though the wise men started out going the right direction, they, like some of us, were attracted to a cheap glory. Matthew tells us that they first went to Herod at the palace. It was only natural to look for the glory of a king in the palace that glittered with gold. As humans, it is natural for us to look for glory in the places of wealth and power. But they got back on the right path when they once again saw the star. As long as they followed the light of the star, they were on the right road to find the glory of God. The light of truth will always lead us to Jesus.

When they came to Jesus, they opened their treasures and offered them to the Christ child. Jesus said where our treasures are, there our hearts will be also (see Matthew 6:21). The question for us to consider is, when we open our hearts, what treasures do we have to offer Jesus? He first desires our hearts.

The wise men came before Jesus and rejoiced with exceeding great joy (see Matthew 2:10). These two words *rejoice* and *joy* come from the Greek word *chairo*, which is the ultimate of happiness and relates to the joy of God's grace. This is a key for us in our coming before Christ, by continually entering the presence of the Lord with worship and rejoicing.

The Lord told the wise men through a dream not to go back to Herod, so they went home another way. They violated political protocol and yielded to the will of the Lord. When going for the glory, we must have the priority of being obedient to the plan God has for us.

The Magi started their journey looking for a nameless, faceless king of the Jews. Their trip ended in a personal audience with Jesus, the Christ, the manifest glory of God.

Are you going for the glory? The example of the wise men serves as an example still today:

> Go to God
> Look for his light
> Open your heart
> Rejoice in him
> Yield to his will

&‑*Brenda*

＊　＊　＊

Glorified Lord, I come to you with an open heart full of worship and praise. I yield myself to your will for me today. Hear my prayers for the military today: give them right missions, wise judgments, and your favor. + *Amen.*

Anchor Points

That time of darkness and despair will not go on forever. The land of Zebulun and Naphtali will be humbled, but there will be a time in the future when Galilee of the Gentiles, which lies along the road that runs between the Jordan and the sea, will be filled with glory. ✛ ISAIAH 9:1

> *Hope is not wishful thinking.*
> *Hope is not yearning.*
> *Hope is not simply cheery optimism.*
> ~LLOYD JOHN OGILVIE[1]

Hope is a certainty in our heart of what is to come. Hope is a confidence in the promises of God. The writer of Hebrews says in Hebrews 6:19, "We have this hope as an anchor for the soul, firm and secure" (NIV).

The anchor usually thought of in this Scripture is that of a ship, but I like to think of the anchors used in rock climbing. As climbers make their ascent up the face of a precipice, they establish anchor points along the way. If they grow weary, they can let the anchors hold their weight while they rest. Or if they slip and fall, the anchors secured in solid rock will catch them before they go very far down. The hope of Christmas is the message that Christ is the anchor to which we can hold.

The world does not need a message of wishful thinking, yearning, and cheery optimism. The world needs the message brought by a babe in a manger. His birth became the bridge of the hopelessness of humanity. The prophet Isaiah wrote the words of today's Scripture long before Christ's birth. He spoke of a time when the land would be filled with the glory of God. On the night of the birth of Jesus, the angels sang to the shepherds of the glory of God. Now those whose lives have been transformed by the saving grace of Jesus can sing of the glory of the Lord to the world. In this Christmas season, let your song bring adoration to the King.   ⮞*Brenda*

✶   ✶   ✶

Hope of the ages, you are the song of my heart today. I hold on to you as the anchor of my soul. There are many without hope today—right here in my neighborhood, and far away in war-torn lands. I ask your blessing on them today. May the message of your saving grace pierce their darkness and provide them a new song. ✛*Amen.*

---

[1] Lloyd John Ogilvie, *A Future and a Hope* (Nashville, TN: W Publishing Group, 1988), 47–48.

December 28
He Knows

The Word became human and made his home among us. He was full of unfailing love and faithfulness. And we have seen his glory, the glory of the Father's one and only Son.
✝ JOHN 1:14

I asked several friends who have experienced deployment to share some of the challenges they encountered. The list included loneliness, relinquishing a spouse to the fear of the unknown, as well as the awareness of turning to other things for comfort whether they be food, shopping, or alcohol. One idea that came up several times was the idea of the lack of understanding by others. Here it is in their words:

> Our society teaches that the holidays are all about friends and family and everyone being together. So it's not really Christmas because Daddy's not here? Or we can't be thankful because we aren't all together?

> The condolence look—you know, the one that comes out when you find out someone died. They get the look, and they say "I'm so sorry"—and proceed to talk about how they don't understand how we do it, they've never been away from their husband for more than a weekend retreat. Well, on a good day, that's only annoying. On a bad day, it can lead to a full-on pan-of-brownies pity party.

> Everyone else was living in normal land, but our circumstances, feelings, and thoughts were on a whole different planet. This meant I needed to work harder to connect with people. Though people were wonderfully gracious, unless they had been there, they did not understand and I did not know how to help them understand what I barely understood myself.

The celebration of Christ's birth is a celebration of a Savior who entered the world as a baby just as each of us did. He came to live and experience life. The Gospel of John describes Jesus as One who was tired and thirsty. He wept, bled, and died. He was a real person. "He took on Himself sinless human nature and identified with us in every aspect of life from birth to death. 'The Word' was not an abstract concept of philosophy, but a real Person who could be seen, touched, and heard."[1]

Whatever you are going through today, be encouraged that Jesus knows, understands, and cares. *≈Brenda*

✶   ✶   ✶

Lord, you are my great High Priest who has entered heaven, Jesus, the Son of God, so I hold firmly to what I believe. Thank you for understanding my weaknesses, for you faced all of the same testings I do, yet you did not sin. So I come boldly to the throne of my gracious God. Here I will receive your mercy, and I will find grace to help me when I need it most (Hebrews 4:14-16, paraphrased). ✝ *Amen.*

---

[1] *The Bible Exposition Commentary* (SP Publications, 1989).

You Will Find Me

"In those days when you pray, I will listen. If you look for me wholeheartedly, you will find me. I will be found by you," says the LORD. "I will end your captivity and restore your fortunes. I will gather you out of the nations where I sent you and will bring you home again to your own land." ✛ JEREMIAH 29:12-14

Jeremiah has written a letter from Jerusalem to all who had been exiled to Babylon. He is telling the people of Israel not to be tricked by those who would tell them things that are not true. He also lets them know that the Lord has said they would only be in Babylon for seventy years and then be returned to their land. These verses for today come just after the famous verse quoted in Jeremiah 29:11, which reads, "'I know the plans I have for you,' says the LORD, 'They are plans for good and not for disaster, to give you a future and a hope.'"

As my military husband would leave to go to the field for extended separation, I would always quote that Scripture to him. Whenever our sons had times of frustration or hurt, I reminded them that the Lord has great intentions and a future planned for them. He has no intent of disaster for those who love him.

In my Christian life, there are three characteristics of my faith that I hold very dear. They are grace, mercy, and hope. Were it not for those characteristics of God the Father and his salvation in my life, I would not be here today. I have held onto those characteristics through many a night as a military wife while going through times of military separation. I held onto God's mercy as our sons would wake up with high fevers, and I would be there alone to pray over them, give them medications, and wait until morning to take them to a clinic.

I held on through those times with the hope that God promised that when I prayed to him, he was listening. When I looked for him, I would find him.

Military wives, military parents, and other family members of those deployed in harm's way this Christmas season, God is with you. You will find him waiting for you when you pray and when you call out to him. He is the hope for the future of your loved one. ❧*Carol*

✱   ✱   ✱

Jehovah Shalom, thank you for the hope that comes with knowing you are there when I call to you. I ask for your grace, mercy, and hope for those serving our country. ✛*Amen.*

December 30
Steady Spiritual Legs

It is God who makes both us and you stand firm in Christ. He anointed us, set his seal of ownership on us, and put his Spirit in our hearts as a deposit, guaranteeing what is to come.
✦ 2 CORINTHIANS 1:21-22, NIV

Throughout this year we have looked at ways to stand firm and strong in the midst of whatever life brings our way. There is no way to know what a year will bring. No way to look into the future to see the joys or sorrows that will come. There is also no way we can stand firm in Christ on our own. When we stand on our own strength, we find that it doesn't take long before we fall. Hopefully, through the devotional thoughts that have been shared, you have a better grasp on how God helps you to stand firm. The key to steady spiritual legs is the Holy Spirit. Paul tells us three ways God works in us with his Spirit.

1. He anoints us. Anointing in the Bible always refers to special empowerment from God. People were anointed to show that God placed his special power or ability on them. The anointing of the Spirit reminds us that we don't accomplish anything spiritual on our own. The only way we can stand firm in Christ is with God's help.

2. He set his seal of ownership on us. The mark of the Spirit lets us know that God claims us as his. His Spirit bears witness with our spirit that he is our heavenly Father.

3. He put his Spirit in our hearts as a deposit. We know that heaven is real and that all the promises God makes to us will come to pass because he has given us his Spirit. Knowing the good things to come helps us stand firm now.

Ask the Lord to help you stand firm today. You can be an overcomer today, with the help of God's Spirit in you.   ≈*Brenda*

* * *

Lord, I thank you for your anointing, your seal of ownership, and your Spirit in my life. May I stand firm and strong, always leaning upon and pressing into your Spirit. ✦ *Amen.*

December 31
Keeping Watch

No, dear brothers and sisters, I have not achieved it, but I focus on this one thing: Forgetting the past and looking forward to what lies ahead, I press on to reach the end of the race and receive the heavenly prize for which God, through Christ Jesus, is calling us. + PHILIPPIANS 3:13-14

As a child, I remember attending watch-night services at church on New Year's Eve. The congregation would come together to begin the new year with fellowship and worship. There was always a message with the theme of setting godly goals for the coming year and the challenge to watch for God to work in our lives as we commit the days ahead to him. It has been a long time since I attended a watch-night service, but I do practice a type of watch service of my own each January.

I set a goal to find some time in January to reflect on the passing year. It is important to remember and put in perspective the things experienced and learned in the past. However, the Christian faith is one of looking forward in hope and expectation of what God is going to do. We look back only to view life from the perspective of the Cross of Christ in laying the foundation of our salvation. We are to say with Paul, "Forgetting the past, and looking forward to what lies ahead."

My January watch includes prayerfully selecting a Scripture that will serve as focus and direction for the year to come. I am challenged to focus on areas of spiritual discipline with the desire of growing deeper in my knowledge of Christ. I am also challenged to grow in the area of outreach, service, and awareness of what God is doing in the world. I ask him to clarify how I may join him in his work in this coming year.

As this new year begins, guard yourself from being bogged down with past failures and disappointments. Look ahead with hope and expectation for all God will do in and through you—just watch!   *Brenda*

* * *

Thank you, Lord, for another year to love and serve you. I pray for a spirit of hope and expectation for your work in my life and in the world. I pray for your guidance for those who are pressing on toward the goal of bringing peace to areas of the world characterized by conflict. In Jesus' name I pray. + *Amen.*

About the Authors

BRENDA PACE

Brenda Pace has a BA in elementary education from Lee University in Cleveland, Tennessee, and an MEd in early childhood education from Columbus State University, Columbus, Georgia. She is presently a student at Liberty Theological Seminary studying Christian Leadership.

An active speaking ministry has allowed Brenda opportunities to address a variety of audiences here in the United States, as well as Japan, Korea, Germany, Italy, and Turkey. She has been involved in the development of a weeklong summer conference for wives of deployed soldiers. This conference, which ministers to women and their children, has had a positive impact on military families.

Brenda has served in various leadership roles for military organizations. For ten years, she enjoyed serving on the national board of Protestant Women of the Chapel–International, where she held the positions of USA president, vice president, advisor, and most recently resource coordinator. She would tell you that her greatest joy, aside from being a wife, mom, and now grandmom, is sharing with women the message that God can use their lives for his Kingdom work!

Brenda lives in Washington, D.C., (military move number thirteen!) with Richard, her husband of thirty-four years. Richard is a U.S. Army chaplain assigned to the Pentagon as the director of personnel for the army chief of chaplains. He was deployed for one year with Operation Enduring Freedom and Operation Iraqi Freedom while serving as the Division Chaplain for the 82d Airborne Division. They are the parents of two married sons and the proud grandparents of two.

As a result of her desire to encourage military spouses, Brenda has coauthored a devotional book entitled *Medals above My Heart*.

CAROL McGLOTHLIN

Carol McGlothlin earned a BS in psychology from Belmont University in Nashville, Tennessee, and studied speech pathology and special education at East Tennessee State University. She has been trained in personality styles, group development, conflict management, and the stages of grief.

Throughout her husband's military career, Carol has served in many volunteer positions, including board positions with the Protestant Women of the Chapel, Officers' Wives Club, and Musettes, as well as facilitator for the Pre-Command Spouse Orientation Program at Fort Leavenworth, Kansas. She is part of the national leadership team for Wives of Faith (www.wivesoffaith.org).

For many years Carol has spoken to Christian women's groups and led Bible studies in the United States and overseas. She currently still enjoys a connection to military wives' groups. She has a heart for encouraging women to love and support their husbands and pray for their families. Carol has led marriage classes, and she and her husband have led pre-marriage classes.

Carol has also found great joy in challenging community groups and churches to reach out to the families of active-duty and retired military personnel. The publication of *Medals above My Heart* (Broadman and Holman), also co-written with Brenda Pace, has provided numerous opportunities to share her passion for those who serve and have served their country so selflessly. She enjoys writing for various Web sites supporting the military family and for various Christian magazines.

Carol and her husband, Richard (U.S. Army, Retired), have been married thirty-four years and have two grown sons and a precious daughter-in-law. They are actively involved in their church and community in Huntsville, Alabama.

Index of Scripture References

Do-able. Daily. Devotions.

START ANY DAY THE ONE YEAR WAY.

Do-able.
Every One Year book is designed for people who live busy, active lives. Just pick one up and start on today's date.

Daily.
Daily routine doesn't have to be drudgery. One Year devotionals help you form positive habits that connect you to what's most important.

Devotions.
Discover a natural rhythm for drawing near to God in an extremely personal way. One Year devotionals provide daily focus essential to your spiritual growth.

For Women

The One Year® Devotions for Women on the Go	The One Year® Devotions for Women	The One Year® Devotions for Moms	The One Year® Women of the Bible	The One Year® Daily Grind

For Men

The One Year® Devotions for Men on the Go

The One Year® Devotions for Men

For Couples

The One Year® Devotions for Couples

For Families

The One Year® Family Devotions

For Teens

The One Year® Devos for Teens

The One Year® Devos for Sports Fans

For Bible Study

The One Year® Praying through the Bible

The One Year® through the Bible

For Personal Growth

The One Year® Walk with God Devotional

The One Year® at His Feet Devotional

The One Year® Great Songs of Faith

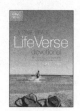

The One Year® Life Verse Devotional

It's convenient and easy to grow with God the One Year way.

CP0145